The SketchUp Handbook for Interior Design

A step-by-step visual approach to planning, designing, and presenting interior spaces

Rebecca Terpstra

Dana Hoffman

The SketchUp Handbook for Interior Design

Group Product Manager: Rohit Rajkumar
Publishing Product Manager: Kaustubh Manglurkar
Book Project Manager: Shagun Saini
Senior Editor: Anuradha Joglekar
Technical Editor: Simran Haresh Udasi and Reenish Kulshrestha
Copy Editor: Safis Editing
Proofreader: Anuradha Joglekar
Indexer: Pratik Shirodkar
Production Designer: Ponraj Dhandapani
DevRel Marketing Coordinator: Anamika Singh and Nivedita Pandey

Publication date: June 2024

Production reference: 2290524

Published by Packt Publishing Ltd.
Grosvenor House
11 St Paul's Square
Birmingham
B3 1RB, UK.

ISBN 978-1-83763-187-2

www.packtpub.com

To my amazing partner, Chris, for consistently providing unwavering support in the pursuit of my aspirations, and gratitude to our charming ballerina, Sophia, whose unique perspective has afforded me a nuanced understanding of the world.

– Becca Terpstra

To my children, Leon and our soon-to-arrive second child, for reminding me how to approach life with curiosity and wonder.

– Dana Hoffman

Contributors

About the authors

As an interior designer, **Rebecca (Becca) Terpstra** uses SketchUp to create beautiful interior and exterior models for designers, architects, and construction professionals. Well versed in LayOut and the photorealistic rendering plugins SU Podium and Enscape, Becca's passion lies in showcasing design details and making the most of SketchUp's fluidity. A content creator on LinkedIn Learning, a presenter at SketchUp Basecamp, and full-time faculty and Chair of Interior Design and CAD programs in Littleton, Colorado, Becca leverages her extensive interior design experience and passion for SketchUp to educate students globally. She focuses on teaching the foundational aspects of SketchUp as a design tool and demonstrates how LayOut can transform mundane construction documents into visually compelling works of art.

This book would not have come to fruition without the invaluable contribution of my students. Through your inquiries and overarching curiosity, you've played a pivotal role in enhancing both my capabilities as a professor and my skills as a SketchUp designer. I am deeply honored that a former student agreed to embark on this book journey with me, and I am so proud she has surpassed the teacher with her SketchUp skills.

A former SketchUp student of Rebecca Terpstra, **Dana Hoffman** has spent thousands of hours in SketchUp. She currently works for Carré Designs, building custom 3D models and creating one-of-a-kind renderings for high-end, world-renowned design firms. Dana lives in Minnesota and collaborates with designers and architects across the United States, reviewing 2D plans, problem-solving design conflicts, and producing 3D virtual experiences for clients. When her mouse isn't in hand, she is likely outside with her family, rain or shine.

First and foremost, I want to express my deepest gratitude to Becca for the indelible mark you've had on my academic, personal, and professional journey. I am fortunate to have had the privilege of being your student and honored beyond words for the trust you've placed in me. To my husband Gabe, your love, patience, and support kept me grounded and motivated throughout the writing process. And to my parents, thank you for giving me opportunities to create.

We are grateful to everyone who played a part in bringing this book to fruition, especially our editor, Anuradha Vishwas Joglekar, and the entire Packt team. Working with such a talented group of individuals has been a privilege and made the entire publishing process a rewarding experience.

Lastly, a huge heartfelt thank you to all the readers who embark on this SketchUp adventure with us. We are beyond grateful to be a part of your SketchUp journey and hope this book enriches your life in some way.

About the reviewers

With over 25 years of experience in the interior design and architecture fields, **Kristi Freeland** has acquired a wealth of knowledge and expertise working on high-end custom homes. Following 15 years as a senior designer and project manager at an acclaimed design firm in San Francisco, she founded Carré Designs, a boutique design studio providing renderings, 3D modeling, furniture design, and CAD services to interior designers and architects nationwide. Her team's passion for this niche within the broader design industry is driven by their commitment to detail, scale, historic relevance, and the importance of communicating cohesively with clients and all parties involved. Kristi thrives on collaborating with designers and architects by adding an extra layer of checks and balances and expertise to the designs that come through her studio. When Kristi isn't hard at work, you can find her hard at play camping, hiking, sailing, skiing, traveling, and exploring with her husband, two daughters, and their especially furry pup.

Dhanish Ahmed is an architect and founder of the Arch'O'Maniac design studio. Apart from architectural design and detailing, he specializes in boosting growth through architectural visual marketing. With his expertise in 3D modeling and visualization, along with both rendering and real-time video creation, he has helped the growth and profitability of the previous companies he worked for. Currently, he's in the UK looking for opportunities to work with companies and firms that could make use of his architectural visual marketing and precise detailing skills.

Table of Contents

3

Extruding along Curves and Other Timesavers   61

Part 2: Working with Floor Plans

4

Importing and Exporting a Drawing   99

5

Creating the As-Built Floor Plan

6

Building Exterior Elements and Using the Extension Warehouse

Part 3: Adding Designer Details to a SketchUp Model

7

Adding Interior Elements and 3D Warehouse Furnishings

8

Modeling Furniture – From the Basics to Intricacy   243

9

Applying and Customizing Colors and Materials   271

14

Photorealistic Rendering with SU Podium   473

Part 5: Bonus Tips for Quicker Modeling

15

Tips and Tricks to Up Your SketchUp Game   537

Preface

Without a doubt, **SketchUp** stands out as one of the most remarkable and powerful 3D visualization tools across a spectrum of design sectors, encompassing interior design, architecture, product design, woodworking, landscape architecture, and beyond. It serves as a valuable asset during the schematic and design development stages, and clients benefit from its ability to bring ideas to life in a visually compelling way. A significant advantage of using SketchUp from the get-go is that you will not need to transfer and manipulate drawings from one program to the next. It can all be done right in SketchUp Pro or Studio!

While AutoCAD and Revit are incredible tools for large and small construction documents, make no mistake – you can create accurate construction blueprints for any project type in SketchUp. When it comes to SketchUp drafting and modeling, any limitations often stem from a user's familiarity and skill level rather than inherent flaws in the software itself. *The SketchUp Handbook for Interior Design* aims to cover sophisticated and innovative ways of planning, designing, and presenting within the software, complete with step-by-step explanations and helpful illustrations.

Embark on a journey through each chapter, where you will enhance your SketchUp Pro skills using its sleek yet robust toolset. Practice models specific to each chapter are found in 3D Warehouse. Dive into creating a cozy residential room from scratch, letting your creativity flow by making your own **Furniture, Fixtures, and Equipment** (FFE). Explore the construction of architectural elements for a commercial building, adding realistic touches that help clients quickly understand the concept and design. Learn the art of crafting attractive presentations, and discover interesting tips along the way. This book is constructed as a fun and relatable exploration of what SketchUp can do for your designs and client interactions.

Who this book is for

Assuming that you have a foundational understanding of SketchUp Pro or Studio's toolbars and camera views, you will be seamlessly transitioned from an intermediate to advanced SketchUp modeler with this book. Written by two seasoned interior designers, it unveils their expert navigation of SketchUp, providing valuable insights and strategies for elevated design proficiency.

What this book covers

Chapter 1, Using Essential Tools and Shortcuts for Space Planning, eases you into SketchUp by reviewing introductory concepts and fundamental tools you should already know, adding an interior design spin to make them relatable.

Chapter 2, Becca's Hierarchy of Modeling and the Designer's Modeling Approach, examines Becca's Hierarchy of Modeling, which is a 10-step process you should repeat every time you perform a SketchUp command. Using this process creates a rhythm your fingers will memorize until it becomes second nature. We also wrap up our review of the basics by going through essential trays (or toolbars).

Chapter 3, Extruding along Curves and Other Timesavers, explores some awesome tools that are often underutilized because they require a good amount of practice to master. The instructions in this chapter will help ease your fears when using Follow Me, Autofold, Solid Tools, and Intersect Faces.

Chapter 4, Importing and Exporting a Drawing, covers how to import a quick two-dimensional hand sketch, construction document, DWG/DXF CAD file, or Revit file, which designers are frequently given to create their SketchUp designs. When those imports into SketchUp are done, we trace on top of the content to create three-dimensional models. These processes imply a method of refining or enhancing the initial imported elements, creating a more detailed and accurate representation within the SketchUp software.

Chapter 5, Creating the As-Built Floor Plan, walks you through the beginning steps to create architectural elements of a commercial building. That includes creating walls, cutting holes for doors and windows, and constructing stairs. Drawing on axes and using tags are essential parts of this process.

Chapter 6, Building Exterior Elements and Using the Extension Warehouse, shows you how to build a flat roof with a plain parapet, add additional architectural elements to a building's exterior, and create branding signage using 3D text. This chapter (finally!) introduces you to the Extension Warehouse interface, which has been mentioned in many chapters of the book so far, and covers how to create sections.

Chapter 7, Adding Interior Elements and 3D Warehouse Furnishings, walks you through how to set up CAD elevations in SketchUp and then use the elevations to model custom interior architectural elements, such as pocket doors and intricate trim. In this chapter, we also take a deep dive into 3D Warehouse, discuss the best practices for downloading and importing objects into your model, and introduce Live Components.

Chapter 8, Modeling Furniture – From the Basics to Intricacy, teaches you how to model furniture, starting with a simple coffee table to create a more complex furniture piece, using the manufacturer's specifications for accuracy. We will also share helpful extensions to model furniture more quickly.

Chapter 9, Applying and Customizing Colors and Materials, introduces SketchUp's Paint Bucket tool and built-in collections of materials, enabling you to quickly experiment with adding color. Then, we will dive into editing materials directly in SketchUp and introduce creating and working with custom materials.

Chapter 10, Enhancing a Model with Details for Final Presentation, discusses tools and techniques for augmenting and showing a SketchUp model to prepare for a final presentation, including shadows, geo-location, and SketchUp styles.

Chapter 11, Exporting Images and Animations, shows you how to prepare final scenes for presentations, export various quality images, create a simple walkthrough animation in SketchUp using the camera tools and scenes, and correctly set up a SketchUp scene to be exported to scale as a PDF.

Chapter 12, SketchUp LayOut Part I – The Interface, explains the interface of SketchUp LayOut, a second powerful application that users are automatically given when purchasing SketchUp Pro or SketchUp Studio. LayOut is the paper space for SketchUp's model space or the software to create beautiful presentations or construction documents.

Chapter 13, SketchUp LayOut Part II – Paper Space Content, enables you to experiment with LayOut's panels and explore its features in the context of paper space. Discover techniques such as stacking viewports and crafting impressive presentations or construction documents.

Chapter 14, Photorealistic Rendering with SU Podium, explores SU Podium, which is an easy-to-use rendering plugin for SketchUp that creates realistic lighting, materials, and reflections for your models. You will learn how to produce a photorealistic rendering using a practice model.

Chapter 15, Tips and Tricks to Up Your SketchUp Game, is loaded with extra juicy tips and tricks that we have learned through the years. The last section of the chapter provides helpful links, books, and courses to explore to continue your education.

To get the most out of this book

We assume that you have a foundational understanding of SketchUp Pro or Studio's toolbars and camera views.

Software/hardware covered in the book	Operating system requirements
SketchUp Pro or SketchUp Studio	Windows, macOS, SketchUp Pro or Studio 2022 or newer (images are from SketchUp 2024)
SketchUp LayOut	
SU Podium	
SketchUp 3D Warehouse	
SketchUp Extension Warehouse (available online or inside SketchUp)	

Before installing any software or plugins, check the system requirements from Sketchup.com *and* suplugins.com.

This book uses the designs and models created by Carré Design Studio, Heather Hilliard Design, JayJeffers Inc., jbA Architecture, Kelly Hohla Interiors, Madeleine Draper, Nat Ellis, Picciotti Design, and SketchUp School for demonstration purposes with their approval.

Measurements in the book are presented in US customary units.

Links to download practice models from 3D Warehouse are provided in the Technical requirements section of the respective chapter.

If you are accessing 3D Warehouse within a SketchUp file, avoid directly inserting it into your existing model. Instead, download it as a separate SketchUp file to preserve the scenes we've created. If you need help with how to do this, consult Chapter 7 for 3D Warehouse guidance.

This book focuses on SketchUp for Desktop software, whether SketchUp Pro or SketchUp Studio, which are paid subscriptions within SketchUp's suite. Pro and Studio include SketchUp LayOut, which we will also teach and use in this book (Chapters 12 and 13). You will require the following:

- *A SketchUp Pro or SketchUp Studio subscription*
- *A Trimble ID SketchUp login and an internet connection to access 3D Warehouse*

Download the example files

You can download the practice files for this book from **3D Warehouse**. The specific links are provided in the *Technical requirements* section of the respective chapter. Images in the book are available as XCF files here: `https://static.packt-cdn.com/downloads/9781837631872_Resourcefiles.zip`

Download the color images

We also provide a PDF file that has color images of the screenshots and diagrams used in this book. You can download it here: `http://www.packtpub.com/sites/default/files/downloads/Bookname_ColorImages.pdf`.

Conventions used

There are a number of text conventions used throughout this book.

Bold: Indicates a new term, an important word, or words that you see on screen. For instance, words in menus or dialog boxes appear in **bold**. Here is an example: "From the **File** menu, choose **Import**."

> **Tips or important notes**
> Appear like this.

Get in touch

Feedback from our readers is always welcome.

General feedback: If you have questions about any aspect of this book, email us at customercare@ packtpub.com and mention the book title in the subject of your message.

Errata: Although we have taken every care to ensure the accuracy of our content, mistakes do happen. If you have found a mistake in this book, we would be grateful if you would report this to us. Please visit www.packtpub.com/support/errata and fill in the form.

Piracy: If you come across any illegal copies of our works in any form on the internet, we would be grateful if you would provide us with the location address or website name. Please contact us at copyright@packt.com with a link to the material.

If you are interested in becoming an author: If there is a topic that you have expertise in and you are interested in either writing or contributing to a book, please visit authors.packtpub.com.

Share Your Thoughts

Once you've read *The SketchUp Handbook for Interior Design*, we'd love to hear your thoughts! Scan the QR code below to go straight to the Amazon review page for this book and share your feedback.

https://packt.link/r/1-837-63187-5

Your review is important to us and the tech community and will help us make sure we're delivering excellent quality content.

Download a free PDF copy of this book

Thanks for purchasing this book!

Do you like to read on the go but are unable to carry your print books everywhere?

Is your eBook purchase not compatible with the device of your choice?

Don't worry, now with every Packt book you get a DRM-free PDF version of that book at no cost.

Read anywhere, any place, on any device. Search, copy, and paste code from your favorite technical books directly into your application.

The perks don't stop there, you can get exclusive access to discounts, newsletters, and great free content in your inbox daily

Follow these simple steps to get the benefits:

1. Scan the QR code or visit the link below

https://packt.link/free-ebook/9781837631872

2. Submit your proof of purchase
3. That's it! We'll send your free PDF and other benefits to your email directly

Part 1: Applying the Basics to Interior Design

In the first part of the book, we review the SketchUp for Desktop (SketchUp Pro or Studio) interface by applying the foundational tools and concepts to the design field, with industry-specific examples. We ensure a thorough understanding of precision modeling fundamentals, including reviewing inferences and essential tools and panels (like the sometimes challenging Follow Me). We also provide a beginner's workflow if you have not established one yet. Along the way, you may come across a tip or two that adds efficiency to your modeling process!

This part has the following chapters:

- *Chapter 1, Using Essential Tools and Shortcuts for Space Planning*
- *Chapter 2, Becca's Hierarchy of Modeling and the Designer's Modeling Approach*
- *Chapter 3, Extruding along Curves and Other Timesavers*

Using Essential Tools and Shortcuts for Space Planning

SketchUp shines as a premier 3D visualization tool embraced across diverse design sectors, from interior design and architecture to construction and landscape design.

It transforms concepts into reality during schematic and design development phases without the headache of switching between different programs.

Authored by two seasoned interior designers, this book is packed with intermediate-to-advanced tips, tricks, and techniques tailored for SketchUp for Desktop users, whether SketchUp Pro or SketchUp Studio. Leveraging your foundational SketchUp skills, we dig into practical applications within the design field while enhancing your modeling proficiency.

By the book's conclusion, you'll command SketchUp's capabilities from a designer's standpoint, refining your workflow strategies for optimal efficiency. You'll know how to use SketchUp for your whole project, collaborate seamlessly with your design team, and craft vibrant presentation documents to show off your work.

In this first chapter, we will ease into SketchUp by reviewing the introductory items you should already know, but we will add an interior design spin to make it relatable. You will learn how to effectively use 2D applications, the importance of utilizing inferences, and how to create your own shortcuts. Finally, we will delve into the complexity of components and how they can improve your workflow productivity.

By the end of this chapter, you will probably pick up a tip or two that you didn't know to make your modeling time more efficient!

In this chapter, we will cover the following topics:

- Using camera views for 2D space planning
- Modeling accurately using SketchUp's tools and inferences

- Creating 2D space plan items
- Mastering components for repeated elements
- Building information modeling and other data extraction

Technical requirements

This book focuses on **SketchUp for Desktop** software, whether **SketchUp Pro** or **SketchUp Studio**, which are paid subscriptions within SketchUp's suite. Pro and Studio include **SketchUp LayOut**, which we will also teach and use in this book (*Chapter 12* and *Chapter 13*).You will require the following:

- A SketchUp Pro or SketchUp Studio subscription
- A **Trimble ID** SketchUp login and an internet connection to access **3D Warehouse**

> **Images in the book**
>
> Our images might look different than what you see on your screen. This is simply based on your version of SketchUp, your computer operating system, and the extensions we have chosen to install on our machines. Most screenshots in this book are from a Windows computer using SketchUp 2024.

Using camera views for 2D space planning

You are already familiar with SketchUp's interface, so we will bypass the overview of the modeling window. Let's jump into the **menu bar** options to set up a view for **two-dimensional** (**2D**) space planning:

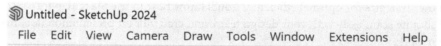

Figure 1.1: Menu bar in SketchUp 2024 (Windows)

When space planning in 2D, it is best to model using the **Camera** setting **Top** view to ensure we are modeling on top of the ground plane.

In the menu bar, click **Camera**, then go down to **Standard Views**. A flyout will give you seven view options: **Top**, **Bottom**, **Front**, **Back**, **Left**, **Right**, and **Iso**. These views are based on the original drawing coordinates (x, y, z):

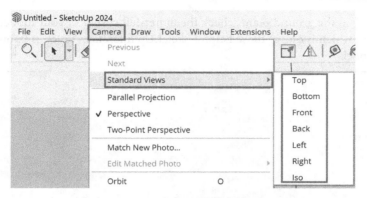

Figure 1.2: Standard Views flyout under Camera menu

Click on **Top** to choose a top-down look at the ground plane.

SketchUp modelers using a Windows computer have access to a toolbar called **Views**, which has icons for each of the seven views, and it can save a bit of time by single-clicking the icon. *Figure 1.3* shows this toolbar:

Figure 1.3: Views toolbar in Windows OS (from left to right) Iso, Top, Front, Right, Left, Back, and Bottom

MacOS users will discover identical icons within the **Tools** menu, presented individually rather than as a lengthy toolbar.

> **Finding tools**
>
> Can't remember where to find *additional toolbars*? A quick way to access toolbars is by right-clicking in the gray toolbar area (underneath the **Menu** bar), which produces a list of available toolbars. Find the toolbar you want to use and click once on its name for it to open.
>
> A second way to access toolbars is in the menu bar. For Windows users, click **View**, choose **Toolbars**, check the box next to the toolbar(s) you want to use, then click **Close**. On macOS, click **View** | **Tool Palettes** | and select the tool palette you want to use.
>
> You can also use the search function or command for any type of tool or command (available in 2022 and later versions) by clicking the **Search** icon (or the shortcut *Shift* + *S*), typing top view, and clicking on the correct selection.

Now, looking down at the ground plane, check the upper-left corner of your modeling window. It should read **Top**, which is one of those helpful SketchUp inferences to let us know how we are oriented in our model:

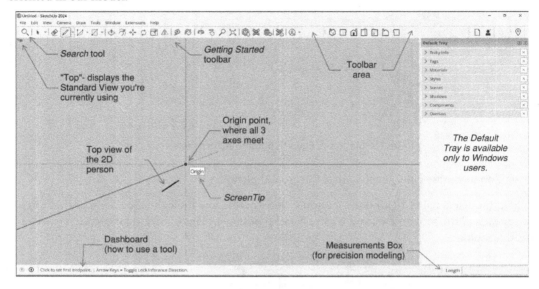

Figure 1.4: Top view, looking down on the ground plane (Windows)

In this section, we set up our modeling window to draw two-dimensionally. Let's go to the next section for a list of tools and commands to help us draft precision-based objects.

Modeling accurately using SketchUp's tools and inferences

Creating accuracy in SketchUp requires the knowledge and use of the following tools and commands. You might already be familiar with some of these, but their importance will be outlined as we go along.

Measurements toolbar

Think of the **Measurements toolbar** or **Measurements box** as your side view mirrors while driving. When we drive, we should consistently monitor those mirrors to avoid accidents. The same goes for the **Measurements** toolbar.

The **Measurements** box is a major way to draft accurately in SketchUp. Many designers believe that creating precision drafting is impossible with SketchUp, but it is done flawlessly by correctly typing in dimensions.

Depending on the template you are using (we are using the **Inches** template for this book), there is a default unit of measurement. However, you are not locked into using the template's units. Typing in additional information after the number value will change the unit of measurement for the command you are performing:

- **Inches**: Type `"` after the number, then *Enter* or *Return* on the keyboard. Example: 6 ".
- **Feet**: Type `'` after the number, then *Enter* or *Return* on the keyboard. Example: 6 '.
- **Millimeters**: Type mm after the number, then *Enter* or *Return* on the keyboard. Example: 6mm.
- **Centimeters**: Type cm after the number, then *Enter* or *Return* on the keyboard. Example: 6cm.
- **Meters**: Type m after the number, then *Enter* or *Return* on the keyboard. Example: 6m.

Inferences

As a beginner to SketchUp, you should have learned about the inference types. SketchUp comes equipped with little "helpers" to make sure you are getting the most out of each tool. Here is a list to remind you of your helpers:

- **ScreenTips**: Yellow boxes of black text that pop up when you hover over anything in the model while in a command or tool (other than **Select**). The ScreenTip quickly tells you what your mouse is hovering over (whether it's an endpoint, component, edge, etc.).
- **Cursor/Icons**: Your cursor will look like the icon of the tool you are using. The icons themselves give a glimpse of what the tool does. For example, the **Tape Measure** tool looks like a tape measure.
- **Point inferences**: Each point (endpoint, midpoint, face, grouped endpoint, grouped midpoint, etc.) has a different color and, sometimes, a different shape. These are helpful for snapping to precise areas.
- **Shape inferences**: While using a shape tool (rectangle, circle, arc), we can see the shape at the tip of our cursor. It will change color based on which axis we are drawing. A ScreenTip will pop up when we have created a half circle with the arc tool, a golden section with the rectangle, or a perfect square (all four sides equal) with the rectangle.
- **Linear inferences**: These are the most common types of inference because they include most other inference types: point, shape, axes colors, and ScreenTip. Locking in any axis will show the linear inference by referencing the axes colors: red for the x-axis, green for the y-axis, and blue for the z-axis. We will discuss this more later on.
- If you are using SketchUp 2024 or newer, your file's title will include an asterisk (*) to the right of the name, just like in other software programs, indicating that you need to save your work.
- **Dashboard**: The dashboard at the bottom of the modeling window gives instructions on what to do with the tool you chose based on your operating system. For example, when using the **Select** tool on a Windows computer, it shows this information:

⚲ ⓘ Click or drag to select objects. Shift = Add/Subtract. Ctrl = Add. Shift + Ctrl = Subtract.

Figure 1.5: Dashboard with Select tool activated

> **More information**
>
> For more information about inferences, head over to `https://help.sketchup.com/en/sketchup/introducing-drawing-basics-and-concepts` to refresh your memory.

Locking in the axes (another type of inference)

To be more efficient when modeling, tapping **arrow keys** on the keyboard will easily lock in a particular axis. This is much more efficient than holding down *Shift* to lock it in for many reasons, such as easily switching the axis when the wrong one was chosen and the ability to perform a command without *Shift* hindering you from doing so.

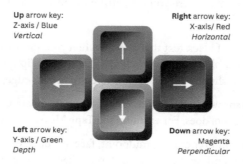

Figure 1.6: Keyboard arrow keys compared to the axes in SketchUp

To lock in an axis, tap the corresponding arrow keys. When you do, you will notice the line turns from a regular line thickness to a bold one:

- *Right arrow* key = red or x-axis (horizontal)
- *Left arrow* key = green or y-axis (depth)
- *Up arrow* key = blue or z-axis (vertical)
- *Down arrow* key = magenta; draw a line perpendicular to another

> **Important note**
>
> For those with some form of color blindness, the colors of the axes can be changed under **Window | Preferences | Accessibility** on Windows, or **SketchUp | Settings | Accessibility** on macOS.

As beginning modelers, it was important to practice drafting along an axis to get comfortable drawing accurately in the interface. If you have not already, you can begin drafting off the axes. However, note that you will still draft using axes approximately 80–90% of the time and should always try to lock in an axis, whether a novice or pro.

The Flip tool

The **Flip** tool is mentioned at this point in the chapter because it relies on the axis colors to use, though some users only rely on the rectangular plane it creates for flipping. Whichever method you rely on for the **Flip** tool, here are the basics to using it.

The **Flip** tool is for flipping or mirroring an object along an axis (x/red, y/green, or z/blue).

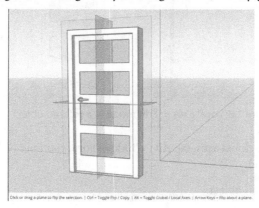

Click or drag a plane to flip the selection. | Ctrl = Toggle Flip / Copy. | Alt = Toggle Global / Local Axes. | Arrow Keys = Flip about a plane.

Figure 1.7: Door with Flip tool activated and the Dashboard with instructions for the tool

As mentioned in the *Locking in the axes* section, anything that uses axis colors means you can use the arrow keys to toggle through x, y, and z. Once you activate the **Flip** tool, you see the three planes. Lock in the plane to the corresponding axis using the *right arrow* for red (x-axis), *left arrow* for green (y-axis), and *up arrow* for blue (z-axis).

The **Flip** tool is also used for mirroring an object while copying it.

You can find the **Flip** tool in **Tools | Flip**, or in toolbars such as **Getting Started** and **Large Toolset**. It does not have a default shortcut, but you can assign one to it.

You can flip any object, whether a group, component, or loose geometry.

While most find it easier to select the object to flip first, you can activate the **Flip** tool and then click on the object to flip.

Objects are flipped along the central point of the object, where the three planes intersect. If you want to change where the objects flip from, click and drag the plane (not in Copy mode) to change the point where the flip happens.

Objects are flipped based on where the axes lie. If you get into **Edit** mode of a rotated component, for example, the **local axes** (inside **Edit** mode) are likely different from the model axes (called **global axes**). In *Figure 1.8*, the door on the right was rotated 30 degrees. In **Edit** mode of the group, the local axes have changed to match the rotation:

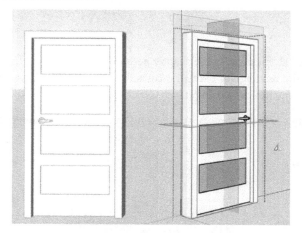

Figure 1.8: Local axes in Edit mode of a rotated object

If you prefer to flip along the global axes, tap *Alt* (Windows) or *Command* (⌘, macOS) to toggle the axes between **global** and **local**.

Here's how to flip or **mirror** an object:

1. Select the object and activate the **Flip** tool (or vice versa).

2. Click once on a plane to flip the object along the x-, y-, or z-axis, or tap the corresponding axis' arrow key one time.

3. That's it! Your object will be flipped.

Here's how you can copy with the **Flip** tool:

4. Select the object to copy.

5. With the **Flip** tool active, tap *Ctrl* (Windows) or *Opt* (macOS) to start **Copy** mode. You will see the plus sign inference attached to the cursor, which means you are in copy mode.

6. Click and drag a plane to the desired spot for copying.

> **Tip**
>
> You can snap the copy to a point or edge for precision. While you are getting used to the tool, some find it easier to copy the original to line up with the object they are mirroring and then use the **Move** tool to place the object.

7. When you release your mouse button, SketchUp creates a mirrored copy of your selected geometry.

The **Flip** tool is a great addition to SketchUp! Those of you who enjoyed Flip Along (the previous mirroring tool) will eventually come to like Flip (it took us a bit before we finally relinquished our loyalty).

Undo and redo (your new best friends)

If you are familiar with the **Undo** command in other software, it is the same in SketchUp.

Typing *Ctrl/⌘) + Z* will undo the last step you performed in SketchUp (though remember that the default undo cache holds no more than 100 undo actions).

To **Redo** a command after accidentally (or purposely) using Undo, use *Ctrl/⌘) + Y.*

Remember, once you close out of a SketchUp model and re-open it later, you can no longer use undo or redo work prior to closing out of the model (though one workaround for this is using **Version History**, which will be discussed in *Chapter 3*).

SketchUp Modeling Tips from the Pros: Shortcuts

Tip 1: You should always have one hand resting on the keyboard and the other hand on your three-button mouse (or 3D mouse).

Tip 2: Use keyboard and mouse shortcuts to boost productivity!

Using a three-button mouse

Who doesn't want to increase their productivity? You will save a lot of time using a three-button mouse to navigate the modeling window rather than clicking the icons or tapping the keyboard shortcuts. You save time because you do not need to exit out of a command to navigate around the model and then get back into the command. You can perform the command and navigate all at the same time!

Mouse navigation shortcuts

Learning how to effectively use the mouse navigation shortcuts can take a bit of time to feel comfortable with, but once you get the hang of it, you will understand why it is so important. Give yourself time to practice using these shortcuts over and over:

- **Orbit** = scroll wheel: Orbit is how you move three-dimensionally within the model, circling around objects. Hold down the scroll wheel in short increments, moving your mouse in all directions. Every now and then, lift your finger and put it down again so you don't run out of room.

- **Zoom** = scroll wheel: Move your cursor to the object or area you want to view better. Then, move the scroll wheel up (unless you inverted your scroll wheel). To zoom away from the object, move the scroll wheel down.

Cursor placement is vital to making this work properly! Your cursor should be on the object or area you are scrolling to or away from. If you scroll randomly in your modeling window, your zoom may take you to Timbuktu. Be purposeful with your cursor placement. Do the same when scrolling out so you do not become stuck.

> **SketchUp Modeling Tips from the Pros: Zoom In!**
>
> Zoom in for accuracy! Modeling further away from the object you are editing negates SketchUp's precision. For example, zoom in on existing points before adding a line, or make sure you selected a single face (or multiple) before adding materials.

- **Pan** = *scroll wheel + Shift*: Pan takes you up and down and side to side. Hold down the *scroll wheel* and the *Shift* key at the same time. Just as with orbit, hold down the scroll wheel in short increments while moving your mouse to go where you want, toggling between lifting your finger and holding it down again.

Note that you can also use *scroll wheel + left-click*, though some find this difficult depending on the preferred finger for the scroll wheel.

Other mouse tips

There is much more to the mouse than navigating through SketchUp. The mouse is another powerful tool within SketchUp, allowing users to find hidden tools and effectively select and deselect one or more objects at one time:

- **Right-clicking in SketchUp**: Whether you are in the modeling window or on an object, this quickly leads to additional tools within the **Context menu**. Right-click often!

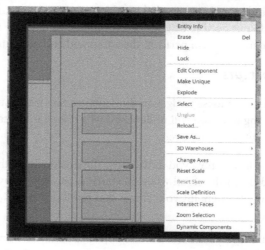

Figure 1.9: Context menu (accessed by using a right-click on a component)

- **Ways to select objects with the mouse**:

  - We always select an object with a left-click; however, there is an important tip for this: do not hold down the button. You will almost always release the mouse before moving to the next step. The mantra for this tip is click and release, click and release.

  - When working with 2D shapes, edges and faces that are loose geometry, double-click the face to pick up the connected edges and faces that make up that shape.

  - When selecting 3D forms that are not yet grouped, triple-click (a fast 1-2-3) any of the faces to choose all connected shapes and edges that create the form.

  - After selecting, you can add other objects to the selection by holding down the *Ctrl* or *Opt* keys and left-clicking the new selections.

  - Holding down the *Shift* key allows you to add or subtract objects from the selection.

  - Ways to use the crossing windows:

    - Left-to-right crossing window (solid line): Clicking to the left side of the entities and dragging right, which is called a window selection or bounding box, selects only those elements completely within the selection rectangle.

    - Right-to-left crossing window (dotted lines): Clicking from the right side and dragging to the left, which is called a crossing selection, selects any elements within the selection rectangle, including those that are only partially contained in the rectangle.

  - With one or more edges selected, right-click and choose **Select**, and there are options based on what you have selected.

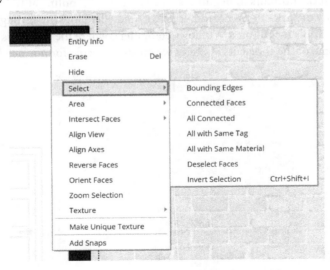

Figure 1.10: Right-click Context menu for the Select flyout

- **To invert the scroll wheel, do the following**:

  - On Mac, click the **SketchUp** menu | **Preferences** | **Compatibility**. Then, in the **Mouse Wheel Style** area, check **Invert** and click **OK**

  - On Windows, click the **Window** menu | **Preferences** | **Compatibility**. Then, in the **Mouse Wheel Style** area, check **Invert** and click **Close**

Using a three-button mouse is critical to your success with the software. SketchUp is intuitive and powerful, but it cannot read our minds. We must choose the correct command and move our mouse purposefully, creating a symbiotic relationship between ourselves and our computer.

> 3D mouse compatibility
>
> If you prefer using a **3D mouse**, also referred to as a space mouse or CAD mouse, rest assured that SketchUp Pro and Studio support most brands. Whether it's a compact travel-size 3D mouse or the robust **3dconnexion SpaceMouse Pro**, many SketchUp users find great satisfaction in utilizing their 3D mouse within the SketchUp environment.

Creating keyboard shortcuts

While the SketchUp icons are a helpful visualization of a tool, using shortcuts will (you guessed it) shave a lot of time off modeling. If you do not have a list of shortcuts, one of our favorites— with corresponding large-scale shortcut graphics—comes from Matt Donley of Master SketchUp (`mastersketchup.com`).

You can also find a list of shortcuts in beginners' SketchUp books, online at `https://help.sketchup.com/en/quick-reference-cards`, and when looking through the menu bar. *Figure 1.10* shows the **Tools** menu (on a Windows computer), where the shortcuts are listed to the right of the name. Some of the shortcuts are ones we created specific for our needs, so they won't match yours:

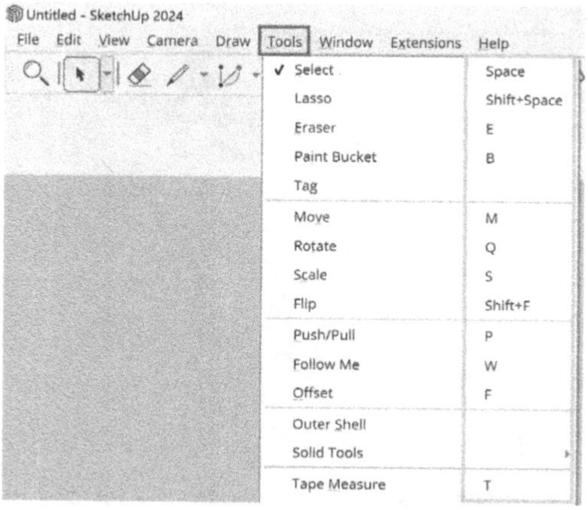

Figure 1.11: Shortcut letters to the right of a tool's name

Creating your own shortcuts is imperative to a good modeling workflow. There are a few stipulations to creating your own shortcuts, but almost anything native to SketchUp can have a shortcut (and many of the plugins can, too!). Here are some basic rules for creating them. If you break one of these rules, you will see a popup telling you to choose another one:

- You can use modifier keys in the command, such as *Shift* or *Option* (*Opt*).

- The shortcut cannot start with a number due to conflicting with the **Measurements** box.

- You cannot use shortcuts that are specific to your computer's operating system. For example, *Ctrl* + *P* is not allowed on a Windows computer because that is the system's shortcut for printing.

- If there is a SketchUp default shortcut that you do not use and want to assign to another, you can reassign the shortcut. For example, the default shortcut *G* creates a component of the selected objects, but the authors of this book carefully pick and choose what should be made a component, so we do not need a shortcut for it. However, every object in our model should be grouped, so we reassigned *G* to **Make Group**.

Another command we use often is **Paste in Place**, which does not have a default shortcut.

What is **Paste in Place**? Sometimes, we need to move or copy an object from inside a group to outside a group or vice versa. This is done by cutting it—*Ctrl*/⌘ + *X*—or copying with *Ctrl*/⌘ + *C*, then pasting it in the exact same place outside the grouping using **Paste in Place**. It is also a great way to paste to the exact location in an identical SketchUp file.

To manually use **Paste in Place** after copying or cutting an object, use the **Edit** menu and arrow down to **Paste in Place**. To create a shortcut for the **Paste in Place** command instead, follow these steps:

1. In the menu bar, select **Window | Preferences** (Windows) or **SketchUp | Settings** (macOS).

2. A dialog box called **SketchUp Preferences** appears. In the sidebar (on the left), select **Shortcuts**.

3. In the **Filter** box, start typing the name of the command you want to add a shortcut to. In this instance, type paste. Under **Function**, the menu bar where the tool or command can be found is listed first:

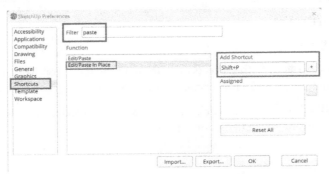

Figure 1.12: Adding a shortcut for Paste in Place (Windows)

4. Highlight the correct field (**Edit/Paste in Place**) to add a shortcut.

5. For Windows users, click the box underneath **Add Shortcut**. Then, do the following:

    * For this shortcut, we are using a modifier key (*Shift*) plus the letter *P*. So, hold down the *Shift* key to make it auto-populate to the **Add Shortcut** field, then tap *P*.

    * Click the + sign next to the field. The shortcut will now show up in the **Assigned** box.

    * Click **OK** if you are done, or continue adding shortcuts.

6. For macOS users, click the text box in the lower-left of the **Shortcuts** pane and type the keyboard shortcut that you want to assign to the command:

    * Hold down the *Shift* key to make it auto-populate to the **Add Shortcut** field, then tap *P*.

    * Your assigned shortcut then appears in the **Key** column. Do not hit *Enter*, or the shortcut will be deleted.

    * You can continue adding shortcuts, or close out of the dialog box.

7. If you try to override a shortcut already in the system, a popup like this one will be displayed. You can select **Yes** to reassign the shortcut, or **No** to choose another command:

Figure 1.13: Shortcut warning dialog box

Other software-to-software shared shortcuts will also work in SketchUp, and are already enabled, some of which we already mentioned:

* **Copy** = *Ctrl*/⌘ + *C* = Copy

* **Paste** = *Ctrl*/⌘ + *V*

* **Cut** = *Ctrl*/⌘ + *X*

* **Select All** = *Ctrl*/⌘ + *A* (this selects everything in the model or, when in edit mode of a group or component, it selects everything inside that grouping)

* **Deselect All** = *Ctrl*/⌘ + *T* or click a blank area in the modeling window (this is not a software-to-software shortcut, but one that should be mentioned)

> **Note regarding Copy and Paste**
>
> Do not make a habit of using the shortcuts for **Copy** and **Paste** in your model when copying objects. Use the **Move** + **Copy** commands (copy is activated with a modifier key after activating Move (*M*) so you copy along the axis).

Guide lines and guide points

The **Tape Measure** tool not only measures objects, but its default purpose is to create guides for precision modeling. Both types of guides do not interfere with regular geometry and can be easily deleted or hidden using the **Edit** or **View** menus.

Here are tips for creating guides:

- To create **guide lines** (dashed lines that stretch on infinitely), click an edge, face, or midpoint of an object, move your mouse in the direction of the measurement, and type in an increment. Note that you can lock in the tape measure movements (axes) using the arrow keys.

- If a guide is not created, the **Tape Measure** tool might be in measure mode. You will know by looking at your cursor. When using the **Tape Measure** tool, if your cursor looks like a tape measure without a plus sign, it is only measuring. In the command, tap the modifier key (*Ctrl* on Windows or *Opt* on macOS) once, and a red plus sign will show above the **Tape Measure** tool. Try creating a guide line again.

- To create a **guide point**, a dotted line with a black point at its end, click an *endpoint*, and move your mouse towards another endpoint, typing in the desired increment.

  - The beauty of a guide point versus a guide line is that objects can easily snap to the point. Whether you are moving an object to the point or creating a line or shape that begins or ends at that point, guide points are much easier to use as references than lines or guide lines.

  - If a guide point is not created, follow the steps for the guide line to ensure you are not in measure mode. Otherwise, make sure you are clicking an endpoint to create the guide point. It will not work if you first click a midpoint or edge.

Also, remember that the **Protractor tool** creates guide lines on a specific angle, which is great for roof pitch and other angled guides.

In this section, we reviewed multiple ways to model efficiently, including using mouse and keyboard shortcuts, inferences, and guides. In the next section, we will look at how to create a 2D sofa for a reusable space plan item with step-by-step instructions.

Creating 2D space plan items

A large part of the programming phase in interior design includes space planning, which influences how people interact, communicate, move, work, play, and feel (mentally). It also ensures that a room can be used to its maximum potential when incorporating **Furniture, Fixtures, and Equipment** (FFE).

Creating space plan items in the 3D SketchUp world makes it easier to visualize how the items will interact while considering the volume of the space. Space planning in 2D CAD programs is fine but does not allow for a quick 3D view to determine spatial equity. Additionally, going between CAD and SketchUp can ultimately be a waste of time if most of the work will be done in SketchUp anyway.

For this example, we will create a 90" L x 33" D sofa to use for space planning; this is the kind of item that can be used over and over again:

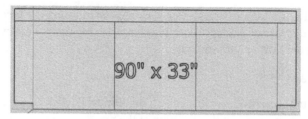

Figure 1.14: Completed sofa

To create any 2D Space Planning Objects in SketchUp, follow these steps:

1. Set the Camera view to **Top** view.

2. Zoom in to the origin point of the model, where all three axes meet.

> **SketchUp basics reminder**
>
> We should always begin modeling close to the origin point and then outward from that point to avoid future issues, such as clipping planes.

3. We will first create the seat or base of the sofa, which is 78 " L x 29 " D:

    I.   Activate your **Rectangle** tool by either clicking on the icon or tapping the shortcut *R* on your keyboard. Your cursor will change to a pencil with a little rectangle attached (another one of those awesome SketchUp inferences!).

    II. Lock in the blue/z-axis by tapping the *up arrow* key.

    III. Click once on the origin point and lift up your finger (do not hold down the mouse button).

    IV. Move your mouse up to the right, diagonally from where you started.

    V.   Now, remember how you should always keep an eye on your **Measurements** box? The text in the box has now changed to read **Dimensions**. This means it wants us to type in the dimensions of the rectangle. You do not need to click inside the **Measurements** box; in fact, you cannot. Instead, type 78 , 29 and hit *Enter/Return*. In top view, the first number is the red/x-axis, and the second is the green/y-axis.

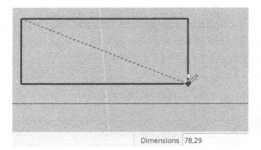

Figure 1.15: Create a Rectangle in Top view

Note regarding measurements

This exercise uses the inches template/units. Because we used a template that is in inches, we do not need to type the inch marks (") after each number set. If you are not using an inches template, you must type " after each number set.

    VI.   End your command by hitting the *spacebar* or clicking the **Select** tool icon.

4.   Next, immediately make the rectangle a group by double-clicking on the face (to pick up the face and the edges that created it), right-clicking on the shape, and choosing **Make Group**.

Important note regarding groups

Every object in your model should be grouped so that the geometry does not stick together. You can make an object a group before you started creating it, by right-clicking a blank area in your model and selecting **Make Group**, or immediately after you create the object. Make one of these options a habitual part of your workflow.

---

5.   We will now create the arms for the sofa, which are 6 " W x 27 " D:

    I.   Activate the **Rectangle** tool, click the top-right endpoint of the rectangle group we made in the last step, release your mouse, and move it down the right. Type 6 , 27 and hit *Enter/Return* on your keyboard.

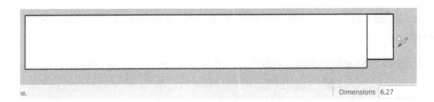

Figure 1.16: Create the first sofa arm

II.   Make that arm a group (or a component because it is a repeated object), then copy it over to the opposite side of the sofa, endpoint to endpoint:

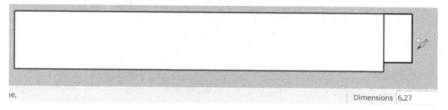

Figure 1.17: Copy the sofa arm to the opposite side

6.   Now let's create the back of the sofa, which is 90 " L x 4 " D:

I.   This time, let's change it up by creating a group first. Right-click in the blank modeling window and choose **Make Group**. By doing this step first when drawing a shape, we will already be creating a group within edit mode, which is one less step to remember:

Figure 1.18: Right-click in the modeling window and choose Make Group

II.   Activate the **Rectangle** tool and lock in the blue/z-axis (using the *up arrow* key). Then, click an **Endpoint** on the sofa, move the mouse to the opposite corner, type 90 , 4, and tap *Enter*:

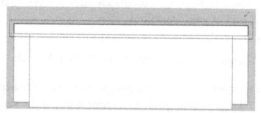

Figure 1.19: While already in Edit mode of a group, create the sofa back

7.   Now, check the dimensions by using the **Tape Measure** tool. To accomplish this, use the following steps:

I.   Activate the tool by clicking the **Tape Measure** icon or using shortcut *T*.

II.   Find an endpoint inference by hovering around the square until you see an inference point and/or the yellow ScreenTip that says **Endpoint**; then, click that point. (As mentioned in the *Using a three-button mouse* section, zoom in! That way your measurements will be accurate.)

III.   Hover over the opposite endpoint and look at your **Measurements** box, or the ScreenTip, for the correct length.

8. From here, you can add lines for cushions or other details or leave it as-is.

9. When you are done, select all the sofa pieces (groups and geometry) and make them one overall group:

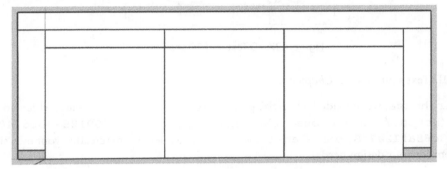

Figure 1.20: The completed and grouped sofa

10. Now, we will add 3D text to the shape so you can easily distinguish the variety of space plan items you will create in the model:

I.   In the **Tools** menu or **Large Tool Set**, choose **3D Text**.

II.   There are many options inside the **Place 3D Text** dialog box. Here, you can choose the font, size, color, and extrusion:

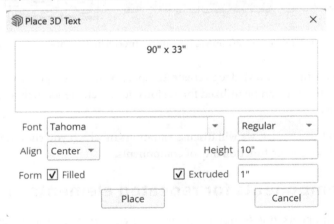

Figure 1.21: 3D Text dialog box

III.   Once you have filled out the options, click **Place** and move the text on top of your 2D shape.

11. You can use the **Scale** tool (shortcut *S*) to quickly size up or down the 3D text after placing it.

12. Plus, you can get into **Edit** mode to add color to the text.

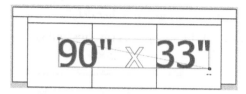

Figure 1.22: 3D Text and 2D shapes

We cover 3D Text a bit more in *Chapter 6*.

In 3D Warehouse, we uploaded a SketchUp file called Space Plan Items, which you can download (https://3dwarehouse.sketchup.com/model/82259125-3bbd-40d1-a569-ae2c65af12a7/Space-Plan-Items) to use as a reference for creating your own shapes (or use them for your design needs).

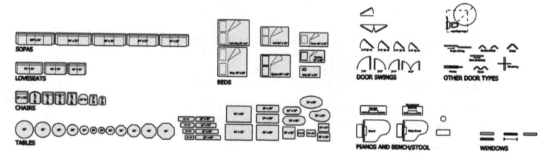

Figure 1.23: Becca's 2D Space Plan Items model in 3D Warehouse

You are now equipped with the knowledge to create 2D space planning shapes. The method outlined in this section is versatile and can be utilized for various design elements such as 2 x 4s, doors, windows, and columns.

In the final section of this chapter, we will discuss situations in which you should use components instead of groups and review the functionality of components.

Mastering components for repeated elements

To level up using components, this section begins by reviewing what you should already know and addressing the commonly asked questions when differentiating a group from a component. From there, more advanced component knowledge will be discussed that references **Building Information Modeling (BIM)**, data extraction, and object classification.

Groups in SketchUp are vital to modeling success. Groups are when all geometry of an object—whether shapes, lines/edges, or forms—are fused together so they cannot be modified accidentally or mess up another object. We must reiterate what was stated earlier in this chapter because of its importance: every single item in your model must be grouped. The most visible reason for this is so objects do not stick to other objects. The technical reasons include loose geometry slows down the modeling file, creating lags, and this can create glitches.

Now, what is a component? A **component** is a group of geometries that will be reused more than once in a model. Components possess additional capabilities that groups do not, allowing modelers to edit linked objects (i.e., copied components) simultaneously, whether adding materials, changing the scale, adding or removing geometry, and more. Components require us to think ahead when modeling and efficiently plan when objects will be reused. A component does not appear to be more than a group until it has been copied.

When learning components, the most often-asked question is this: are components groups? The answer is yes; components are groups! After that answer, the second question is this: Do you need to make an object into a group before making it a component? Technically speaking, no, because making loose geometry a component automatically forms a group. That said, sometimes software is glitchy. Every now and then, we create a component of nongrouped objects, but for whatever reason, SketchUp does not group the objects. To be extra cautious, make it a habit to group an object before making it a component. Doing this ensures all geometry is fused together, regardless of glitches.

Let's look at some additional questions that arise when learning components:

- *Can a group become a component?*

  Yes. A quick way to do this is to right-click on the group (not in edit mode) and choose **Make Component**.

- *I created a component, but it is acting like a group. Why?*

  After creating the component, you will not see its functionality until it is copied and then edited.

- *Can I just make everything a component so I don't have to worry about what to make a group or what to make a component?*

  That is entirely up to your workflow. Some prefer making all objects components, while others use them sparingly.

- *Can a component become just a group?*

  No, not without exploding the entities (which we should avoid).

A component can be made unique, by right-clicking on a component and selecting **Make Unique** so it is no longer tied to other components. However, it is still a component. To make it a group - which is something we only suggest doing once you have a thorough understanding of how components work - you can explode the component and regroup it.

We can also make multiple objects unique together by selecting them all at one time and choosing **Make Unique**. This is helpful when you want to break the link between a series of components, but a few items should still link to each other.

- *Why do we not recommend exploding a component?*

We are not fans of exploding any object unless it is necessary because the geometry becomes separated, leading to issues such as glitches, **bug splats** (crashes), slowing down the model, and more. Another major problem that occurs has to do with tags. When a tagged object is exploded, the entities inside the grouping will take on the tag name. That is why we love the **Paste in Place** function mentioned in the *Creating keyboard shortcuts* section of this chapter, because if any geometry needs to be moved from one group or component to another while remaining in the same location, **Paste in Place** saves us from exploding.

- *I created a component of copied objects, but when I edit one, nothing happens to the rest of the copies. Why not?*

This answer comes in the form of a question. Did you create the component after making the copies? 99% of the time, their answer is yes. A component must be created before copying the object, which is why we should plan ahead when modeling. In instances like this, all but one of the groups should be deleted; the remaining group becomes a component, and then the component should be copied (again).

- *Do I need to name components? What about groups?*

To answer the first question, yes, you should name components. We name components to find and edit them easily, and for data extraction (discussed later in this section). Naming components should happen when you generate them (when the dialog box for creating them appears). Always name components what they are, though you may have to be specific if your model has more than one type.

For example, we typically have more than one window size in a building. If you are creating a 38" x 50" casement window component, name it Window-5080 or name it by window type CSMT-5080. Another window size, 28" x 40", is created as a component named Window-2840 or DH-2840 (for double-hung).

To answer the second question, no, you do not need to name groups.

Naming groups takes extra legwork, especially when everything in your model should be grouped. It is very rare that professional modelers will name every group due to the time it takes. Naming groups must happen either in the **Outliner** toolbar (right-click and choose **Rename**) or in the **Entity Info** toolbar (type the name in the **Instance** box).

Note that in the **Outliner** toolbar, we can change the name of one instance of a single component's entity, but it will not change all components to that name.

- *How do I know if a grouped object is a group or a component?*

One of three ways, as follows:

- Select the object and look at the **Entity Info** toolbar. The object type, whether **Component**, **Group**, **Edges**, or **Faces**, will be written at the top:

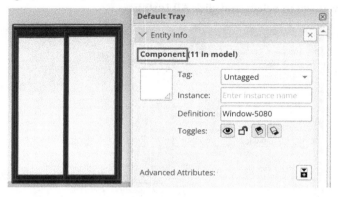

Figure 1.24: A selected component and its properties shown in the Entity Info toolbar

- Right-click on the object and see if you have the option to **Edit Group** or **Edit Component**. If **Edit Group** is shown, the object is a group, and if **Edit Component** is shown, the object is a component (*Figure 1.25*).

- In the **Outliner** toolbar, the name of the object you selected is highlighted (*Figure 1.25*). Alternatively, clicking on a line item in **Outliner** will show its location in the model with a selection box. An object is recognized as a component in **Outliner** by the presence of a specific graphic to its left, which consists of four small black boxes forming one square. Objects in the **Outliner** that are groups have only one solid black box to their left.

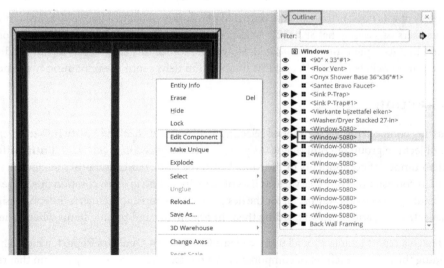

Figure 1.25: Edit component option when right-clicking on a component
(left) and component shown in Outliner (right)

An additional (and awesome) capability of components emerges when you aim to select all instances of a component, meaning you want to simultaneously select every linked component. Right-click on the component, arrow down to **Select**, and click **All Instances**.

Figure 1.26: Right-click | Select | All Instances

Hopefully, the review of groups and components in this section has been helpful. Becca hears these questions each semester when beginner and intermediate students start to modify objects, and she wants to ensure you fully understand the differences (and similarities) between the two.

Building information modeling and other data extraction

One of the goals of this book is to dispel the outdated perception of SketchUp. We've heard criticisms from previous users suggesting that SketchUp lacks precision for 2D plan views, space planning, or BIM functions, and that its capabilities are outdated. However, most of this chapter has already addressed and debunked those beliefs (hooray!), and this final section delves into the remaining two aspects.

Data extraction

When discussing components, we mentioned selecting an object and checking **Entity Info** to determine whether an object is a group or component. As you may have noticed in *Figure 1.24*, **Entity Info** also displayed the number of components in the model with the same name and other attributes, which is 11. SketchUp consistently compiles various lists of data, including groups, components, edges, and more. This feature proves incredibly useful for the design team, comprising architects, interior designers, estimators, electricians, and plumbers, aiding them in organizing and pricing items when ordering.

SketchUp created a report template for all users, called a **Component Qualities Report**, which is helpful for determining the units of each set of components in a model. These are the steps to run that report:

1. To see a list of generated data, click on the **File** menu and arrow down to **Generate Report**:

Figure 1.27: Where to find Generate Report

2. In the lower-right corner, click **Run**.

Figure 1.28: Click Run to see report data

A tallied list of groups and components within the model is generated. Based on the information in this report, naming the groups in this model would be beneficial:

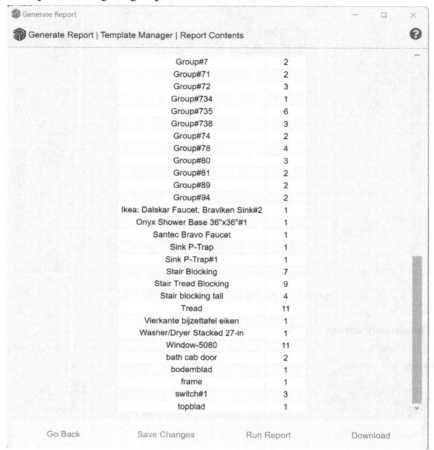

Figure 1.29: Report tallying all groups and components in the model

3. You can download a .csv (CSV) file to sort the data and produce a report (you do not have a choice on the type of download it creates; it only creates a CSV). To produce the file, click **Download** in the lower-right corner.

4.   Open the CSV file, and it will look like this:

	A	B
1	Definition Name	Quantity
2		531
3	33500780-3D_dxf-1103889-_3D_#1	1
4	90" x 33"	1
5	90" x 33"#1	1
6	Component#3	1
7	Drain	1
8	Floor Vent	1
9	Group#101	1
10	Group#116	2
11	Group#132	2
12	Group#137	2
13	Group#145	2
14	Group#146	3
15	Group#148	2
16	Group#151	2
17	Group#158	2
18	Group#193	1
19	Group#318	4
20	Group#319	2
21	Group#35	1
22	Group#359	22
23	Group#40	1
24	Group#42	2
25	Group#44	1
26	Group#452	2
27	Group#47	1
28	Group#533	1

Figure 1.30: The downloaded report creates a .CSV file

Afterwards, you can format the CSV file to suit any Excel functions and utilize the data for purchasing.

> **More information**
>
> To learn more about generating and customizing report data, check the `https://help.sketchup.com/en/sketchup/classifying-objects` section called Set up a template to customize report data.

Classifying BIM objects with IFC

If you have not heard about object classification in SketchUp, it is a hidden gem that is native to SketchUp (part of it was covered in the data extraction report we just made).

When working in SketchUp's **Architectural Template**, classifying objects is easy because there are already IFC imports available (specifically IFC2x3 and IFC4).

Now, what is IFC? It is the **international foundation class** (**IFC**). Using objects in SketchUp that are classified with the IFC file structure are, in fact, **building information modeling** (**BIM**) objects. However, unlike other BIM file formats, IFC files are platform-neutral and can be read and edited by any BIM software.

These steps take you through setting up objects for classification:

1. In SketchUp, using the IFC classification first takes place in the **Window** menu; then, choose **Model Info**. In the left sidebar, choose **Classifications**.

2. You must import IFC systems to **Classifications** by first clicking **Import**:

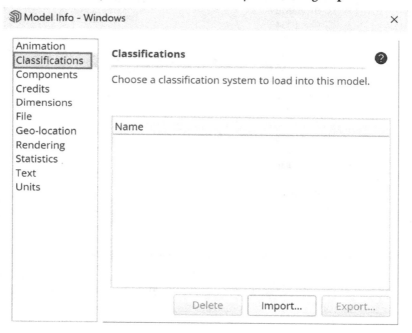

Figure 1.31: Classifications is found in the Model Info toolbar

3.   Choose the classifications you want to load into SketchUp and click **Open**:

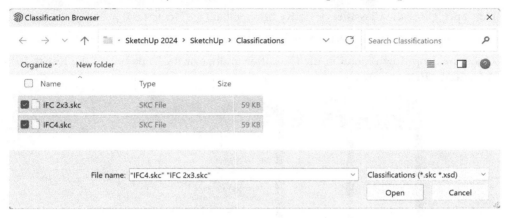

Figure 1.32: Loading Classifications from SketchUp program files (Windows)

You can select more than one classification to import at a time.

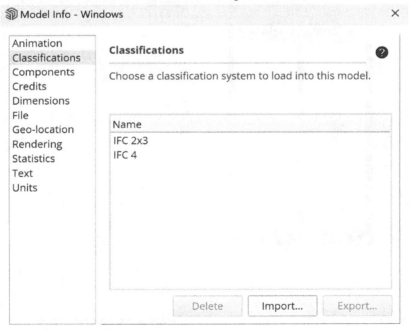

Figure 1.33: After loading the classifications that come with the Architectural Template

4. Once imported, close out of the **Model Info** toolbar by clicking the **X** in the corner.

5. Now open either the **Classifier** or **Entity Info** toolbar (see *Figure 1.34*).

6. In the modeling window, select the component to classify.

7. Open the drop-down menu in the **Classifier** toolbar or the **Type** box of the **Entity Info Advanced Attributes** area:

Figure 1.34: Classifier toolbar (top) and Entity Info- Advanced Attributes (bottom)

8. Click the arrow next to the classification system, such as **IFC 2x3**, and select an object type. Alternatively, you can type the name of the object in the **Filter** box.

Classifying groups and components

You can only classify objects that are either a group or a component. When dealing with a grouped object, you need to utilize the **Classifier** toolbar; groups do not offer the **Advanced Attributes** option within **Entity Info**.

Choosing one component that is linked to multiple objects will result in all instances being classified at the same time.

> **More information**
>
> There is more to this tool and other ways to use classification. Read more about classifying objects (and generating data reports), including the ability to uniquely classify one component, at `help.sketchup.com/en/sketchup/classifying-objects`.

Using extensions for BIM modeling

We will discuss **Extension Warehouse** and plugins in *Chapter 6*, but because we are on the subject of BIM, we will briefly introduce it here.

SketchUp is an incredible tool for the predesign, programming, and schematic design phases. There are limitations to SketchUp, but these are rectified with the use of plugins (also called extensions or ruby scripts due to their file type `.RBZ` or `.rbz`).

Performing a search in Extension Warehouse by typing `bim` (it is not case-sensitive) will result in many plugins that are specific to BIM functions.

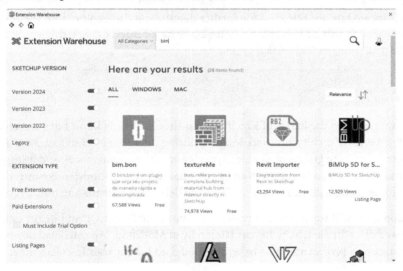

Figure 1.35: BIM search in Extension Warehouse

We also suggest an internet search for the best BIM extensions for SketchUp. Because some extensions do not include the word BIM, an internet search will offer additional information on which plugins are out there, and include their pros and cons.

Here are links to a few SketchUp BIM extension sites, most of which are also found in the Extension Warehouse.

- **Profile Builder** or **Quantifier Pro** by Mind Sight Studios: `mindsightstudios.com`

- **PlusSpec** for architects and builders: `plusspec.com`

- **Estimator** for SketchUp by John Brock: `estimatorforsketchup.com`

Many third-party sites allow for downloading plugins, which the authors of this book have done often. If you are concerned about downloading viruses, a trustworthy source for obtaining plugins that are not available in Extension Warehouse is `SketchUcation.com/PluginStore`.

This briefly introduces data extraction and BIM functions within SketchUp. Be sure to read more about these functionalities at SketchUp's website and investigate extensions that streamline tasks (we cannot wait for *Chapter 6* when we show you how to use extensions!).

PreDesign with SketchUp

The mention of predesign at the start of this section prompted us to highlight another remarkable SketchUp feature before concluding this chapter. The **SketchUp PreDesign Tool** is included with a SketchUp Pro or Studio subscription and offers early-stage design analysis tools. It helps architects and designers explore environmental factors such as sunlight, shading, and energy efficiency, allowing them to make informed decisions during the initial phases of design.

PreDesign is located under **File**, and for further details, you can explore it in the SketchUp Help Center through this link: `https://help.sketchup.com/en/predesign-sketchup/getting-started`.

Summary

In this chapter, we reviewed the basics of SketchUp you should already know but expanded on their importance in the worlds of architecture and design. Utilizing timesaving techniques, such as keyboard and mouse shortcuts, making groups of all objects, paying attention to inferences, and using the correct camera views, move you from a beginner to an intermediate SketchUp modeler. We introduced more advanced techniques using data extraction for BIM and delved into the ins and outs of components.

In the next chapter, we will wrap up our review of the basics of SketchUp and begin establishing a tried-and-true workflow for SketchUp: Becca's Hierarchy of Modeling. We will detail our step-by-step approach to beginning a project and how to set the model up for any user to collaborate.

Becca's Hierarchy of Modeling and the Designer's Modeling Approach

Allow us to present **Becca's Modeling Hierarchy**. What exactly is this hierarchy? It's a structured sequence of 10 steps to follow whenever you modify a SketchUp object. Using this process creates a rhythm your fingers will memorize until it becomes second nature.

This chapter further explores fundamental concepts relevant to the design realm. We'll delve into key toolbars (referred to as **panels** on macOS) essential for your daily modeling tasks. These include **Scenes**, **Tags**, **Entity Info**, and the **Large Tool Set**, all of which enhance your efficiency and precision.

This chapter covers the following topics:

- Becca's Hierarchy of Modeling: 10 steps for modifying an object
- What are tags? How are they used?
- Creating a client-worthy scene
- Using the Large Tool Set and other trays

Technical requirements

This chapter requires the following software and files:

- SketchUp Pro or Studio (SketchUp for Desktop versions)
- To follow along with the tutorials in the book, you'll need to download the practice file from 3D Warehouse named Chapter 2- Hierarchy or download it from https://3dwarehouse.sketchup.com/model/f34472bb-411a-42d3-811f-dceae533e301/Chapter-2-Hierarchy.

If you are accessing 3D Warehouse within a SketchUp file, avoid directly inserting it into your existing model. Instead, download it as a separate SketchUp file to preserve the scenes we've created. If you need help with how to do this, consult *Chapter 7* for 3D Warehouse guidance.

Becca's Hierarchy of Modeling – 10 steps for modifying an object

We all know that repetition when learning leads to the mastery of any skill. As a college professor teaching introductory and advanced SketchUp courses, Becca created the **Hierarchy of Modeling** to help students repeat the necessary steps to perform commands that require modifying objects, such as extruding, moving, copying, and rotating. The first semester the hierarchy was taught was so successful, it became a staple in each semester's introductory course curriculum. The 10 steps are proven to be effective when practiced regularly, even when variation is necessary. After outlining the steps, we will show you examples of how to use them.

The 10 steps for productive modeling are as follows:

1. Determine whether you should be in **Edit** mode of a group or component. If yes, double-click the mouse as many times as necessary to be inside the correct grouping, or right-click on the object and choose **Edit Group** or **Edit Component**.

2. Using the **Select** or **Lasso** tool, select the object(s) you will be modifying.

3. Activate the tool (or command) by using a *shortcut* or clicking an icon.

4. Click a *point* (endpoint, center point, or midpoint) on the object to start the action, then release the mouse (lift up your finger).

5. Move the mouse slightly in the direction the command should be performed.

6. Lock in the *axis* with one of the arrow keys.

   You could use the *Shift* key to lock in the axis, after finding the correct one, but it is much faster to use the arrow key because you can use other tools while also locking in the axis.

7. Type the measurement (such as distance or length) and tap *Enter* or click the mouse again to complete the command.

8. End the command by tapping the *spacebar*.

9. Save your file.

10. Double-check the measurement with the **Tape Measure** tool.

These steps may seem like simple instructions, or you may wonder why we must perform these steps every time. Performing these steps will create a healthy foundation for clean modeling, especially as you start working on large, complex SketchUp files, saving you time down the road. Students still thank Becca years later for solidifying this framework into their practice. Let's give it a go with some examples!

Step-by-step Hierarchy of Modeling example 1 – Extruding

First, download the `Chapter 2- Hierarchy` practice model. Then, click on the `Hierarchy Practice` scene.

Example 1 is for beginners but is often not correctly performed by some intermediate modelers. We will use the **Push/Pull** tool to add depth (height) to a floor, as shown in *Figure 2.1*.

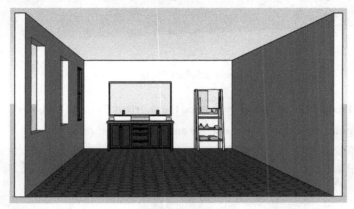

Figure 2.1: View of the Hierarchy scene

We need to add depth to the floor because all objects in the view should be three-dimensional.

Now, follow these steps to add depth (or height) to the floor:

1. Get into **Edit** mode of the flooring by double-clicking the group or right-clicking the object and choosing **Edit Group**.

Figure 2.2: Right-click and select Edit Group

2. Select the face to extrude by clicking on it once. Because this object is still two-dimensional, we can select the top or bottom face with a single click because they are one and the same. However, orbiting underneath allows us to better see what will happen in the subsequent steps.

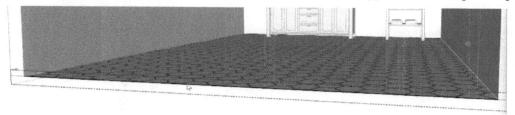

Figure 2.3: Select the face

3. Activate the **Push/Pull** command by tapping the shortcut *P* on the keyboard.

4. Click an endpoint or midpoint of the shape and release the mouse.

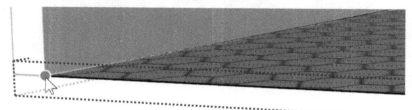

Figure 2.4: Click an endpoint of the face

5. Move the mouse slightly downward, which tells SketchUp that the extrusion will happen underneath the surface. Why are we moving down instead of up? If we were to extrude upward, we take away from the overall wall height (if the walls have been drawn).

Note regarding materials

Add the material or texture to the top face *after* you extrude. Sometimes, the texture will disappear to the inside face, leaving the top face with the default color.

---

6. *Step 6* in *Becca's Hierarchy of Modeling* tells us to lock in the axis. However, since there are no options to deviate from the current path during a push/pull extrusion, this step can be skipped.

7. We need to type in the height of the flooring. This is where real life and SketchUp-land will differ. Sometimes, we need to be dramatic with the depth in SketchUp, giving more than we would in an actual project. At other times, we can downplay by not adding as much depth as is truly necessary. For flooring, this is a category where almost any depth is acceptable. Usually,

¼" or ½" depth is enough. If there is another story underneath, however, the depth should be as close to the real-life value as possible. For our example, we will use 1/4". So, type .25 and press *Enter/Return* on the keyboard.

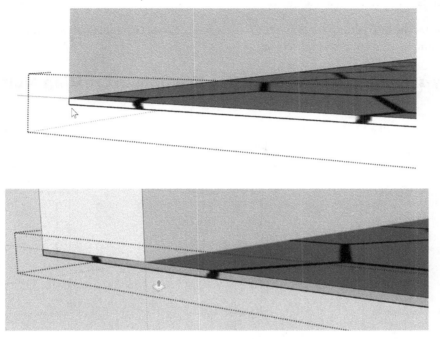

Figure 2.5: Push/pull the floor down

8. Tap the *spacebar* to stop the **Push/Pull** command and get out of **Edit** mode by clicking the modeling window or tapping the *Esc* key.

9. Save your model (*Ctrl*/⌘ + *S*).

Saving versus Auto-save

Have you heard of or used **Auto-save** in SketchUp?

Auto-save settings are found in the **Window** menu | **Preferences** (Windows) or **SketchUp** | **Settings** (macOS), then choosing **General** on the left sidebar. You can create a backup file and auto-save every few minutes (you input the increments). These are great options to use when modeling (we should always have backups of our files, right?). With that said, don't rely on the backup or **Auto-save** to save for you. Why not? Because technology is amazing when it works, but sometimes it fails us. If **Auto-save** is set to save after five minutes, what happens when you've spent four minutes creating an object and your file crashes? You've lost those four minutes. You will also notice that the larger your model is, the longer **Auto-save** takes to, well, save. On huge models, it can take over a minute to save, during which you cannot work on the model (you see the spinning wheel of death circling around).

We are getting you into the habit of saving often and not relying on the software to do it for you.

10. Use the **Tape Measure** tool (shortcut *T*) to measure the flooring, ensuring that you have extruded the correct height.

That completes the instructions for example 1 of how to use Becca's Hierarchy of Modeling. Let's take a look at example 2: creating multiple copies.

Step-by-step Hierarchy of Modeling example 2: Creating Multiple Copies

In example 2, we will add a variation to *step 7* in *Becca's Hierarchy of Modeling* by adding the copy modifier key, to create two copies of a window, as shown in *Figure 2.6*.

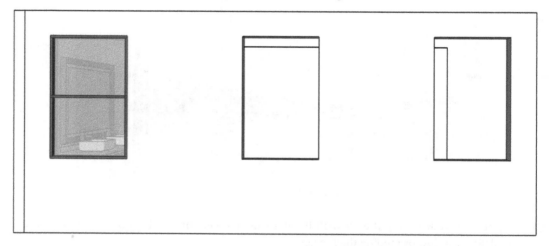

Figure 2.6: Our task is to make two copies of the existing window

The multiple copy modifier key is *Ctrl* on Windows or *Option (Opt)* on macOS.

Now, orbit to the side of the bathroom, so you are looking at the same view shown in *Figure 2.6*. If you select the **Left** standard view, that will make accessing the view faster.

1. We will not go into **Edit** mode of the window to copy, so there is no need to double-click. Try not to move, copy, or rotate in **Edit** mode unless necessary, to avoid messing up geometry. Now, follow these steps to add the variation:

2. Select the existing window with one click.

3. Activate the **Move** command by tapping the shortcut *M* on the keyboard, then to activate **Copy**, tap the modifier key *Ctrl* on Windows or *Opt* on macOS. Your cursor should now look like a **Move** tool icon with a black plus sign attached to one corner (shown in *Figure 2.7*).

4. Click an endpoint at one corner of the object (in our case it is a window) and release the mouse. Don't forget to zoom in to ensure you are clicking the correct endpoint!

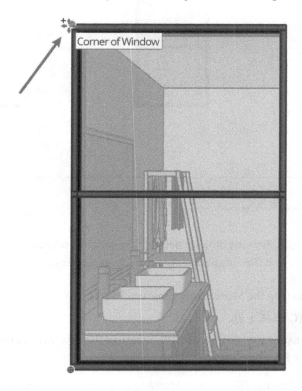

Figure 2.7: Zoom into an endpoint and click to start the command

5. Move the mouse slightly in the direction of the copy (again for us, it is to the right).

6. Lock in the axis. With the way the window is facing, we need to lock in the green/y-axis. So, tap the *left* arrow key.

7. Now, type in two numbers:

    *   The first is the distance between each window, which is 7 ' - 6 ". Type 7 ' 6 and press *Enter/Return* on the keyboard. Alternatively, you can copy along the green/y-axis and click the same corner of the subsequent window. Do not get out of the command yet.

    *   We want two copies, at the exact same distance apart from the first window (for a total of three windows). Immediately type x2 or 2x (for two times the copies) and press *Enter/Return* on the keyboard.

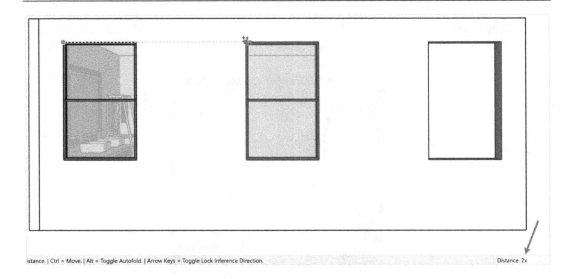

istance. | Ctrl = Move. | Alt = Toggle Autofold. | Arrow Keys = Toggle Lock Inference Direction.   Distance 2x

Figure 2.8: Type the distance between the windows or click (left)
and then the number of copies (2x or x2) (right)

8.   Tap the *spacebar* to stop the **Move/Copy** command.

9.   Save your model (*Ctrl/⌘ + S*).

10. Use the **Tape Measure** tool (shortcut *T*) to measure the distances between each window, confirming that we have the correct spacing.

Try practicing the steps of *Becca's Hierarchy of Modeling* again and again, whether moving, copying, extruding, rotating, or scaling. The repetition of these steps will improve your modeling precision!

Next up, we head into the world of tags where we will discuss the right and wrong ways to use them.

What are tags? How are they used?

What are **tags**? Tags are a way to organize your model and control the visibility of objects in the model.

There is a right and wrong way to use tags. The difference between the two is simple: no edges or faces should be on named tags. Only overall groupings, whether groups or components, should be on named tags.

Organizing objects with tags

In this section, we will look at a few important rules for organizing objects with tags.

Modeling on Untagged

Always model on **Untagged**. This guarantees there will not be tag/layer issues in the future.

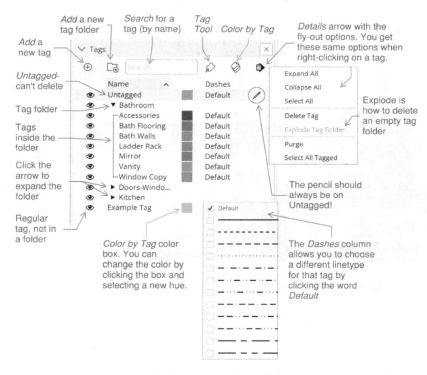

Figure 2.9: The Tags toolbar

The pencil in the **Tags** toolbar or panel (macOS) tells you which tag you are drawing with. *Never move the pencil from Untagged*! The reason for this is that the pencil tells us which tag we are using when modeling. We should always model edges and faces on **Untagged**, so geometry stays where it should, which means the pencil should stay on **Untagged**.

Using Entity Info

The toolbar or panel that goes hand in hand with the **Tags** toolbar is **Entity Info**.

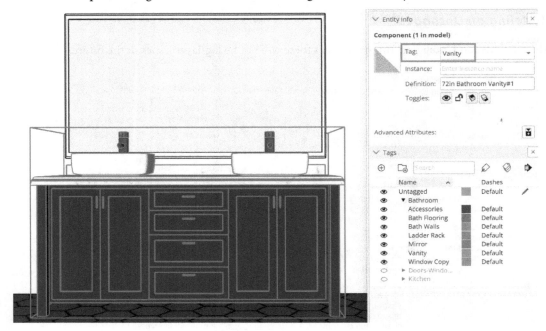

Figure 2.10: Entity Info shows us which tag an object belongs to

Using **Entity Info** and **Tags** toolbars together has two main benefits:

- First, when you select an object, **Entity Info** shows you which tag it belongs to.
- Second, **Entity Info** is one of the main ways to move an object to a named tag.

More about **Entity Info** will be explained later in the chapter, under *Putting it all together*.

Naming tags

How you name tags is important, because chances are someone else will be using or looking at your model. Oftentimes, you will need to update a model weeks or months later, like swapping out a light fixture after a client decides on another one. Therefore, having tags named appropriately will make it easy to pick up where you left off.

With that in mind, be purposeful in naming tags and the items you put on them. A good rule of thumb is to stick with the architectural standard of naming layers in AutoCAD, such as A-Wall for an architectural wall. However, not starting a tag name with an architectural designator like *A* is fine if differentiation between types is made. Keeping with our wall example, there could be a tag named `Wall-Exterior` and another tag named `Wall-Interior`.

Deleting tags

When you need to delete a tag, make it a habit of not deleting all the entities. Instead, merge the geometry with another tag, such as **Untagged**. This will save you from accidentally deleting something important! Let us see this with an example.

In this example, we are deleting the **Accessories** tag. The items that are currently on the **Accessories** tag are the candles on the ladder rack. We no longer want the **Accessories** tag, but still want to keep the candles in the model. Should we move those items to the **Ladder Rack** tag? The answer is no because doing that would limit which tag those items can be on; it's better to move them to **Untagged**. Should we use **Entity Info** to move the candles to Untagged? We could, but that does not also delete the **Accessories** tag. Instead, we can accomplish both tasks at once by deleting the **Accessories** tag (right-click and select **Delete Tag**), then **Assign** it to **Untagged** (see *Figure 2.11*). This is the correct way to **merge tags**.

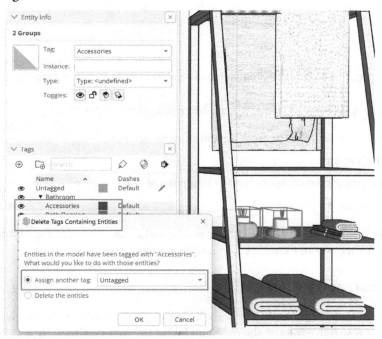

Figure 2.11: Merge (or reassign) tag entities instead of deleting them

You don't have to be in **Edit** mode to merge tags, as depicted in *Figure 2.11*; we did that to emphasize the candles for reference.

Tags and Entity Info

If you select an object and look at **Entity Info** to see which tag it belongs to, but the tag area is blank, that means you have selected an object that uses more than one tag. Another reason is that you have selected more than one object with differing tags. Be cognizant of what you are selecting.

Another way to move objects to a tag, whether named or **Untagged,** is by using the **Tag** tool. This will not delete the existing tag, as with merging a tag.

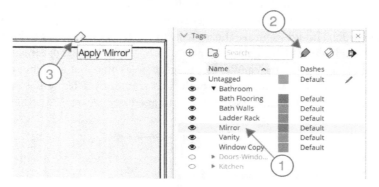

Figure 2.12: Using the Tag Tool to move the mirror to the correct tag

Employ the following four steps to use the **Tag** tool, as you refer to *Figure 2.12*:

1. Click once on the tag name to move an object (or objects) to.
2. Activate the **Tag** tool.
3. Choose the group(s) or component(s) to assign to the tag.
4. Press *spacebar* to exit the **Tag** tool.

Now that we have familiarized ourselves with the fundamental rules of organizing objects with tags, let's put all this together into an example to see how to use tags correctly.

Using tags correctly

Not every group or component needs to be tagged. How to tag grouped objects does not come with clear-cut rules, because it depends on the object and what the user needs visible at different times. A good rule of thumb is to tag the overall grouping. This means that after all the parts of an object have been made into a group or component, tag the grouping when outside of edit mode. Only tag the pieces inside the grouping when necessary for visibility.

Let's look at one example of the authors' way of using tags correctly for a window (refer to *Figure 2.13*):

- When a basic window is created, for this example it is 3 ' wide x 5 ' high x 5 " deep (the frame), all pieces are modeled on **Untagged**. They are extruded to give depth, using manufacturer dimensions.

- One rail piece is created and made a component, then copied twice (one of the copies acts as the sash).

- One stile (vertical frame) piece is created, made into a component, and then copied once.

- The glass is made as one overall group.

- Once all the pieces are modeled and made into groups or components, all the pieces are grouped together. That one group is put on the tag named `Windows`, where all of the other windows in the model, whether groups or components, are placed.

- Additional tags inside the window group are not necessary, because all parts of the window should be viewed at one time (*Figure 2.13*).

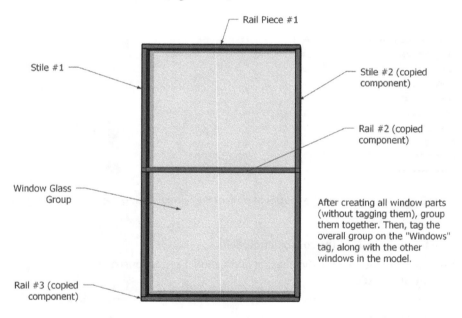

Figure 2.13: Parts of the window (left) and Entity Info (right)

- The window treatment, in this case, a shutter, is its own separate group that is also tagged separately from the windows. This is because sometimes, we might need to see the window without the shutters, and sometimes with the shutters on. We can easily control the visibility of the shutters by opening and closing the eye, as shown in *Figure 2.14* (right).

- The shutter consists of numerous components and a few groups. These groups and components are then consolidated into a single overarching group, which is subsequently relocated to the `Shutter` tag. The shutter parts are the frame, rails (top, mid, and bottom), rotation pieces, slats or louvers, and stiles. You can view how we organized the shutter's components and groups by clicking on one of the `Kitchen` scenes in the practice model and zooming in on the shutter. Select different parts of the shutter while looking at **Entity Info** to see the tally of groups and components.

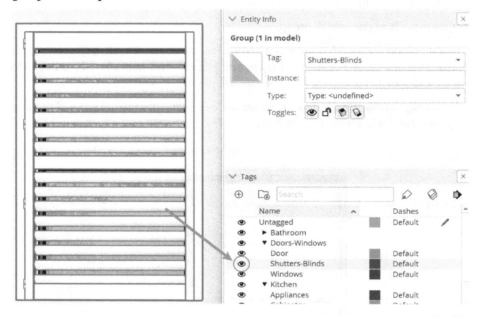

Figure 2.14: Easily show and hide the shutter in front of the window using the corresponding tag

---

A side note to our friends in the construction field

Tagging is important for creating the phasing of the model as per construction standards, just as layers are in AutoCAD.

By now, you should be feeling comfortable with naming tags. Now, we will investigate how tags and scenes work together for our clients.

Creating a client-worthy scene

Scenes provide an excellent platform for displaying and **presenting** our designs to clients or the design team, while employing presentation techniques.

What is a client-worthy scene?

First, let's talk about a *client-worthy scene*. What does that mean?

You've likely noticed that many clients prefer consistency in the views presented when making decisions, whether it's swapping out furniture options or assessing exterior elevations. Maintaining the same viewpoint each time helps clients visualize differences more effectively. Utilizing the **Scenes**, **Tags**, and **Entity Info** toolbars makes that easy!

There are additions we should make to our models to make them client-worthy:

- **Show a complete design**: Whether finishing out the architectural details to look true to life or adding décor items for realism, you will sell the design better by adding as many realistic touches as possible.

- **Only show the necessary edges**: Play around with the **Edge Style** settings to see which edges or **profiles** you can do without:

  - A quick way to access **Edges** or **Profiles** is from the **View** menu. Arrow down to **Edge Style** and *uncheck* (click) **Edges** or **Profiles** to hide them (or follow the steps again and *check* to show them).

  In *Figure 2.15*, you will see that we have created shortcuts for **Edges** and **Profiles** because we use these options often.

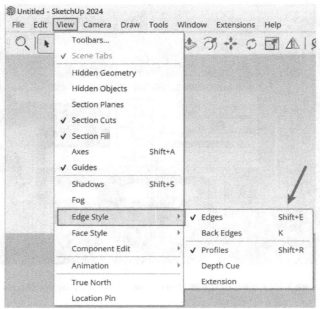

Figure 2.15: View menu with Edge Style flyout

For a more detailed look at **Edge Settings**, you can use the **Styles** panel (which will be discussed in *Chapter 10*):

- On macOS, access **Edge Settings** through **Window | Styles**, which opens the **Styles** panel. Under the thumbnail at the top, click **Edit**. Click the first icon on the left, which is **Edge Styles**.

  - On Windows, access **Edge Styles** through **Default Tray | Styles**. Just like with macOS, under the thumbnail at the top, click **Edit**. The first icon on the left is **Edge Styles**.

- **Use authentic material images**: Show off your SketchUp and product knowledge by importing and using images from material manufacturers. This is an incredible resource with which to present and make design decisions, allowing us to see how a product will look in an actual space. We will examine how to create and apply materials in *Chapter 9*.

- **Add shadows or exterior images**: If your scene includes windows, add shadows or an exterior image through the glass texture. We will go through both of these features in *Chapter 10*.

Now, let's practice using scenes, tags, and entity info for client options in the following section.

Putting it all together

In the practice model, click the 3D Warehouse and download the SketchUp model titled Chapter 2 Practice - Kitchen.

Figure 2.16: A view of the kitchen in the Chapter 2 Practice file

Using the Kitchen - Front View scene, we will create and update scenes to give our clients two bar stool options for their large kitchen island. You can follow these steps:

1. Hopefully, after you downloaded the model, you took some time to peruse the contents. You should always acquaint yourself with someone else's model; look at the tags, scenes, groups, components, and other goodies you are given. Select objects and edit them, clicking around to see how another person has created them. You can get great tips from viewing others' work.

> **Important Note**
>
> Sometimes, we're given a rather messy model, leaving us clueless about where to start. Check out *Chapter 4* for helpful tips on assessing someone else's model.

2. There are already two kitchen scenes in this model: Kitchen - Front View and Kitchen - Top View. The top view shows the top of the kitchen without the ceiling on, for easier editing. The front view is the starting scene we will use to create two furniture choices for our client, having them choose between two bar stools.

3. Let's put the bar stools at the island on a tag. First, we need to make a tag. Create a tag in the **Tags** toolbar/panel named Bar Stool 1. (You can even go one step further to create a Furniture folder and have your furniture tags inside it.)

4. If you highlight the Kitchen folder and then click **Add Tag**, the new tag will be created inside the folder.

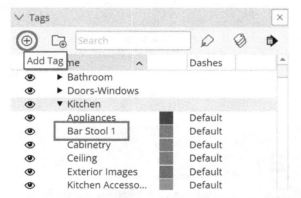

Figure 2.17: Create a tag named Bar Stool 1 inside the Kitchen folder

5. Select all three white bar stools at the island and, using **Entity Info**, add them to the Bar Stool 1 tag (or use the **Tag** tool.)

6. We will now create a new scene for the first bar stool option. Right-click on the **Scene** tab called Kitchen - Front View. Click **Add...** to add a new scene. Right-click on the new scene, select **Rename** and name the scene Bar Stool 1. (You can also use the **Scenes** toolbar/panel to perform these steps. The tabs, however, are more convenient.)

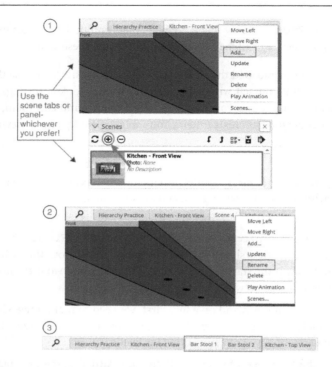

Figure 2.18: Right-click on the Front View scene tab and select Add… (top), right-click on the new scene and choose Rename (middle), all the scene tabs in the model (bottom)

7. The second bar stool option still shows in this scene, which is the stool to the left of the island. Create another tag called Bar Stool 2 and use **Entity Info** to add that stool to the new tag.

8. Turn off the visibility to the new tag, Bar Stool 2, so only Bar Stool 1 is showing. Update the Bar Stool 1 scene with this change by right-clicking that **Scene** tab and selecting **Update**.

Figure 2.19: Bar Stool 1 updated scene

> **Reminders about scenes**
>
> You can use the **Scene** tab for almost every scene option, except creating the first scene in the model. If you prefer, use the **Scenes** toolbar in **Default Tray** (Windows) or **Scenes Window** (macOS) to accomplish all scene tasks. Remember, every time you make a visual change within a scene, whether you have altered the view using orbit or pan, added shadows, or modified the style, you should *update* the scene (or add a new one).

9.   Have you saved your model recently? *Get into the habit of saving frequently and not relying on Auto-save. Use the Ctrl + S or ⌘ + S shortcut often until it becomes a reflex.*

10. Right-click on the **Scene** tab Bar Stool 1 and add a new scene. Rename it Bar Stool 2.

11. For this scene, turn off the visibility of the Bar Stool 1 tag and turn on the visibility of the Bar Stool 2 tag. Update the Bar Stool 2 scene tab with this change.

12. Move, rotate, and copy Bar Stool 2 so the three stools sit at the kitchen island.

     You do not need to update your scene after doing this, because there is not a view or style change, just a rearrangement of furniture.

Figure 2.20: Bar Stool 2 scene

If you would like a third option for your client, repeat the same steps to add another bar stool option and a new tag and scene. Whatever you do, remember to make it a client-worthy scene by adding realistic elements, shadows, and styles (which are discussed in *Chapter 10*). When you are done, use the scene to export images to send to your client or design team (learn helpful tips in *Chapter 11*). Scenes are also used to create animations, exported as .mp4 files. We will study this further in *Chapter 11*.

SketchUp Viewer app for scene presentations

SketchUp Viewer application is an excellent presentation tool, allowing you to view and present models in read-only mode. It is available as **Viewer for Desktop** – a free download to your computer, or **Viewer for Mobile** – compatible with macOS and Android devices. It's great for showcasing different design phases created in SketchUp, whether you're on-site or in the office! Logging in with your **Trimble Connect** account allows you to orbit, pan, and zoom around a model or cycle through scenes. Additionally, in **Viewer for Mobile**, you can utilize **augmented reality (AR)** to visualize the design in its real-world context. (You need a SketchUp Go, SketchUp Pro, or SketchUp Studio subscription for AR.) There are also collaborative and impressive ways to experience **virtual reality (VR)** with **Viewer for VR** technology and hardware.

Apple OS: `https://apps.apple.com/us/app/sketchup/id796352563`.

Android: `https://play.google.com/store/apps/details?id=com.trimble.buildings.sketchup&hl=en_US&gl=US&pli=1`.

Learn more about SketchUp Viewer here: `https://www.sketchup.com/en/products/sketchup-viewer`.

`https://help.sketchup.com/en/sketchup-viewer/sketchup-viewer`.

Being tech enthusiasts, we're all about staying in the loop with the latest and greatest, and SketchUp keeps pace with the times. If you're itching to model while on the move, **SketchUp for iPad** does more than **SketchUp Viewer**—you can perform actual 3D modeling. To get started, you need an iPad Pro with an Apple Pencil, a Bluetooth mouse, or a touchpad. If your iPad has a keyboard, using SketchUp shortcuts makes modeling even faster! You also need a SketchUp Go, Pro, or Studio subscription. **SketchUp for iPad** is a handy tool in the field, allowing you to annotate drawings and models directly at the job site. It also incorporates **artificial intelligence (AI)** capabilities such as photorealistic rendering with **SketchUp Diffusion** (check out *Chapter 15* for more) and 3D LiDAR room scanning. While all the tools of **SketchUp for Desktop** are at your fingertips, you might need some time to discover where they all live on the iPad.

More information

Learn more about SketchUp for iPad at this site: `help.sketchup.com/en/sketchup-ipad`.

Using the Large Tool Set and other trays

In this section, we'll explore how to utilize the Large Tool Set toolbar along with various other toolsets and trays.

Large Tool Set

The **Large Tool Set** is a toolbar that may be unfamiliar to some users, yet it's an excellent resource due to its extensive range of included tools.

In *Chapter 1*, we reviewed how to access the toolbars available in your model. Whether on a Mac or Windows operating system, you have the Large Tool Set toolbar. The Windows version, which is a long toolbar and is meant to dock on the right or left side of model space, looks like this:

Figure 2.21: The Large Tool Set (Windows version)

The reason this toolbar is so appealing is that it gives quick access to tools we use often. Some call this tray the **all-purpose** toolbar because it shows all the basic tools (**Principle** and **Drawing**), along with **Edit**, **Construction**, and **Camera**.

The following icons/tools, found in the Large Tool Set, are particularly beneficial for Mac users who lack comparable toolbars found in Windows systems:

- **Section Plane** (for Windows, this is part of the **Section** toolbar)

- **Position Camera**, **Walk**, **Look Around**, and the option to undo the previous camera view (for Windows, these are part of the **Camera** toolbar)

- **Tape Measure**, **Dimension**, **Protractor**, **Text**, **Axes**, and **3D Text** (for Windows, these comprise the **Construction** toolbar)

Dimensions in SketchUp

Regarding SketchUp dimensions and text: The authors of this book do not care for using dimensions or text in SketchUp, though these are sparingly used (such as dimensioning or annotating a smaller number of objects). The reason for this is that the scale of the dimensions and text does not change when zooming in and out and sometimes overtakes the model. (However, this does not happen with 3D text, which is discussed in *Chapters 1* and *6*.) For a construction set or presentation document, use SketchUp LayOut for dimensioning. We will practice dimensioning in LayOut in *Chapter 13*.

In the next section, let's take a look at some other useful trays and toolbars.

Other trays, panels, or toolbars

SketchUp provides various trays, panels, windows, or toolbars, that cater to the different purposes one might use SketchUp, such as woodworking, architecture, or 3D printing. Some toolbars are available in Windows and Mac operating systems, while others are specific to only one operating system.

Important Note

It is worth noting that SketchUp users often use the terms trays, panels, windows, and toolbars interchangeably. For instance, referring to the Tags panel as the Tags tray or Tags toolbar is acceptable. We mention this because we will change how we refer to them throughout the book.

Let's explore a few other toolbars or panels that a designer or architect will use.

Outliner

If you are not familiar with the **Outliner** toolbar, it is another way to organize and find objects in your model. (With the **Components** toolbar, you only see components, where **Outliner** indicates groups, as well. It also lists **section planes** and **hidden geometry**.)

Outliner is found in the **Default Tray** for Windows users and under the **Window** menu on macOS. **Outliner** displays objects along with their nested positions, whether they are groups, components, or a mixture of both.

The top of **Outliner** has a **Filter** (or search) area. You can search for objects by name, which is another great reason to name your components (as mentioned in *Chapter 1*). Under **Filter** is the name of the model. *Figure 2.22* shows the model's name is Chapter 2- Hierarchy.

Components are listed first, as long as they are not nested within groups. You can tell they are components by the icon on the left of the object's name: four small black boxes creating a square.

After all components and their nested objects are listed, then groups come next. You can tell they are groups, whether named or not, by the icon: one black square.

Figure 2.22 has blue arrows pointing to the component and group icons, to help you see the difference.

You should be familiar with another icon in **Outliner**, the same visibility *eye* from the **Tags** toolbar. You can turn the visibility of individual objects off and on from **Outliner** by clicking the *eye* icon.

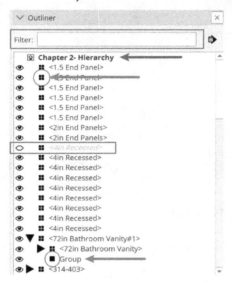

Figure 2.22: Outliner

In *Chapter 1*, we mentioned that you should try right-clicking on anything in the model to see whether there are additional options. The same goes for **Outliner**. When right-clicking on any line item, additional options will be displayed, such as **Hide** or **Lock**. If a line item is grayed out, that means it is hidden or not visible (such as one of the **4in Recessed** components in *Figure 2.22*). Click the eye to make it visible and it will no longer be grayed out, or right-click on the name and choose **Unhide**.

Section planes are listed at the bottom of **Outliner**, unless they are part of a nested grouping.

More information about **Outliner**, including options with the **details arrow**, can be found at this site: help.sketchup.com/en/sketchup/working-hierarchies-outliner.

Entity Info

We have talked quite a bit about **Entity Info**, but there are a few additional tidbits that should be mentioned.

If you select an object and look in **Entity Info**, there are attributes to read about. As you may be aware, the information provided varies depending on the type of object you select, whether it's a singular face, edge, group, or component.

An important attribute to note for construction projects comes from selecting a group or component, an edge or edges, or a face. When a 3D group or component is selected, we have an attribute called **Volume** that shows the total volume of a 3D object. Selecting a single edge, or multiple edges, shows the length (45', as shown in *Figure 2.23*). We are also given options to smooth or soften the edge.

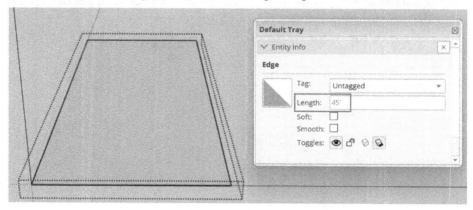

Figure 2.23: Two selected edges in Entity Info show the length

If we select only the face of the object, for example the floor in *Figure 2.24*, **Area** is calculated (675ft²):

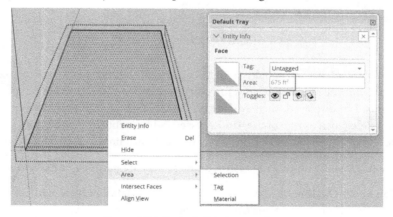

Figure 2.24: Entity Info's *Area* attribute

Additional area calculations

In *Figure 2.24*, you can see additional area calculations when you right-click on an object. After arrowing down to **Area**, choose **Selection**, **Tag**, or **Material**.

There are quick-use toggles underneath the measurement attributes, which are **Hide** (which can also be done by right-clicking on an object and choosing **Hide**), **Lock** (again, this can be done by right-clicking and choosing **Lock**), **Don't receive shadows**, and **Don't cast shadows**.

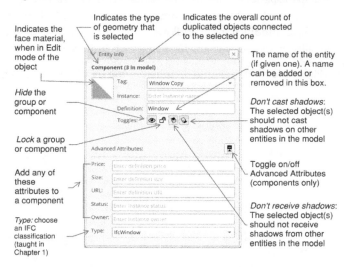

Figure 2.25: The Entity Info window

Begin exploring toolbars that you frequently use to ensure you haven't overlooked any updates. As creatures of habit, it's common for us to stick to familiar routines and overlook some hidden gems along the way.

For example, Windows users, were you aware that you can relocate the **Default Tray** to one of four docking areas by simply moving it and locating the four rectangles positioned in the middle of the screen?

Figure 2.26: Move the Default Tray to choose one of four docking areas

Drag the tray to the rectangle that matches where you want it docked, then release your mouse.

Try to figure out a tool or tray you have yet to peruse or explore customizing your own. There are plenty of undiscovered treasures in SketchUp waiting to be used!

Summary

In this chapter, we wrapped up the basics that are relevant to design disciplines, offering valuable nuggets for initiating or reviving your practice. Employing Becca's Hierarchy of Modeling provides a solid framework for enhancing object modification workflows, while also emphasizing the importance of understanding the functionality of organization and modeling tools in SketchUp for increased efficiency.

In the next chapter, we will explore tools, tips, and preferences you should be using as an intermediate SketchUp modeler.

3
Extruding along Curves and Other Timesavers

In SketchUp, numerous tools and functions prove beneficial, though some present a steeper learning curve. This chapter explores underutilized tools due to the significant practice needed to master them. Nonetheless, incorporating these tools enhances productivity and streamlines workflow, ultimately saving time.

The instructions in this chapter will help ease your fears when using **Follow Me**, **Autofold**, **Solid Tools**, and **Intersect Faces**. We will practice creating trim (molding), a light fixture shade, and a roof gutter, applying real-life principles to these daunting tools.

We will wrap up this chapter by introducing lesser-known time-saving techniques, specifically **Version History**, **Purge Unused**, and **Match Photo**.

This chapter will cover the following main topics:

- Extruding with **Follow Me**
- Autofolding your way to lighting
- Applying **Solid Tools** versus **Intersect Faces**
- Learning lesser-known timesavers

Technical requirements

To complete this chapter, you'll need the following:

- SketchUp Pro or SketchUp Studio
- A working internet connection and your Trimble ID for Trimble Connect (for the *Version History with Trimble Connect* section)

The easiest way to login or create a Trimble ID is at https://www.sketchup.com/, then click the outline of a person at the top-right corner of the window, next to **Buy SketchUp.**

You will need two practice models for this chapter:

- For most of the chapter, you will need to download the practice model from 3D Warehouse named *Chapter 3- House*, or download it from https://3dwarehouse.sketchup. com/model/16b99e2c-09b7-404f-a686-f1bef13b8424/Chapter-3-House

- For the *Solid Tools* and *Intersect Faces* sections, you can follow along by downloading the second practice model from 3D Warehouse named Chapter 3- Solid Tools, or download it from https://3dwarehouse.sketchup.com/model/5dc980a4-8cd2-4e66-ae30-d8c91a1b5f12/Chapter-3-Solid-Tools

Extruding with Follow Me

The **Follow Me** tool is the second native SketchUp way to extrude an object after the **Push/Pull** tool. The importance of the **Follow Me** tool – and its difference from the **Push/Pull** tool – lies in its ability to extrude around curves and irregular lines. Unlike the **Push/Pull** tool, the **Follow Me** tool can go around corners and curves without difficulty, creating a beautifully linked extrusion:

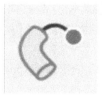

Figure 3.1: The Follow Me tool's icon

Many people feel anxious whenever the **Follow Me** tool is mentioned. We often encounter statements like, "I can't seem to make it work" or "I'll never figure this out!" Our aim is to assist you in becoming more comfortable with this incredibly valuable tool, even though it sometimes feels challenging.

Working with the Follow Me tool

Let's break down how the **Follow Me** tool works. To extrude an object with **Follow Me**, you need two things:

- A path of connected edges

- A face (surface), usually a profile, of the object you want to extrude

Making sure this tool operates effectively hinges on two key factors: selecting the correct path of edges and ensuring that both the path of edges and the face to extrude are grouped together (whether in the same group or a component). *We must be able to select the face and path without going into another grouping or out of the current one.* Another key factor: The path of edges should not be selected at the same time as the face or profile. Something worth noting is that the path and the face do not need to be touching.

The **Follow Me** tool can create a wide range of cool objects, from spheres to fountains to cars and more. The beauty of using this tool is how smooth and lifelike the extruded objects appear.

The most common interior design uses of the **Follow Me** tool are as follows:

- Bullnoses, whether around countertops or nosing on stairs; creating trim such as crown molding; lamps; table legs; dishes; plumbing fixtures; other lathed designs; a simple sofa cushion and piping; HVAC ducts; and a lot more.

- On the exterior, you can quickly create rooftop elements such as facia, trim, gutters, and eaves; planters and other landscaping features; and more.

You can access the **Follow Me** tool from these toolbars or windows:

- The **Large Tool Set**
- The **Tools** menu (Windows)
- The **Tool** palette (macOS)

The are two main ways to use the **Follow Me** tool:

- **Manual extrusion**: The first way is to select **Follow Me**, then click and release your mouse on the face, and move your mouse around the path. This way, the extrusion will happen behind your mouse, following it around the various curves. This is the slower way to use **Follow Me**.

- **Automatic extrusion**: The fastest – and easiest – way to use **Follow Me** is to select the path of edges for extrusion, choose **Follow Me**, and then click once on the face or profile. If the path has been properly created (with all edges touching), you'll finish up in no time.

What happens when all edges of the path do not touch?

When right-clicking your mouse on an edge, have you ever seen the word **Weld**? This is a handy context tool in SketchUp to use with **Follow Me**. Using **Weld** will – just like its name suggests – weld edges together so that there is one continuous path. That way, **Follow Me** won't get stuck as it tries to make its way around the curves. Try it out!

It's time to put this tool to use! In the following section, we'll practice using the **Follow Me** tool.

Practicing with Follow Me

To practice using **Follow Me** tool, download the Chapter 3- House SketchUp model from 3D Warehouse. This is what the model looks like once you've opened it:

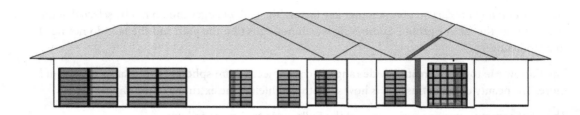

Figure 3.2: The Chapter 3- House SketchUp file

Cycle through the different **scenes** to see how this partially completed home looks. There are a few room names listed inside for you to get your bearings. We will work together in the Great Room and Kitchen areas.

Click on the scene tab called **View Southeast**. A line has been drawn around the entire open area in the middle that follows the top of the inside walls. In *Figure 3.3*, the group has been selected and is highlighted in blue so that you can visualize it. This is the rectangular path of edges we'll use in conjunction with **Follow Me**.

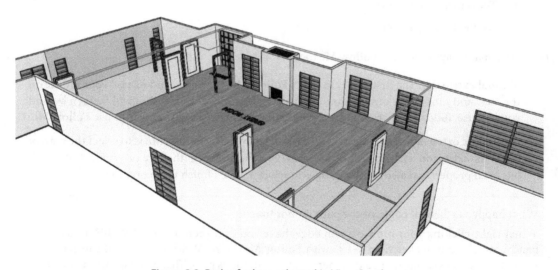

Figure 3.3: Path of edges selected in View Southeast

Zoom into the area near the **Entry** and you will spot the profile of crown molding that was created for you to extrude. When you get into **Edit** mode of the path, you'll notice that the profile is attached to the path of edges, all within the same group:

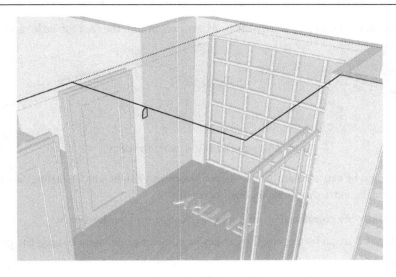

Figure 3.4: In edit mode of the profile to extrude

Follow these steps to practice using the **Follow Me** tool using automatic extrusion (fastest way) with **Becca's Hierarchy of Modeling** (see *Chapter 2*):

1. If you're not already in **Edit** mode of the path and face group, double-click on them so that you are.

2. Select all the edges that make up the path by triple-clicking one of the edges. Or, you can right-click an edge, arrow down to **Select**, then click **All Connected**.

3. Now, you must deselect the profile or face/surface you will extrude by holding down the *Shift* key and double-clicking the face. This should only deselect the face and the edges that created the face (profile). If not, deselect them again by using *Shift*. Only the path of edges should be selected:

Figure 3.5: Select the path of edges first

Remember, the path the face or profile takes cannot be selected at the same time as the profile; otherwise, extrusion will not happen.

4. Activate **Follow Me**, whether from the **Large Tool Set**, **Tools** menu (Windows), or **Tool** palette (macOS).

5.   Then, click on the face once to extrude it. Always zoom into the face for easier access.

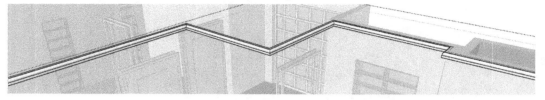

Figure 3.6: Extruded shape along the path

The face should be extruded around the **Great Room** and **Kitchen** areas. **Orbit**, **Pan**, and **Zoom** to make sure the extrusion has happened correctly.

6.   End the **Follow Me** command by tapping the *spacebar* on your keyboard.

7.   Stop editing the group by tapping the *Esc* key or clicking somewhere outside the group.

8.   **Save** your model.

9.   Zoom out and orbit around the model to see how the crown turned out. You can even make the Walls-Interior tag visible to get the full effect.

Having practiced the automatic extrusion method using **Follow Me**, the next section shows how to troubleshoot when the tool is not working.

Troubleshooting Follow Me

Let's learn how to troubleshoot **Follow Me** when it's not working. For this exercise, we will add a gutter to the roof.

1.   Click the scene tab named Gutter:

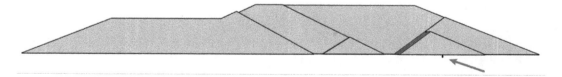

Figure 3.7: Gutter scene

The arrow in *Figure 3.7* points to the gutter profile we created for you.

2. Zoom into the gutter profile and enter **Edit** mode of the roof group. Once inside the grouping, you will see two additional groups: one for the roof and the second for the gutter profile.

    To extrude the gutter profile, we need a clear path of edges that follows the perimeter of the roof. The edges along the bottom of the roof provide the exact path we need to take, and they have already been drawn for us.

3. Get into **Edit** mode of the roof.

4. Double-click the bottom face of the roofline, which will select all the edges around the perimeter.

    You can leave the face selected without any concerns because we're utilizing all the edges that are part of the face. However, if you want to extrude a profile around only a few edges rather than the entire area, exclude the face before proceeding to the next step.

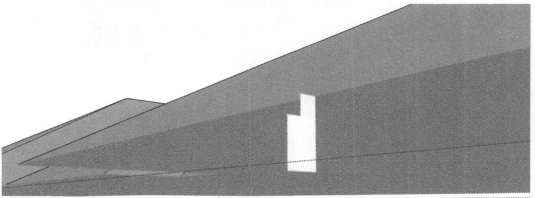

Figure 3.8: Double-click the bottom face of the roofline to access the path of edges

With a larger edge selection like this one, if you are new to **Follow Me**, orbit around to ensure all edges are selected.

5. Activate the **Follow Me** tool.

6. Click the gutter profile.

    The outcome should be a bad one, based on the step we overlooked to make this work properly. This is how ours turned out:

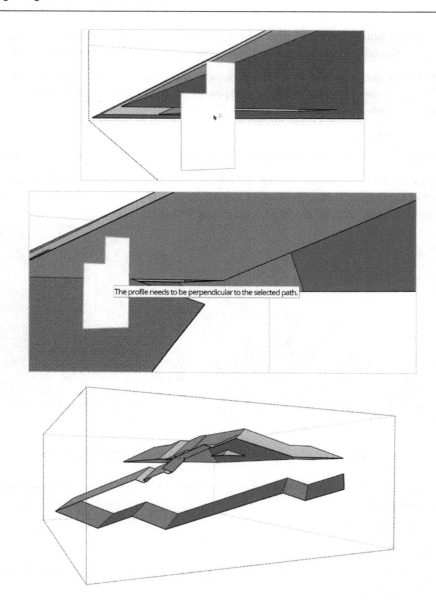

Figure 3.9: Following the first few steps, our roof is now in disarray

Don't worry, we will fix it!

7. Tap *spacebar* to end **Follow Me**, so we can troubleshoot.

8. Undo the extrusion using *Ctrl* or ⌘ *Z*.

The problem with the extrusion is that the roofline path of edges and the gutter profile are in separate groups. To successfully select both elements together, they need to be in the same grouping. Previously, when we clicked on the gutter profile, SketchUp mistakenly interpreted it as choosing the face of the roofline, so it attempted to extrude the same profile as the path. Obviously, this approach won't work with Follow Me!

Let's change the steps starting after *step 4*:

5. Copy the face and edges you selected in *step 4*, with *Ctrl* or ⌘ *C* or **Edit | Copy**.

6. Get into **Edit** mode of the gutter profile group.

7. Paste the roofline copy exactly where it is in the roof group, using **Edit | Paste in Place**.

    Double-check they are in the same group by selecting the path of edges and the gutter profile at the same time. You should be able to do this if they are in the same group:

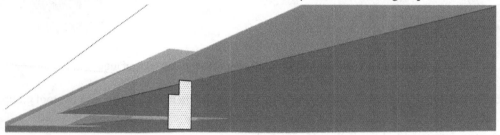

Figure 3.10: The path of edges and the gutter profile are now in the same group

Deselect the gutter profile before going onto the next step (hold down *Shift* and click to deselect). Additionally, develop a habit of zooming into objects you need to select – or deselect – to ensure accuracy.

8. Activate **Follow Me**.

9. Click the gutter profile.

Now, zoom out to admire your work:

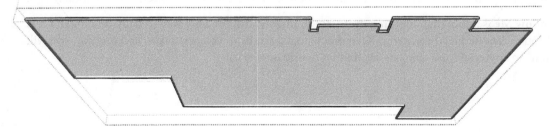

Figure 3.11: The completed gutter

While not a significant issue, there is an extra face on the bottom of the roof. This is because we copied the edges and face of the existing roofline for the extrusion, when we only needed the edges. (The extra face is pointed out in *Figure 3.12*). Erase or delete the roof face from the gutter group:

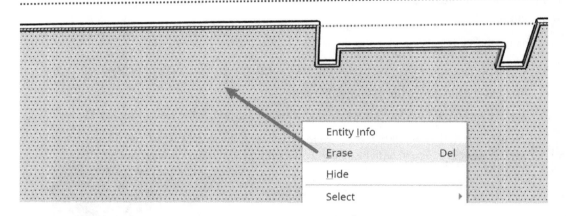

Figure 3.12: Erase the face brought over with the copied roofline

You should not notice a difference after deleting the face because there is already one in the roof group.

Other ways to troubleshoot Follow Me

There is more than one way to fix the extrusion error we covered here. Instead of copying the roofline to the gutter group, another option would be to copy the gutter group into the roof group and then explode it. However, this method presents a drawback because it puts the gutter and roof in the same group, which makes adding new elements or materials to individual areas trickier.

A third fix would be tracing the roofline inside the gutter group, which creates the path of edges for the face to follow. In SketchUp, there's usually more than one method to accomplish a task!

To finish out the gutter, get into **Edit** mode and add a material. (You can do the same for the roof.) Then, save your model once more. For information on adding textures to objects, check out *Chapter 9*.

Follow Me is a tool that often requires time to master, and the only way to truly understand it is through repeated trial and error. Keep practicing, learn from your mistakes, and one day, you will come to appreciate and enjoy its capabilities (we guarantee it)!

> **Follow Me extensions**
>
> Throughout this book, we will mention a few of our favorite **extensions** (or **plugins**) that make modeling in SketchUp even faster. In *Chapter 6*, we will go over how to install and use extensions. For now, we want to mention *MAJ FollowMe*, by Majid M; it is a free plugin that can be found in the **Extension Warehouse**. This extension does a few extra things that SketchUp's native **Follow Me** tool cannot, such as allowing you to change the length or height of the profile by typing in increments and name a profile so that you can draw with it in 3D without having to create a path first.

Now, let's examine a SketchUp function that is less commonly used: **Autofold**.

Autofolding your way to lighting

Autofold is a method of using the **Move** tool (shortcut *M*) to create folds or creases in existing geometry. For **Autofold** to function, you need two touching surfaces, which can be rectangular or circular. As mentioned previously, there is more than one way to complete a task in SketchUp. (We're sure you've figured that out already!)

When would you use **Autofold**? **Autofold** is great for creating bevels around objects (such as cabinetry, mirrors, or millwork), projecting objects outward while still being connected to other geometry (such as awnings), and tapering objects (as we will do in the next exercise).

To practice using **Autofold**, we will create a pendant light fixture that can be found at **Crate and Barrel** called *Weston Black Mid-Century Modern Pendant Light* (if you want to look up the product online). Part of the light fixture has been created for you to save time, using the manufacturer's specifications. You can find it in the `Chapter 3- House` model by clicking the scene tab named `Pendant:`

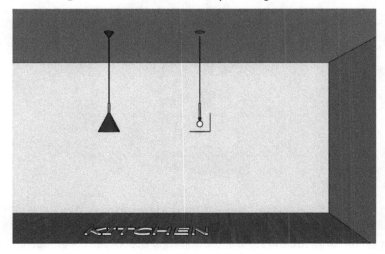

Figure 3.13: View of the Pendant scene

The left-hand side of *Figure 3.13* shows the completed pendant that we will create. The unfished pendant on the right will allow us to practice making cone shapes with **Autofold**, for the canopy and shade.

Before we get started on the light, here are some tips for using **Autofold**:

- You need two sets of shapes (edges and faces) that are touching, are different sizes, and in the same grouping. You can perform **Autofold** before grouping the objects to fold, if that is easier for you, or group them first and get into **Edit** mode.

- **Autofold** occurs when you use the **Move** tool along any one of the three axes – x (red), y (green), or z (blue). Locking in an axis with the correct **arrow key** is crucial to making this work.

    If you are not familiar with keyboard arrow keys and their coordinating SketchUp axis, refer to the chart below:

    You could also use one of the modifier keys (*Alt* on Windows or ⌘ on macOS) to toggle **Autofold** on and off, instead of locking in the axis.

- For the exercise in this chapter's practice file, we will use the z-axis (blue); however, **Autofold** can be done on any of the axes, as long as the object(s) is already rotated in that direction.

Time to practice using **Autofold**! As we go through these steps, remember to use **Tags** to turn off the visibility of objects that get in your way while modeling, such as walls or the ceiling:

1. First, we will create the shade by using the large circle at the bottom of the pendant. *Zoom* into that area.

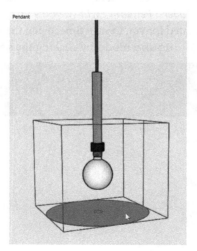

Figure 3.14: Zoom into the shade grouping

2. Click once on the large circle to see that the objects at the bottom are grouped.

3. The objects are grouped, so double-click to enter **Edit** mode. Select the face or edge of the smaller *inside* circle.

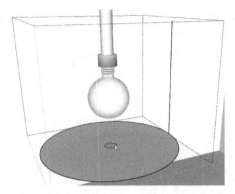

Figure 3.15: Select the face or edge of the inside circle

It doesn't matter if you select the face or an edge. It is more important to select the correct shape.

4. Activate the **Move** tool (shortcut *M*) and click on any point of the inside circle.

5. Move your mouse upward and lock in the blue/z-axis with the up arrow key.

6. Enjoy experimenting with **Autofold** by moving your mouse up and down, observing how it behaves when it is near the larger circle. Notice how it gradually transforms into a taller cone as it moves further away from the large circle.

7. Move your mouse up to meet the top of the vertical edge we drew for you. This is the stopping point for the fold. Click on the **Endpoint** at the top (see *Figure 3.16*).

8. Get out of the **Autofold (Move)** command by tapping the *spacebar*. Then, save your model.

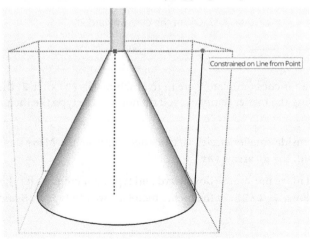

Figure 3.16: Click the endpoint at the top of the vertical edge to stop autofolding

After using Autofold, delete the vertical edge. We no longer need it, and it is not part of the light fixture.

9.   Now, move up to the canopy, or the top of the pendant at the ceiling (see *Figure 3.17*), and go into the canopy group's **Edit** mode.

10. The circle on the ceiling does not have two shapes. As mentioned previously, we need two shapes for **Autofold** to work. Use the **Offset** command (shortcut *F*) to offset the circle inward 2 inches (2 ").

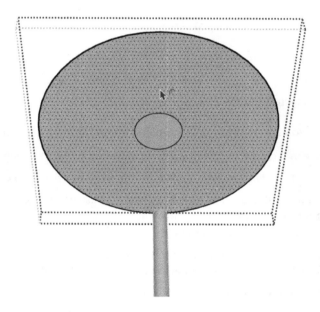

Figure 3.17: Offset the circle inward 2″

Reminder

If you are not using an inches template, type in the inch marks (") after 2, then press *Enter/Return*. If you are using the inches template, you do not need to type the inch marks.

---

11. Again, select the inside smaller circle's face or edge. Activate the **Move** command and lock in the blue/z-axis with the *up* arrow key.

12. This time, we will move our mouse downward and type an increment for the fold. We need the canopy to come down 2-1/2". In the inches template, we can type 2.5 and tap *Enter/Return*.

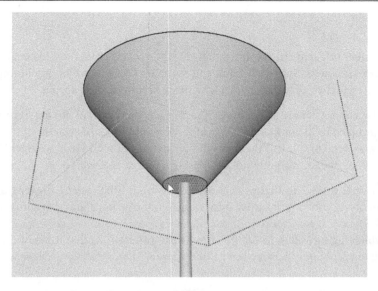

Figure 3.18: The inside circle autofolded down 2-1/2" to create the canopy

13. As usual, end your command by tapping the *spacebar*, getting out of **Edit** mode, and saving your model.

14. At this point, you can add texture to the shade and canopy (inside edit mode) and group all parts of the pendant together (outside edit mode).

Now you know another fantastic SketchUp function to incorporate into your toolkit – **Autofold**! Try this new technique the next time you're designing an object with tapered features.

Our next section goes over **Solid Tools**, a powerful set of tools used for combining or cutting one 3D form from another, and how they differ from **Intersect Faces**.

Applying Solid Tools versus Intersect Faces

In this section, we'll learn about **Solid Tools**, which are used to trim, split, intersect, and combine solid objects. If you have not used **Intersect Faces**, we will give you a brief overview. Using **Solid Tools** or **Intersect Faces** is helpful when you are not familiar with extensions or plugins SketchUp offers, you prefer using native SketchUp tools, or you need to make a quick and easy change in the model.

As with the other tools you've learned about in this chapter, give yourself some time to understand how they work and be patient when you make mistakes.

For this section, download the second practice model for the chapter titled Chapter 3- Solid Tools from 3D Warehouse. There are scene tabs for you to cycle through for each tool.

Let's dive in!

Solid Tools

Solid Tools is a toolbar or palette in SketchUp that gives you six different ways to create new shapes: **Outer Shell, Intersect, Union, Subtract, Trim,** and **Split**. This is achieved by combining one object with another object, whether it's to carve out a new shape or join existing shapes.

You need at least two objects to use **Solid Tools**. The caveat is that both (or all) objects must be solid, whether a solid group or solid component. This may seem odd because even though SketchUp 3D objects are hollow, we tend to think of them as solid forms. A true solid form in SketchUp is a shape without holes, meaning the form should not be missing a face or an edge.

You might be wondering, how do I know if something is solid? That's where **Entity Info** comes in. When we select an object and look at **Entity Info**, we gain information about that entity (as discussed in *Chapter 2*). We know if it is a group, component, edge, or face; its measurements, such as area or length; and on which tag it resides. In *Figure 3.19*, **Entity Info** tells us that the roof on the Outer Shell scene and tag is not only a group but a **Solid Group**. That is exactly what we want!

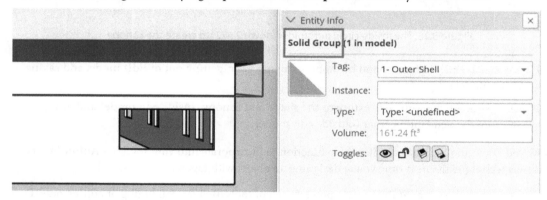

Figure 3.19: Entity Info reads Solid Group

Furthermore, when using **Solid Tools**, the objects must intersect. You need to keep an eye on your **Dashboard** (the bar at the bottom of the modeling window), which helps guide you when using these tools.

Here are some additional tips and rules for using **Solid Tools**:

- Some people like to turn on the **X-ray** face style while using **Solid Tools** to help visualize what is happening. (You can do this with **Intersect Faces** as well.)

- With most of the tools, except **Subtract** and **Trim**, you can preselect all the objects and then click the tool you want to use.

- The **Subtract** and **Trim** tools must be chosen before selecting solid objects because the order in which they are clicked changes the outcome.

- When using **Solid Tools**, we should *not* be in **Edit** mode of either solid grouping.

- Solid objects should only be divided by one level of grouping, which corresponds to their individual group or component. Additional groupings should not be used to separate them. For instance, if the first solid is enclosed within a group while the other solid stands as its own grouping, you won't be able to access the first one.

Figure 3.20 shows that Solid Group 2 is grayed out (or lighter than other objects), indicating that you cannot select it for use with Solid Group 1. (Your practice model does not have this error.)

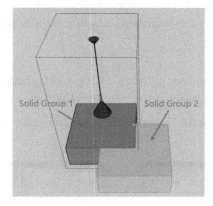

Figure 3.20: Solid objects cannot be separated by more than one group

- Tagged groups or components will automatically switch to Untagged after any solid tool is used to modify or merge groupings.

- If an object is not displayed as a solid in **Entity Info**, use the free **Solid Inspector** [2] extension from the **Extension Warehouse** to identify and resolve any issues. (*Chapter 6* covers how to use the Extension Warehouse.) You can also view the **Solid Inspector** [2] extension on the web: https://extensions.sketchup.com/extension/aad4e5d9-7115-4cac-9b75-750ed0902732/solid-inspector.

All six of SketchUp's **Solid Tools** are only available with a subscription or paid version, including **SketchUp for iPad** and **Go**. Only one tool is included with all of SketchUp's applications: the **Outer Shell** tool.

To find **Solid Tools** in SketchUp Pro or Studio, look in these places:

- The **Solid Tools** toolbar

- The **Tools** menu (**Tools** | **Outer Shell** or **Tools** | **Solid Tools**, then select a tool from the submenu)

- **Tools** palette (macOS)

This is what the **Solid Tools** toolbar looks like with all six icons. These icons give us a little hint as to what each tool does:

Figure 3.21: From left to right, the tools are Outer Shell, Intersect, Union, Subtract, Trim, and Split

Let's explore these six tools and their functionalities. You can use the practice model to explore with us by cycling through the **Scene** tabs, each named according to the **Solid Tool** function.

Outer Shell

This tool is available with all free versions of SketchUp. It gets rid of internal objects, keeping just the outer shell. You can select as many solids as you want with this tool.

In *Figure 3.22*, we combined the exterior walls with a raised roofline so that they are one group, without edges separating them.

Figure 3.22: Before (left) and after (right) using Outer Shell

We accomplished this task by selecting all the exterior wall and roof groups at one time, then clicking **Outer Shell**. You also have the option to select two groups, activate the **Outer Shell** function, and then click on the third group. Give it a try in the practice model!

Intersect

This tool intersects solids but only keeps the intersected part. It converts two groupings into one.

Figure 3.23 shows how two solid pieces were combined to leave the smaller box in the middle, taking on the color properties of both original boxes:

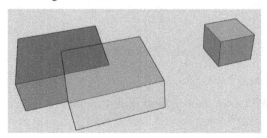

Figure 3.23: Original intersecting solids (left) created one box where they intersected (right)

We made this happen by choosing **Intersect**, clicking one box, and then clicking the other.

Don't forget to check your Dashboard to determine what you need to select. *Figure 3.24* shows the steps taken in the Intersect example, with the Dashboard prompts:

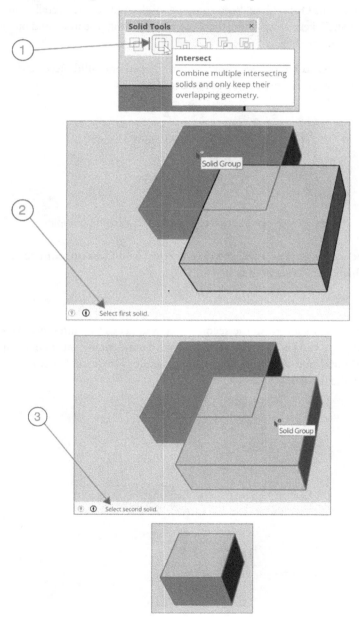

Figure 3.24: The steps taken in using Intersect, showing Dashboard prompts

With **Intersect**, it does not matter which grouping is selected first; the end result will be the same.

Union

Union is almost exactly like **Outer Shell**. Both combine solids to form one overall grouping. However, **Union**, unlike **Outer Shell**, keeps everything that is combined – both the inner and outer parts. (**Outer Shell** only keeps the outer parts.)

Using the same boxes from **Intersect**, we chose **Union**, clicked one solid piece, and then clicked the other. This created one overall grouping of both pieces:

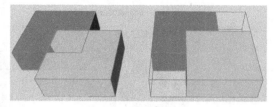

Figure 3.25: Using Union to combine solids into one grouping

When you **Edit** the new group, you will see that all edges and faces are connected. With **Union**, it doesn't matter which piece is selected first.

Subtract

This tool subtracts the first solid from the second solid and keeps the difference. With **Subtract**, it matters which solid piece you click first because you could accidentally get rid of what you intended to keep. This will be a trial-and-error tool, like many commands in SketchUp. If it does not work one way, undo it and try the other way.

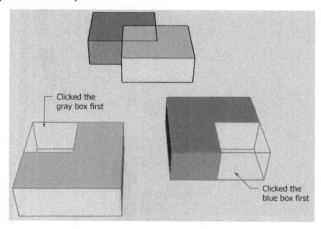

Figure 3.26: Subtract is used to convert two shapes to one, based on which one is clicked first

In *Figure 3.27*, The blue shape on the front left was formed by activating the **Subtract** function, clicking on the gray box intersecting with the blue box, and then selecting the blue box. This action removed the gray box from the area where it overlapped with the blue, resulting in the remaining portion of the blue box. Similarly, the gray shape on the right was created following the same steps, but by selecting the blue box first. When using a free version of SketchUp, **Intersect Faces** can be used instead of **Subtract** because the outcome is similar.

Trim

This tool is similar to **Subtract** in that it trims the first solid against the second solid, but unlike **Subtract**, it keeps both solids. This tool uses another object to create a cut based on the shapes of both objects. **Trim** is another solid tool when it matters which solid you select first. In the practice model, try using Trim twice on the joinery, alternating which object you click first after activating **Trim**. *Figure 3.27* shows what the pieces look like after using the tool then moving them away from each other:

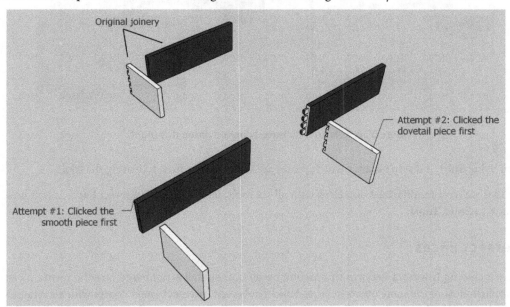

Figure 3.27: Trimmed the smooth piece against the dovetail (left),
then the dovetail piece against the smooth (right)

Clicking the smooth edge first causes the other piece to transition from a dovetail to a basic butt joint. Conversely, clicking the dovetail piece first and then the smooth one results in a flawless interlocking dovetail joint.

When using a free version of SketchUp, **Intersect Faces** can be used instead of **Trim** because the outcome is similar.

Split

This tool intersects solids and keeps all results (it leaves an imprint). It converts two groupings into three groupings.

Going back to our example of the two intersecting boxes, using **Split** creates three separate solid groups at the intersecting points. In *Figure 3.28*, the three new groupings were moved apart to better understand the concept:

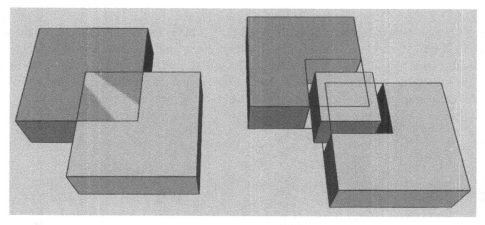

Figure 3.28: Split created three separate groupings (right)

When using **Split**, it doesn't matter which pieces are selected first after activating the tool.

Now that we have familiarized ourselves with all six tools, let's see what **Intersect Faces** is and how it relates to **Solid Tools**.

Intersect Faces

We are including **Intersect Faces** in this section because, though it is not based on solid forms, it can accomplish most of the same outcomes that **Solid Tools** can. **Intersect Faces** comes with all versions of SketchUp – whether free or paid, unlike Solid Tools. A big plus to **Intersect Faces** is that it can be used on all objects: edges, faces, groups, and components.

When using a free version of SketchUp, **Intersect Faces** can be used to achieve a similar result as the **Subtract** or **Trim** tools. (If you have a paid version or subscription, we suggest utilizing **Subtract** for the example in this section, as it offers a quicker solution with fewer steps.)

An example of how to use **Intersect Faces** is shown in *Figure 3.29*, and on the `Intersect Faces` scene of the practice model. The baseboard was created with the **Follow Me** tool. However, an entrance to the room was not considered initially, resulting in the baseboard overlapping the doorway.

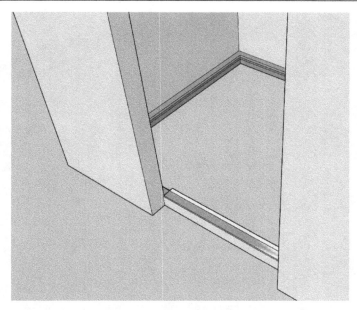

Figure 3.29: We need to remove the baseboard from the doorway

We added a block to intersect the area of the baseboard to be cut. It is the width of the opening (3 ') and slightly overlaps each side of the baseboard. With **Intersect Faces**, the objects need to be in the same grouping and, of course, intersecting. One object can be grouped, however, so we made the block a group – just to see what would happen.

There are two ways to access **Intersect Faces**. Follow these steps to find the tool:

1. Select the objects you wish to intersect. Triple-click the baseboard to pick up all edges and faces, then hold down *Shift* and click the block.

2. Right-click on the selection and choose **Intersect Faces**. Alternatively, choose **Edit | Intersect Faces**.

A flyout will appear (shown in *Figure 3.30*), presenting three options to select from. Choose one option to communicate with SketchUp what you wish to intersect the faces with: **With Model**, **With Selection**, and **With Context**. That said, you will not always see three options. If you are not using a grouping within another grouping, **With Context** will not appear.

Additional reading

There's a lot more that Intersect Faces can do, such as intersecting visible geometry with **hidden geometry**, using the **With Model** option. To read more about Solid Tools, Intersect Faces, and a description of what the three options mean, check out SketchUp's Help Center: `https://help.sketchup.com/en/sketchup/modeling-complex-3d-shapes-solid-tools`.

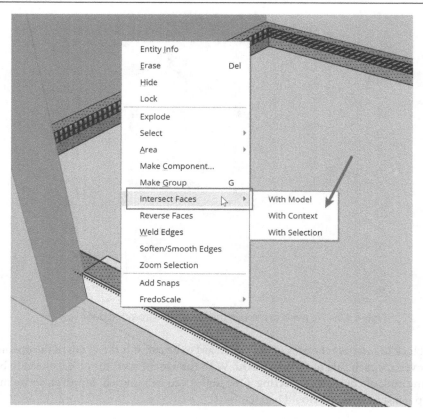

Figure 3.30: The Intersect Faces flyout in the context-menu

The crucial aspect to understand about **Intersect Faces** is that it connects the edges and faces of your selection. This enables you to carve out new geometry and delete what you don't need, thus editing the three-dimensional form(s).

Let's see how that looks when we choose one of the options for our baseboard example:

1.   We chose **With Context** so that the **Intersect Faces** tool only intersected the areas we selected in **Edit** mode. In reality, you can use any of the three options, though choosing **With Model** could take extra time for the intersection to finish.

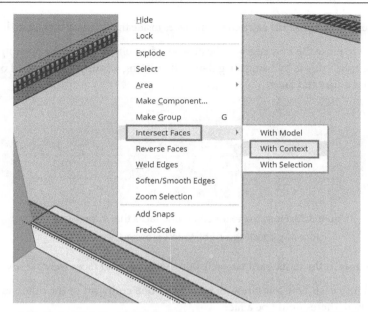

Figure 3.31: Right-click the block, choose Intersect Faces, then select With Context

You will not see any immediate difference to your selection after doing this.

2. Next, we orbited inside the room to face the doorway from the opposite side.

3. Then, we moved the block away to reveal the edges created in the baseboard by intersecting the block with it. (Alternatively, you can delete the block because we no longer need it.)

When you move the block away or delete it, you will see the two new edges in the baseboard that flank the door opening.

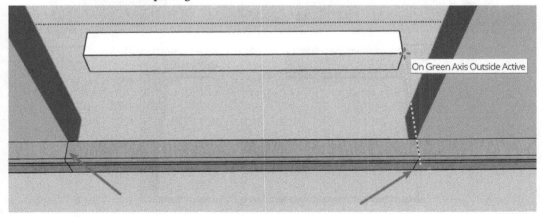

Figure 3.32: Move the block away from the baseboard to see the newly created edges

4.   Next, we deleted (erased) all the extra edges and faces inside the doorway that we no longer needed.

Take care not to erase the new edges in the baseboard on either side of the opening! The easiest way to accomplish this is by using a right-to-left crossing window (the dashed one) to select only the inner edges and faces:

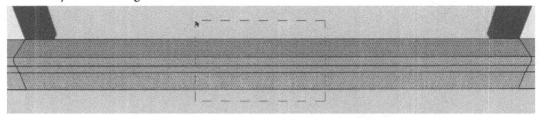

Figure 3.33: Erase the extra edges and faces that impede the
doorway by using a right-to-left crossing window

There was a hole in the baseboard on each side that edges and faces were removed.

5.   We zoomed into each hole and drew an edge from one endpoint to the other, just to remind SketchUp where there should be a face.

We then added the baseboard material to the new faces.

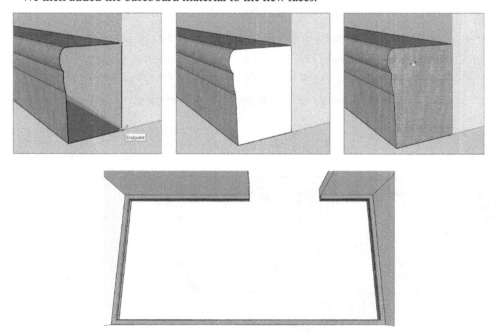

Figure 3.34: Fill in the hole by drawing an edge from endpoint-to-endpoint
(top), and after adding the material we're done (bottom)

And with that, we're done! Using **Intersect Faces** adds a few extra steps than the **Subtract Solid Tool** would need, but it is another way to achieve the same result in SketchUp.

> **Tip**
> We are particularly fond of using **Intersect Faces** following the creation of a pitched roof. This handy tool streamlines the task of blending together the intersecting segments of the pitch, ultimately enabling us to trim away surplus elements and finish with a roof that seamlessly integrates all its parts.

Now, let's move on to the final section of this chapter, where we will introduce you to three lesser-known timesavers for boosting productivity.

Learning lesser-known timesavers

To round off this chapter of *Timesavers*, we want to make sure you know about three timesaving options within SketchUp: **Purge Unused**, **Version History**, and **Match Photo**. There is not much to explain with the first two, but they are important SketchUp gems to know because of how they save time.

Purge Unused

You may have noticed or been taught certain things within SketchUp that slow your model down, causing it to lag from time to time. With the newer releases of SketchUp, the SketchUp team has done an incredible job of updating the graphics engine so those lag times are significantly reduced. However, we should continue employing the basics, as reviewed in the first three chapters of this book, to streamline our models.

One approach is navigating to the **Components**, **Materials**, and **Tags** toolbars, where you can select **Purge** or **Purge Unused** from the **Details** arrow.

A faster way to do this is from **Window | Model Info | Statistics**, then click **Purge All**. This is the faster approach because it purges all toolbars at once: unused **Materials**, **Components**, **Styles**, and **Tags**!

Figure 3.35: Model Info's Statistics menu allows us to purge all unused items in our model simultaneously

Another great part of the **Statistics** box is all the additional information it gives. Essentially, this one button is a performance improver! This area gives us a count of almost everything in the model, such as how many edges or faces there are, the number of groups or components in the model, and ways to find and fix errors in the model (by clicking **Fix Problems**).

That's all there is to **Purge Unused**. We try to purge our model once per day or every couple of days because we work on large files that need all the extra oomph they can get.

Version History with Trimble Connect

What happens when you have gone further than undo can go back or have closed out of a model and cannot undo, but you desperately do not want to recreate the object you created 2 days ago? Some say, "Use the backup file!" Yes, you can do that if there is one. But what if there isn't? Well, friends, we introduce you to **Version History**. Bonus – this is available in all SketchUp paid formats, including iPad! This is brought to you by **Trimble Connect**, using your **Trimble ID** login.

When you purchased SketchUp, you created a **Trimble ID** account. It's shared and used by other **Trimble** applications – the same account that allows you to download items from **3D Warehouse** (we'll talk more about that in *Chapter 7*) and **Extension Warehouse** (wait for *Chapter 6*!). Trimble Connect is another application from Trimble, automatically built upon the identity you made when creating a Trimble ID login. Trimble Connect was explicitly created as a collaboration tool for securely storing files and sharing data in the cloud.

What can Trimble Connect do for you?

- Provides unlimited online file storage in Trimble's cloud service

- Allows for automated file syncing between computers (using **Trimble Sync**)

- Keeps multiple **Version History** files for recovery purposes

- Delivers remote modeling collaboration abilities (using the **Collaboration Manager**). We will talk about this a bit more in *Chapter 4*.

Follow these steps to get started with **Version History**:

1. Open the Trimble Connect toolbar:

Figure 3.36: The Trimble Connect toolbar

The icon on the left looks like a page or piece of paper. This icon means that your file has either not been saved yet or has been saved locally. It's important to remember this as we progress through the steps.

2. Then, to upload the model you are working on to Trimble Connect, use the **File** menu (*Figure 3.37*).

3. The first time you are uploading a version, arrow down to **Save to Trimble Connect…**, though you can also select **Save A Copy to Trimble Connect…**.

Make sure you are connected to the internet, or this will not work.

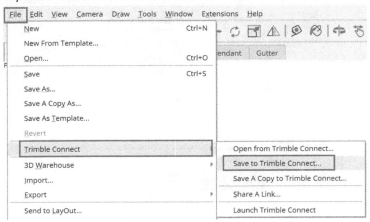

Figure 3.37: File | Trimble Connect | Save to Trimble Connect

4. Once you're in **Trimble Connect**, double-click on the SketchUp folder (see *Figure 3.38,* top). This will take you to another area of folders – if you have created or collaborated on any.

5. If you already have a folder for the project, click on it. If not, click the **Add New Folder** icon (*Figure 3.38,* bottom), then name the folder accordingly.

Figure 3.38: In Trimble Connect, click SketchUp (top) then Add New
Folder, or select a folder you already created (bottom)

Each company or individual has a method of naming folders. For good file management and ease of use, be consistent when naming files. Larger firms tend to name files by project number or name, inside another folder that is named with the year the project began. There are examples of this in *Figure 3.39*.

6. Click on the folder name to go into it or click **Save As** to save the model in this location.

7. We went into the folder named *Chapter 3*. Inside this folder, we can add another folder, or choose **Save As** to publish the model to the **Trimble Connect** cloud.

    Wait! Before you publish the model, add a date or other information to the file name so that you know which version is inside the folder. (There is information attached to the model, such as the date, but adding something to the filename saves you time.) In *Figure 3.39*, we have three versions of our Chapter 3- House model, all with different publish dates added to the file name:

Figure 3.39: Click Save As after adding a date to the filename

8. The next time you work on your model and go to publish a different version, follow the same steps again. The only change is to choose **Save A Copy to Trimble Connect…** instead of **Save to Trimble Connect….** The rest of the steps are the same. It will act like a regular save, so you won't see a confirmation when it's done.

9.   To access a previous version within any SketchUp model, navigate to the **File** menu, then select **Trimble Connect**, and choose **Open from Trimble Connect…**.

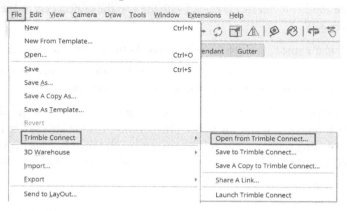

Figure 3.40: To open any version or file from Trimble Connect, choose Open from Trimble Connect…

Wait for **Trimble Connect** to open.

10.   Select the version you want to work with.

11.   Double-click the version name or highlight the name and click **Open**. It will open to the last saved view, exactly as it was when you uploaded that version to **Trimble Connect**.

Remember back on *step 1* when we had you open the Trimble Connect toolbar? After saving a model to the cloud, the toolbar will look different – where there was once an icon of a piece of paper there is now an icon of a cloud. The cloud icon is telling you the model was successfully uploaded:

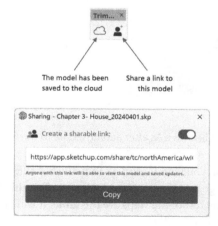

Figure 3.41: The Trimble Connect toolbar after saving a model to the cloud (top) and creating a link to share your model (bottom)

To the right of the cloud is an icon called **Share a link to this model**. The icon is an outline of a person's head with a plus sign next to it. By clicking on the icon, you can generate and copy a link of the model to send to anyone, allowing them to view your model- and any updates you make to it- in **SketchUp for Web** (a free version). It will be a read-only file, meaning they cannot edit it but can view your progress.

After you create a link, the `Share a link to this model` icon will change, showing outlines of two people, rather than one:

Figure 3.42: The Trimble Connect icons after creating a link

You can also create and share links through **File | Trimble Connect | Share a Link...**.

> **Additional reading**
>
> Learn more about Trimble Connect on SketchUp's website: `https://help.sketchup.com/en/sketchup/managing-models-using-trimble-connect`.

There is so much more you can do with your Trimble ID and SketchUp Pro or Studio subscription! Visit SketchUp's official forum, **SketchUp Community,** at `https://forums.sketchup.com/` to stay up with the latest and greatest product information, get answers to questions, and find awesome tutorials!

Our last section of the chapter is a quick overview of **Match Photo**; a fast way to model real-life elements.

Modeling real-life elements with Match Photo

We considered devoting a whole chapter to **Match Photo** (or **Photo Matching**), but there's already too much packed into this book. Given that this chapter is already extensive, we'll provide a brief overview of Match Photo to pique your interest – just enough to inspire you to delve deeper into it!

There are two ways to use Match Photo: One way is to apply parts of an image to an existing model. That way, you don't have to draw extensive details or add materials to multiple entities. (See *step 8* below.)

The second way is importing an image into SketchUp using **Match New Photo** to seamlessly translate 2D images into immersive 3D environments. Here's a breakdown of this capability and workflow:

1. **Snap your photo**: First, begin by capturing a representative photograph of the scene you wish to model. Whether it's an architectural structure, an interior space, a landscape, or a furniture item, this serves as the foundation for your digital reconstruction.

For images of existing spaces or exterior shots, the photo should be taken at a 45-degree angle, and you need at least one right angle.

2. **Import the photo**: You will import the image to SketchUp using one of three ways:

    - **File | Import**, select the image to import, click the radio next to **Use Image As: New Matched Photo** (see *Figure 3.43*), then click **Import**. MacOS, instead of clicking the radio, because there isn't one, click the dropdown next to **Format** and select **Use As New Matched Photo**.

    - **Camera | Match New Photo...**, select the image file to use, then click **Open**.

    - The third way is for Windows users only and came with SketchUp version 2024.0. In the Default Tray, open the **Match Photo** toolbar. Click the *plus sign* at the top-left, which is the **New Matched Photo...** button. It will prompt your file browser to open, allowing you to select the image. You can click the image and select **Open** or double-click the image.

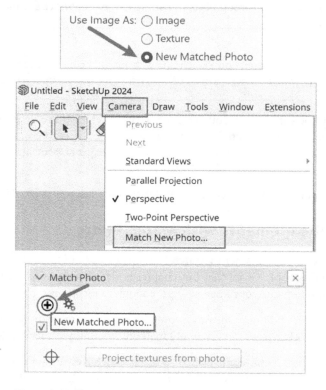

Figure 3.43: Three ways to import an image for Match Photo

3. **Set up your axes**: After the Match Photo is imported, SketchUp guides you through aligning your 3D workspace with the perspective of your photo. This involves defining the vanishing points (changing the red/x-axis and green/y-axis) and aligning them with the lines of perspective in the image.

4. **Draw your guides**: With your scene set, you can start sketching directly onto the photo, marking key points and lines to help SketchUp understand the scale and angles. Strategically position guides and reference points directly onto the photograph, accurately relocating dimensions and proportions into the 3D realm. It's like giving your 3D model GPS directions!

5. **Start modeling**: Now, the fun begins! Commence the construction of your 3D model within SketchUp, utilizing the photograph as a guiding template. This phase involves iteratively refining geometric elements to mirror the elements observed in the image. (It's like tracing but cooler!)

6. **Fine-tune your model**: As you work, SketchUp keeps updating the view to show how your model fits with the photo. You can tweak and adjust until everything lines up just right.

7. **Add those details**: Enhance your 3D creation by incorporating intricate details, textures, and material properties. This step adds depth and realism to the model, elevating its visual appeal and contextual authenticity. (This topic is discussed in *Chapter 10, Enhancing a Model with Details for Final Presentation*.)

8. **Blend it all together** (optional): Additionally, you have the choice to integrate your 3D creation with the photo, seamlessly fusing digital and real-world components. This is done with match photo's feature called **Project Photo** or **Project textures from photo**.

This tool is a game-changer! Match Photo is like wielding a magic wand for architects, designers, and urban planners. Picture this: with just a snapshot, you're able to conjure up jaw-droppingly precise 3D models that seamlessly integrate into real-world environments.

Learn more about Match Photo

We're big fans of Match Photo, relying on it to swiftly create both interior and exterior architectural designs, furniture, and landscaping projects. You can read more about it here: `https://help.sketchup.com/en/sketchup/matching-photo-model-or-model-photo`, or watch this YouTube video: `https://youtu.be/_VKAdKmSHEI?si=zg7nGdDfZlR4_OI6`.

In **3D Warehouse**, SketchUp modeler Wouter C. has an impressive model called `Veranda Match Photo`. This model showcases a stunning home renovation achieved using Match Photo, with all elements included for transparency in the process. You can download the model from this link to see firsthand how Match Photo can effortlessly bring designs to reality: `https://3dwarehouse.sketchup.com/model/ae461d10-d6c2-4e4b-9ff3-08b8415460c9/Veranda-Match-Photo`.

Trimble Connect Version History, **Purge Unused**, and **Match Photo** are three lesser-known timesavers within SketchUp. Familiarizing yourself with these techniques and tools will not only save you time in the future but also add an enjoyable element to your work!

Summary

In this chapter, we went through some heavy artillery for making more complex objects in SketchUp by practicing how to use **Follow Me**, **Autofold**, **Solid Tools**, and **Intersect Faces**. You learned how to increase both your and SketchUp's performance by purging the model and saving different versions of a project to Trimble's cloud service, Trimble Connect.

In the next chapter, we start integrating other drawing files, such as AutoCAD and Revit, with SketchUp. We will also outline the key considerations when working in a SketchUp file someone else created.

Part 2:
Working with Floor Plans

The second part is a comprehensive guide to crafting architectural elements, from walls and floors to stairs and roofs. Establish yourself as a skilled designer by mastering the art of importing and resizing hand-drafted floor plans, and using DWG/DXF plans to create 3D models (no AutoCAD knowledge is necessary!). Discover the efficiency of extensions for faster modeling, add section cuts to establish interior architecture, and gain insights into acclimating to SketchUp models drafted by others.

This part has the following chapters:

- *Chapter 4, Importing and Exporting a Drawing*
- *Chapter 5, Creating the As-Built Floor Plan*
- *Chapter 6, Building Exterior Elements and Using the Extension Warehouse*

4

Importing and Exporting a Drawing

Designers are frequently given a two-dimensional (2D) hand sketch, plotted **construction document set (CDs)**, CAD (DWG/DXF) file, or a Revit (RVT) file to create their SketchUp designs. When those imports into SketchUp are done, we trace on top of the content to create three-dimensional (3D) models. Conversely, sometimes, we create the draft in SketchUp and might need to export a view to AutoCAD or Revit.

Other times, a SketchUp model is received that requires some touch-ups before tackling the project. Knowing where to start with someone else's work will alleviate stress.

This chapter takes you through how to approach these different scenarios and begin creating a project.

In this chapter, we will cover the following topics:

- Importing an image of a drawing
- Importing a PDF file
- Importing a 2D AutoCAD file
- Importing a Revit drawing
- Exporting a SketchUp file to AutoCAD
- Working with someone else's SketchUp model

Technical requirements

To follow along in this chapter, you will need SketchUp Pro or Studio.

Importing an image of a drawing

When given drawings from reliable sources, such as a hand sketch of a plan revision or as-builts from a CAD file, we can upload almost any type of drawing to SketchUp and trace directly on top of it. This saves a lot of time because you do not have to flip back and forth from the drawing to SketchUp, and both files can be combined as an easy reference right there for you! This section covers how to insert a few different types of files into SketchUp by importing an image of a drawing.

Importing images to use in our SketchUp model is a process we are all familiar with because we use images as materials to add realistic touches. (If you do not feel comfortable using images as textures, check out *Chapter 9*).

When we are given an image of a drafted document, whether a floor plan, elevation, or anything else, we can import the image file to SketchUp to use for two-dimensional drafting. We won't get into the nitty gritty of **raster** vs. vector image files but know this: in SketchUp, you can import and export raster image files, with the more common offerings being **Joint Photographic Experts Group** (**JPEG**), **Portable Network Graphics (PNG)**, **Tagged Image File Format (TIFF)**, **Bitmap (BMP)**, and **Adobe Photoshop (PSD)**. Typically, we import JPEG (or JPG) and PNG files because they keep the SketchUp file size smaller than other formats, and their colors tend to view similarly across varying graphics cards and computer operating systems. Check the **Import** window's file type dropdown (from the **File** menu) to determine the file types you can import. *Figure 4.1* displays the supported file types for SketchUp Studio for Windows users:

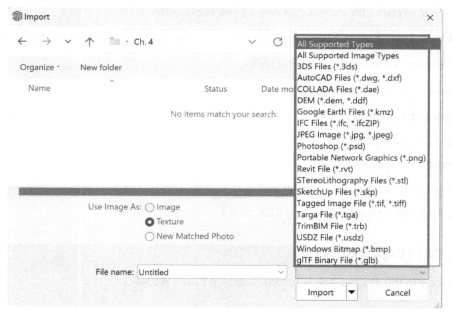

Figure 4.1: File types Windows version of SketchUp Studio will import

If you are not familiar with the word raster, they are image files made up of pixels, which are tiny dots of color. The more pixels an image has, the higher quality it will be (and vice versa). You must be careful when resizing raster images because the pixel numbers are fixed or unchanging, so they can become distorted or blurry when resized. Common raster files are JPEG, PDF, PNG, and GIF images. We give a bit more information about raster images in *Chapter 12*.

> **Additional reading- Raster and Vector**
>
> For additional information about raster and vector images in SketchUp, go to SketchUp's website: `https://help.sketchup.com/en/sketchup/importing-and-exporting-image-files`.

There are two ways to import an image into SketchUp. The first way is to use the **File** menu, and the second is to click and directly drag the image from a file folder into SketchUp.

To use the **File** menu, follow these steps:

1. From the **File** menu, choose **Import**.
2. Navigate to where the image is saved and click on it once.
3. Before clicking **Import**, select the radio (Windows) or dropdown (macOS) called **Use Image As: Image**:

Figure 4.2: Importing a floor plan image as an image

4. After selecting the **Image** option, click **Import**.

The file will be imported to SketchUp.

The second way to import the image is to *click* and *drag* it directly from the file folder on your computer where the image is saved.

1. Simultaneously, with SketchUp open, *click*, *hold*, and *drag* the image file into SketchUp.

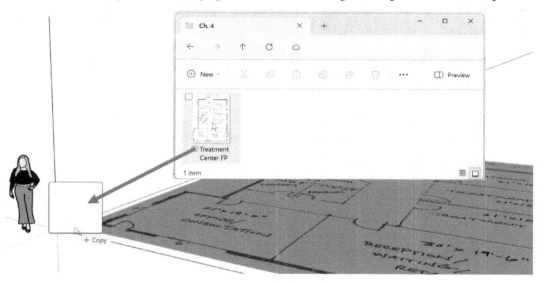

Figure 4.3: Click, hold, and drag the image file into SketchUp

2. After the image file is imported, *release* your mouse.
3. Tap the *spacebar* to exit the **Scale** tool, which is automatically activated after you drag the file into SketchUp.
4. **Save** your model.

Once the image is imported by using either method, you will most likely need to resize the image for accurate drafting. Let's see how in the next section.

Scaling the Image

Some might think that to **resize** or **rescale** an image in SketchUp, we use the **Scale** tool. That is not always true! There are times to use the **Scale** tool, but for resizing a large object to precise dimensions, we use the **Tape Measure** tool. This allows for a uniform rescale without the accidental distortion of the object, which can happen with the **Scale** tool.

First, let's measure a known dimension, preferably a larger dimension. In our example, we are working with a commercial space, a treatment center. We have the overall dimensions of the rooms and can measure one of them with the **Tape Measure** to find out the imported dimensions.

> **No endpoints in an image**
>
> The downside to using an image to draft with (rather than an imported drawing file) is that there is no usable geometry. That means we are measuring blindly, guessing where the beginning and end of the doorway are based on the lines of the image. In other words, we do not have points to snap for measuring. Because of this, drafting from an image can be tricky. Some people think if they explode the image, they can get geometry from it, but that is only the case when importing a PDF. For details, please see the *Importing PDF files* section in the chapter.

Figure 4.4 shows an approximate dimension of the north wall of the Reception/Waiting area measured with the **Tape Measure** tool along the red/x-axis, resulting in a length of 15'-5 3/16". (This number is based on how we brought in the image.)

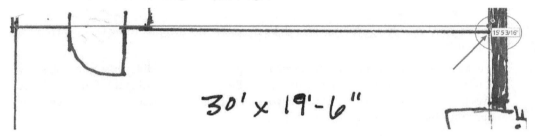

Figure 4.4: Measuring the north Reception wall with the Tape Measure tool

We know, from the drawing notations, that the wall should be 30'. To resize the image to the correct length, it needs to be a group. If you click once on the image and look at **Entity Info**, you will see that rather than being a group or component, the image is categorized as **Image**. As an Image, it cannot be manipulated or edited as a functioning entity, meaning we cannot make changes to its makeup other than moving, rotating, or scaling.

To make the image a group, explode it (right-click and select **Explode**), and then immediately right-click again and choose **Make Group**. Check out **Entity Info** now; instead of *Image*, it reads **Group**. Now, we can use the **Tape Measure** tool to resize the image, following these steps:

1. Get into **Edit** mode of the new image group.

2. Measure the distance again (in this case, the north **Reception** wall) by clicking on one end of the wall and then the opposite end.

    Make sure to measure along an axis, even if the drawing is not perfectly straight (such as in our example).

3. After the second click, before you do anything else, immediately type in the new length of the wall, which is 30'. Type 30' and hit *Enter*.

4. If you have done this correctly, a popup will ask you this: **Do you want to resize the active group or component?**:

Figure 4.5: Popup after resizing inside a group or component

5. Select **Yes**, and your image (or object) will be resized uniformly according to the increment you input.

6. If you are not in a group or component when using this method, a different popup will show. This window asks if you want to resize the model. Be careful when using this function! If you say **Yes** to resizing the model, everything in your model will rescale according to the increment, not just the objects inside a group or component:

Figure 4.6: Popup after resizing outside a group or component (the entire model)

Now that you've imported and resized the drawing image, what's the next step? Let's find out in the following section.

Tracing the Image

Now that you have a reference document for drafting in SketchUp, you will use it for **tracing** on a two-dimensional plane. Once the tracing is done, you can extrude the various shapes you created to produce three-dimensional objects (refer to *Chapters 1* and *2* for extruding objects with **Push/Pull**. *Chapter 3* discusses how to extrude using **Follow Me**).

If working on a plan view, such as a floor plan, the best practice is to be in the **Top** view, as discussed in *Chapter 1*. Some modelers like to be in the **Camera** setting **Parallel Projection** for this work, while others (such as the authors) prefer to stay in the **Perspective** view for toggling back and forth between the **Top** and **Isometric** views.

With hand-drafted documents, the lines tend to be a bit wavy or not drawn straight. For beginning drafters, remember to draw on the axis with precise measurements, even if it deviates from how the image is shown or scaled. You use lines or shapes to create walls or flooring, such as the lower-right rectangle in *Figure 4.7*, which was drawn with the measurements given (30' x 19'-6"):

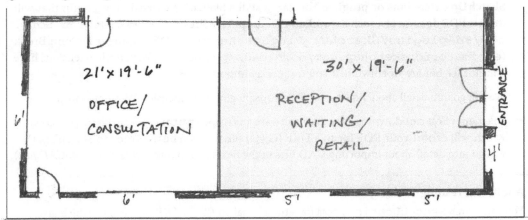

Figure 4.7: Begin tracing the image at precise measurements, using shapes, lines, materials, and groupings

We grouped the rectangle and then added an opaque material inside **Edit** mode. That way, as we continue drafting the remainder of the building, we ensure that all areas are connected as they exist in real life.

Remember to create groups or components to separate geometry as you draft, simplifying your future work and saving time.

Now that we have learned how to import a raster image of a drawing let's look at other options for importing drawings.

Importing a PDF file

If you are using a Mac, you have an advantage over Windows users when importing PDF files to SketchUp; macOS will import PDF files to SketchUp without a need for external applications. Windows does not yet support this function.

To import a PDF to SketchUp on macOS, use **File | Import**, as is customary with most insertions. You can also *click* and *drag* the file into SketchUp, as shown previously in the chapter.

For Windows, there are a few options for bringing your PDF into SketchUp:

- **Adobe Acrobat DC**: If you have Adobe Acrobat DC, first export the PDF to image file(s) and then import the image(s) to Sketchup, whether through the **File** menu or using *click* and *drag*.

- **Snip & Sketch or Snipping Tool**: You can use Snip & Sketch (Windows) or another screen grab application. (We like Snipaste!) MacOS has a built-in screenshot command, but to get a higher-quality shot, you can use a free application, such as **Shottr** (`https://shottr.cc/`) or **Markup Hero** (`https://markuphero.com/`).

- **SketchUp extensions or plugins**: You can install a SketchUp extension or plugin that will import PDF documents, such as **SimLab PDF Importer** (`https://www.simlab-soft.com/3d-plugins/SketchUp_Plugins.aspx`) or **PDF Importer** by John Brock (`estimatorforsketchup.com/downloads/pdf-importer`). Both extensions have a minor fee but are worthwhile if you frequently import PDFs.

  We will go into detail about how to use SketchUp's plugins and Extension Warehouse in *Chapter 6*.

- **Inkscape**: You can download the free software Inkscape (`https://inkscape.org/`), which will export your PDF file to a DXF (CAD) file that can be imported to SketchUp. (We will go into detail about importing CAD files in the next section, *Importing a 2D AutoCAD file*.)

Additional reading - Inkscape

You can search `SketchUcation.com` for a tutorial called *PDF to SKP Conversion*, which gives complete steps for using Inkscape, or click this link: `sketchucation.com/resources/tutorials/426-pdf-skp-conversion`.

Now that we have explored ways to import PDF files to SketchUp, let's jump into importing two-dimensional drawing files.

Importing a 2D AutoCAD file

The great thing about importing a DWG or DXF file to SketchUp is that no prior CAD knowledge is needed, nor do you need the software on your computer! All you need is the file.

Here is some important information about how SketchUp converts DWG/DXF information:

- Only paid versions of SketchUp – SketchUp Pro, Studio, and iPad – will import DWG and DXF formats. You will not have this option using any of the free versions.

- SketchUp will not import dimensions, hatching, text, numbers, XREFs, and some dynamic blocks. It can help to explode blocks and other elements inside the DWG/DXF file, if they are not importing to SketchUp. If you are interested in importing hatching, there is a workaround for this by creating polyline boundaries for the hatches (an internet search will help you with the workaround).

SketchUp will, however, import some of the layers those objects are on if they have geometry attached to them that SketchUp recognizes.

- First, re-save the CAD drawing as a new file to import into SketchUp (such as `Drawing Title_SketchUp Import`). Get into the habit of not using the original CAD files for importing. Then, make changes to the CAD file as listed in the next bullet point.

- Simplify the drawing so it won't take long to import. Most of the suggestions in our list are for lowering the file size of the CAD drawing to make the import seamless:

  - Delete the layers and the objects on them you will not need, such as schedule tables and hatching.

  - Delete or explode unneeded blocks.

  - Delete text and dimensions. Again, SketchUp will not import text and numbers, including dimensions, so this just slows down the import process.

  - Purge the drawing of all these changes and save.

  - Moving the CAD entities to the origin at `0,0` will help the import scale accurately and can prohibit viewing problems later in SketchUp.

There are two ways to import a DWG or DXF file into SketchUp. They are almost identical, except for the first step, so we will explain both at the same time. Both are the same methods we used when importing an image of a drawing: use the **File** menu or *click* and *drag* the drawing file from a folder into SketchUp.

1. The first method is through the **File** menu:

    I. From the **File** menu, choose **Import**, navigate to where the drawing file is saved, and click on it once.

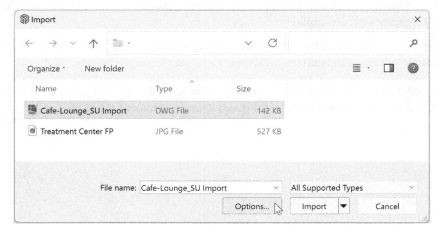

Figure 4.8: Import a DWG file

      II.   Before clicking **Import**, you must click **Options**. Then, go to Step 3.

> **Important note**
>
> If you do not see your file in the folder, make sure the file type dropdown reads **All Supported Types**, as shown in *Figure 4.8*. Alternatively, you can click that dropdown to pick a specific file type.

2.   The second way to import the drawing file is directly from the folder on your computer where the file is saved.

      I.   Simultaneously, with SketchUp open, *click*, *hold*, and *drag* the drawing file into SketchUp. (This is the same maneuver used when importing an image of a drawing.)

      II.   A dialog box called **Import AutoCAD DWG/DXF Options** will pop up. Go on to *step 3* to learn what to do with these options.

3.   Select the following in the **Import AutoCAD DWG/DXF Options** box (*Figure 4.9*):

- **Geometry**: Use these settings for Geometry:

  - Check the top two boxes, **Merge coplanar faces** and **Orient faces consistently**. By checking these boxes, you are choosing to have the edges line up and touch where possible.

  - You will not usually choose the **Import Materials** option. When that is checked, it imports the CAD Layer colors.

- **Position: Preserve drawing origin** should be checked if you are bringing in a stacked drawing, such as a building with two or more floors. The authors of this book do not typically check this box because the drawing should be brought in at SketchUp's 0 , 0 origin point, keeping the geometry where it should be.

- **Scale**: You can set the **Units** to match the drawing by choosing **Model Units**, which is helpful if you do not know the units in the drawing, or, you can choose another unit.

4.   Finally, click **OK** to save the above settings. These settings will be saved to your computer, so you will not need to re-select them the next time you import a drawing.

5.   Then, click **Import** to bring the drawing into SketchUp.

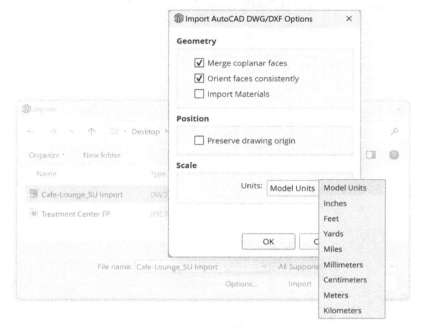

Figure 4.9: The Import AutoCAD DWG/DXF Options box

Click and Drag Import

If you are importing the drawing using the click-and-drag method, you will skip *step 5*, clicking **Import**, because that option is not available to you.

---

6.   SketchUp will take a few moments to import and then share the **Import Results** window (*Figure 4.10*).

If the **Import Results** window does not pop up, the file most likely did not import correctly, and you need to retry your import.

To ensure a successful import, you might need to save the CAD file to a version that's a few years older than the version of SketchUp you're using.

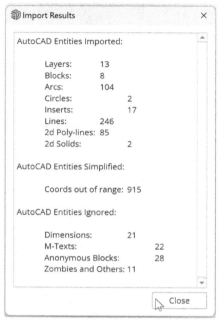

Figure 4.10: Import Results

You do not need to read or memorize the results. All the information is found in various toolbars and panels within SketchUp.

7.   You can **Close** the Import Results.

8.   As a fail-safe, you should immediately check a known measurement with the **Tape Measure** tool. If the measurement is not correct, remember that you can use the tape measure tool to scale your entire floor plan correctly by resizing the model or the grouping, as we did in the *Scaling the Image* section.

SketchUp requires a closed group of edges, which is not something CAD produces; this is why there might not be any faces to your imported floor plan. By checking **Merge coplanar faces** and **Orient faces consistently** before importing, we come close to creating closed edges, but there is no direct translation between the two software types to create faces on import. That is not something to worry about, though, because we will not use the import to draft. We will trace over it instead, so we leave the reference untouched.

Sometimes, we consolidate all CAD layers into a single SketchUp tag, but this choice depends on our workflow preferences. Yet, there are situations where keeping individual CAD layers accessible proves beneficial. In such cases, we organize them within a tag folder named, for instance, CAD Plan, allowing easy reference later on. The drawback is that SketchUp doesn't allow duplicate tag names, so if a CAD layer name matches a desired SketchUp tag name, one of them must be modified.

Figure 4.11: CAD layers upon importing (top), after moving them to a folder,
and after merging into one tag called CAD PLAN (bottom)

You will notice that the drawing comes in as a **Component**. You should lock it so you do not accidentally delete any needed references. Right-click on the component and choose **Lock**. Or you can lock it in the **Entity Info** toolbar by clicking the **Lock** icon.

Tracing the Drawing

After importing a CAD file or any other type of drawing file, use the import to create the two-dimensional shapes by tracing the drawing. Then use a SketchUp extrusion tool to create three-dimensional objects. We will go further into this in *Chapter 5*.

The next section will highlight some of the processes for integrating **Revit** with SketchUp.

Importing a Revit drawing

While importing a Revit file (RVT) directly into native SketchUp isn't currently possible, a **SketchUp Studio** subscription offers enhanced sharing and collaboration features, including the capability to integrate Revit drawings using **Revit Importer**. However, macOS users should note that **Revit Importer** is currently compatible only with Windows computers. That said, there are workarounds to importing a Revit model, which we will discuss a bit later. Those on Windows computers using SketchUp Pro can get a 7-day trial version of **SketchUp Studio** with **Revit Importer** through the **Extension Warehouse**.

When you open the Install window for **SketchUp Studio**, there is an option to add **Revit Importer** (and **Scan Essentials for SketchUp and LayOut**) to the installation:

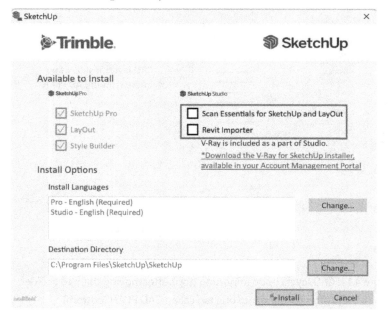

Figure 4.12: Install window for SketchUp Studio

If you check the box next to **Revit Importer** before clicking **Install**, it will automatically be added to your SketchUp program files. Then, you can import the Revit file by using **File | Import** (the same way we imported the AutoCAD drawing).

> **Important note**
> If you forget to check the box or decline to have it installed, you can later download **Revit Importer** from the **Extension Warehouse**.

What will **Revit Importer** do? It will import any Revit file (RVT) without the software having to be installed on your computer, if the Revit file is newer than 2011. SketchUp will automatically convert Revit information to be used within SketchUp (the following information comes from `Sketchup.com`):

- **SketchUp components**: Revit families and repeated identical objects are converted into SketchUp components. The converted components are automatically named using Revit's family name or family type.

- **SketchUp materials**: Revit materials import to SketchUp as flattened, solid color components, but appropriate opacity is maintained for translucent or opaque materials. If you are familiar with Revit, the SketchUp color matches the appearance of Revit's **Consistent Colors** option. If you are not replacing a solid color, you will likely need to rename the materials because their name usually begins with `RevitLink`.

- **SketchUp sections**: Sections from Revit translate slightly differently in SketchUp. They are created from Revit levels, but they point downward, and the Section Plane is 4' above the Revit level.

- **SketchUp tags**: Revit families automatically receive tags named after their Revit categories. You might need to clean up the tags after importing to merge objects and reduce the number of tags. *Chapter 2* reviews how to merge tags.

- **Geometry optimization**: Because there is no true curve in SketchUp, just a series of points and triangles, SketchUp reduces the segment count on curves and decreases repeated triangulation for imported 3D objects. You might see slight texture variations with chamfered and other curved objects.

- **Revit Links support**: When an imported Revit project contains one or more linked RVT files, **Revit Importer** creates a proxy or alternate object for each file. The proxy objects appear in a SketchUp tag called `<Revit Missing Link>`.

> **Additional reading**
>
> Find out more about importing to SketchUp with Revit Importer by clicking one of these links: `help.sketchup.com/en/revit-interoperability/revit-to-sketchup` or `https://help.sketchup.com/en/revit-interoperability/importalternatives`, or `https://blog.sketchup.com/article/six-tips-tomaximize-the-revit-importer`.

If you are not a **SketchUp Studio** subscriber, or on macOS, you can import a Revit file to SketchUp by changing the file type to another CAD format. That means you or someone you are working with must have access to a Revit software license.

You can generate an AutoCAD drawing from Revit through three distinct export options from within Revit:

1. To export a Floor Plan (2D view) from inside Revit, go to **File | Export | CAD Formats** (refer to *Figure 4.13*). Then, select the file type, DWG or DXF, and the plan views to export. Finish the export by clicking **Next** and saving the file.

Figure 4.13: Revit 2024 Export menu

We suggest selecting one Revit plan view at a time for faster importing to SketchUp, but that is your call.

2. To export a 3D view from inside Revit, follow the same steps as above but choose 3D views. Again, we suggest exporting one Revit view at a time (singular files).

3. You can also import Revit as an **IFC import**. (We discussed IFC in *Chapter 1*). In Revit, select **File | Export | IFC**, then finish the export.

In all three instances, import the CAD file to SketchUp from **File | Import**.

Importing 3D blocks

You can import 3D files as well, either by utilizing **File | Import** or by employing the click and drag method. Why might you choose to do this? It could be to incorporate **3D CAD blocks** (in DWG or DFX formats) or 3ds models (in **3DS** format) into your model, thereby eliminating the need to recreate objects that have already been designed. Once imported, you can edit them just like any other element within SketchUp.

Let's take a break from importing and move on to exporting drawings from SketchUp.

Exporting a SketchUp file to AutoCAD

In SketchUp Pro or Studio, you can export vector images and drawing files. We will discuss exporting image files in *Chapter 11*, and also how to export a drawing to a PDF.

To export a SketchUp model to an AutoCAD file, first set up a view and scene. Will you set up an elevation view or a plan view? Here are some helpful tips for setting up a successful drawing export:

- Use the Camera's **Standard Views** and **Scenes** to create the best view. Any time you change or update the views or styles, update the scene.
- For two-dimensional views, which are the most-used drawing exports, use the Camera setting **Parallel Projection** to create an orthographic view.
- Use **Section Planes** to create **Section Cuts,** which not only saves time but creates a clean drawing export.
- Utilize tags to hide the visibility of objects not necessary for the CAD file, such as accessories or décor items. These items do not typically export cleanly to CAD, creating a lot of extraneous lines.
- Decide on the **style** of the view, such as showing or hiding edges, using a pre-made style, such as *Sketchy Edges*, or using a section cut. (Check out *Chapter 10*, where we talk more about SketchUp's **Styles** panel.)

In the example below, the SketchUp model is a kitchen elevation scene set up using **Parallel Projection**, the **Back** camera view, a **Section Cut** with the **Section Plane** hidden, a gray **Section Fill**, and **Profiles** are turned off. The tags for accessories, flooring, and lighting are also turned off. There is a blank area at the top-right where the crown molding atop the cabinets turns towards the camera view.

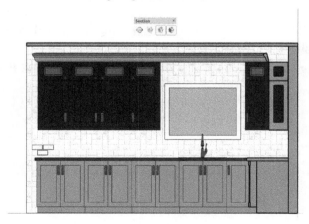

Figure 4.14: SketchUp Elevation view using Parallel Projection

Follow these steps to export a SketchUp model to a 2D AutoCAD file:

1. After setting up the 2D view, export the SketchUp file from the **File** menu.

2. Click **Export** and select **2D Graphic**.

3. Name your file and choose the export type next to the **Save as type** dropdown:

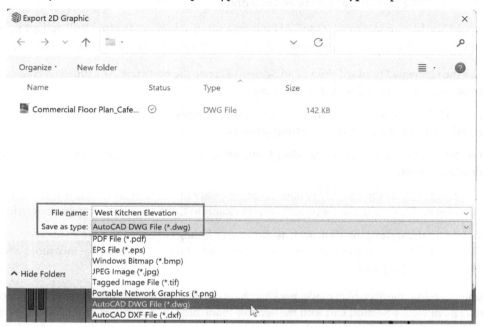

Figure 4.15: Select the DWG or DXG file types for exporting to AutoCAD

4. You can click **Options** to change the scale of the drawing, though it defaults to `Full Scale 1:1` so that might not be necessary.

5. Click **Export** or go into **Options** to play around with the **DWG/DFX Export Options** box (*Figure 4.16*).

As a reference, this is what the **DWG/DFX Export Options** box looks like when `Full Scale 1:1` is selected, without making any changes to other settings::

Figure 4.16: Options box for exporting to a DWG or DXF file

In *Chapter 11*, we will show you how to use a similar options box to export a drawing to a particular scale.

6. After clicking **Export**, your computer will take a few seconds (or minutes) to export.

Once it is done, a popup in SketchUp will read, **DWG/DXF Export is Complete:**

Figure 4.17: Export is complete

Figure 4.18 shows what the exported kitchen SketchUp drawing looks like in AutoCAD. You will see that a few things were not exported: the tile backsplash in SketchUp is mostly an image, not tiles created with edges and faces. The only tiles showing are the three on the left that were drawn and given depth in SketchUp. The axes and section toolbar were showing in SketchUp but were not exported to CAD.

The drawing is brought in without anything grouped how it was in SketchUp. You can edit and add lines as usual in AutoCAD.

Figure 4.18: SketchUp exported to a 2D DWG file (AutoCAD)

The steps for exporting a SketchUp file to a drawing or other file are easy to understand after a bit of practice. The important thing is to make sure you are modeling well, using groupings, tags, scenes, and the other basics we have discussed throughout the book so far. Try exporting your SketchUp model to another drawing type, play with different views and options, and see what you can create!

Now that we know how to import and export drawings in SketchUp, let's look at the next section to learn how to work with someone else's SketchUp model.

Working with someone else's SketchUp model

Collaborating with designers or architects is a typical part of our jobs. With this comes sharing drawing files, like AutoCAD and Revit, and also SketchUp models. Receiving any type of drawing file that we did not originally create can be irritating because we all feel our drawing standards are the best. Receiving someone else's SketchUp model is no different. We cannot tell you how many times we have opened a SketchUp model someone has sent us, only to throw our hands in the air and say, "Oh, come on!" (You know you have done that, too.)

Here are some tips to get you started.

- Save the model with a new name (or a new date). You are likely going to be making changes to the model, and you do not want to mess up the original.

- Check the file size. Large file sizes may indicate complexity or excessive detail, which could impact performance. If the file is too large, consider simplifying or breaking it down into smaller, separated files. Simplifying complex models can improve performance and ease of editing.

- Acclimate yourself to their model:

  - Use **Zoom extents** to see the entirety of what you are working with; then, use **Orbit**, **Pan**, and **Zoom** to investigate different areas.

  - Check out their **Scenes**, if there are any. If not, create scenes for easier viewing of different areas.

  - Evaluate the accuracy of the model. Are dimensions and proportions correct? Check for any errors or discrepancies that need to be addressed.

  - Are components and groups used effectively to organize the model? Well-organized models are easier to work with and modify. Click into groups and components. Is everything grouped separately from each other as it should be? Are repeating objects linked together as components?

  - Take a look at the **Tags** panel. Are there any tags? Do the names make sense? Turn the visibility of each one off and on and see what objects reside where. As you know, proper tag management helps with visibility and control over different parts of the model. Are any edges and faces tagged? Move them to **Untagged** to save yourself geometry issues in the future (refer to *Chapters 1* and *2* for SketchUp basics reminders).

  - Investigate sections and hidden geometry with the **Outliner**.

- Decide what must be fixed to do your part of the project or what can be overlooked to save time. For example:

  - It must be fixed: Many or all objects are fused together without separation.

All objects must be grouped separately from each other. Sometimes, this takes a ton of time to fix, but in the end, it is worth it. You decide what absolutely must be separated into groups to make your life easier, even though you may not be paid for it.

Other 3D file formats

It is also common to receive a SketchUp file that was originally a **3ds Max** file (or different 3D modeling software) that was converted to SketchUp. If this is the case, there's a chance that the file has no groups or tags at all. Again, you must decide what is necessary to make into groups and how to organize your tags. Unfortunately, sometimes, it is easier to rebuild a space from scratch in SketchUp rather than using the converted file. The plus side is that the converted file is the best resource for building the new file!

- Some things can be overlooked to save time: Components were not made of repeating objects.

  You must decide how much billable time it will take to make a group a component and copy it around the model, or if editing a few extra groups will save time.

  - Should you move everything closer to the **Origin Point** to avoid clipping planes and other issues? Or will that make it harder for other tools you might use for collaborating, such as **Paste in Place?**

  - Should you **Purge Unused** items in the model or keep them in case there might be something you can use later? (This is one people often regret!)

- Is the model running slow or lagging a bit? Consider using a fast style (covered in *Chapter 10*, section *Exploring SketchUp's Styles panel*) or disabling shadows if they are toggled on. We cover other tips for how to keep your model clean in *Chapter 15*.

- If you have questions for the original modeler, ask them right away before you get too deep into the model. However, refrain from criticizing the modeler's modeling skills; everyone learns and uses software their own unique way.

- If available, review any reference material provided along with the SketchUp file, such as plans, elevations, site photos, or design briefs. Understanding the context and requirements of the project will help you work more effectively.

These tips will get you started when given another person's model. By thoroughly reviewing these aspects of the SketchUp file, you can better understand the project's scope and ensure a smooth workflow!

Summary

This chapter is all about importing and exporting various drawing file types. We learned how to import image, PDF, AutoCAD, and Revit files, and how to export our SketchUp model to AutoCAD. We also covered some tips on what to do when you receive a SketchUp project you did not originally create.

In the next chapter, we will continue from where we left off, following the import of an AutoCAD file. We will trace over the imported AutoCAD file, create the architectural details (such as walls and floors) of a commercial building, and extrude those elements into 3D.

Creating the As-Built Floor Plan

Using a downloadable SketchUp file from 3D Warehouse, this chapter walks through the beginning steps to create the architectural elements of a commercial building by creating walls and floors, cutting holes for doors and windows, and constructing stairs. Tags and drawing on the x-, y-, or z-axis are essential parts of these processes.

This chapter will cover the following topics:

- Creating walls and floors by **tracing** an AutoCAD plan
- How to cut in window and door openings
- Constructing stairs

Technical requirements

To follow along with this chapter, you will need the following:

- SketchUp Pro or SketchUp Studio
- The SketchUp practice file called `Chapter 5- Commercial Plan` for this chapter. It can be downloaded from `3D Warehouse` inside SketchUp or from `https://3dwarehouse.sketchup.com/model/91ece689-7151-46b1-a5d2-690ef3cf8d4e/Chapter-5-Commercial-Plan`.

Creating walls and floors by tracing an AutoCAD plan

In this chapter, we will be working on a SketchUp model with an imported AutoCAD drawing (review *Chapter 4* for how to import a DWG/DXF file). The drawing is a commercial project, a coffee and lounge space with a mezzanine level. We will start by tracing over the CAD drawing two-dimensionally and then create three-dimensional elements.

The *Chapter 5* practice file includes an image of the CAD plan to use as a reference for items that were not imported to SketchUp, such as dimensions. There is also an imported CAD drawing. The drawing came in as a component, which is locked so it cannot accidentally be edited. As another reference for you, we have kept the imported CAD layers but put them in a tag folder named CAD PLAN. This is how the drawing looks:

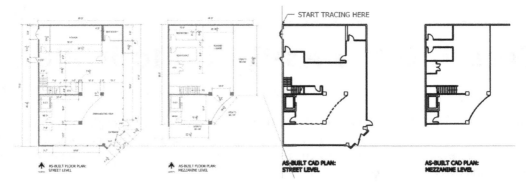

Figure 5.1: Chapter 5 practice file

Other than the default solid linetype, a dashed line is shown for the items on the GLAZE-HIDDEN tag, which is the see-through resin wall on the mezzanine level. Linetypes can be changed in the **Tags** toolbar, underneath the **Dashes** column. Click the **Dashes** dropdown on each tag line to select a different linetype. (Tags were reviewed in *Chapter 2*. If you need more information, refer to the *What are tags? How are they used?* section of that chapter.)

Lineweights in SketchUp

When looking at the imported AutoCAD drawing, you will see that lineweights were not brought in. That is because all edges or lines are of the same width or weight throughout native SketchUp. You can change the edge profile to be heavier or lighter in the **Edge Styles** toolbar, but that only affects the outline of all connected edges, whether grouped or ungrouped.

Varying lineweights are created in **SketchUp LayOut**, not in SketchUp itself. We will introduce LayOut functions in *Chapters 12* and *13*.

To create the architectural details of the drawing, specifically the walls and floor, we will trace over the drawing with lines or edges; we can also use the rectangle shape.

The steps for tracing the drawing begin in the next section.

Tracing the drawing in 2D

As we discussed in previous chapters of this book, we should draft in **Top** view of a plan view for drawing accuracy. When drafting in top view, you are drawing two-dimensionally on the ground surface of the model. You can access **Top** view using the **Views** toolbar or by navigating through **Camera | Standard Views | Top**.

> **Reminder: How to draft on a computer**
>
> As you draft, keep one hand lightly posed on the mouse and the other lightly over the keyboard. You will model more efficiently with this technique, especially if you take advantage of the keyboard and mouse shortcuts.

Once you have selected **Top** view, follow these steps:

1. Zoom into the `Street` or `Ground Level` CAD floor plan (the plan on the left). Be sure to zoom in on the CAD drawing and not the image to the far left. In the model, there is text marking where to start that reads, "`START TRACING HERE`".

    You should always zoom in to select precise points, not further away from the area in hopes of selecting the correct point. As a general rule of thumb for workflows, be consistent with where you start and end your drafting points so you always know where you began. The authors draft from the upper left and work our way down and around to the right. You decide where you want to begin and be consistent each time. (See *Figure 5.2* for where we started.)

> **Important note**
>
> The tool we choose for *step 3* will determine how we go about tracing the drawing, though your approach can change from one area to the next. For less experienced modelers, starting with the **Line** tool, coupled with locking in each axis, is the best practice. For more experienced modelers, using the **Rectangle** tool – and locking in the blue/z-axis – is another way to approach the tracing process.

2. Let's start with the exterior walls first, tracing over all the walls, windows, and doors for each individual wall area. What is meant by individual wall area? For interior designers, it is a good idea to separate walls – such as north, south, east, and west walls – into individual groups and then place them on tags with the same names. This approach makes it easier to edit one wall by turning off the visibility to the rest of the walls that are in the way of modeling. (It is also beneficial down the road when creating and exporting scenes, which was discussed in *Chapter 2* and will further be covered in *Chapter 11*.) This is not necessarily the best approach for architects. Choose the method that works for you.

3. For now, activate the **Line** tool (shortcut *L*). *Figure 5.2* shows you how that looks when zoomed into the upper-left corner of the Street Level (Ground Floor) plan:

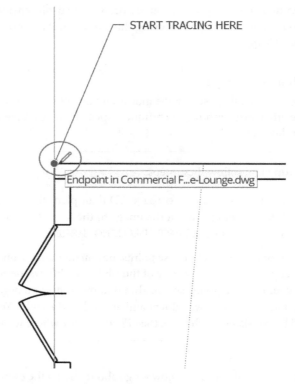

Figure 5.2: Tracing over the north wall of the ground floor using the Line tool

4. Click your mouse on an endpoint, release the mouse, and move it across along the red/x-axis to the opposite end.

   Remember to lock in the x-axis by tapping once on the *right arrow* key.

5. Click the endpoint at the opposite end, move your mouse down the width of the wall, which is 8 ", and click the Endpoint there (*Figure 5.3*). Remember to lock in the green/y-axis by tapping the *left arrow* key.

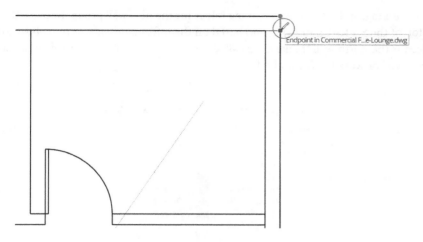

Figure 5.3: Click the Endpoint along the green/y-axis for the wall width

6. Finish up the remaining two endpoints, along the red/x-axis and green/y-axis, which should then create a face.

7. Once the connecting edges form a face, double-click on the face to select both the edges and the face itself. Then, right-click on the face and choose **Make Group**.

Figure 5.4: Make the wall shape a group

Don't forget to save your model!

Grouping walls separately

Some modelers do not like to group walls separately. As interior designers, we added this workflow method to our repertoire after years of modeling. We have found that grouping walls individually from the get-go saves time when modeling more complex buildings or individual interior spaces. Some photorealistic rendering engines are unable to render through a section cut, which further emphasizes the necessity to separate walls for this purpose, thereby speeding up the process. As with anything else in this book, use *your* preferred method!

The next step can be done now or after you are done creating all the exterior walls.

8. Now, create a tag, and – if you want – a tag folder for the new wall group. Because this wall is at the top of the SketchUp drawing and based on the information about the job site, the wall we traced is the north wall. Make a tag called EXT-WALL-NORTH, or name it according to your personal or work CAD standards.

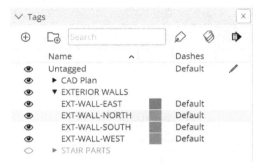

Figure 5.5: Created exterior wall tags in a tag folder

Next, trace the exterior walls on the east, or the right side, of the ground floor. This time, practice using the **Rectangle** (shortcut *R*) tool.

9. Click an endpoint at the top of the drawing, just below the first wall group you made.

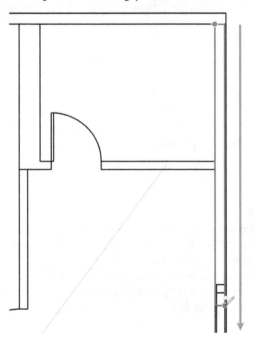

Figure 5.6: With the Rectangle tool, click an endpoint at the top of the drawing

10. Continue the rectangle down the entire length of the wall, encompassing window and door areas as well, until you reach the bottom of the wall.

Why are we covering the windows and doors with the wall group?

If we were to leave openings for all windows and doors, that would cause extra work in the future after you push/pull up the wall height. Later in the chapter, we will show you how to cut a hole for the windows and doors.

---

11. The east and south walls were cut off a bit early due to the entry and exit doors at a 45 degree angle. The entrance wall area is also oddly shaped. Stop the east wall rectangle just past the door opening (*Figure 5.7*) and pick up the rest of the wall in another group (*Figure 5.8*).

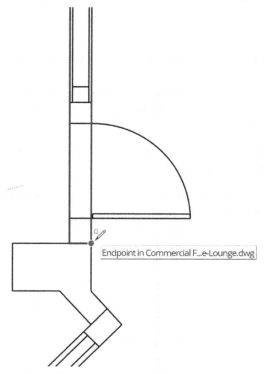

Figure 5.7: End the rectangle just past the door opening

12. Exit the **Rectangle** tool (*spacebar*), make the wall a group, and tag it using EXT-WALL-EAST (or your own tagging method).

Now, because the rest of the east wall is oddly shaped, use the **Line** tool to trace around its edges, making sure to zoom into each endpoint.

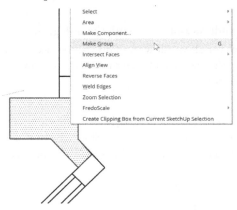

Figure 5.8: Use the Line tool to trace the oddly shaped wall

After tracing the wall, make the edges and face a group. Then, tag that group. (Will you put it on the east wall tag or another? It is up to you. We will put ours on a new tag named ENTRANCE WALL, but it can be changed later if necessary.)

Continue creating the remaining exterior walls, making groups and then tags. Complete the perimeter of the ground floor, then continue on to the next steps.

Figure 5.9 shows the SketchUp model with the CAD plan's visibility turned off, so you can see how all exterior wall groups were constructed:

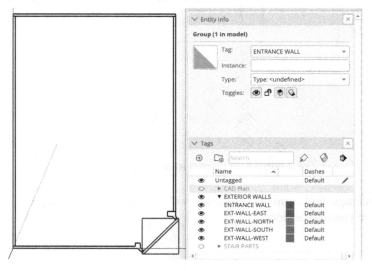

Figure 5.9: All ground floor exterior wall groups are created

For the wall at the entrance/exit, we created a separate tag just for that area called ENTRANCE WALL. As always, you can create tags that best fit your CAD standards.

The next step in tracing can either be to create the flooring shape or begin outlining the interior walls. Let's touch on the flooring.

Wherever SketchUp can make a face, it will. If you did not create groups after making each wall section, it is likely that a face appeared in the middle of the drawing. You can use that face to make the subfloor or flooring; just double-click on it and make it a group.

If there is no face there, trace around the drawing to create either sectioned-off flooring area groups, if there will be more than one type of flooring material, or one entire flooring group.

To make this easier, turn off the visibility to all CAD plan entities and use the exterior wall groups you created to draw inside the exterior walls. Use lines and/or rectangles to accomplish this task. Make sure you stay in top view as well.

Figure 5.10 shows the creation of the flooring using two rectangles and the **Line** tool. We also started the process by right-clicking in the window and selecting **Make Group**, so we were already in **Edit** mode to create the flooring.

Figure 5.10: Use lines and rectangles to create the flooring

Rectangles and lines can be fused by erasing overlapping edges to create one continuous face. *Figure 5.11* shows the completed flooring after removing the overlapping edges:

Figure 5.11: The completed flooring group

If you did not start the flooring as a group, be sure to immediately made it a group. Then, tag the group immediately after it has been created.

For now, pause tracing the drawing to learn a quick way to extrude walls. You can come back to this drawing later to continue practicing drawing over the plan. With increased practice, your speed will improve, enabling you to discover your optimal workflow.

Extruding walls

Because we are creating the As-built Floor Plan, we need to decide what to extrude three-dimensionally. For example, there could be walls we are removing, changes to the exterior, and so forth. In this exercise, you will learn how to extrude a few exterior wall shapes and cut in walls and doors as they are drawn now (even though there might be architectural changes you want to make to this plan).

The first thing to do is set up the view. When extruding, try to see the beginning area to apply the extrusion tool (whether **Push/Pull** or **Follow Me**), as well as the ending area. Because of this, we will set up an isometric view. Also, decide what should be visible for each view. In this case, you are extruding only the exterior walls, so the other parts of the model are not necessary. Thus, turn off the visibility to the unneeded objects in the **Tags** folder.

The second thing is dimensions or measurements; we need to know how high to extrude the walls. Based on the dimensions from the Reflected Ceiling Plan (you do not have this), we know that the ground floor wall height is approximately 11' high, with dropped ceilings and soffits scattered throughout. For this exercise, we will extrude all exterior walls up 11' high.

Let's go through the steps to extrude the wall using **Becca's Hierarchy of Modeling** (from *Chapter 2*):

1. Get into **Edit** mode of one of the wall groups.
2. Select a face to be extruded.
3. Activate the **Push/Pull** command (shortcut *P*).
4. Click and release the mouse on an endpoint of the wall.
5. Move your mouse up, which tells SketchUp that this is the direction of the extrusion.
6. We do not need to lock in the axis because we can only go up or down using the **Push/Pull** tool in this instance, so we are skipping that step in the hierarchy.
7. Type 11' and *Enter*, making the wall 11' high.

> **Important note**
>
> As mentioned in *Chapter 1*, if you are using another system of measurement while in the inches template, typing the unit information after the number value will change the unit of measurement for the command:
>
> **Millimeters**: Type mm after the number, then press *Enter* or *Return* on the keyboard.
>
> **Centimeters**: Type cm after the number, then press *Enter* or *Return* on the keyboard.
>
> **Meters**: Type m after the number, then press *Enter* or *Return* on the keyboard.
>
> You can, of course, start with a template with a different unit of measurement instead.

8. Tap *spacebar* to get out of the command.
9. Save your model.
10. Use the **Tape Measure** tool to double-check that the extrusion height is correct.

The more you become familiar with SketchUp, the less you will need to perform the last step, which is double-checking the measurement. That said, just as accountants always double-check their numbers, we should do the same.

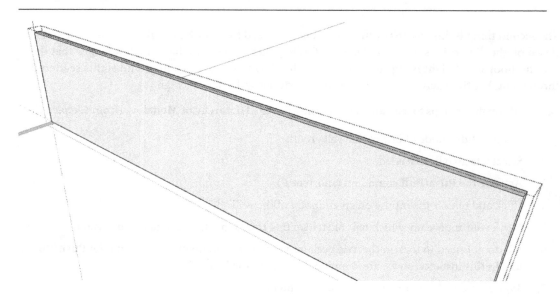

Figure 5.12: Push/Pull the exterior wall up 11' high

Because all walls we are extruding are 11' high, there is a shortcut to raise the rest of them quickly. SketchUp remembers the last measurement, so rather than having to type 11' and press *Enter/Return* each time you push/pull, you only need to double-click the face.

Here are the steps to use the double-click shortcut on each wall:

11. Get into **Edit** mode of another wall group.

12. Select the face to extrude.

13. Activate the **Push/Pull** command (shortcut *P*).

14. Double-click the face with the **Push/Pull** tool. This is the shortcut for extruding to the same height as the last push/pull!

15. Tap *spacebar* to get out of the command.

16. Save your model.

17. Check the increment with the **Tape Measure** tool to see whether the extruded wall is 11' high.

As long as you did not type another increment before you double-clicked the face with **Push/Pull**, or accidentally clicked and released your mouse, this shortcut should have worked. Pretty cool! In SketchUp, double-clicking certain tools can trigger different shortcut actions. For example, with the **Offset** tool, when you double-click on another face right after creating an offset, it will automatically apply another offset to the face, using the same distance as the previous one. This concept is similar to what we did with the **Push/Pull** tool in the previous exercise and can be used with the **Arc** tool.

Now, follow *steps 11* to *16* to extrude the remaining exterior walls up 11 ' high.

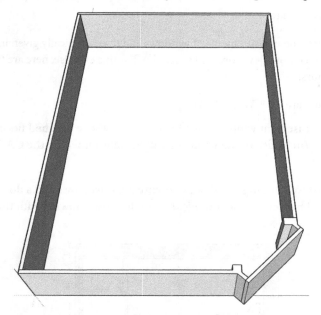

Figure 5.13: All exterior walls extruded to 11' high

To extrude the flooring group, simply push/pull the flooring down (to not take away from the overall ceiling height). We discussed this way of extruding flooring in *Chapter 2* when going over *Becca's Hierarchy of Modeling*. You can refer to that chapter for help.

Next, let's finish making one exterior wall by cutting openings for windows and doors.

How to cut in window and door openings

In order to cut an opening for windows and doors, there are two parts involved. The first is to make the shape for the hole, which involves precision drafting for accurate measurements. The second part is creating the hole, which is a quick extrusion. We will break up the steps to make it easier to understand.

Making the shape for the windows and doors

We will use the CAD plan to create the openings for windows and doors. (If you turned off the visibility to the CAD plan in the *Tracing the drawing in 2D* section, turn it on again now.) Cutting openings requires the use of the following SketchUp tools:

- **X-ray** face style or **Back Edges** edge style (or switch between the two) to see the CAD plan through the three-dimensional wall

- The **Tape Measure** tool to create *guide lines* and *guide points* (as discussed in *Chapter 1*)
- The **Line** or **Rectangle** tool

You will also need to know the measurements of windows and doors, typically given in the construction document set (door and window elevations and schedule). For this exercise, here are the measurements of the windows and doors:

- The exterior doors are 36" W x 80" H
- The windows are casement windows that begin at 36" **above finished floor** (**AFF**) and have a height of 72". The width of the windows will be determined by the CAD plan, which we will practice next.

Let's cut through the east wall of the ground floor because it has windows and a door to practice with. The wall to edit has a red border around it in *Figure 5.14*. It is also showing with the **X-ray** face style already applied:

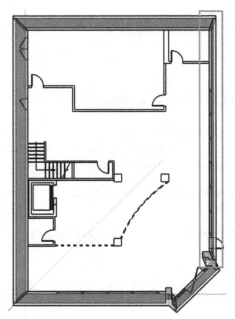

Figure 5.14: Cut through the east wall, highlighted by a red rectangle in this figure

Here are the steps for making the shape to create the window and door openings:

1. Get into **Edit** mode of the east wall. *This first step is a crucial one and most overlooked.* Always remember that you must be in **Edit** mode to make changes to a group or component. We are starting from inside the building, looking east.

2. Turn on the **X-ray** face style (the **View** menu | **Face Style** | **X-ray**), or **Back Edges** (shortcut *K*).

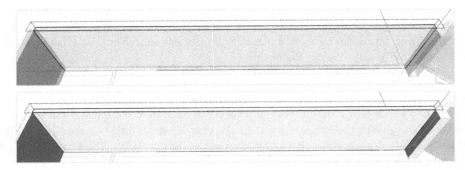

Figure 5.15: Both the X-ray face style (top) and Back Edges (bottom) allows
us to see the CAD plan through the bottom of the wall

Using one of those style options, you should be able to see the CAD plan through the bottom of the wall, as shown in *Figure 5.15*, even while in **Edit** mode. We only need to create holes where the windows and doors are located. Let's begin with the windows.

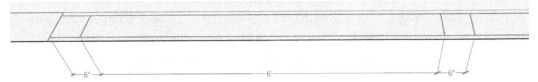

Figure 5.16: Window and mullion widths are found on the CAD plan

If you measure the windows of the CAD plan, they are 6 ' wide, with a 6 " mullion separating each one.

3. While still in **Edit** mode, activate the **Tape Measure** tool (shortcut *T*). We will create one continuous guide line at 36 " AFF, because that is the bottom of each window.

You can copy that guide line up 72 " (or 6 '), which is the height of the windows. Do not forget to lock in the blue/z-axis so you are creating the guide lines up from the wall's bottom edge. (This is another area where people tend to mess up when cutting holes. Make it a habit to draw on an axis, whether x, y, or z!)

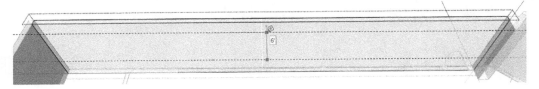

Figure 5.17: Create two horizontal guide lines for the window heights

Quick tip

Thinking ahead as modelers is a critical part of efficiency. What is another way you can create a line for the sill height? Using the existing wall line at the bottom, copy it up 3 6 ". Then, copy the header or lintel line down to quickly create the line for the window height. That is a slick way to accomplish the same task in SketchUp!

4. Now, create guide points or edges for the vertical measurements, by zooming in as close as possible to a window or mullion. This guide point or edge creates the first point in which to snap to when drawing the window opening. To carve out individual windows and mullions, we made it easier for you by adding additional lines to the CAD plan. The first guide point or edge should be 9 ' AFF. That will put you at the same height as the upper guide line.

With **X-ray**, you might be creating lines inside the wall, which does no good when making the shape for the window because it will not extrude through the entire wall. Again, make sure to lock in the blue/z-axis so you create the guide points up from the wall's bottom edge. Use SketchUp's **inferences** to ensure you are creating the guides or edges on top of the wall's faces, such as axis colors and point or line inferences.

You can also toggle between **X-ray** (or **Back Edges** by tapping shortcut *K*) and a regular face style (or no back edges) to avoid making mistakes when placing guide points or guide lines.

In our example, we are starting with the first window on the far left, on the inside of the building. We created a guide point from the inside edge of the mullion, moving 9 ' up the blue/z-axis. (Use one of the extra edges we drew for you. That way, you won't need to find, draw, or snap to the correct area for the first guide point.)

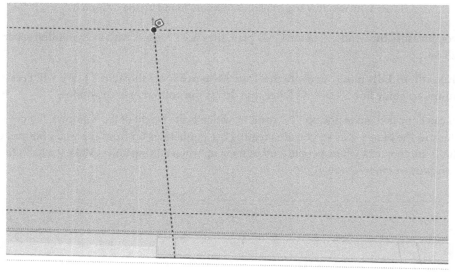

Figure 5.18: Zoom in closely to make sure you are selecting points and edges not inside the wall

Figure 5.18 shows that we have created a guide point for the vertical measurement.

5. Now, create a shorter guide point at the right side of the window to create a second snapping point, which is the bottom of the wall to the bottom of the window (3 ' AFF):

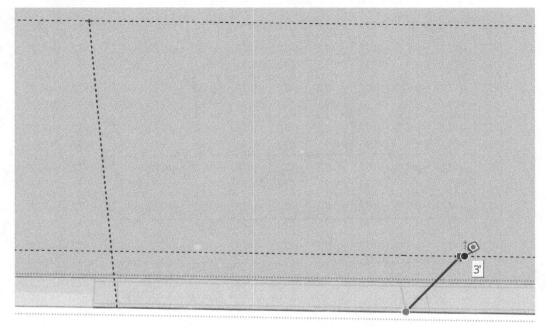

Figure 5.19: Create a second guide point 3' AFF

For the next step, you can leave your view as **X-ray** or **Back Edges**, or change the face or edge settings back to the default.

6. Still in **Edit** mode, activate the **Line** (*L*) or **Rectangle** (*R*) tool and draw the window according to the given dimensions, using the points, lines, or edges to snap to. Whichever tool you use, make sure to draw on axes!

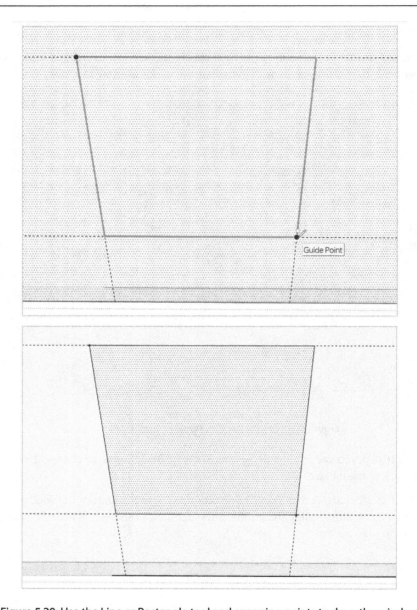

Figure 5.20: Use the Line or Rectangle tool and snapping points to draw the window

Figure 5.20 shows the window drawn with a rectangle and default face and edge settings.

7. Because all the windows on the east wall are the exact same dimensions, you can copy the face and edges you created in *step 6* across the east wall. Use the endpoints of the CAD plan for precise placement while copying (*Figure 5.21*).

Copying the edges and faces across means you do not have to create guides for each window. However, if you have windows with varying heights and placement, you will need to create guides for each dimension and draw edges accordingly.

We used the multiple copies method reviewed in *Chapter 2* to make 5 copies of the window across the green/y-axis, according to the window placement on the CAD plan:

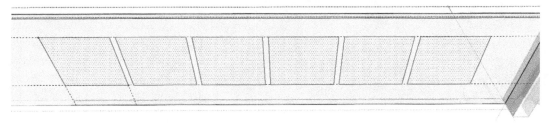

Figure 5.21: Copied the edges and faces of the window across the east wall

You can follow *steps 1* to *6* to create the shape of the door opening at the end of the wall.

> **Door dimensions**
> The dimensions are 36" W x 80" H. (You should also use the CAD plan to determine the width and door placement).

Another method to creating the door shape is to draw three lines, still in **Edit** mode:

1. Activate the **Line** tool and click the bottom endpoint of the door opening. Move your mouse up the blue/z-axis, type 80", then tap *Enter/Return*.

2. Move your mouse across the green/y-axis, locking it in with the *left arrow* key, then move your mouse down to the CAD plan and click the endpoint that is the width of the door opening (36").

3. Move your mouse down the blue/z-axis, clicking the endpoint at the bottom of the door opening on the CAD plan.

When you are done creating the door shape, it will look like this:

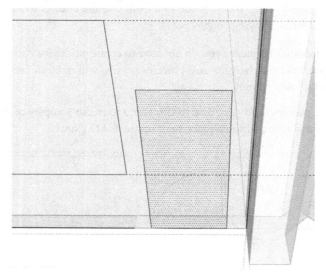

Figure 5.22: Door opening created with three edges

In *Chapter 7*, we walk through the steps for making the shapes for windows and doors using imported CAD elevations rather than the **Tape Measure** tool and guide lines.

The next step of cutting the opening is to extrude the shapes created in this section. Let's see how!

Creating the holes for the windows and doors

We are done with the guides for creating the shapes, so those can be deleted. Delete these guides by navigating to **Edit | Delete Guides**. We also no longer need to use the **Back Edges** edge style or the **X-ray** face style, so you can turn those settings off. To turn off **Back Edges**, tap the *K* key on your keyboard. To turn off **X-ray**, navigate to **View | Face Style** and uncheck **X-ray** (by clicking on it).

With the guides, face style, and edge style back to their default, and out of **Edit** mode, the view of the east wall now looks like this:

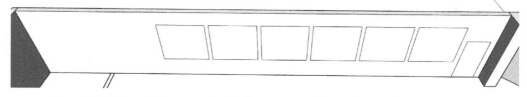

Figure 5.23: View of the east wall with shapes created for window and door openings

Creating the hole for the windows and door – and any other similar object – is the fun part! Not only is it easy, but it is also cool to see the effect of a hole punched through a wall. It is helpful to know the dimension of the object you are pushing through. For this example, we are pushing the window and door shapes through an 8" thick wall.

To create the hole, follow these steps. Once again, we are using the *Becca's Hierarchy of Modeling* taught in *Chapter 2*:

1. Enter **Edit** mode of the object you are cutting the hole in, specifically the east wall.

2. Click on the face of one of the shapes you made, whether it is for a window or the door.

3. Activate the **Push/Pull** command (*P*).

4. Click once on an endpoint or midpoint of the shape.

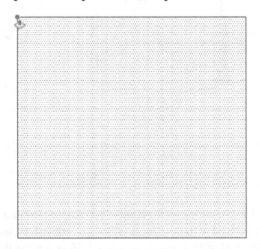

Figure 5.24: Click an endpoint or midpoint of the shape to extrude

---

Reminder from Chapter 2

You should click a point instead of the face for accuracy before using push/pull. However, clicking the face of the shape will almost always end in the same result.

---

5. Move your mouse toward the opposite side of the wall that the face is on.

6. Once again, we can skip the step to lock in the axis from *Becca's Hierarchy of Modeling*, because with **Push/Pull**, we are limited to one direction or the other.

7. Type 8" and press *Enter/Return* to extrude the shape through the wall. Another way to do this is to click an edge on the opposite side of the wall.

8. Get out of the **Push/Pull** command by tapping *spacebar*.

9. Get out of **Edit** mode by tapping the *Esc* key once.

10. Save your model.

We do not need to double-check the measurement with the **Tape Measure** tool because there is an obvious hole in the wall.

When you are done with *steps 1* to *10*, you should have a hole in your wall like this:

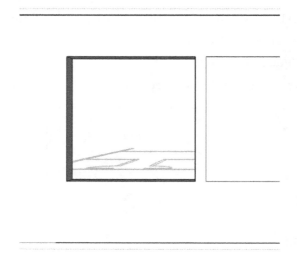

Figure 5.25: One window hole cut through the wall

Follow *steps 1* to *10* to cut out the remaining window and door shapes. Alternatively, and much quicker, you can use the double-click method with push/pull, which we used previously to bring the walls up 11 ' because it will remember the last increment we entered. Here is what the final wall of windows should look like when all the holes have been created:

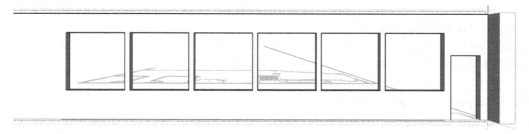

Figure 5.26: All window and door openings have been cut out in the east wall

You have completed the tasks to trace walls and floors and cut out holes for windows and doors.

In the next section, *Constructing stairs*, we look into one way of constructing the stairs up to the mezzanine.

Constructing stairs

There are many ways to construct stairs in SketchUp. If you are looking for fully constructed stairs, such as with stringers and cleats, the **Extension Warehouse** has many plugins to make quick work of a variety of stair types and configurations. (Look up `Medeek Wall` and `1001-bit tools`.) However, when you do not need to show the construction details of a staircase, creating one with a few shapes and **Push/Pull** is easy.

Constructing basic stairs

When constructing basic stairs, there are a few easy methods that have been taught in many SketchUp books and tutorials throughout the years.

> **Additional material**
>
> Because the methods of constructing basic stairs are readily available for learning, here is a link to a YouTube video tutorial on doing so in SketchUp: `https://youtu.be/MCmW394TyMA`. This video is made by Justin of *The SketchUp Essentials*, who is a great resource for learning SketchUp! The video is called *7 Ways to CREATE STAIRS IN SKETCHUP!*, if you want to search for it.

One method has been referred to in the *SketchUp for Dummies* book as the **Copied Profile Method**. This method was used to create the stair stringers for the *Chapter 5* practice model.

Click the `Stairs` scene tab. This scene takes you to where the stairs are located on the floor plan and turns off most of the tags so you can view the stairs task more easily. You need to turn off the exterior wall and flooring tags to view the stairs elements shown below:

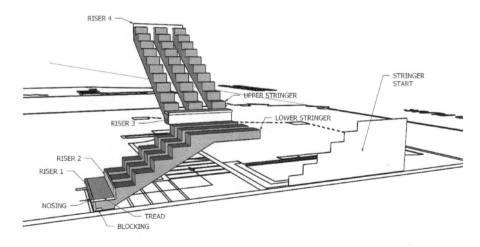

Figure 5.27: Stairs scene with EXTERIOR WALL and FLOORING tags not visible

To the right of the stairs is what looks like the beginning of a staircase, marked as STRINGER START, with stair steps drawn using the **Line** tool. The appropriate calculations were done to determine the slope, stair rise, and overall run of the staircase. Based on those calculations, individual riser and tread dimensions began, starting with an edge drawn up the blue/z-axis 7 ½" for the rise (height), then over on the green/y-axis for a 12" run. Once a few edges were drawn, they were then selected and copied multiple times, as shown in *Figure 5.28*.

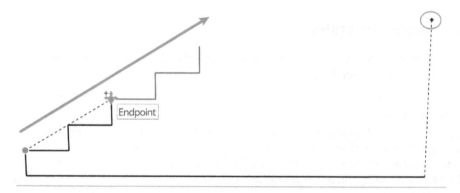

Figure 5.28: Copying the stair edges (or profile)

Once the risers and treads were correct, the rest of the stringer pieces were carved out, so to speak, using edges. Then, depth was added using **Push/Pull**. This is a great method for stringers and a quick way to create a basic staircase because it is easy and fast.

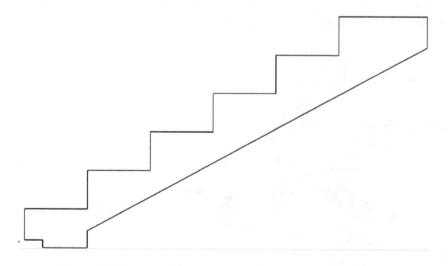

Figure 5.29: The rest of the stringer profile carved out using edges

Let's look at another quick method of creating a staircase, using components.

Creating a staircase using components

A favored way to create quick stairs in SketchUp is by making the various elements of the stairs into components, then copying them. This is an easy method to create L-shaped staircases, like we have in the *Chapter 5* practice file.

Still looking at the `Stairs` scene, this view also shows the pre-made parts of the stairs, most of which are components:

- Stringers
- Risers (four different sizes)
- Blocking (or thrust block)
- Treads
- Nosing (in this file, the nosing is separated from the tread for easier editing. You can make the nosing part of the tread component)

The parts of the stairs are labeled in the practice file and also shown in *Figure 5.30* for easy reference.

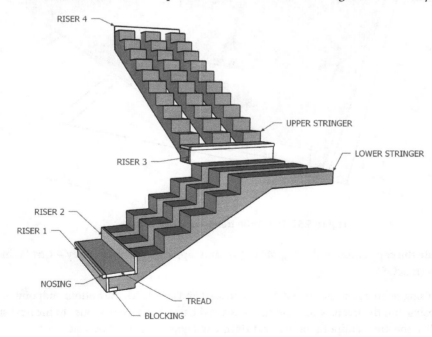

Figure 5.30: Stair terminology for the practice model

Take time to look at the parts of the staircase by entering **Edit** mode to see how the components and groups are constructed and by using your **Tape Measure** tool to understand the dimensions.

Now, we need to finish out the staircase by copying three pieces from the bottom to the top: the nosing, tread, and main riser. If it helps, turn off the visibility to the `Stringer Start` and `Stair text` tags, making note of where **RISER 2** is so you can copy it.

Follow these steps to finish the staircase:

1. Zoom in to the bottom of the staircase. Select the tread, nosing, and riser as shown in *Figure 5.31*.

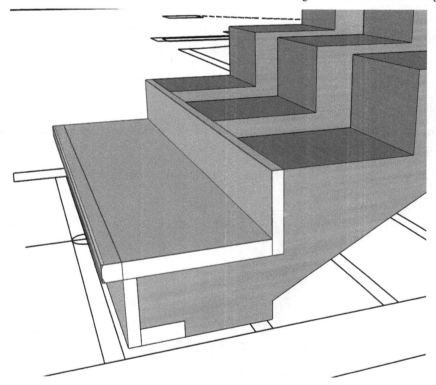

Figure 5.31: Select the tread, nosing, and riser

Activate the copy command using **Move** (*M*) and tapping the modifier key – *Ctrl* (Windows) or *Opt* (macOS).

2. Copy using reference points to know where to start and end. Click the bottom endpoint between the nosing and the tread, where the riser ends at the top. Move your mouse to the next step up and click the same endpoint of the next riser. Use *Figure 5.32* to guide you:

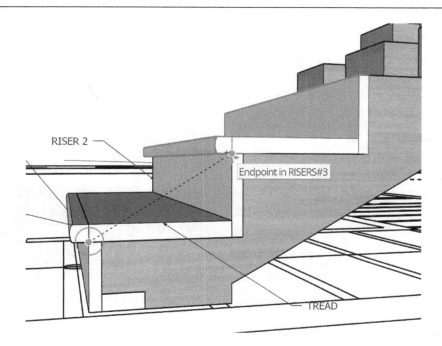

Figure 5.32: Copy the components from the first riser to the second

3. Immediately after clicking the second endpoint, type 6x and press *Enter/Return*. This will make six copies of the original tread, all spaced evenly up the lower staircase.

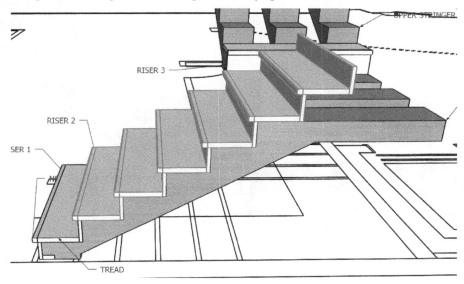

Figure 5.33: The six copies of the stair components are highlighted in blue

This also gives us one extra set of components to rotate and then use for the upper staircase.

4.   Select the last copied set of components – the nosing, tread, and riser – at the top of the lower staircase. Activate **Rotate** with the *Q* shortcut key and lock in the blue/z axis. Type 90 and press *Enter/Return* to rotate all three components 90 degrees so they are facing the correct way for the upper staircase.

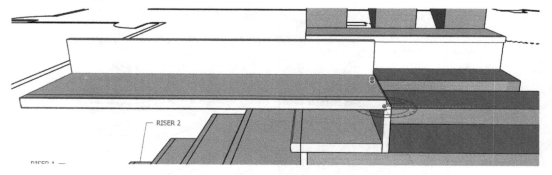

Figure 5.34: Rotating the stair components toward the upper staircase

5.   Move the components so they rest precisely on the upper staircase, above the existing tread and risers for that staircase (refer to *Figure 5.35*).

6.   Once placed, you might notice there is a gap underneath the nosing where a riser should be (the red arrow in *Figure 5.35* is pointing at that gap). Whoops! Copy the riser down to fill in the gap.

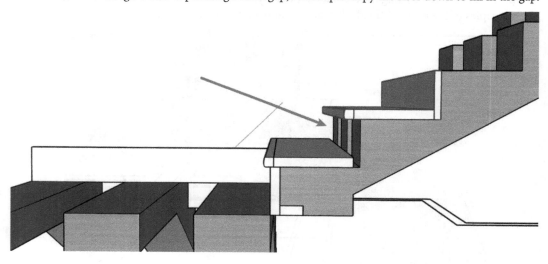

Figure 5.35: Rotated and moved stair components and a gap where the riser should be copied

Returning to the lower staircase, we have a couple of extra copied pieces to deal with. The fifth tread from the bottom is the landing area of the lower staircase. We need to extrude the tread so it covers the entire landing area, but because it is part of linked components, we should make it unique.

7. First, you can delete the extra riser; we will not need it.

8. Then, right-click on the tread and choose **Make Unique**:

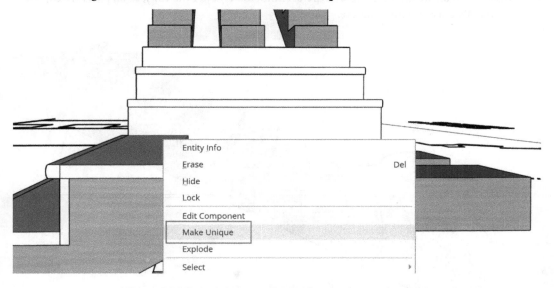

Figure 5.36: Delete the extra riser and make the tread unique

9. Then, get into **Edit** mode of the tread and **Push/Pull** it toward the elevator wall until it meets the end of the stringer (3 ' – 3 "):

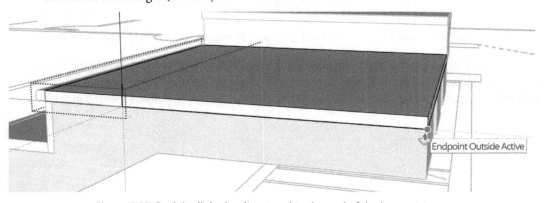

Figure 5.37: Push/pull the landing tread to the end of the lower stringer

To finish the rest of the upper staircase, you will need to perform almost the exact same routine as *steps 1* to *3*:

10. Select the three components that you moved and rotated – the nosing, riser, and tread.

11. Use a reference point to copy the three components to the next step up on the staircase. Use the **Move** tool and a modifier key to copy.

12. This time, to create multiple copies, type 8x immediately after the copy, so all parts are copied at equal distances up the staircase.

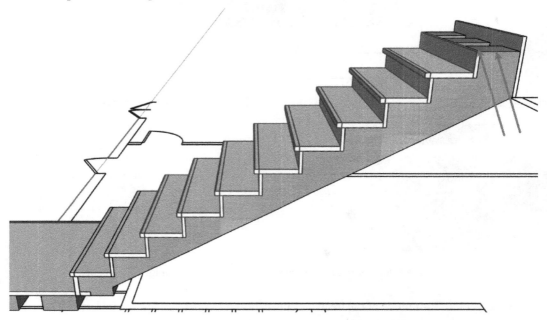

Figure 5.38: Copy the components on the upper staircase

13. The top step is missing the tread and nosing, as pointed out in *Figure 5.38*, so copy those parts up.

Can you believe how easy that was? The great thing about this type of staircase is that the staircase pieces are components, so anything you do to one will happen to the others. For example, if you **Edit** one tread or one nosing component to add a material, all the other treads or nosings will change as well.

Figure 5.39: After adding materials to the components

Or, if you want to add a railing, **Edit** one tread to draw the railing, and it will be added to all of them. You will, of course, have to add it to the landing area that was made unique, but it still is much faster than having to redraw again and again.

> **Important note**
>
> Some people have experienced bug splats when creating railing in **Edit** mode; therefore, constructing railing outside of **Edit** mode is also acceptable. It is important, however, to utilize components whenever possible.

If you turn on the visibility to the `Railing` tag, you will see a stair railing all the way up the staircase. It was created using components, groups, and a free extension called *MAJ Follow Me*, from the Extension Warehouse. This railing was not created in **Edit** mode of the staircase, which has its benefits. The staircase railing isn't flawless, but it was crafted quickly with the extension. Unless you zoom in closely, the imperfections are not too noticeable.

Figure 5.40: The completed staircase with railing

There are other things you can practice with the imported plan drawing, such as creating the architectural elements of the mezzanine level and inserting windows and doors on both floors. In *Chapter 7*, we will go over how to create custom interior architectural details using imported CAD elevations and how to search and download items from **3D Warehouse**. You can find already-created windows, doors, elevators, and more in 3D Warehouse.

Summary

In this chapter, we delved into the creation of fundamental interior architectural elements sourced from an imported CAD plan, specifically focusing on walls and stairs. You gained valuable insights into hole-cutting techniques for windows and doors, and a quick intro to a few staircase crafting methods.

In the next chapter, we will guide you through constructing a parapet roof on the *Chapter 5* practice model and other exterior features. Additionally, we'll demonstrate how to add the client's branding to the exterior and leverage the **Extension Warehouse** for expedited modeling.

Building Exterior Elements and Using the Extension Warehouse

After working with the *Chapter 5* practice file, our *As-Built Floor Plan* is almost complete; we now need to construct the exterior elements. We will build a flat roof (not the roof deck or sheathing but the visible part) with a plain parapet, add architectural elements to the building's exterior, create branding signage using 3D text, and learn how to use sections. This chapter (finally!) introduces you to the **Extension Warehouse** interface, which has been mentioned in many chapters of the book so far. The bulk of this chapter is for architects and commercial designers who frequently need to focus on a building's exterior.

Our main topics are as follows:

- Creating a flat roof with a plain parapet
- Using the Extension Warehouse
- Adding architectural elements to a building's exterior
- Carrying a client's brand from inside to outside
- Including sections
- Other valuable exterior tools

Technical requirements

To follow along in this chapter, you will need the following:

- SketchUp Pro or SketchUp Studio
- A Trimble login for the Extension Warehouse and 3D Warehouse
- Practice exercise file Chapter 6- Exterior in 3D Warehouse or from: https://3dwarehouse.sketchup.com/model/ea89dedc-4ae3-4336-a97d-d96bb08286b0/Chapter-6-Exterior

Creating a flat roof with a plain parapet

There are many ways to create roofs in SketchUp using only its native tools, such as **Line**, **Offset**, **Follow Me**, and **Protractor**. Because this chapter is a continuation of *Chapter 5*, where we worked on a commercial building, we will use the same project to create a low slope roof (or flat roof) and add a parapet and other features to showcase a visually appealing building exterior.

When thinking about creating a basic flat roof in SketchUp, without the need for the intricacies of real-world construction, you are going to have to remove yourself from real-life design. That means we are not building roof joists, a deck, insulation, or a membrane. This is SketchUp-land only, where we will show only the visible, more attractive parts of the roof for the purpose of showing a client the schematic design. We won't even worry about the roof pitch. (We recognize this goes against everything you know!)

This also might bring up another question – can you draw the joists, deck, insulation, and so on in SketchUp? Absolutely! For those who use SketchUp in all design phases, including construction documents, there is a surplus of extensions to help quickly draw all parts of a roof that are necessary for design development and bidding. We will show you such an extension in the next section, *An introduction to extensions and plugins*.

From inside SketchUp's 3D Warehouse, download the Chapter 6- Exterior practice file. You can also download the model from the web using this link: https://3dwarehouse.sketchup.com/model/ea89dedc-4ae3-4336-a97d-d96bb08286b0/Chapter-6-Exterior.

Figure 6.1 shows what the practice model looks like. It is a continuation of the commercial building we started working on in *Chapter 5*.

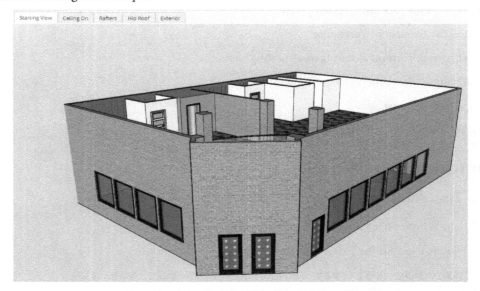

Figure 6.1: The Chapter 6- Exterior practice file

Take a minute to look around the model and acquaint yourself with the finishes and other additions we have made since *Chapter 5*. There are also a few changes, such as the placement of doors and windows.

It's time to create a flat roof! Follow these steps:

1. Click the scene tab called Ceiling On. You are now in **Top** view of the building.

2. Right-click in the modeling window, not on top of another object, and choose **Make Group**.

Figure 6.2: Right-click somewhere in the modeling window and choose Make Group

Choosing **Make Group** first allows us to draw while already in **Edit** mode, so we do not accidentally mix up new geometry with old.

3. While in **Top** view and with the **Line** tool, trace the outline of the exterior walls all the way around the building. Unlike when creating the ceiling, we are using the outer edges of the walls, not the inner edges. Be sure to zoom in for accuracy. When you are done tracing the lines, it should look like *Figure 6.3*:

Figure 6.3: Drawing the roof outline in Top View

Now, we need to add some height for realism, pretending that real-life architectural roof elements are hidden inside.

4. Push/pull the roof up 12" by typing 12 and press *Enter/Return*.

5. Still in **Edit** mode, click the top face of the roof.

6. Activate the **Offset** tool (using the *F* shortcut). Offset the shape outward by 12" (type 12 *Enter* or *Return*).

7. Double-click the new face you created and **Make Group**.

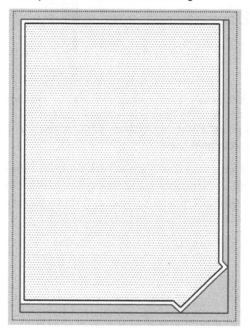

Figure 6.4: Offset the shape by 12" and make it a group

This new group is the beginning of our parapet.

8. Go into **Edit** mode of the new parapet group. Make the parapet 3'-0" high by push/pulling it up 36" (type 36 *Enter* or *Return*).

Figure 6.5: Give the parapet a height of 3'-0"

9.   Exit **Edit** mode. Select the overall roof group and move it to the ROOF tag.

10. Turn on the tag named COPING. You will see a group containing a profile of coping, surrounded by a path of edges.

     If you created the roof as outlined in the first 8 steps, the coping profile should rest on the parapet. If not, move the coping down so that it is on top of the parapet:

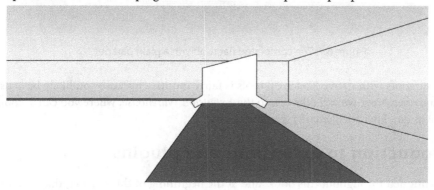

Figure 6.6: The coping group on top of the parapet

What is coping?

If you are not familiar with what coping is, it is a material used to cap the wall top for both visual and practical weatherproofing purposes. It needs to allow water to run off its surface, which is why it is sloped on both sides. The slope also helps the building façade from staining.

We will now use the coping created, in conjunction with the **Follow Me** tool, to quickly create coping around the top of the building:

11. In **Edit** mode of the coping group, *triple-click* the coping profile so that the entire path around the parapet is selected. We do not want the coping profile and its edges to be selected, however, so hold down the *Shift* key and *double-click* the face.

12. Activate the **Follow Me** tool from the **Large Tool Set** or **Tools | Follow Me**. Click once on the coping profile (face).

13. Add materials or textures to the roof pieces you created. If you would like, there is a material in the model called Ext. Limestone that you can use.

    We cover all things materials-related in *Chapter 9*.

14. Finish off the roof by creating fascia or a soffit. Turn on the visibility of the Fascia tag to see what we have created using only lines (edges) and the **Follow Me** tool. *Figure 6.7* shows the completed parapet roof, including coping and fascia.

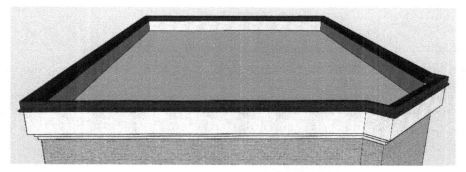

Figure 6.7: The completed flat roof with a plain parapet

Creating basic roofs with native SketchUp tools is fairly intuitive because you likely have used the tools over and over. Now, we will take you to the *Extension Warehouse*, where you can accomplish a lot more just as quickly with SketchUp plugins.

An introduction to extensions and plugins

We have mentioned throughout this book, and at the beginning of this chapter, that extensions or **plugins** can be added to SketchUp that will accelerate how you model. We must tell you, our new friends, that plugins and extensions are game-changers!

Let's first address the words *plugins* (or plug-ins) and *extensions*. These two words are used interchangeably when discussing third-party applications that can be added to SketchUp. When plugins were first introduced to SketchUp, they were called rubies, rubiz, or ruby plugins. This is because the file extension for SketchUp plugins is .rbz (RBZ). (Are there any old-school SketchUp modelers among you who remember the ruby stone icon that used to be the link to the Extension Warehouse? We remember, too!) When the Extension Warehouse rolled out with SketchUp 2013, things changed for us old-school modelers, as we did not have to download every RBZ file from the web and then move each file to our operating system's program files. The Extension Warehouse gets better and better, now housing over 600+ third-party extensions. There is also a plethora of direct links to outside plugins (i.e., RBZ files) that have to be downloaded from the web, but they can be easily uploaded to SketchUp through the **Extension Manager**.

OK, so what are extensions, plugins, and rubies? They are applications that are added to SketchUp Pro or SketchUp Studio (i.e., paid versions of SketchUp only) to streamline your workflow. Want to create kitchen cabinetry quickly, with just a few clicks? There's an extension for that! Need to chamfer corners to create true curves in SketchUp? There's a plugin for that! (See how we are using the terms *plugins* and *extensions* interchangeably? You will see that a lot.) Want to create roof joists or trusses? Let's find an extension for that together!

The Extension Warehouse

Inside SketchUp, using any blank file or working model, open the **Extension Warehouse**. You can find it under **Extensions | Extension Warehouse**. You can also click the Extension Warehouse icon in the **Getting Started** toolbar, which looks like a blue and white X (see *Figure 6.8*).

Figure 6.8: The Extension Warehouse icon in the Getting Started toolbar

If you prefer to view the Extension Warehouse on the web, here is the link: `https://extensions.sketchup.com/`.

> **Accessing the Extension Warehouse**
>
> The Extension Warehouse, like 3D Warehouse, needs an internet connection. If there are issues getting into either warehouse unrelated to logging in, there is most likely a problem with online connectivity. Check your internet connection.

When opening the Extension Warehouse, you might be prompted to log in using your **Trimble ID**, which is most likely the same email and password you use to log in to SketchUp.

Learning to use the Home screen

The first window that opens in the Extension Warehouse is the *Home* screen.

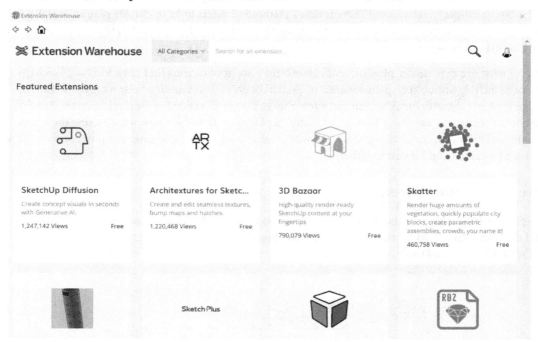

Figure 6.9: The Extension Warehouse Home screen

> **Images of the Extension Warehouse**
>
> This book shows you images of the Extension Warehouse as it appears to us at the time of writing. SketchUp periodically changes what is viewed on the Home and other screens. Do not worry if your view differs from the images in this chapter.

Let's break down what you can see on the home screen, starting with the top-left area.

- **The left and right arrows**: The arrows allow you to go backward and forward during searches. When first opening the Warehouse, you cannot use them because you have not searched for anything. After your first search, you will be able to use the left arrow to go back.

- **The Home button**: The icon shaped like a house will take you back to the home screen.

- **The All Categories dropdown**: Click the dropdown to search by category (though you don't have to select a category to search). Currently, the categories are these:

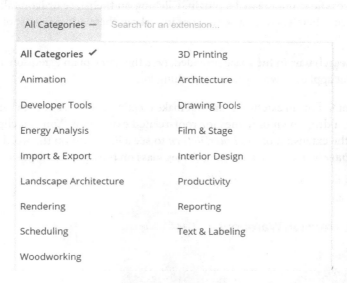

All Categories —	Search for an extension...
All Categories ✓	3D Printing
Animation	Architecture
Developer Tools	Drawing Tools
Energy Analysis	Film & Stage
Import & Export	Interior Design
Landscape Architecture	Productivity
Rendering	Reporting
Scheduling	Text & Labeling
Woodworking	

Figure 6.10: You can search by one of these categories

Click a category to go to a list of extensions within that category. You can scroll down through the list and also use the search bar to look for extensions that apply to that category, without having to go back to the home screen.

- **Search bar**: To the right of **All Categories** is the search bar. We will come back to this one in a minute.

- **User profile**: To the right of the search bar and magnifying glass is your user profile. It could be a circle with your initials or, if you uploaded one to your Trimble account, a picture or avatar. Click on the circle to see the following:

  - **My Downloads**: A list of extensions you downloaded

  - **Settings**: Not much to see here unless you want to upload an extension you created

- **Featured Extensions**: Underneath the search bar are the featured extensions. These are extensions that SketchUp developers like to highlight so that users are aware of them. They change at random times, depending on when SketchUp developers have time to update.

- **Top Extensions**: Underneath featured extensions, top extensions list some of the most currently popular extensions. This list will change, depending on when SketchUp developers have time to update the data.

- **Top Developers:** Get to know the extension developers who make your life easier! Some developers work directly for SketchUp, and others are advanced modelers who found a need to improve workflow and created a plugin. Clicking on their face or icon takes you to their developer page, where you might see a bit of info about them and a full list of the extensions they created.

- **Back to the search bar:** In the space provided, type the name of an extension, or begin typing a keyword that applies to what you are searching for.

For example, we want to find an extension that will make creating a complex roof easier. Typing `roof` in the search shows a dropdown of names for roof-related extensions. You can click one to open information about the extension or tap *Enter/Return* to see a list based on the word you typed. Or, instead of tapping *Enter*, you can click the magnifying glass on the right-hand side of the search bar.

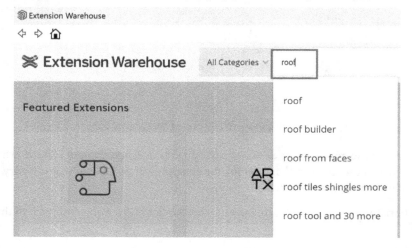

Figure 6.11: Type roof in the search bar

The next section takes you through finding and downloading an extension.

How to use the Extension Warehouse

Earlier, we began searching for an extension to build a roof. Let's go through the steps to find and download a roof extension.

In the search bar, type `roof` and tap *Enter/Return*. After searching, you will see the results screen.

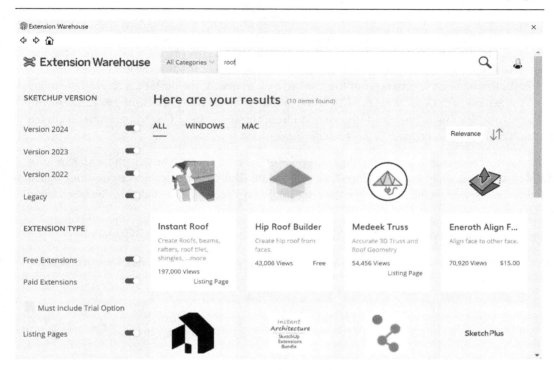

Figure 6.12: The results screen after searching for roof

The sidebar on the left gives you filters to choose from, which can narrow down your search. Choose a particular SketchUp version year and extension type – free, paid, include a trial option (check the box), or **Listing Pages**. An extension with a listing page is shown in the Extension Warehouse, but it must be downloaded from another website. A link to the site is provided on the details page.

In the main area of the results screen, underneath **Here are your results**, are three tabs: **ALL**, **WINDOWS**, and **MAC**. This means you can view all extensions that apply to the roof by:

- all operating systems
- only Windows systems
- only macOS systems

Looking at the thumbnail, or a quick view of each extension, you can see brief information about the extension. For example, in the top row of extensions after our search (*Figure 6.12*), there is **Instant Roof**, **Hip Roof Builder**, **Medeek Truss**, and **Eneroth Align Face**. The **Instant Roof** extension says it **Creates Roofs, beams, rafters, roof tiles, shingles, …more**. At the bottom, it shows how many views the extension has and, at the right, its listing page. You now know that a listing page means you will need to click a link to download the extension from another website. (We will practice that in the next section, *Downloading an RBZ file from the web*).

If the quick view does not say **Listing Page**, the price of the extension will be written there. **Hip Roof Builder** says **Free**, while **Eneroth Align Face** says **$15.00**. This can be helpful when deciding which extension to view. Sometimes, however, the price might say **Free**, but that could only be when using a trial version.

Take a few minutes to play around with the filters and scroll down to see all the results.

Now, find an extension called **1001bit Tools**. Click anywhere on the extension quick view to be taken to a new window.

1001bit Tools (...

Collection of useful tools for architectural works.

2,204,478 Views   Free

Figure 6.13: The 1001bit Tools quick view

The new window has more information about the **1001bit Tools** extension.

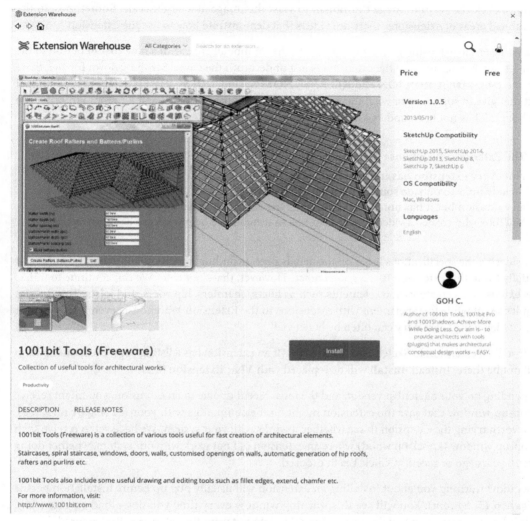

Figure 6.14: The 1001bit Tools details page

On the details page about the **1001bit Tools** extension, a lot more information is given. The sidebar on the right shows the price (**Free**), the most recent version number, the last modified date, SketchUp year compatibility, operating system compatibility (both Mac and Windows), and languages in which information is given. Underneath that is information about the developer, **GOH C.**

On the left is an image showing one way to use the extension. Underneath the image are two thumbnail images; click the second image thumbnail to view the image at a larger scale. Sometimes, in the thumbnail areas of extensions, there are videos that demonstrate how to use the extension.

The name of the extension is shown underneath the thumbnail area, with a blue **Install** button to the right. A quick description of the extension is just underneath the name. Scrolling down further, there are two tabs – **DESCRIPTION** and **RELEASE NOTES**. Under **DESCRIPTION**, there is additional text that gives a summary of what the extension can do. At the bottom is a link to more information (although it has not been updated in a few years).

The Extension Warehouse details page

Not every extension has information about how to use the extension, nor do they always include links to outside sources such as videos or blogs. If you need help learning how to use an extension but it has not been provided by the developer, chances are there is someone on YouTube who created a video about it. Do a bit of searching to help you learn about an extension.

Considering the specifications listed on the details page, including SketchUp compatibility, you might initially think this extension isn't a good choice. However, that's not true! We can continue to utilize this extension to create various elements such as fillets, chamfers, hip roofs, and joists. This implies that it's worthwhile to experiment with extensions in the Extension Warehouse, even if they appear outdated. Giving them a try can often be beneficial!

To install an extension to SketchUp, click **Install**. (If an extension has a listing page, the **Install** button will not be there. Instead, **Install** will be replaced with **Visit Extension Site**.)

Depending on your SketchUp version and the most recent update to an extension, you might receive a pop-up window that says the extension might not be compatible with your file (*Figure 6.15, top*). It is worth trying the extension to see whether it works with your system. We have yet to receive such a pop-up window (knock on wood) where an extension did not work with our system, whether doing this 10 years ago or recently. Click **Yes** to proceed.

A window warning you about installing an extension will usually pop up before installation begins (*Figure 6.15, bottom*). You will see this warning window every time you download an extension. This is helpful if you accidentally clicked **Install** but do not want the extension. Rest assured that the Warehouse is checked for spam, and it is most likely fine to download the extension. It is also a good reminder to acquaint yourself with the top developers because they have extensions you can trust.

Figure 6.15: Two warning windows you might see before installing an extension

Click **Yes** on both windows to download the extension. (It's safe- don't worry!)

A final window popup will let you know that the extension has finished installing:

Figure 6.16: The extension installed successfully

Click **OK** to close the window.

When you are done searching for extensions, click the **X** or *close* button in the upper-right corner of the extension window to exit and begin using the extension.

The next section, *Finding and using extensions*, shows you how to navigate extensions in SketchUp. It also takes you through how to use the roof tools in the **1001bit Tools** extension toolbar.

Finding and using extensions

After downloading an extension to SketchUp, a quick fail-safe to finalize the download process is to exit SketchUp and reopen it. This can help push through the extension, just like restarting your computer after installing an update.

Upon restarting SketchUp, you need to find the extension. The extension description in the warehouse might tell you where to find it once installed. If not, here is a list of places you might find it:

- In the **Extensions** menu
- In the **Tools** menu
- As a new toolbar. Use **View | Toolbars** to search for it and add it to your window
- Right-clicking (or context-clicking) on an object and searching the **Context** menu

1001bit Tools comes with a new toolbar automatically added to SketchUp upon installation. Once you find it and add it to your modeling window, you will see it as a long toolbar with a lot of tools. You can squish it into a more manageable box, like we did here:

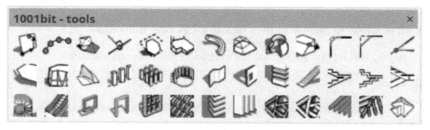

Figure 6.17: The 1001bit - tools toolbar

To find out what each icon or button is for, hover over each one to see its name. They all perform different, incredibly helpful tools. If you are interested in creating chamfered or fillet edges, look for the icons shown in *Figure 6.18*.

Figure 6.18: The 1001bit - tools fillet (left) and chamfer (right) icons

1001bit Tools also has sections for creating stairs, an escalator, windows, and more!

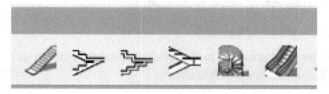

Figure 6.19: The 1001bit - tools stairs and escalator icons

There is so much to this toolbar we aren't going to cover, so we included a YouTube link to a SketchUp expert – Justin of *The SketchUp Essentials* – who reviews how to use all the 1001bit Tools: `https://youtu.be/bsBEh9QRhKw?si=kNuJEtEIzuJFkIby`.

Help with using an extension

Remember, the *dashboard* in SketchUp is incredibly helpful when learning how to use a tool or refreshing your memory on how to use it. The dashboard is the long, filled box at the bottom of your screen that stretches from the left to right of the entire window. After activating a tool, check the dashboard for what to click or see a list of modifier keys to use in conjunction with the tool.

There are three icons dedicated to roofs, which we will use in our practice model:

Figure 6.20: Create rafters/joists from a face (left), auto-create ridge
rafters (middle), and auto-create a hip roof (right)

Now, let's go through the steps to create rafters and a hip roof quickly with the free **1001bit - tools** toolbar.

First, we will add rafters. We can do this with either the *Create rafters/joists on selected face* icon or the *Automatically create ridge rafters, rafters, and battens/purlins* icon:

1. Click the scene tab called `Rafters`.

   There are two shapes in this scene. One is a flat shape, and the other looks like an angled roof:

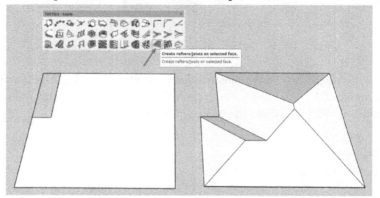

Figure 6.21: Select the flat shape on the left

The angled roof on the right will be used later to create rafters at the precise angles of the shape.

2. Go into **Edit** mode of the flat shape on the left. That shape is there so **1001bit Tools** extension knows where to add the rafters.

3. Click the icon in **1001bit - tools** called *Create rafters/joists on selected face* (shown in *Figure 6.21*).

4. A window will pop up called **Create Roof Rafters**.

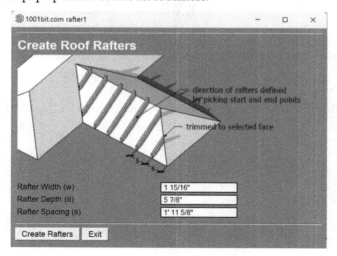

Figure 6.22: The Create Roof Rafters window

Don't worry if you do not know what to type in the boxes. If you do not like the rafters once they are made, you can *undo (Ctrl/⌘ Z)* and remake them with different settings.

5. Change the settings for **Rafter Width**, **Rafter Depth**, and **Rafter Spacing** by typing numbers in their boxes. You can also leave them as-is. (We are leaving them as-is for the example.)

6. Click **Create Rafters** when you are done with the settings.

   Check the dashboard for what to do next as you continue following our steps.

7. The dashboard will say, **Please pick a face**. (However, if you selected a face first it will not say that, so go to the next step.) Click once to select the face.

8. Now, the dashboard will say, **Please pick a point**. Click any endpoint inside **Edit** mode. There will not be a ScreenTip to help you find the endpoint; however, the curser will jump slightly when you are on one.

9. After you click and move your mouse, the dashboard will read, **Please pick direction of rafters**. If you do not know which way they go, guess. Otherwise, click an *endpoint* opposite or parallel to the first point you chose.

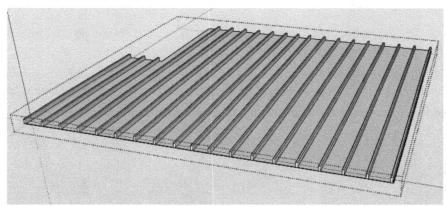

Figure 6.23: Rafters created on the flat shape

Voila! Rafters were created on the flat shape using *Create rafters/joists on selected face*.

Now let's create rafters on an angled roof, rather than a flat shape, using a different **1001bit Tools** tool:

10. Go into **Edit** mode of the angled roof group.

11. Triple-click on a face to select all faces.

    If you do not select the faces first, the tool will not work because it does not know which face you want to create rafters with.

12. Click the icon in **1001bit - tools** called *Automatically create ridge rafters, rafters, and battens/purlins* (shown in *Figure 6.24*).

13. We now have a different window called **Create Roof Rafters and Battens/Purlins**:

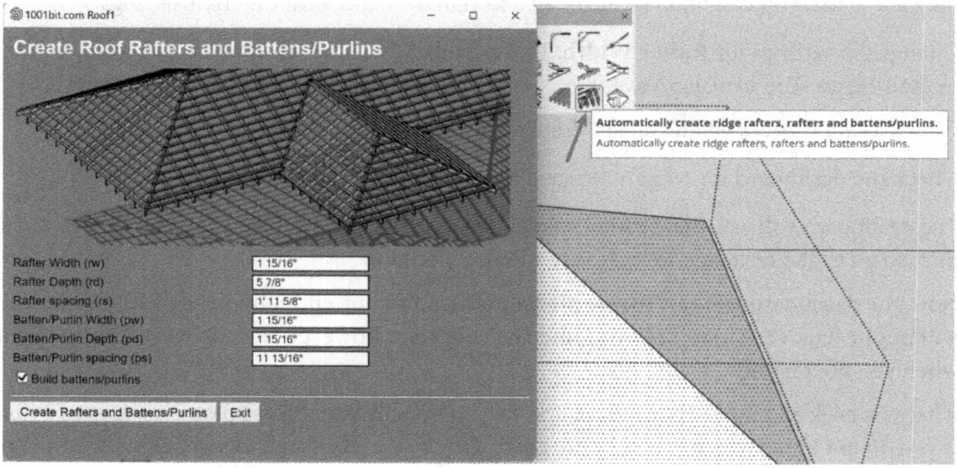

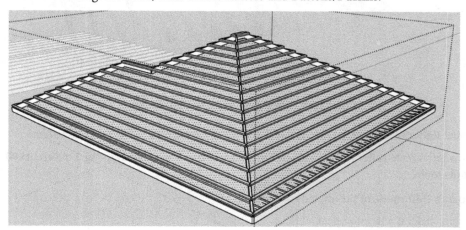

Figure 6.24: The window for Create Roof Rafters and Battens/Purlins

This window is different from **Create Rafters** in that there are additional lines for batten/purlin width, depth, and spacing.

14. You can change the settings on each line or leave them as-is. If you do not need to build battens or purlins, using this tool to solely create rafters on complex angles, uncheck **Build battens/purlins**.

15. When the settings are done, click **Create Rafters and Battens/Purlins**.

Figure 6.25: Completed rafters, battens, and purlins for the angled roof

Play with the new groupings that were automatically created. There is one group for the rafters, another one for the purlins, and a third one for the battens.

Let's finish this extension demonstration by creating your own hip roof:

1. Click the scene tab named `Hip Roof`.

   The rafters from the previous scene will disappear when you click the new scene tab. If you want them back, turn on the visibility of the `Rafters` tag. To create the roof, however, it might be easier if the rafters do not show.

2. Go into **Edit** mode of the group.

3. Click the top face once to select it.

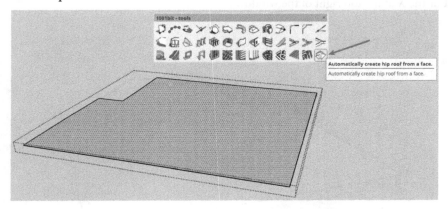

Figure 6.26: The Hip Roof scene – Edit mode

If you do not select the face first, the tool will not work because it does not know where you want to create the hip roof.

4. In the **1001bit - tools** toolbar, click the *Automatically create hip roof from face* icon (shown in *Figure 6.26*).

5. A window will pop up called **Create Hip Roof**. It wants you to type in the roof pitch (or the degree of the highest peak) and a distance for the roof overhang.

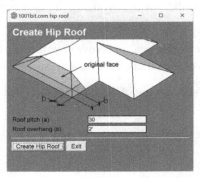

Figure 6.27: Type the roof pitch in the first field and the roof overhang distance in the second

We will create our roof pitch at 30 degrees, with a 2' overhang. As always, if you do not like it once it is made, you can *undo* (*Ctrl/⌘ Z*) and remake the roof.

> **Architects who use ratios**
>
> Architects typically use ratios instead of angles. You can type ratios in the **Roof pitch** field, such as 8/12 or 8:12.

6. Once your settings are input, click **Create Hip Roof**. (If you decide not to make the roof, click **Exit** or the *X* at the top right of the window.)

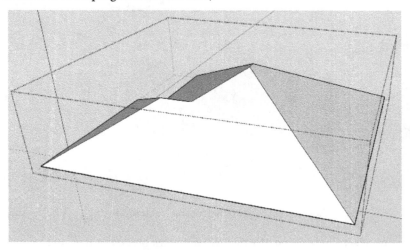

Figure 6.28: The completed hip roof

Orbit around to see your creation! Double-check that it looks the way you want it to, in pitch and overhang. Again, if you do not like the results, you can *undo* and remake the roof.

You might have noticed that two new groups were created. The extension automatically created a group for the new hip roof and another for the overhang. It's nice that it does this so that you can modify one but not the other.

Turn on the Rafters tag, and then orbit, pan, and move objects to see how they fit within your roof. Use a section cut to see the effects of the rafters, battens, and purlins inside the hip roof.

When you have time, play around with the rest of the 1001bit - tools. All modelers will find something helpful in this toolset!

Our next and last subsection covering the **Extension Warehouse** is *Downloading an RBZ file from the web*.

Downloading an RBZ file from the web

Do you remember when we first introduced the Extension Warehouse and discussed listing pages inside the Extension Warehouse? As a reminder, many developers add information about their extensions to the Extension Warehouse but include an outside link to download the RBZ (or `.rbz`) file. Other times, you come across extensions while perusing the internet. This section covers how to add an RBZ file to SketchUp.

One of our favorite places to get extensions is *sketchUcation [sic]*. (Most of the extensions on sketchUcation are part of the listing pages in the Extension Warehouse.) Here is the URL to sketchUcation extensions site: `https://sketchucation.com/pluginstore`. This site requires you to create a free login, but afterward, you can download to your heart's content. Some plugins cost money, while others are free.

To continue our chapter topic on exterior elements, we will show you a cool extension for walls. This will also outline the steps to download the RBZ file to your computer:

1. In the search bar, type `medeek` or `medeek wall`, and tap *Enter*/*Return* on your keyboard.

sketchUcation
Community
Resources
Shop
Servi
Sketchup Plugins
medeek wall
Full list
---- Authors ----
---- Categories ----

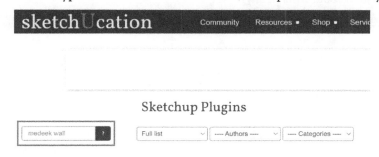

Figure 6.29: Search for medeek on sketchUcation

2. The results will show **Medeek Engineering**'s extensions listed on the site. They all start with **Medeek Engineering** and then the name of the extensions – **Medeek Electrical**, **Medeek Engineering**, **Medeek Wall**, and so on. Scroll down to find **Medeek Wall**.

   (The version shown in *Figure 6.30* is the most recent at the time of writing. Chances are there will be a newer version when you read this book.)

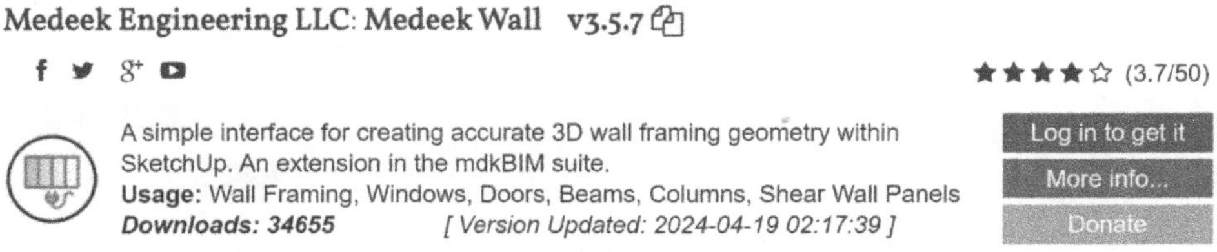

Medeek Engineering LLC: Medeek Wall v3.5.7
(3.7/50)
A simple interface for creating accurate 3D wall framing geometry within SketchUp. An extension in the mdkBIM suite.
Usage: Wall Framing, Windows, Doors, Beams, Columns, Shear Wall Panels
Downloads: 34655
[Version Updated: 2024-04-19 02:17:39]
Log in to get it
More info...
Donate

Figure 6.30: The Medeek Wall extension box on sketchUcation

The extension box for **Medeek Wall** shares a great deal of information, most of which is shown with all extensions in *sketchUcation*. We can see the version number and when it was last updated, a brief description of the interface, its rating, and three buttons – **Log in to get it** (or **Download** if you already logged in), **More info…**, and **Donate**:

- Click **Log in to get it** to open a login or signup window.

- Click **Download** to begin downloading the RBZ file.

- Click **More Info…** to read more about the extension. Sometimes, that is not necessary because all the information the developer provided might be right there in the extension box.

- Click **Donate** to donate money to the developer, which helps them create new or update old plugins.

For Medeek extensions, it is helpful to go into the next screen of information to access their website link. Their website gives information on how to use and pay for their extensions.

3.   Click **More Info…** in the plugin information box to possibly find out more about the extension and information about costs (if any).

Figure 6.31: More information about Medeek Wall

Developers sometimes include additional information on this page or tabs at the top, such as links to video demonstrations, directions on using the extension, or images. Medeek Wall shows 20+ images of what the extension can create in SketchUp.

4. Read through the information about Medeek Wall. It mentions that purchasing the extension costs **0.00 USD**, but having purchased it, we know that the trial version is free, but the full extension is not. About halfway down is a link to Medeek's website. Click the link to go there. We have also provided it here: `http://design.medeek.com/resources/medeekwallplugin.pl`.

On Medeek's website, there is a lot more information about the extension, including video tutorials to use it. (We love it when developers do that!) They also list in detail the other tools that come with Medeek Wall: roofs, doors, windows, panels, columns, beams, stairs, and more. Medeek's extensions are **BIM**-functioning, which helps estimate a project. When you can, peruse the site and see other tools and extensions they offer.

There are three different pricing options for Medeek Wall and the ability to download the trial version. A trial version is a great way to get to know an extension and see whether you want to purchase it. Just make sure to pay attention to how long the trial version is. Sometimes, developers have a short 24-hour window, others one week, and some offer an entire month or more.

5. If you would like to try Medeek Wall free for thirty days, click the **Download Now** button on their website:

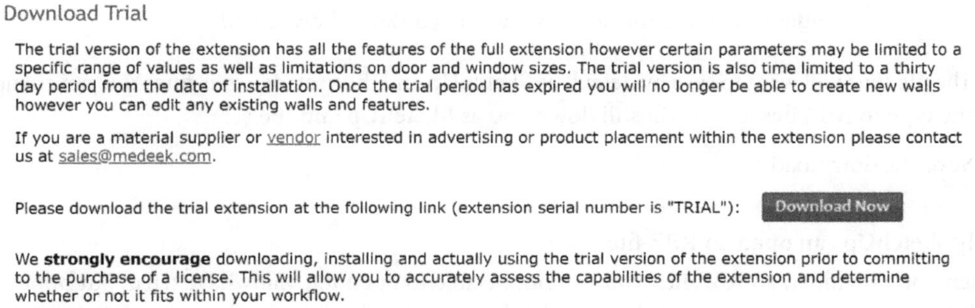

Download Trial

The trial version of the extension has all the features of the full extension however certain parameters may be limited to a specific range of values as well as limitations on door and window sizes. The trial version is also time limited to a thirty day period from the date of installation. Once the trial period has expired you will no longer be able to create new walls however you can edit any existing walls and features.

If you are a material supplier or vendor interested in advertising or product placement within the extension please contact us at sales@medeek.com.

Please download the trial extension at the following link (extension serial number is "TRIAL"):   Download Now

We **strongly encourage** downloading, installing and actually using the trial version of the extension prior to committing to the purchase of a license. This will allow you to accurately assess the capabilities of the extension and determine whether or not it fits within your workflow.

Figure 6.32: The Download Trial section of the website

A new window will pop up, wanting to know where to save the RBZ file.

6. Navigate to where you want to save the file. Some people prefer these files in their *downloads* so that they can quickly delete them after installing them in SketchUp, while others save RBZ files in a file folder, like this:

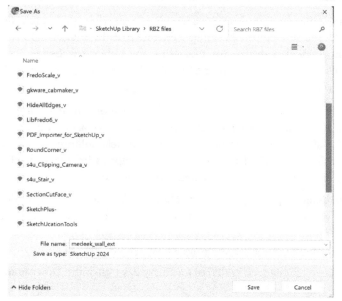

Figure 6.33: Save the download where you know how to find it

The file type will want to save by default as **SketchUp** and the year, which is fine. You can change the type to **All Files**, but it will still download as **SketchUp** and the year.

7. **Save** the download.

> **Only SketchUp can open an RBZ file**
>
> When you download an RBZ file, you will not be able to open it. (Many have tried, but none have succeeded.) The purpose of the download is to immediately upload it to the **Extension Manager** for use within SketchUp.

Our next section, *The Extension Manager*, goes through uploading an RBZ file to SketchUp. This is also the last bit of information we need to share about the Extension Warehouse before letting you explore on your own.

The Extension Manager

The **Extension Manager** is used to upload RBZ files to SketchUp and also to manage extensions you already have installed.

Here are the steps to upload an RBZ file to SketchUp:

1. Open the **Extension Manager**. It is found under the **Extensions** menu.

    The icon for the Extension Manager is in the **Getting Started** and other toolbars. It is the same X icon for the Extension Warehouse, but it also has a gear in front of the X:

    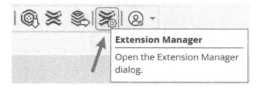

    Figure 6.34: The Extension Manager icon is on the far right

    After clicking the icon or opening from the **Extensions** menu, the **Extension Manager** window will open.

2. When you first see the **Extension Manager,** you will be on the **Home** tab. The **Home** and **Manage** tabs are almost identical.

    Your **Extension Manager** window might look different from our screenshots because we could have installed some extensions that you may not have, or vice versa.

    Figure 6.35: Extension Manager | the Home tab

On the **Home** tab, you can enable or disable an extension by clicking the box under the **Enable | Disable** column. Disabling an extension means you still want to use it later, but perhaps you want to declutter your toolbars or make your model run faster.

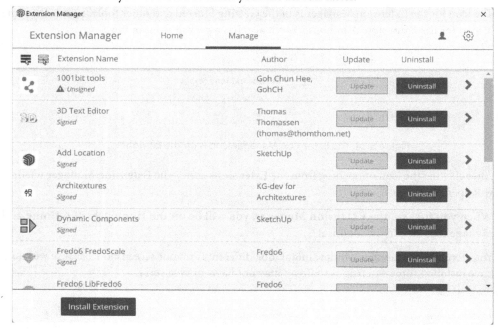

Figure 6.36: Extension Manager | the Manage tab

On the **Manage** tab, you can update or uninstall an extension.

Periodically, when you open a new SketchUp file, you will see a popup at the bottom right of your screen, telling you there is an update to an extension available. Go to the Extension Manager and find the extension(s) that need updating. **Update** will no longer be grayed out, like in *Figure 6.36*, so you can click on it to install the update (*Figure 6.37*). It usually takes just a few seconds.

Figure 6.37: Update is not grayed out, so this extension needs to be updated

To uninstall an extension, click the **Uninstall** button by the extension you want to remove.

If you click the gray arrow at the far right of each line, you will learn a bit more information about the extension, such as the version number, developer's name, and copyright.

Signed versus Unsigned

Underneath the extension name is either the word **Signed** or **Unsigned**. In a nutshell, a signed extension means that a registered SketchUp extension developer is claiming their software property by digitally signing it with a coded format. That signature is tied to the developer's Extension Warehouse account, so you know that the extension is from a trusted source. Does that mean you should not use an extension that is unsigned? The short answer is no. Sometimes, when you install an extension manually, even from a trusted developer, the extension will read **Unsigned**. As long as the extension is usable, go ahead and create with it!

Take a few minutes to look through your **Extension Manager** window. As you scroll down, look at the extensions that are automatically added to SketchUp Pro/Studio. For example, **Sandbox** is an extension you may have used but did not know was an extension.

3. To upload an RBZ file, click **Install Extension**. You can do this from either the **Home** or **Manage** tab.

4. Using the new window that appears, called **Open**, find the location where you saved the extension. Double-click the file to install it, or click the file once and then click **Open** at the bottom of the window.

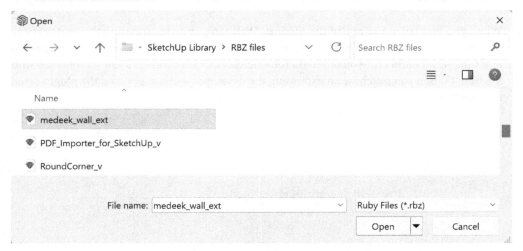

Figure 6.38: Find the RBZ file you downloaded from the web

5. When the file is uploaded to the **Extension Manager**, you will see it in your list of extensions. You can exit the Extension Manager when you are done uploading the RBZ file.

6. Sometimes, an extension's toolbar will automatically pop up in your window after installation. However, to find Medeek Wall's tools, look in the **Extensions** menu | **Medeek Wall**, or right-click on the gray toolbar area at the top of the modeling window. Toolbars are listed alphabetically.

Currently, there are eight toolbars for you to use, and they all start with **Medeek**. Click on one to open the coordinating toolbar:

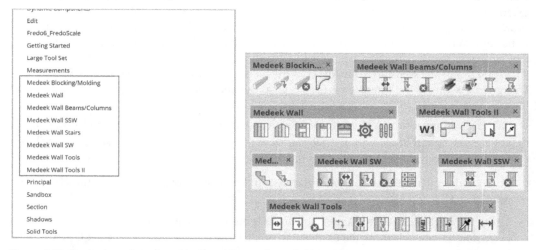

Figure 6.39: Medeek toolbars listed in SketchUp toolbars (left) and added to the modeling window (right)

7. When you first try to use one of the **Medeek Wall** tools and you are using the trial version, *Figure 6.40* shows you a warning – and informational – window. This box tells you where to input the serial number if you purchase the extension. Otherwise, click **OK** to continue with the trial. (When you purchase an extension, the developer will usually send the plugin serial number to your email.)

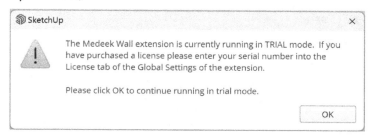

Figure 6.40: Warning window for the trial version

In order to use the extensions you upload, refer back to the *Finding and using extensions* section of this chapter. You can also refer to the developer's website, if there is one, for videos and other information. YouTube has a fountain of knowledge on how to use extensions!

So that you're not left wondering about **Medeek Wall**'s capabilities, you can examine the exterior elevator wall (EXT-WALL-WEST) of the practice model, which was created with the Draw Wall tool. Turn off the WEST-GYPSUM tag to get a better look inside (*Figure 6.41*). Based on settings we selected, it automatically created sheathing, studs, insulation, gypsum, and more. Another tool, Draw

Door, quickly and easily cut out the door openings. (We deleted some of the insulation so you could see what was behind it.) It's truly an impressive extension!

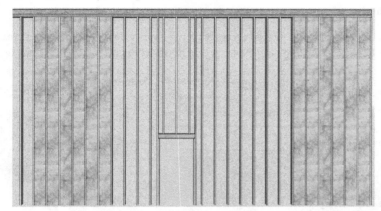

Figure 6.41: Partial west wall of the practice model without the GYPSUM tag visible

This section on the Extension Warehouse covered a lot of information! Here's a key takeaway from this section: using extensions will significantly speed up your workflow. However, it's important to note that while some extensions are intuitive, others may require a learning curve to use effectively. Enjoy experimenting with them and discovering how they can elevate your modeling experience! As you continue reading through the chapters of this book, watch for more information about our favorite extensions.

> **Finding additional extensions for your workflow**
>
> We recommend exploring additional extensions to simplify your modeling process. Websites such as Architizer offer valuable plugin ideas for architectural modeling. Mattersmith has configurable kitchen cabinets to streamline your custom build. Alternatively, you can conduct a targeted browser search, such as `best SketchUp plugins for architecture` or `SketchUp plugin for furniture`. We also include a list of must-have extensions in *Chapter 15*.

Our next section, *Adding architectural elements to a building's exterior*, gives tips on adding beautiful details to the exterior building shell.

Adding architectural elements to a building's exterior

Architects and commercial designers often show the exterior of the building, which helps our clients see the entire scale of the project. For interior designers, it is important to add architectural elements to a building's exterior to finish out the design and show how the interiors carried the architectural and design styles from outside to inside.

Now that the roof is complete, let's look at the exterior. How do you think you could update the façade of this building? Do you need to create items from scratch or download them from 3D Warehouse or a third-party site?

Click the Exterior scene tab. *Figure 6.42* shows what the scene would look like if you created the roof and coping in the *Finding and using extensions* section of this chapter. The FASCIA tag is also visible.

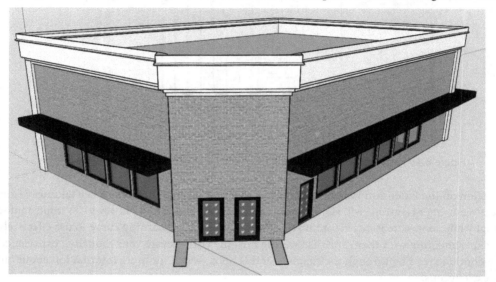

Figure 6.42: The Exterior scene tab

We have created a few items to make the exterior more interesting, then added them to the model. You will see how easy it is to add architectural features in SketchUp.

Creating architectural elements from scratch

Although the elements for the exterior are already added in this model, we will give some brief instructions on how we created the soffits and pilasters:

- **Soffits**: There are two soffits; one on the east side and the other on the south side of the building.

  - The soffit on the east wraps around to the north side, which was accomplished using the **Follow Me** tool.

  - Both soffits were constructed using the **Rectangle** tool to exact measurements. Then, after using **Push/Pull** to add downward height to the soffit, we orbited underneath to offset the remainder of the soffit structure. A manufacturer-specific texture image was added to the soffit shell and the interior.

- In this model, we aren't showing how the soffits are secured to the building because it is not necessary for our purposes.

Figure 6.43: A close-up of the underside of a soffit

All in all, after researching and discussing which soffit we wanted, it took less than five minutes in SketchUp to create them.

- **Pilasters**: On three of the corners are contemporary-style pilasters:

  - They are linked components, meaning if you edit one, they all change simultaneously. They are purely decorative, serving no purpose but to add interest to the building.

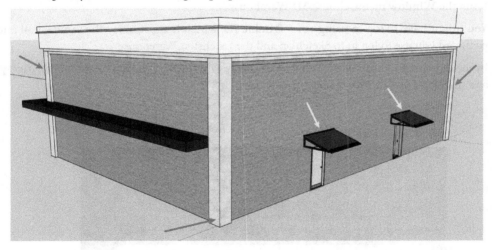

Figure 6.44: Pilasters on three corners and two decorative awnings at the back entrances

- The great thing about creating the pilasters in SketchUp first is that we were able to experiment with different sizes – widths and heights – and eventually settled on the size we felt best fit the area. We also tested different stones for all the decorative features, including the fascia, and found limestone to be the best. Using SketchUp for schematic design and development helps save time and costs!

> **Have you noticed you cannot see underneath the ground plane?**
>
> We are using a **background style** called *Show Ground from Below* that has zero transparency. That means we cannot see underneath the ground plane or, in the case of this building, the underground garage. This style makes the model even more realistic because you cannot see through the ground plane to what is below, and when you orbit underneath the ground, you cannot see through the ground to the sky. (The downside is it sometimes causes a flickering face when it interacts with the flooring.) You will learn more about **Styles** in *Chapter 10*.

Now, we will download an architectural element from 3D Warehouse so that you can see how easy it is.

Downloading architectural elements from 3D Warehouse

We created a cantilevered canopy to add to the storefront and uploaded it to **3D Warehouse**. Let's download it and add it to the entrance of the building.

The steps in this section show how to download the canopy to our model. We will go further into 3D Warehouse and what it has to offer in *Chapter 7*.

1. From the **Window** menu, choose **3D Warehouse**.
2. You might have to log in using your Trimble ID, which is most likely the same email and password you use to log in to SketchUp and the Extension Warehouse.
3. In the search area, underneath **What can we help you find?**, type `cantilever canopy`, and then tap *Enter* or *Return* on your keyboard.

Figure 6.45: Type cantilever canopy in the search bar

Alternatively, instead of tapping *Enter/Return*, you can click the magnifying glass on the far right of the search bar.

4. At the top of the next window, which are the results of the search, you should be on the **Models & Products** tab.

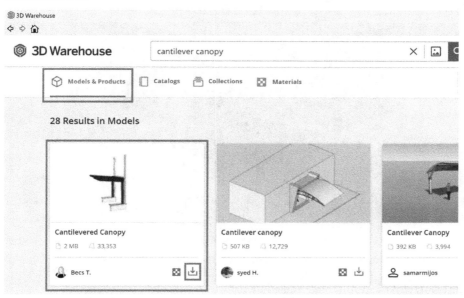

Figure 6.46: The cantilevered canopy file on the Models & Products tab

You can scroll through the results to see what other modelers created and named *Cantilever Canopy* or *Cantilevered Canopy*. You will download the model notated with a red square in *Figure 6.46*, by *Becs T.*

5. To download it, click the arrow in the bottom right of that box.

Whenever you select **Download** in 3D Warehouse, a pop-up window appears, asking whether you want to load the object directly into your model, as shown in *Figure 6.47*. We usually advise against this for a few reasons, which we will cover in *Chapter 7*. However, we created and uploaded this object to 3D Warehouse specifically for this book, so it's okay to do it this time.

Figure 6.47: Click Yes to download the canopy into your model

6. Click **Yes** to download the canopy into your SketchUp model.

7. The canopy comes into your model attached to your cursor with the **Move** tool activated. Move your mouse near the entrance (storefront) and click to place.

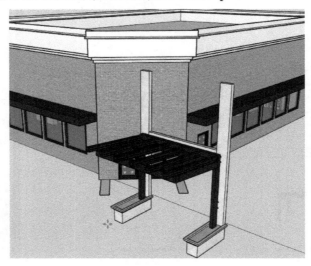

Figure 6.48: Place the canopy near the building's entrance

Don't worry! We can still rotate and edit what we downloaded.

Have you noticed the random rectangles near the entrance? They are highlighted in blue in *Figure 6.49*:

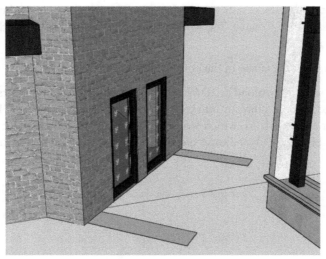

Figure 6.49: Rectangles at the building's entrance

Those rectangles show you where to line up the decorative limestone planter boxes.

8. Using the rectangles as your guide, rotate and move the canopy so that the planter boxes line up exactly with the rectangles. We suggest moving one outside endpoint of a planter box to an endpoint of a rectangle, then using the rectangle to guide the rotation.

Figure 6.50: The canopy aligned to the building's entrance – front view (left) and a lower side view (right)

Check the back of the canopy and limestone. The limestone should be flush with the building façade.

Now, let's look at our finished exterior and display it with materials added and a bit of **Ambient Occlusion** stylizing:

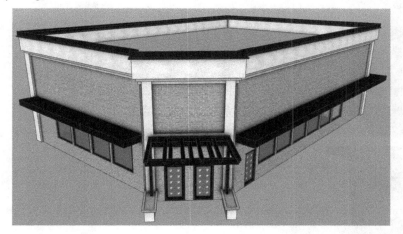

Figure 6.51: All the exterior architectural elements and exterior materials added

Wow, the exterior is looking good! In the next section, we will finish the model by adding the client's brand to the façade.

Carrying a client's brand from inside to outside

Commercial designers and architects know the importance of helping carry a client's brand from inside to outside. One approach to this, besides using images, is to use SketchUp's 3D text to write the company's name on the outside. This section will explore a couple of ways to finalize our building's shell by applying the branding in name and color.

Text options in SketchUp

SketchUp has three types of text options, which can all be found in the **Tools** menu or the **Large Tool Set**. Let's look at each of these options:

- **Text**: This is used to create leaders of text. You can add callouts that include numbers, can be moved (with the **Move** tool), and can be edited. When you right-click on the leader or text, there are additional options to change how the arrow or leader is displayed (see *Figure 6.52, top*).

- To change the font size and style, click on the text once and open **Entity Info**. You can change the size of the text using the number box, or click **Change Font** (or **Font** on macOS), shown in *Figure 6.52* (*bottom*), to change the font style and other attributes.

  You can also change the properties of all the screen text in your model from **Window | Model Info**. Choose **Text** on the left sidebar to see your options.

  The downside of **Text** is that when you zoom in and out, the text does not maintain its size. It tends to run into other entities in the modeling window or, when orbiting, can disappear.

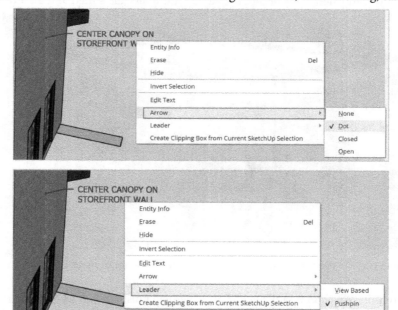

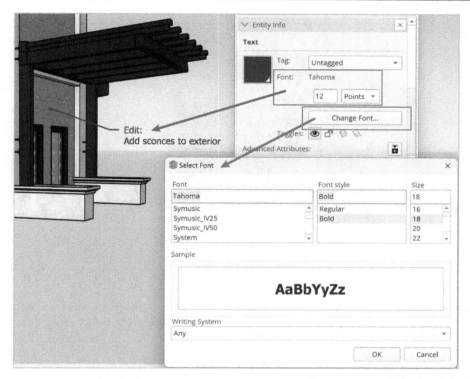

Figure 6.52: Text in SketchUp: Right-click menu for Arrow and Leader (top) and font settings (bottom)

- **Dimensions**: We are not going to sugarcoat how we feel about dimensioning in SketchUp – it's awful. It functions almost exactly like **Text**, which means you can edit the font and size, but when you zoom in and out, the text does not maintain its size. Just like other text, there are additional options when you right-click on one. Or, preferably, you can change the properties of all the screen text in your model from the **Model Info** window, under the **Window** menu. Choose **Dimensions** on the left sidebar to see your options.

Dimensioning in SketchUp is fine if you need to dimension a smaller number of objects from one view only. If you need multiple dimensions, use SketchUp LayOut instead. LayOut's dimension settings are much easier to use and are drawn uniformly. We will go into further detail on SketchUp LayOut and dimensioning in *Chapters 12* and *13*.

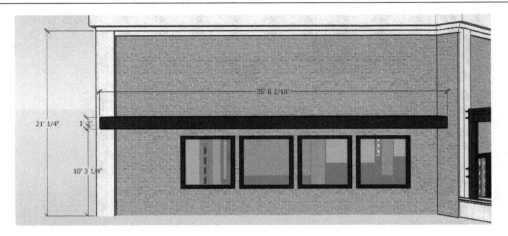

Figure 6.53: Dimensions in SketchUp

> **Read more**
>
> You can read more about **Text** and **Dimensions** here: `https://help.sketchup.com/en/sketchup/adding-text-labels-and-dimensions-model`.

- **3D Text**: Adding **3-dimensional** (**3D**) text to SketchUp is quick and relatively painless. There are multiple fonts to choose from, and once placed, you can move and scale the text.

  The downside to **3D text** is that it cannot be edited. If you make a mistake or need to change it later, you must recreate the text. Make a habit of writing down the settings you used in order to recreate it the same way the next time. (Yes, there is an extension that will edit 3D text! Search for `3D Text Editor` in the Extension Warehouse, by ThomThom. It's free!)

> **Why create 3D text and not 2D?**
>
> Creating text that is 3D and not 2D is important for one major reason. 2D text, just like other 2D faces, becomes hard to see when placed on another face due to lack of depth or extrusion. Depending on the camera view, the text might disappear or flicker between the 2D text material and the texture of the face behind it.

Next, let's insert **3D Text** into the exterior wall of our *Chapter 6* practice file.

Adding 3D text

3D Text can be found in a few places – the **Large Tool Set**, **Construction** toolbar, and the **Tools** menu| **3D Text**. For macOS users, it can also be found in the **Tool** palette. *Figure 6.54* shows the window that will open, called **Place 3D Text**. The settings in the window will default to the last time **Place 3D Text** was used in any model.

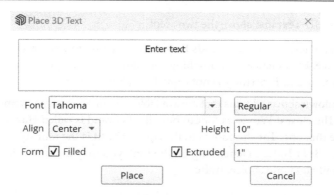

Figure 6.54: The Place 3D Text window

We will now go through the steps to place **3D Text** on the building façade.

> **A macOS note**
>
> Your **3D Text** window will look slightly different from the one shown here, but everything functions the same.

1. Click the Exterior scene tab and orbit so that you are facing one of the banks of windows:

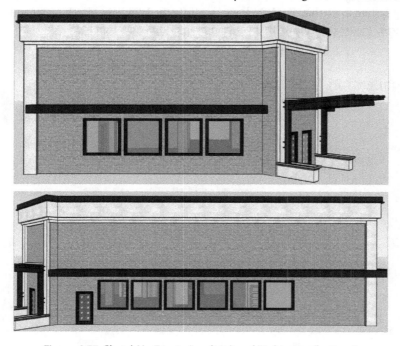

Figure 6.55: SketchUp Front view (top) and Right view (bottom)

We will add the **3D Text** just above the two soffits.

2. In the text box, where it currently reads **Enter text**, highlight those words and type the text you want to place. For practice, type anything you want! We will type the business name of our client, called *young and Free* (the *y* is not capitalized, but the *F* is).

3. The **Font** dropdown shows all fonts that are available in your operating system, whether macOS or Windows. The closest Windows font to our client's brand is called **Harlow Solid Italic**, so we will choose that one. The dropdown to the right of **Font** is the font style (such as **Regular**, **Bold**, **Italic**, or **Bold Italic**). Depending on the font, you may not have the ability to change the style. We only had one choice, **Italic**.

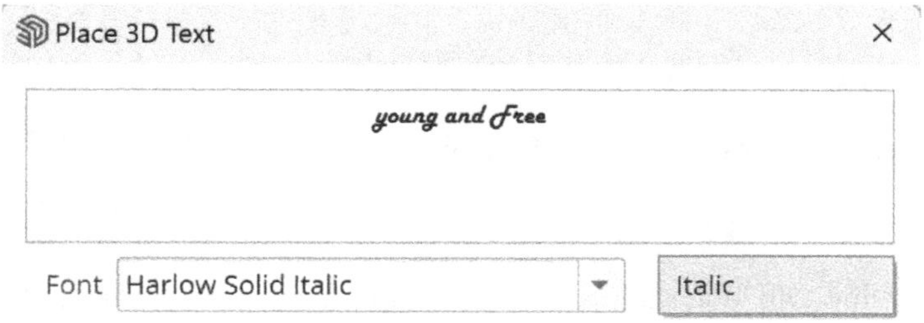

Figure 6.56: 3D Text settings through step 3

If you want to import a font into SketchUp that is brand-specific, use the settings for your operating system to do that. For Windows users, use the Windows search menu and type `Font Settings`. *Figure 6.57* shows that you can drag or upload a font file.

Figure 6.57: Install fonts to Windows 11

On macOS, check the **Font Book** app from your `Applications` folder. You will find more info there and online.

Let's continue the steps for adding 3D text:

4. The **Align** dropdown relates to multiple lines of text. For single-line text, whether you center, right, or left-align text, it does not really matter because you can move it after placing. If you have multiple lines of text, **Align** will be your friend. Give it a try on your own.

5. **Height**, of course, is important, but if you get this wrong, it's not a big deal because you can scale the text after placing. For our exterior sign, we will change the **Height** setting to 2 ' or 24 ". This means that the tallest letter will be 2 ' high.

6. **Form**: Almost 100% of the time, you will fill in the letters so that they have faces, not just edges. That way, if you hide edges or photorealistic render, you can still view the text. Make sure **Filled** is checked.

7. **Extruded** should also be checked. If not checked, the text will be 2D and not 3D. When this is checked, you will need to type a number in the box to the right. This tells SketchUp how much of a projection you want for the text.

For example, in *Figure 6.58*, we created a 4 ' extrusion. Looking at the side view after placing the text, we can see it projects 4 ' out from the wall and looks, well, weird.

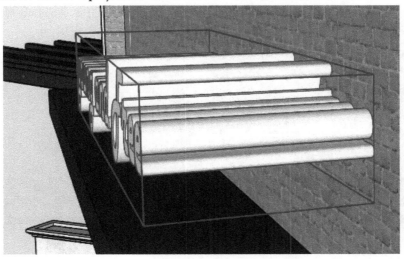

Figure 6.58: 3D Text extruded (projected) 4' out from the wall

The good news is, if you accidentally make a mistake like this, you can use the **Scale** tool to squish back the text.

For our client's brand, we will set **Extruded** to 6 " by typing that in the box.

Figure 6.59: The Place 3D Text window with all our settings

We have added all necessary information to this window, so we can now add the text to our model.

8.   Click **Place**.

The 3D text will now be attached to your cursor. As you mouse around the model, notice how the text will change its angle depending on where your cursor is. It is also ready to be placed on a face; 3D text expects to be on a surface, so it will try to snap to a face.

9.   Click on the wall above a soffit to place the text.

Figure 6.60: Click to place the text on the wall

A ScreenTip will pop up just before you click that says **On Face in Group**.

10. Move the text so that it is centered on the bank of windows, no matter which side of the building you apply the text to.

Figure 6.61: Center the text on the bank of windows

The bottom of the *y* should land approximately 10" above the soffit.

3D text comes in as a component. When you get into **Edit** mode, you will see that the text is now geometry, made up of many lines and faces.

11. Get into **Edit** mode to add color(s) or texture(s) to the text geometry:

    * You can apply an identical color or texture to each face by using a selection tool to choose all surfaces simultaneously. If you select all the letters and apply color to only one, even though the edges and faces are not connected, all selected letters will receive the color.

    * Alternatively, you can select individual letters, either by triple-clicking a letter or using a selection window. That allows you to apply a variety of colors or textures to multiple letters.

Figure 6.62: Select one letter by triple-clicking the letter

    * Then, after the selection is made, use the **Materials** toolbar to add a texture, or import an image of a material.

Our client, *young and Free*, uses a bright white for their brand on all letters, so we will paint all the letters white.

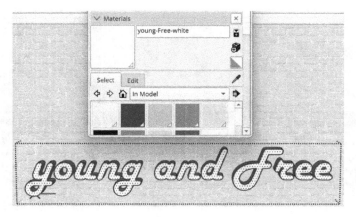

Figure 6.63: Paint all the faces simultaneously by first selecting them

It's hard to tell that all our letters changed to white, but you can check yours with the **Sample Paint** dropper (or **Color Picker** on macOS) to make sure the letters changed. (Learn more about colors and textures in *Chapter 10*.)

Take some time to play around with the text component. Try using the **Scale** tool to make it larger or smaller or squish the extrusion inward and outward. (Do not use the **Scale** tool while in **Edit** mode of the component. Make those changes to the overall component grouping, outside of **Edit** mode.)

Also, you might not be able to move the text along one or more axes. This happens sometimes with 3D text. The quick fix is to *explode* the component and then quickly **Make Group**. Easy enough!

Now, you have to decide whether you will rotate and copy the text to the wall on the other side of the entrance or create new 3D text. The choice is yours! All the settings are the same, using *steps 1* to *10*.

Figure 6.64: The other side of the building with 3D text added

One final 3D text tip is that sometimes, after clicking **Place** in the **3D Text** window, text will disappear. That is because some fonts cannot be created at smaller scales. If that happens to you, try recreating the 3D text using a different font. Chances are that will fix the issue.

3D text in SketchUp is a great way to carry your client's brand from inside to outside, especially because you can load any brand-specific font into your computer's operating system. Further, 3D text can be photorealistic rendered, which means text can light up with any LED color or typical lamp setting. Have some fun with 3D text!

Inserting a client's logo

You probably have noticed throughout the *Chapter 6* practice file that the exterior doors have a logo on the glass. Our client sent us a transparent PNG file to add to the glass, just like we will do in the real-life project.

> **Importing brand images and logos**
>
> *Chapter 9* tackles how to import and customize images. The information in that chapter can be used to integrate a client's brand not just with text but with their actual logo images.

You can incorporate these details into your exterior as well. Turn on the tag called `Brand-Signs`. You will see that the **young and Free** logo has been placed above the 3D text and on the entrance façade:

Figure 6.65: The full brand on the building's exterior

Isn't this amazing? SketchUp is so intuitive and can create such personalized details.

Working with client branding

Proficiency in photo editing software such as Photoshop or Sketch is essential when working with client branding to guarantee that logos appear sharp and polished. Frequently, it becomes necessary to adjust what the client provides to deliver a high-quality end product. For example, when it comes to printed items such as vinyl, it's crucial to use the logo in a high-resolution format to guarantee sharp and clear printing. Vector formats, such as EPS, are ideal, since they can be resized to any dimension without compromising quality (not to mention the ability to change the Color mode to the printing standard CMYK). Another thing to keep in mind is the distance from which the logo will be viewed, such as the building in this example. Tweak the logo's details to make it viewable from any angle, such as adding a heavier stroke or using a solid background.

To make this design even better when we show it to our clients, we will use an extension, **SketchUp Diffusion**, to add landscaping and other realistic touches. This **Artificial Intelligence (AI)** extension, created by the SketchUp team, uses text prompts to create AI-generated images:

Figure 6.66: An AI-generated exterior view using SketchUp Diffusion

SketchUp Diffusion will be introduced in *Chapter 15*. We're sure you have played around with its settings already, so for now, these are the settings and prompts we used:

- **Style – Aerial Masterplan**
- Prompts – `building off busy black street, dark red brick building, cement roof, black aluminum awnings, urban downtown, dusk.`

We created the parking garage entrance to the west side of the building, which we use in the next and final part of this chapter to explain sections.

Including sections

We would be remiss if we wrote a book about SketchUp without reviewing **sections**. As mentioned earlier in the book, we assume you are familiar with the basics of SketchUp, including creating a section plane, cut, and fill, and modifying them. For architectural drafters or interior designers, incorporating and utilizing sections is a routine aspect of their work. We'll provide a brief review of this crucial feature.

After the practice file for this chapter was uploaded to 3D Warehouse, we added an underground parking garage beneath the building. Your model won't include the parking garage shown in this section.

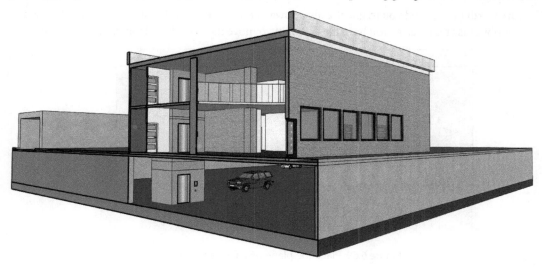

Figure 6.67: Underground parking garage added to the model shown using a Section Cut

Here is our scenario for creating the section – for an upcoming client presentation on this project, they requested a section cut revealing both floors of the building and the parking garage.

1. To achieve this, the initial step is to create a section plane. Begin by opening the **Section** toolbar.

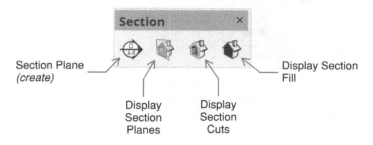

Figure 6.68: The Section toolbar

The icons in the **Section** toolbar, from left to right, are **Section Plane**, **Display Section Planes**, **Display Section Cuts**, and **Display Section Fill**.

2. Click the **Section Plane** icon or create the plane from **Tools | Section Plane**.

You will first see that there is a square attached to your cursor. Depending on where you move your mouse, it will be the color of one of the axes. When it turns magenta, it either follows a sloped area or is parallel to another object.

3. To initiate the cut, click on the specific area or object you wish to section.

It's worth noting, and you might already be aware, that the exact point of your click on that area or object isn't critical, as you have the flexibility to move the plane later to fit your requirements.

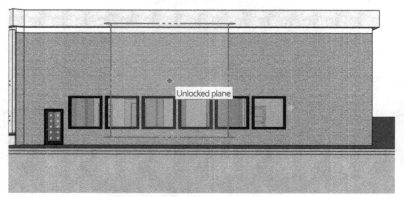

Figure 6.69: Place the plane on a face and click

Also, keep in mind that the plane will include everything within the model unless you're working within a group or component.

4. A pop-up window will then ask you to name the section and give it a number, letter, or combination.

As mentioned in *Chapter 2*, you should always name your sections because you can then find them easily in the **Outliner** toolbar.

Figure 6.70: You should name and number the section cut

5. At this point, you should see an orange section plane in your model. Click on it once, and it will change to blue, indicating that it's ready for manipulation.

6. You should also be able to partially see inside your building or object. If that's not the case, it suggests the cut isn't active. Verify this by right-clicking on the plane, bringing up a new menu related to section planes:

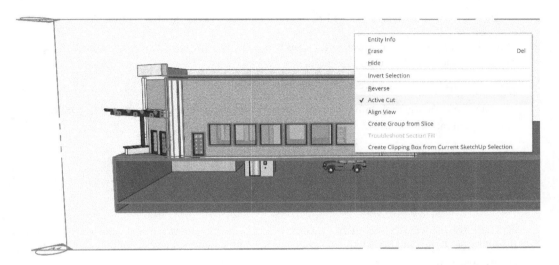

Figure 6.71: Context menu for section planes

7. Make sure **Active Cut** is checked.

    Take note of the additional choices available in the context menu:

    *   **Reverse** flips the direction of the cut.

    *   **Align View** changes your viewpoint to match the orientation of the section plane, giving you a clear and aligned view of the model where it was cut along that plane. If you are in a 3D isometric view, it will adjust your camera to look at the cut in a straight-on, more 2D view.

    *   **Create Group from Slice** is a powerful tool. It forms a group from the edges (or geometry) that the slice touches. This geometry can then be utilized to craft new shapes or modify existing ones.

    *   **Troubleshoot Section Fill** is helpful when parts of the geometry are not filled. This occurs when there isn't a closed loop of edges to generate a fill. Selecting this option will highlight areas without closure with a red circle. If there are not issues with the section fill, this option will be grayed out.

8. Now that the section plane has been added to an object, adjust the cutting area. There are two methods:

   - Activate the **Move** (*M*) tool, click anywhere on the section plane (there's no need to choose a specific point because there aren't points), and then move your mouse to expand or decrease the cutting area

   - Alternatively, you can also use the **Rotate** (*Q*) tool, which helps create an angled view of an area.

9. Once the section plane shows the view you want, click to stop the move (or rotate) or type a distance/angle, and then tap *Enter/Return*.

10. The next step is to create a scene.

    A scene conveniently maintains the view, eliminating the need to constantly orbit, pan, toggle tags, or generate a new cut.

> **Scenes**
>
> We covered scenes in *Chapter 2*, in the *Creating a client-worthy scene* section. We will not go further into scenes in this chapter.

As you know, objects in SketchUp don't have solid interiors, so when we make a section cut, there's often empty space left. This is where section fill comes in handy—it helps us fill in that empty space created by the cut.

To toggle a section fill off and on, use the icon at the far right of the **Section** toolbar. Alternatively, you can utilize the **View** menu to check or uncheck **Section Fill**.

11. To change the color of the section fill, use the **Styles** toolbar. On Windows, that toolbar is found in the default tray. For macOS, you can find it in **Window | Styles**.

12. Click the **Edit** tab within the **Styles** toolbar, then just underneath that, choose the blue grid box on the far right. When you hover over it, a ScreenTip reads **Modeling Settings**.

In the **Modeling** dialog box, most of the information on the right applies just to sections and section fills:

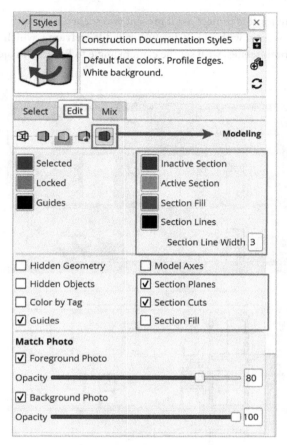

Figure 6.72: The Modeling settings for sections are outlined in red

> **More about styles**
>
> In *Chapter 10*, in the *Exploring SketchUp's Styles panel* section, we will explore built-in styles in the **Styles** toolbar to craft an impressive presentation model.

The settings in this dialog box are user-friendly and self-explanatory, thanks to the clear text descriptions. If you want to change colors, just click on the box next to the description. And if it's the **Section Line Width** setting you want to tweak, pop a new number into the box on the right.

You might have noticed that many of the features in the **View** menu are also in this dialog box. It's a neat reminder that, in software, there's often more than one way to get things done, which is always handy!

To complete the section cut for this project, we'll present two scenes, each with a different style – one featuring textures and the second with a built-in style called **Wireframe**, which is devoid of textures (refer to *Figure 6.73*). For both scenes, we'll set the camera angle to **Parallel Projection**, transforming the view from 3D to 2D.

Figure 6.73: Two section cuts of the building and parking garage with differing styles

In the wireframe style, the bottom view displays a diagonal line, indicating the ramp cars use for entering and exiting the parking garage.

> **More information**
>
> Want to know more about sections in SketchUp? Here's a link to SketchUp's help page: https://
> help.sketchup.com/en/sketchup/slicing-model-peer-inside.

Other valuable exterior tools

Commercial designers and architects often show only the exterior of a building, using existing site images to show and incorporate changes to the façade, create a sun study, and determine possible site locations based on topography. Although we do not have enough space in this book to show how SketchUp makes this easier for you, we want to mention the tools within the software so that you can search for and learn more about them:

- **Geo-location**: Geo-locate your model to, or begin modeling from, a precise location anywhere on Earth. You can add satellite images from the imported site map and import pre-existing terrain into SketchUp. SketchUp harnesses the capabilities of **Trimble Maps**, showcasing pristine imagery and the most current map data.

  - If you are using SketchUp version 2024.0 or newer, there are two ways to start geo-locating:

    - **File | Add Location**
    - Open the **Add Location** toolbar and click the (only) icon. (We will also discuss **Add Location** in *Chapter 10*. This tool is complementary to both chapters.)

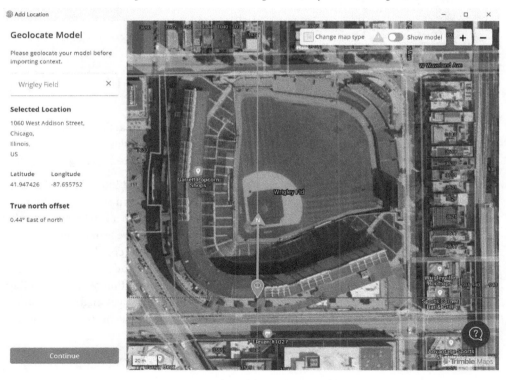

Figure 6.74: The Add Location window

- Here is a helpful link to get you started: `https://help.sketchup.com/en/sketchup/add-location`

- For our friends using SketchUp 2023 or older, you will find **Geo-location | Add Location** under the **File** menu, or in the **Location** toolbar (*Figure 6.75*). Though the newer SketchUp versions have incredible graphics and updated data, you can accomplish most of the same tasks without having to upgrade. This link takes you through how to use it: `https://help.sketchup.com/en/sketchup/importing-preexisting-terrain-sketchup-and-geolocate-model`

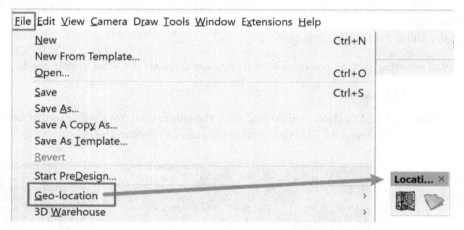

Figure 6.75: Find Geo-location in SketchUp 2023 and older

Something to note: You can view your geo-located model in **Google Earth** by exporting it to a KMZ file. For more information on how to use this feature, explore the following link: `https://help.sketchup.com/en/sketchup/viewing-your-model-google-earth`.

- **Sandbox tools**: This toolbar is actually an extension that is integrated into all paid SketchUp software. Importing existing terrain can be easier than creating it from scratch, but there are times when you might need to create it yourself. The tools in this toolbar can be used together or separately, depending on what you need to accomplish. Those tools are **From Contours** (used when importing existing terrain with **Add Location**), **From Scratch** (creating a new terrain), **Smoov** (used after creating a mesh with **From Scratch**), **Add Detail** (adding additional edges to selected triangulated edges made by **Smoov** to create higher resolution terrain), **Flip Edge** (improving smoothness and adding realism to by flipping triangular edges made with **Smoov**), **Stamp** (creating a flat foundation on bumpy terrain), and **Drape** (projecting or dropping a set of edges onto bumpy terrain to create roads and other surfaces).

- Where to find it: **Tools | Sandbox,** and then choose a tool from the submenu, or the **Sandbox** toolbar.

- Helpful links to get you started: `https://help.sketchup.com/en/sketchup/ placing-models-and-objects-your-terrain`

- Something to note: Sandbox tools can also be used to create more detailed objects, such as creating the realistic rise and fall of dirt in a pot or making lumpy mashed potatoes. (We're not kidding! Becca created a LinkedIn Learning video showing how to create lumpy potatoes.)

Figure 6.76: Bowl of lumpy mashed potatoes made with Sandbox tools (bowl created with Follow Me)

- **Trimble Scan Essentials**: Trimble Scan Essentials is an extension toolset for architecture, engineering, construction, and surveying professionals. It's designed to efficiently manage and analyze point cloud data generated by 3D laser scans. By leveraging point clouds, it enables us to work seamlessly with large-scale scans, create precise models, take accurate measurements, and visualize detailed 3D representations of real places.

  - Where to find it: The great news is if you subscribe to **SketchUp Studio** you already have access to the extension! (Sorry, hardware not included.)

  - Helpful links to get you started: `https://help.sketchup.com/en/scan- essentials-sketchup`

Figure 6.77: Trimble Scan Essentials toolbar

We really wish we had more time to go into all the amazing things that SketchUp can do in this realm, but we are not making a SketchUp encyclopedia. (Maybe that will be our next book!) For now, we hope this section has helped you learn about other resources that you can use for the exterior elements of your model.

Summary

This chapter covered a lot of enhancements that architects and designers can add to a building's exterior. Although we did not have time to cover all of the tools for exterior modeling, we were able to cover some valuable tools that you may not know about. And, of course, we finally introduced you to the Extension Warehouse! Your workflow will take off when you find hidden gems you never thought possible. Keep exploring each chapter where we mention our favorites, and hopefully, you will learn something new to add to your repertoire. Extensions are amazing for reducing billable hours that clients do not want to pay for.

In the next chapter, we move from commercial exteriors to residential interiors. Using a beautifully crafted living room, you will continue learning to use an imported AutoCAD drawing for 3D modeling, this time to create elevations and details. You will also learn best practices for navigating and using 3D Warehouse!

Part 3: Adding Designer Details to a SketchUp Model

When you incorporate personalized and custom details into your SketchUp models, your designs gain a distinctive edge. This part guides you through adding custom furnishings, colors, materials, and architectural elements. Elevate your SketchUp projects with techniques that prepare you for an impressive final presentation. Get ready to turn your designs into engaging and visually stunning creations!

This part has the following chapters:

- *Chapter 7, Adding Interior Elements and 3D Warehouse Furnishings*
- *Chapter 8, Modeling Furniture – From the Basics to Intricacy*
- *Chapter 9, Applying and Customizing Colors and Materials*
- *Chapter 10, Enhancing a Model with Details for Final Presentation*

7

Adding Interior Elements and 3D Warehouse Furnishings

This chapter gets the ball rolling for *Part 3, Adding Designer Details to a SketchUp Model*. It is time to incorporate the fun interior elements that make your design unique. (Yay!) The chapter starts by walking through how to set up imported AutoCAD elevations. We will also cover how to use drafted elevations to model interior architectural elements, such as pocket door details, intricate trim, and more.

In the latter half of this chapter, we will dive into the 3D Warehouse world. If you have been following along in this book from the beginning, you will know that we have had multiple practice models available to download on 3D Warehouse, so you are likely familiar with the interface. Now, in this chapter, we will go into greater detail on how to navigate, search, download, and import models from 3D Warehouse. We will also introduce Live Components.

In this chapter, we will cover the following topics:

- Building a room using imported AutoCAD elevations
- Creating interior architectural details from imported AutoCAD elevations
- 3D Warehouse I – Accessing and searching
- 3D Warehouse II – Downloading, reviewing, and importing

Technical requirements

This chapter requires the following software and files:

- SketchUp Pro or Studio
- A Trimble SketchUp login for 3D Warehouse
- An internet connection to access 3D Warehouse

- Download the practice file from `3D Warehouse` named `Chapter 7- Living Room Elevations` or download it from `https://3dwarehouse.sketchup.com/model/d076c461-3ee1-45ef-86a8-49cb8694c3af/Chapter-7-Living-Room-Elevations`.

Building a room using imported AutoCAD elevations

We are often given drafted elevations with interior architectural elements already drawn. In this chapter, we will show you how to use imported AutoCAD elevations to build a living room, complete with interior details such as baseboards, crown molding, a fireplace, and more.

Let's get started by setting up a SketchUp file with imported AutoCAD elevations.

Setting up the elevations

From `3D Warehouse`, download the SketchUp model titled `Chapter 7- Living Room Elevations`. You will see imported AutoCAD elevations on the left and an imported AutoCAD plan on the right when you open the file. (Review *Chapter 4* for how to import a DWG/DXF file into SketchUp.) This is what the model looks like when opened:

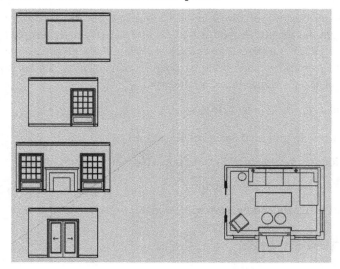

Figure 7.1: SketchUp practice file, Chapter 7– Living Room Elevations

When the CAD elevations were imported, before they were given to you, they were all together in one large component. The component was edited to make each individual wall elevation its own separate group. The imported CAD layers were merged and a tag folder named CAD was created, which is where you will find the CAD plan and elevations. Lastly, a known measurement was checked using the **Tape Measure** tool. In this case, the overall wall height should be (and is) 9'-0".

Click on the **Scene** tab named `Living Room - Elevations Set Up`. We have already set up the CAD elevations by copying, moving, and rotating each elevation group so that they line up appropriately on top of the floor plan group. Then, we locked each elevation and the plan so they could not accidentally be edited. *Figure 7.2* shows what the model looks like from a bird's-eye perspective.

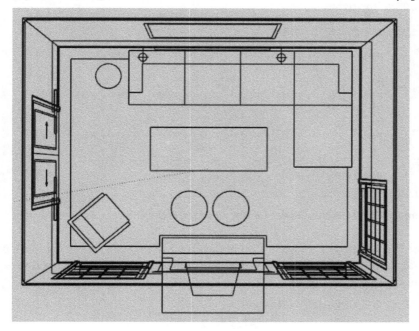

Figure 7.2: A bird's-eye view of CAD elevations set up on top of the floor plan group

If you would like to practice setting up the CAD elevations yourself, click on the **Scene** tab called `Living Room - Imported Elevations`. These elevations are not locked. (If you feel comfortable with this process, you can skip ahead to *Reviewing the practice model*.)

Before getting started, here are some important things to note when setting up CAD elevations in SketchUp:

- The elevations need to be exactly perpendicular at a 90-degree angle to the floor plan, locked in on either the red/x-axis or the green/y-axis.

- The elevations should be placed on the inside of the wall rather than the outside of the wall.

- The lines representing the floor on the elevations should be touching the floor plan. In other words, the elevations should not be floating above the floor plan.

- Everything on the elevations needs to line up perfectly with the floor plan. The pocket doors on the elevation need to align with the pocket doors on the floor plan, the fireplace on the elevation needs to align with the fireplace on the floor plan, and so on.

Let's set up the pocket door elevation together:

1. Start by making a copy of the pocket door elevation group by using the **Move + Copy** command (*Ctrl* on Windows, *Opt* on macOS). Lock in the red/x-axis and move the copied elevation group 20' to the right.

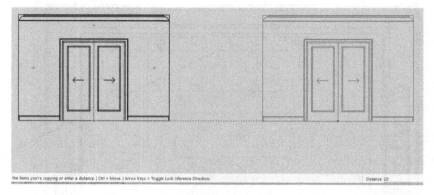

Figure 7.3: Use Move plus Ctrl key (or Opt) to copy the elevation group 20' to the right

2. Activate the **Rotate** tool (shortcut *Q*), tap the *up* arrow on your keyboard to lock in on the blue/z-axis, and rotate the group 90 degrees counterclockwise (type 90 and press *Enter*). Remember to click on endpoints.

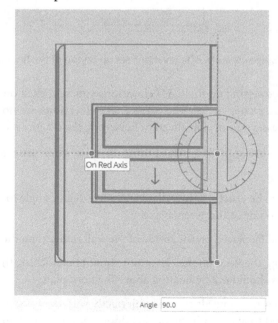

Figure 7.4: Rotate the elevation group on the blue/z-axis 90 degrees counterclockwise

3. Activate the **Rotate** tool again, but this time, tap the *left* arrow to lock in on the green/y-axis. Rotate the group 90 degrees clockwise (type 90 and press *Enter*).

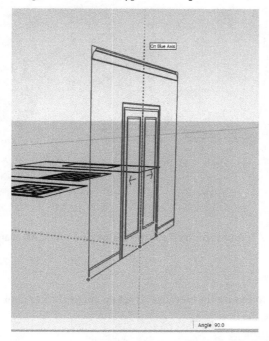

Figure 7.5: Rotate the elevation group on the green/y-axis 90 degrees clockwise

We are now going to move the elevation group so that it sits on top of the floor plan.

4. Activate the **Move** tool (shortcut *M*) and hover your mouse over the bottom-right corner of the group until you see the **Corner of Group** ScreenTip pop up. Select this bottom corner endpoint as the first click.

Zoom in to ensure you are snapping to the correct spot.

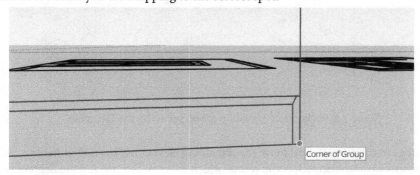

Figure 7.6: Your first click is the Corner of Group endpoint on the elevation

5.   Move the elevation group over to the corner of the floor plan where the inside walls meet. You should see the **Endpoint in CAD Plan** ScreenTip. Select this endpoint as your second click.

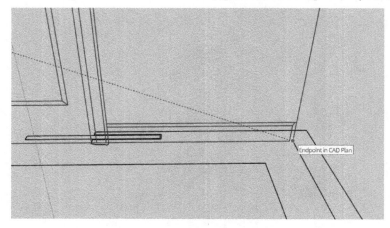

Figure 7.7: Your second click is the endpoint on the CAD plan

6.   Save your model.

Zoom out and orbit around to ensure the elevation is set up correctly. Remember, the elevation group should not be floating above the floor plan.

Figure 7.8: Pocket door elevation group set up on the CAD plan

Repeat these steps to copy, rotate, and move the remaining elevations. The only difference will be the rotations. In other words, the direction you rotate, which axis you lock in, and the degrees you rotate will be different for each elevation.

> **Note for rotating the south (fireplace) elevation**
>
> After you copy the south elevation (which is the fireplace elevation), you will rotate the group 180 degrees. If you do not rotate it 180 degrees, it will not line up with the floor plan properly.

When you are done, your work should match what you see in the **Scene** tab named `Living Room – Elevations Set Up`. If it does not match perfectly, you will run into issues later. Adjust your work if needed and then lock the elevations when they are in the right spots.

Next up, it's time to familiarize yourself with the model, if you haven't already.

Reviewing the practice model

Have you reviewed the model yet? Whenever you open a SketchUp file for the first time, it is always a good idea to review it (as mentioned in *Chapter 2*). Click the **Zoom Extents** icon, cycle through the scenes, and check out the **Tags** panel. If you haven't yet, take some time to poke around in this practice model.

You may have noticed there are tags that are turned off. Go ahead and turn the visibility on for all the tags.

Surprise! The walls have already been constructed with openings for the three windows and fireplace. The floor has also been constructed. We still need to cut an opening for the pocket doors. Let's do that now.

Cutting an opening for the pocket doors

In *Chapter 5*, we discussed how to use the **X-ray** face style or the **Back Edges** edge style to view the CAD plan through the walls when cutting openings for the windows and doors. Since we are using CAD elevations for this exercise, we do not need to change the face or edge style, and we will not need to create any guide lines. Instead, we will trace on top of the elevations and use them as guidance for where to cut an opening in the wall for the pocket doors.

Let's begin!

1. Click on the **Scene** tab named `Living Room – Elevations Set Up`. Turn on the visibility for all tags. Update the scene.

2. Get into **Edit** mode of the wall group with the pocket door. (Remember, getting into **Edit** mode is a critical step when cutting openings!)

3. Trace the pocket doors, excluding the casing, from the imported CAD elevation using the **Line** tool and/or **Rectangle** tool. Even though we are tracing, it is still important to lock in on axis when drawing.

When you are done tracing, there should be a new rectangular face on top of the pocket doors:

Figure 7.9: Select the new face that is created

4. Use the **Push/Pull** tool (shortcut *P*) to cut the opening in the wall, which is 4 . 5 " deep. (Review *Chapter 5* for detailed instructions on cutting openings.)

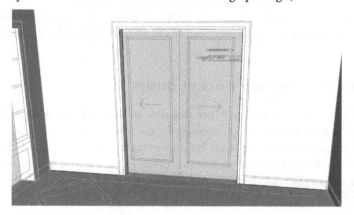

Figure 7.10: Cut opening for pocket doors using Push/Pull

Don't forget to save your model! We are now ready to add the interior architectural details.

Creating interior architectural details from imported AutoCAD elevations

Great design lives in the details! The same can be said about 3D models. Adding elaborate crown molding and unique fireplace designs to your SketchUp models will take your projects to the next level. We will use the imported CAD elevations to build the interior architectural details of our living room.

Building the pocket doors

Let's start by building the pocket door casing. Make sure the visibility of all tags is on. Zoom in on the pocket doors on the floor plan. Notice how the exact profile of the pocket door casing is drawn on the CAD plan. We will use the profile for tracing:

1. Trace the casing profile from the CAD plan on the floor by using the **Line** tool (shortcut *L*) and **Arc** tool (shortcut *A*). Draw on axis when you can. The arched part does not need to be exact, but get as close as you can. Make the face a group.

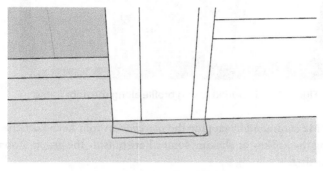

Figure 7.11: Group the door casing profile face

2. Next, we will use the **Follow Me** tool to extrude the face. Get into **Edit** mode of the group. Use the **Line** tool to draw a path for extrusion around the door (three lines).

    Figure 7.12 shows the path to draw, using the edges of the wall as a reference.

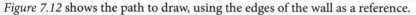

Figure 7.12: Draw the path for extrusion

3. Still in **Edit** mode, select just the path of edges for extrusion. (Remember that only the path edges should be selected, not the profile face, for extrusion to work.)

4. Click the **Follow Me** icon, and then click once on the casing's face. The face should extrude all the way around the door frame.

Figure 7.13: Extruded casing profile along the door frame

5. End the **Follow Me** command by tapping the *spacebar* on your keyboard, then stop editing the group by tapping the *Esc* key or clicking somewhere outside the group. Zoom out to examine the completed casing.

6. Save your model.

    Now, it's time to build the pocket doors.

7. Trace the edges of one of the doors on the imported CAD elevation using lines or a rectangle. Make the face a group.

8. Make the door 1.5" thick using the **Push/Pull** tool (shortcut *P*). Extrude the face away from the room.

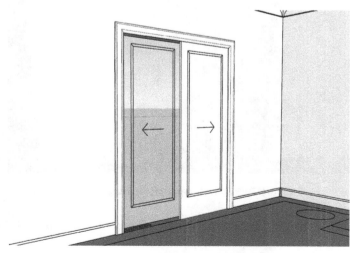

Figure 7.14: 1.5" thick pocket door

Next, we will add the door's paneling.

9. Get into **Edit** mode of the door group if you are not already in it.

10. Trace the exterior edges of the paneling. Use the **Offset** command (shortcut *F*) to offset the traced paneling inward by 1".

11. We will use **Autofold** to create the beveled detail on the paneling. Still in **Edit** mode, select the inside face of the paneling and activate the **Move** tool (shortcut *M*). Click and release on any point of the inside rectangle. Tap the *right* arrow on the keyboard to lock in the red/x-axis. Move your mouse away from the room. Type .75 and press *Enter*.

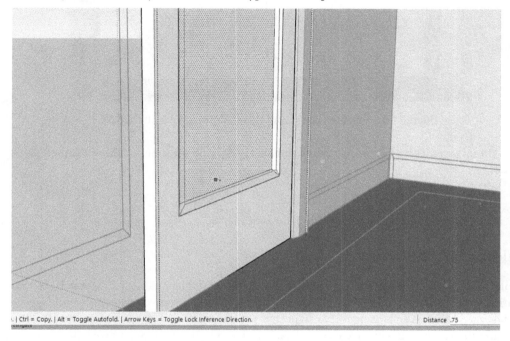

Figure 7.15: Create the beveled detail on the door paneling using Autofold

12. Make the door group a component and name it Pocket Door. Copy the component so that you have two doors side by side, as seen in *Figure 7.16*. You can use the **Flip** tool to make a mirrored copy, as discussed in *Chapter 1*.

Turn off the visibility for the tag folder CAD to view your work.

Figure 7.16: Completed pocket doors with CAD tag folder turned off

13. Group together the two pocket doors and the casing. Add the group to the tag named Wall-West.

14. Save your model.

Look at that detail! Let's continue by building the baseboards.

Building the baseboards

Initially, you may think using the **Follow Me** tool is how we would create the baseboards. In some situations, that is, in fact, how we would do it. For this project, however, we will eventually want the ability to view the room from every perspective without unwanted groups obstructing the view. To ensure this, each wall will have its own baseboard group(s), which means we will not use the **Follow Me** tool.

If you turned off the visibility to the tag folder CAD in the *Building the pocket doors* exercise, turn it on again now. Zoom into the lower corner to the right of the pocket doors, where the two walls meet. There, the exact profile of the baseboards is drawn on the CAD elevations, as shown in *Figure 7.17*. You guessed it! It's time to trace:

1. Trace the baseboard profile by using the **Line** tool (shortcut *L*). Make the face a group.

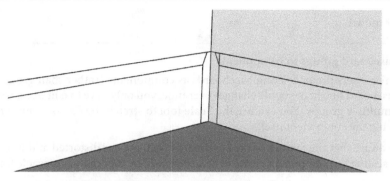

Figure 7.17: Group the baseboard profile face

2. Use the **Push/Pull** tool (shortcut *P*) and extrude the face to meet the pocket door casing.

3. Add a baseboard to the other side of the pocket door by either making a copy of the group we just created or creating a new group from scratch. We recommend making a copy in this scenario since the pocket doors are centered on the wall, meaning the baseboard distance is equal on each side.

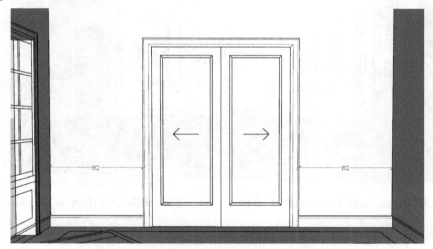

Figure 7.18: Equal distance on each side of the pocket doors

4. Add the two baseboard groups to the `Wall-West` tag.

5. Work around the room and create the remaining baseboards, assigning them to the corresponding wall tags as you go. You can copy, rotate, move, and edit a group already created or create new groups from scratch. It's up to you!

    If you decide to make copies of existing groups, remember to reassign them to the appropriate tags. You do not want the baseboards on the fireplace wall disappearing when you turn off the visibility for the pocket door wall.

6. Save your model.

> **Changing baseboard groups to components**
>
> Some SketchUp users prefer making baseboards as components (rather than groups). This way, if the baseboard height or profile changes over time, you only have to edit one component rather than multiple groups. You can use the **Scale** tool to stretch the component as needed, without altering the component itself.
>
> However, be aware that the texture of the baseboard could appear distorted and unnaturally stretched by scaling the component. Texture distortion will be especially noticeable for wood.

Go ahead and build the rest of the interior details, including the crown molding, windows, and fireplace. Make sure to add a ceiling as well. See *Figure 7.19* for the end result with the `Wall-North` tag visibility turned off.

Figure 7.19: The completed room with all interior architectural details (Wall-North tag turned off)

Here are some tips and reminders as you finish out the space:

- Use the **Follow Me** tool to create the crown molding and fireplace mantle. You do not need to make separate groups for the crown molding on each wall as we did with the baseboards. Unlike baseboards, crown molding usually does not get in the way when viewing a room from different perspectives.

- Use the floor plan as a reference for how deep to make the fireplace surround, mantle, and hearth.

- The three windows are the exact same dimensions and style. Remember to make those components.

- Assign groups and components to **Tags** by using **Entity Info.**

- Create a new tag named `Ceiling` for the ceiling group. You can add the crown molding group to the `Ceiling` tag, or create a new tag just for the crown molding.

- The north wall features framed artwork. We will cover how to import images of art in *Chapter 9*. Make the frame `1.5"` thick.

- Have fun! It is important to take a break when you are feeling overwhelmed. SketchUp and this book will be here waiting when you are ready to give it a go again!

- As always, save your model often.

> **Skip the tracing**
>
> Another method to build the interior details (rather than tracing) is to make a copy of the CAD lines, place the copied lines on a new tag (leaving the original CAD lines on the CAD tag), and then use the copied CAD lines already drawn to create the interior details. With this method, you skip tracing anything, which can save a lot of time when building complex molding profiles that are challenging to trace.
>
> It is worth noting that this technique can result in lots of unwanted loose geometry, so it is especially important to keep tags and groups organized.

Lastly, you will have the opportunity to explore this room professionally built, complete with all interior details, in the *Chapter 10* practice model, when we discuss how to enhance a model for a final presentation.

We are going to dive into 3D Warehouse for the remainder of the chapter.

3D Warehouse I – Accessing and searching

What is 3D Warehouse? It is the largest online source of free, premade 3D models. It is a website that also works seamlessly with SketchUp, where millions of people upload and download models. You can save time by downloading 3D models (such as furniture!) from 3D Warehouse instead of building the 3D models from scratch.

Anyone – beginners and pros – can contribute to 3D Warehouse. You can find entire buildings, rooms filled with furniture, seamless materials, and even accessories such as a bowl of fruit. A link to 3D Warehouse's terms of use is here: `3dwarehouse.sketchup.com/tos/`.

Accessing 3D Warehouse

3D Warehouse is an online open library, meaning that it requires an internet connection. You will also be required to create a Trimble account or log in if you already have one. (If you are using a SketchUp subscription, you already have a Trimble account. Log in to Trimble using your SketchUp subscription credentials.)

Here are two common ways to access 3D Warehouse:

- Locate and click the **3D Warehouse** icon (*Figure 7.20*) in the **Getting Started** toolbar.

Figure 7.20: 3D Warehouse icon in the Getting Started toolbar

---

SketchUp ScreenTip reminder

If you hover your cursor over the icon or any of the icons, SketchUp will display the role of that icon.

- Another way to access 3D Warehouse is on the web; search for `SketchUp 3D Warehouse` in any search engine or type `3dwarehouse.sketchup.com` in the web browser.

No matter how you choose to access 3D Warehouse, you are always directed to the **My 3D Warehouse** page. From here, you can start a search, browse by category, view your saved content, and much more.

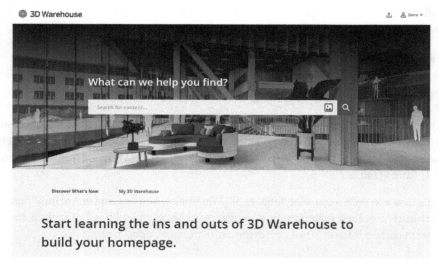

Figure 7.21: The My 3D Warehouse page

To explore the tools and features found on the **My 3D Warehouse** page, visit `help.sketchup.com/en/3d-warehouse/introducing-3d-warehouse-interface`. Let's start searching!

Searching 3D Warehouse

3D Warehouse started as a basic list of SketchUp models with a simple search function. Today, it has grown in content and developed a much more sophisticated search capability, becoming a valuable tool for interior designers!

We are going to search for a round ottoman that we will eventually add to our living room SketchUp model:

1. Let's access 3D Warehouse in a web browser. Open your preferred browser and go to 3dwarehouse.sketchup.com.

2. Type ottoman in the search box, then press *Enter* on the keyboard.

   Wow! This will return a list with a lot of results. Looking at the results in *Figure 7.22*, there are almost 3,000 models and many of them will not work for our purpose as some are rectangular ottomans.

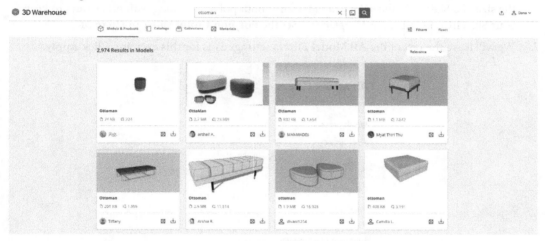

Figure 7.22: Initial results for the "ottoman" search

Oftentimes, it is better to be more descriptive when searching on 3D Warehouse. Let's try again with a bit more description:

3. Type round ottoman in the search box, then press *Enter* on the keyboard. This looks better, but we can still narrow down this list by sorting and filtering results.

You will see the following four tabs at the top:

- **Models & Products** – This tab populates 3D models that are created by anyone, including real-world products from verified companies.

- **Catalogs** – Verified manufacturers can upload an entire catalog of product details, such as appliances or furniture. Catalogs enable users to browse a curated group of models from well-known brands.

- **Collections** – Collections are a way for users to organize 3D models. You can create your own collections of models that appeal to you so you can easily find them again. For example, we could create an Ottomans collection and add ottoman models to it for future use. (In *Chapter 15*, we will cover 3D Warehouse collections when we talk about how to organize your models.)

- **Materials** – When all you want is a material, this is your go-to tab. (We will touch on 3D Warehouse materials in *Chapter 9*.)

4. Different results will populate depending on what tab you select. We want to see 3D models of round ottomans that anyone has created, so click on the **Models & Products** tab.

5. We are going to refine our search by filtering the results. Click on the **Filters** icon in the upper-right corner. A menu box will pop up on the left side with a variety of filter options.

6. We are going to adjust **Polygon Count**. Limiting the number of polygons is one way to manage the size of a SketchUp file. (We will talk more about polygons, along with other ways to keep your SketchUp file clean, in *Chapter 15*.) Set the **Polygon Count** slider to **Up to 3K**.

7. We will leave the rest of the **All Model Filters** settings as-is for this exercise. Click **Apply**.

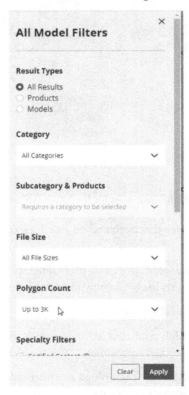

Figure 7.23: Filter your search by Polygon Count

This reduced the number of results to a more manageable amount.

There are also a variety of options for sorting results. By default, search results are sorted by **Relevance**.

Figure 7.24: 3D Warehouse sort options

Visit `help.sketchup.com/en/3d-warehouse/searching-and-downloading-models` for more ways to filter and sort your 3D Warehouse search results.

Scan through the thumbnails of round ottomans. Click on the thumbnail image of any round ottoman that interests you to view the model's *details page*. Here on the details page, you will find information about the model, such as the number of likes, material count, when the model was last modified, and more.

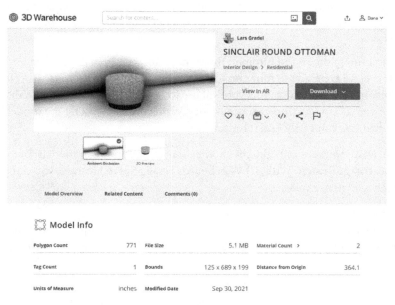

Figure 7.25: Example of a model's details page

You can also preview the model in 3D from the details page. To do this, click on the **3D Preview** option under the model's thumbnail image. You can orbit to view the model from different angles and open the panel on the right to access other tools such as **Views** and **Zoom Extents**.

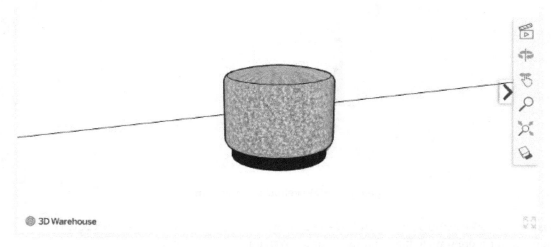

Figure 7.26: In the 3D preview, open the panel on the right side for other tools

> **Tip – Liked models**
>
> Click the *heart* icon if you find a model that you like but are not done searching. Once you are done searching, you can view all your liked models from your profile by clicking your name in the upper right.

Take some time to browse the round ottoman thumbnails and compare details. Once you find one that catches your eye, we are ready to move on to the next section, *3D Warehouse II – Downloading, reviewing, and importing*. This is the model you will use to download and import into the `Chapter 7- Living Room Elevations` practice model. We recommend liking the model by clicking the *heart* icon so that you can easily find it for future use.

Before moving forward, we want to highlight another way to find the right models for your projects on 3D Warehouse: **Image Search**. With 3D Warehouse's **Image Search** feature, you can find models that visually match a reference image.

Simply click the image icon 🖼 in the search box. From here, you can either browse your computer for an image or drag and drop an image. 3D Warehouse will populate similar models based on your reference image. As an example, let's use the following Chesterfield chair as a reference image:

Figure 7.27: Chesterfield chair reference image

See *Figure 7.28* for the search results based on the Chesterfield chair reference image.

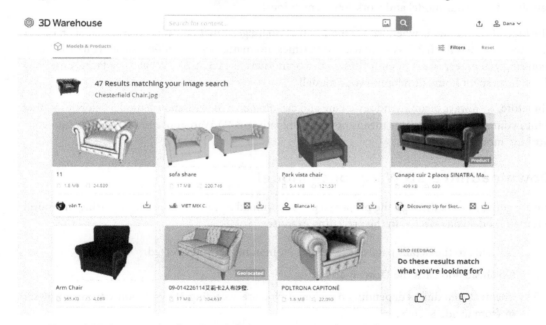

Figure 7.28: An example of 3D Warehouse's Image Search feature using a Chesterfield chair

Isn't this awesome? The **Image Search** feature is especially helpful when you want to illustrate the overall feeling of a design and do not need exact specifications.

We encourage you to explore in 3D Warehouse. It is incredible what you can find. Just to warn you, 3D Warehouse is an interesting rabbit hole you can get lost in for hours! It is also an opportunity to examine and learn how other people build and organize models.

> **Extra tip for finding well-designed models**
>
> When you find a model you like, you can easily access other models by the same author by clicking on the author's name or icon in the upper-right corner of the model's details page.

In the next section, we will walk through the proper way to download, review, and import objects from 3D Warehouse into your own SketchUp models. We will also introduce **Live Components**.

3D Warehouse II – Downloading, reviewing, and importing

A 3D Warehouse model is a complete and independent SketchUp model. This means it has imported images, tags, components, and styles. When you import a 3D Warehouse model directly into your own working model, you are bringing all those elements into your model. This could lead to a lot of unwanted information and geometry, clogging up or even corrupting your file.

For instance, we have seen models triple in size due to unreasonably large 3D Warehouse files. This can slow down your model and workflow tremendously.

The biggest nightmare is when we see models that no longer function properly because of an object directly imported from 3D Warehouse. Sometimes, no matter what you do, you can't fix the issue, requiring you to recreate your entire design in a brand-new SketchUp file. What a headache, especially if you have spent hours developing your model!

Therefore, we always recommend reviewing and cleaning up a 3D Warehouse model before dropping it into your active project. This means never downloading a 3D Warehouse model directly into your working model.

Downloading a 3D Warehouse model

We are going to walk through the proper steps to download a 3D Warehouse file by using the round ottoman model you selected in the preceding exercise:

1. Navigate to the details page of the round ottoman model you selected.
2. Go ahead and click the **Download** button.
3. The next step differs depending on whether you are accessing 3D Warehouse from a browser or from inside SketchUp:

    -   If you are accessing 3D Warehouse from a browser, you will be prompted to select a file type to download. Select **SketchUp File** from the drop-down menu. The file automatically saves to your computer's Downloads folder.

Figure 7.29: Download options from 3D Warehouse browser

- If you are accessing 3D Warehouse inside SketchUp, a popup will appear asking whether you want to load the file directly into your current SketchUp file.

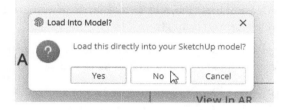

Figure 7.30: Download options from 3D Warehouse inside SketchUp

4. Click the **No** button. This is an important step. If you click the **Yes** button, you are allowing SketchUp to import the entire 3D Warehouse model and all its elements into your current SketchUp file. Remember, this can be dangerous!

5. After clicking the **No** button, a browser will appear enabling you to pick a location to download the file.

Now, you can open the downloaded model as a separate SketchUp file and review the content before importing.

Reviewing (and cleaning) a 3D Warehouse model

Navigate to the downloaded 3D Warehouse file and open it. From here, you can evaluate the model and, if necessary, clean it up to ensure it is ready to be imported. Use the following tips when evaluating and cleaning the file:

- *Condense tags* – Remember, when you import a 3D Warehouse model into your working model, the tags come along too. To avoid confusion and unneeded tags in your working model, delete all tags, leaving everything on the **Untagged** tag.

- *Delete unwanted objects* – Take a close look at the model from all directions. Is there anything you don't need? Now is the time to delete unwanted items. We recommend clicking **Zoom Extents** to check for stray groups or geometry.

- *Adjust the geometry* – You always want to limit geometry. Excessive edges and faces can slow down a model. View hidden geometry by clicking **Hidden Geometry** from the **View** menu. One way to manually reduce geometry is to soften the edges. However, depending on the amount of extra geometry, it may be best to ditch the file altogether and consider another model for your project.

- *Create groups and/or components* – A basic reminder that every face and its edges in a model should be grouped together so the geometry does not stick together. You decide whether to make it a group or a component.

- *Scaling the model* – No doubt, at some point, you will download a bowl of fruit from 3D Warehouse that is larger than a two-story building. Before copying the object to your working model, use the **Tape Measure** tool (shortcut *T*) to determine the current size. Then, use the **Scale** tool (shortcut *S*) to resize accordingly.

- *Purge unused components and materials* – Doing this avoids importing unused things into your working model. (Refer to *Chapter 3* for how to use **Purge Unused**.)

Remember to save the model after cleaning it up!

Following these tips can add extra time upfront to your workflow, but trust us, it will save you time down the road and reduce the chances of something going terribly wrong.

Importing a 3D Warehouse model

After your 3D Warehouse model is cleaned up, importing it into your working model is straightforward:

1. Open the `Chapter 7- Living Room Elevations` practice file if it is not already opened.

2. Choose **Import...** from the **File** menu. Navigate to the round ottoman file you downloaded; make sure you use the cleaned-up version. Select the file and click **Import**.

   SketchUp will return you to the practice model. Without clicking, move your mouse around the screen. You will notice that the round ottoman is connected to your cursor.

3. Click anywhere in the model to place the ottoman.

4. Move the ottoman so that it is in the correct location based on the imported CAD plan. Zoom in to make sure that the object is not floating above the floor. The bottom of the ottoman should be touching the top of the floor.

5. Since there are two ottomans in the space, we will make a copy of it. Make sure the object is a component before copying it. (When a file is imported into a model, it is imported as a component.

It should be a component, but it is always best to check.) Make a copy of the component using the **Move + Copy** command. Remember to click on an endpoint and lock in the axis.

When you are done, this is what your model should look like (with your round ottoman instead):

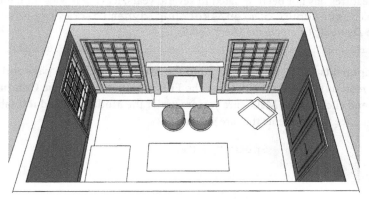

Figure 7.31: Two round ottomans aligned with the CAD plan

6.   Save your model.

> **An alternative way to add a 3D Warehouse model**
>
> Rather than importing a 3D Warehouse model into your working model, you can also select the group/component, press *Ctrl* (or ⌘) + *C*, then click in the practice model and press *Ctrl* (or ⌘) + *V*.

Is it ever okay to import a 3D Warehouse model directly into your SketchUp file from the 3D Warehouse interface? At the beginning of this section, we said to *never* import a 3D Warehouse model directly into an active project. This is a classic *never say never* situation, because the answer is actually *yes*, but only after you have determined that a 3D Warehouse model is deemed clean. It should then be safe to import directly into your model. We recommend that you *like* clean models that you find or add them to a personal collection; that way, you can easily access them in the future. Models that you upload to 3D Warehouse should also be okay to import directly.

We have one last 3D Warehouse feature we want to share before wrapping up this chapter: **Live Components**.

Introduction to Live Components

Live Components are an incredible feature that SketchUp keeps making better and better! They are configurable components that allow you to change parameters and see the updates in real time. They are the newer, more powerful version of **Dynamic Components**.

> **For those who are not familiar with Dynamic Components**
>
> If you are not familiar with Dynamic Components, they are components that have certain parameters and attributes, similar to spreadsheet functions. At the time of writing, the Dynamic Components features has not been updated in several years, leaving it with limitations. Visit `https://help.sketchup.com/en/sketchup/dynamic-components-users-guide` for the *Dynamic Components User's Guide.*

To find Live Components in 3D Warehouse, go to the **My 3D Warehouse** page and click on the magnifying glass icon in the search field. Click the **Filters** icon, turn on **Live Component** under **Specialty Filters**, and click **Apply**. Make sure you are under the **Models & Products** tab. From here, you can find all the Live Components that are available.

Figure 7.32: Turn on Live Components under Specialty Filters when searching in 3D Warehouse

Take a look at the following Live Component of a door already downloaded and imported into a working SketchUp model of a hotel room:

Figure 7.33: Single swing door Live Component

As you can see, the door is too small. We need to adjust the Live Component to fit in the opening. Just like editing a normal component in SketchUp, you can either double-click on the Live Component or right-click and select **Configure Live Component** to edit it. The **Configure Live Component** window will appear. (You can also configure a Live Component directly on the model's details page in 3D Warehouse before inserting it into your working model.)

From the **Configure Live Component** window, we will adjust the width and height of the door to match the opening in the SketchUp model, which is 36" W x 96" H. We will also change the **Paint** color to better match the rest of the room and flip the door swing direction.

Here is what the **Configure Live Component** window looks like after we configured it to meet our needs:

Figure 7.34: Configure Live Component window

It's that easy! There are even options to change the panel style, hardware finish, and more.

At this time, users are not able to create their own custom Live Components. The good news is that SketchUp stated that they are working on this functionality. Fingers crossed that it happens soon!

More on Live Components

Here is a video with more information on Live Components: https://video.sketchup.com/training/watch/h8nPkYqtUMgwASRtCWPP3p.

There you have it! It might take some time and experience to understand how to best navigate and use 3D Warehouse. Once you do, it will become an invaluable resource for design content, ideas, and inspiration.

Summary

This chapter was all about adding interior details to a model. We learned how to set up imported AutoCAD elevations and build intricate interior architectural elements by tracing the elevations. We also took a deep dive into 3D Warehouse, imported a round ottoman to the practice model, and learned about Live Components.

In the next chapter, we will use SketchUp's built-in tools to model a coffee table, an armchair, and a decorative tray. Plus, we will share some of our favorite extensions for modeling furniture.

Modeling Furniture – From the Basics to Intricacy

In *Chapter 7*, we took a deep dive into 3D Warehouse. There is no doubt that 3D Warehouse is a valuable resource for finding hundreds of thousands of ready-made models. However, what happens when your client wants to see the exact coffee table or armchair that you specified in the 3D model? Sometimes, placeholder furniture doesn't cut it.

In this chapter, we will use SketchUp's native tools to model a simple coffee table, a more complex armchair, and a decorative tray. We will also show how to use one of our favorite extensions in the *Modeling an armchair using manufacturer specifications* section, plus share a few other nifty extensions in the final section, *Go-to extensions for modeling furniture*. Like most things SketchUp-related, modeling furniture from scratch requires organization and attention to detail. We will demonstrate techniques throughout the following exercises that will give you the confidence to take on more challenging furniture.

In this chapter, we will cover the following topics:

- Modeling a coffee table
- Modeling an armchair using manufacturer specifications
- Modeling a decorative tray using radial array
- Go-to extensions for modeling furniture

Technical requirements

This chapter requires the following software and files:

- SketchUp Pro or Studio

- Download the practice file from 3D Warehouse named Chapter 8- Modeling Furniture or download it from https://3dwarehouse.sketchup.com/model/7415c5ce-45ad-4abe-8439-0b04adc2872f/Chapter-8-Modeling-Furniture

Modeling a coffee table

To get our feet wet in modeling furniture, we will start with the coffee table shown in *Figure 8.1*.

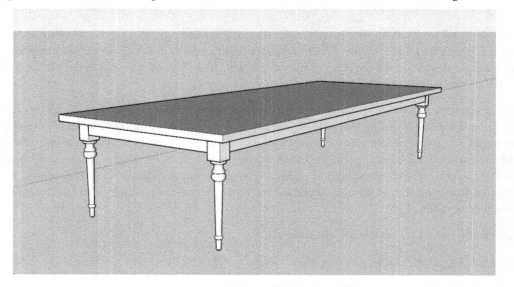

Figure 8.1: Coffee table

For this exercise, we will use only native SketchUp tools.

From 3D Warehouse, download the SketchUp file named Chapter 8- Modeling Furniture. When you open the model, you will see an imported image of a turned table leg on the right and an open space on the left. Use the open space to the left of the leg image to build the coffee table.

> **Reminder to model in the upper-right quadrant**
> It is best practice to always start your model on or near the origin and in the upper-right quadrant.

We will begin by building the top of the coffee table.

Modeling the top of the coffee table

The first step is to model the top of the coffee table. Don't forget to be in **Top** view when creating shapes:

1. Activate the **Rectangle** tool (shortcut *R*), click the *up* arrow to lock in on the blue/z-axis, click and release in the open space to the left of the imported image, type 2 ' 6 , 6 ' 6, and press *Enter*.

Using the Inches template

As we learned in *Chapter 1*, we do not need to type the inch marks (") in the **Measurements** box when using the Inches template, which saves us time.

---

2. Make the top 1 " thick by using the **Push/Pull** tool (shortcut *P*). Extrude the face upward.
3. Triple-click the top and make it a group.
4. Move the group up 1 ' 3 " (lock in the blue/z-axis) so you are not modeling below the red/x-axis. (The overall height of the coffee table will end up at 1 ' - 4 ".)

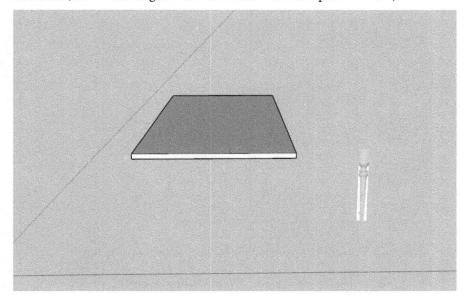

Figure 8.2: Move tabletop group 1'3" up on the blue/z-axis

Next, we will model a table leg using an imported image as a reference.

Modeling the table leg using an imported image

Oftentimes, we are given an image and overall dimensions for furniture. Detailed dimensions are rarely provided. Depending on the quality of the image, you can import it into SketchUp. Then, instead of eyeballing the proportions for elaborate details, you can use the image as a reference for tracing. We use this technique all the time.

Let's try it out with the imported image to create a turned coffee table leg:

5. Zoom into the imported image of the leg. Use the **Front** view camera setting so you begin with a straight-on, accurate view of the leg.

6. Activate the **Line** tool (shortcut L) and hover your mouse over the bottom of the image until you see the **Midpoint in Image** ScreenTip. Click and release your mouse on the midpoint. Move your mouse slightly up and lock in the blue/z-axis by tapping the *up* arrow. Type 12 (or 12 ") and press *Enter*.

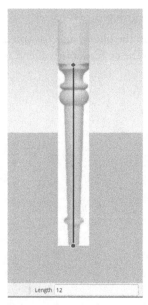

Figure 8.3: Draw a 12″ line starting at the image's bottom midpoint

From here, we will create a face to extrude with the **Follow Me** tool.

7. Trace just the left side of the leg's profile by drawing lines (shortcut L) and arcs (shortcut A). You can overlap edges to create the shape you want, then erase the extra. Make the face a group. Do not worry about the top block for now. We will create it separately.

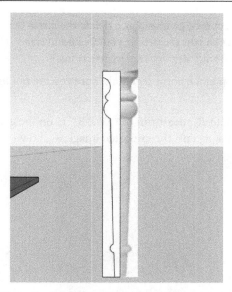

Figure 8.4: Trace the left side of the leg's profile and make it a group

8. Get into **Edit** mode of the group and use the **Circle** tool (shortcut *C*) to create a path for extrusion. The center of the circle needs to align with the lower-right endpoint of the leg profile that we just drew for **Follow Me** to work properly (see *Figure 8.5*).

    This means your first click should be on the lower-right endpoint of the group (or the middle of the image).

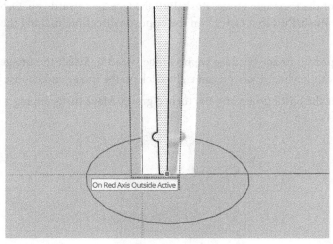

Figure 8.5: The circle's center needs to align with the lower-right endpoint of the group

9. Use the **Follow Me** tool to extrude the face and create the turned portion of the leg.

If everything extruded properly, go ahead and delete the circle that we used for the extrusion path. If not, you may have to edit the profile you created in *step 7*. (Review *Chapter 2* for how to use the **Follow Me** tool with step-by-step instructions.)

Next, we will build the top block of the leg. Make sure you are not in **Edit** mode of the turned portion of the leg:

10. Make a **Rectangle** (shortcut *R*) measuring 2 " W x 3 " H on the green/y-axis. The rectangle's face should be perfectly flat against the imported image, as shown in *Figure 8.6*. Make the face a group.

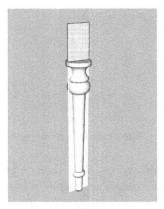

Figure 8.6: Make a 2" x 3" rectangle on the green/y-axis, flat against the imported image

11. In **Edit** mode of the rectangle group, **Push/Pull** the face 1 " toward you. Orbit around to the other side and **Push/Pull** that face 1 " in the opposite direction, making the block a total of 2 " thick.

12. Delete the imported image because we no longer need it. Select the image and tap *Del* or *backspace* on your keyboard, or you can right-click on the image and choose **Erase**.

13. Group together the block group and the turned group. Make the grouping a component and name it `Table-Leg`.

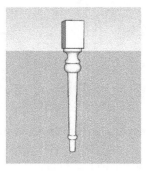

Figure 8.7: The finished table leg

14. Don't forget to save your model!

Now, it's time to connect the table leg to the tabletop by placing guide lines.

Placing the table legs using guide lines

We will use the **Tape Measure** tool to add guide lines to the bottom of the tabletop. We will add the table legs where the guide lines intersect:

15. Orbit under the tabletop. Use the **Tape Measure** tool (shortcut *T*) to create four guide lines, 2 " from each edge. As always, remember to lock in the axis.

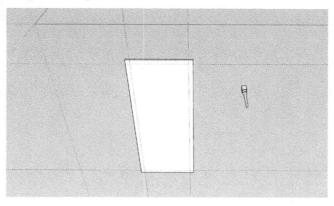

Figure 8.8: Create four guide lines, 2″ from each edge, under the tabletop using the Tape Measure tool

16. Move the table leg component using the **Move** tool (shortcut *M*) to align to an intersection of guide lines. Make sure to grab a corner of the component and look for the **Intersection** ScreenTip to ensure you are snapped to the correct spot.

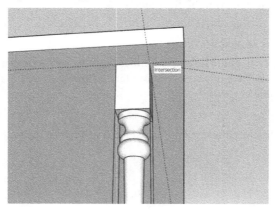

Figure 8.9: Move the table leg to align with the intersection of guide lines

17. Copy the leg component by using the **Move + Copy** command so you copy along the axis and align with the guide lines.

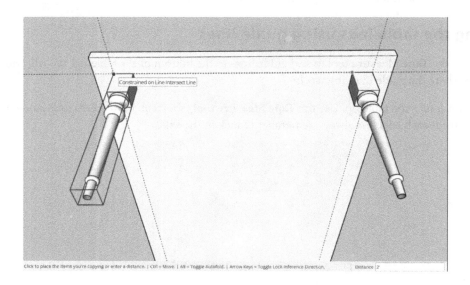

Figure 8.10: Use the Move tool plus the Ctrl key (or Opt on macOS) to copy the leg component

(Alternatively, use the **Flip** tool + *Ctrl* (or *Opt* on macOS) to mirror and copy the leg component to the other side of the table, which is our preferred method. Review *Chapter 1* for how to use the **Flip** tool.)

18. Repeat the steps for the remaining table legs.

19. Delete the four guide lines by erasing them individually. Alternatively, erase them all at once by choosing **Delete Guides** from the **Edit** menu.

Alternative option for creating guide lines

Rather than placing multiple guide lines, sometimes it's more efficient to use the **Offset** tool. For this example, we could have offset the bottom face of the tabletop by 2 " to create guides for where to place the table legs.

We are almost done building our coffee table! We just need to add the apron.

Creating the apron

The last step is to draw the apron:

20. Draw a 1" W x 2" H rectangle at the top of one of the table legs. Do not be in **Edit** mode of the table leg.

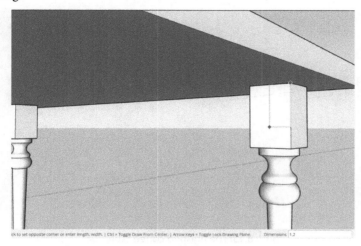

Figure 8.11: Draw a 1" x 2" rectangle

21. Use the **Push/Pull** tool (shortcut *P*) to extrude the face to the opposite leg. Triple-click the apron and make it a component. Name it `Table-Apron#1`.

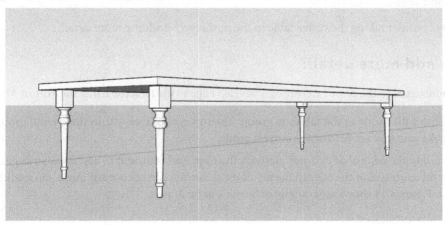

Figure 8.12: Push/Pull the face to the opposite leg and make it a component

22. Copy the apron component with **Move** + *Ctrl* (or *Opt* on macOS) to the opposite side of the table.

23. Repeat *steps 20* through *22* to make and copy the apron on the shorter sides of the table. Name the new apron component `Table-Apron#2`.

24. Zoom out a bit so you can see the coffee table better. We now have a tabletop group, four leg components, and the apron. Select all these entities and make them a grouping.

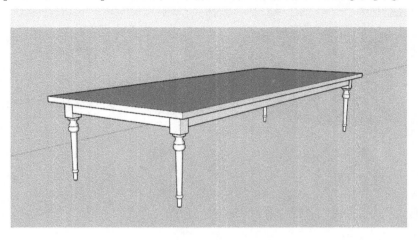

Figure 8.13: The finished coffee table

25. Save your model, and there you have it! The finished coffee table.

If you would like to continue furnishing the living room that we built in *Chapter 7*, go ahead and add the coffee table to that SketchUp file.

Or, you may consider taking the coffee table to the next level by adding more detail…

Want to add more detail?

Let's add more detail to the piece by creating a beveled edge to the tabletop using the **Follow Me** tool:

26. Get into **Edit** mode of the tabletop group. The top group lives within the overall grouping, so make sure you are editing the correct group.

27. Zoom into the edge of any corner. Activate the **Line** tool (shortcut *L*) and draw an angled line from the midpoint of the edge to the top of the table. You can choose any angle you think looks good. *Figure 8.14* shows an example of how it can be drawn.

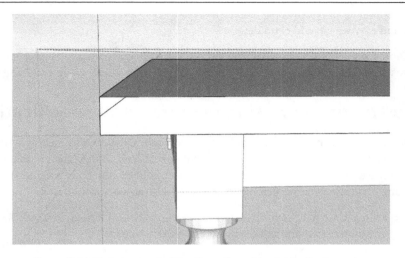

Figure 8.14: Make an angled line from the midpoint to the top edge

Making a chamfered edge

Use the **Protractor** tool to create a 45-degree angled guide line for a chamfered edge. Alternatively, depending on how you are drawing the 45-degree angled line, SketchUp may turn the line magenta as an inference to tell you that the line is at a 45-degree angle. Getting used to the inferencing system takes practice.

28. Still in **Edit** mode, click the top face of the table, activate the **Follow Me** command, and then immediately click the face of the angled corner.

Voila, you created a beveled top!

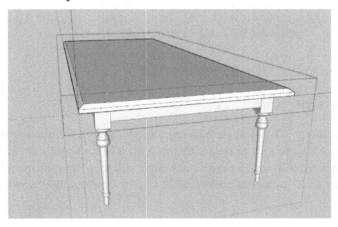

Figure 8.15: Use Follow Me to create a beveled top

This is a quick and easy way to add extra detail!

In the next section, we will build a more complex furniture piece based on manufacturer specifications and images. We will also introduce a nifty extension to enhance your workflow for modeling furniture.

Modeling an armchair using manufacturer specifications

So, your client wants to see the exact armchair you specified in SketchUp? Being able to visualize exact furniture in a space will strengthen the trust that clients have in designers to make the right decisions and may lead to more creative freedom to select bold or expensive furniture. This often requires modeling furniture from scratch based on manufacturer specifications.

In the following exercise, we will walk through how to build the *RH Thaddeus Track Armchair* in *Figure 8.16* using the dimensions and images provided by RH's website.

Figure 8.16: Thaddeus Track Armchair by RH

Before getting started, we will evaluate the armchair and gather information.

Evaluating the armchair

First things first; evaluating. When you are building a model from scratch based on manufacturer information, it is always best to start by familiarizing yourself with the piece of furniture. What are the dimensions? What SketchUp tools or extensions might you use? Does the manufacturer provide images of the furniture piece from multiple angles? This is the time to gather information.

> **Reminder to search 3D Warehouse**
>
> Remember to look in 3D Warehouse before building furniture from scratch. Who knows, maybe someone else already built it! Type the product name or the manufacturer name into the search box. Using variations of the name can help populate different search results. In this example, we could not find a 3D Warehouse model of the *RH Thaddeus Track Armchair*.

In a perfect world, we would have access to detailed AutoCAD drawings of the furniture piece. Then, we could import those drawings into SketchUp and trace them. However, that is rarely reality. So, where do we start? In most cases, we use pictures of the furniture piece along with the dimensions provided by the manufacturer.

Here are the dimensions we gathered from RH's website:

- The overall dimensions are 26¾" W x 32¼" D x 30" H.

- The metal frame is ¾" thick.

In addition, we saved an image of the armchair from RH that we will use throughout the exercise (see *Figure 8.17*). Let's start by building the metal frame.

Building the metal frame

In the previous section, *Modeling a coffee table*, you learned how tracing an image can help with nailing down proportions when we built the coffee table leg. We will use that same technique for building the armchair.

Open the practice model named Chapter 8- Modeling Furniture. Click on the **Scene** tab named Modeling Armchair. You will see an imported image of the armchair's side profile. This image is from the RH website. We know the chair's overall depth is 32.25" and height is 30". The dimensions of the imported image match that.

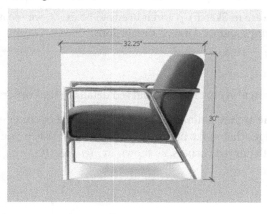

Figure 8.17: The imported image dimensions are based on the overall chair dimensions

We will use this image to build the metal frame by tracing it:

1. Trace the chair arm, arm support, and legs on top of the imported image. Lock in the axis when you can and use guide lines.

    Match what you see in *Figure 8.18*. Remember that the frame is .75" thick.

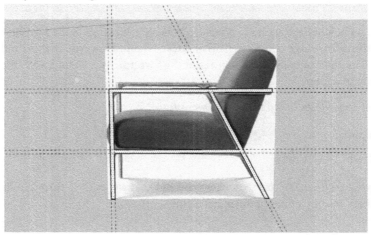

Figure 8.18: Trace the chair arm, arm support, and legs using guide lines

Note about image distortion

It is difficult to photograph anything straight on. That means there is always some distortion in images of furniture. We do the best we can to match the furniture piece and lock in the axis when we know something is supposed to be straight, regardless of how straight it is in the image. For example, you should lock in on the red/x-axis when tracing the top of the chair's arm, even though the line will not perfectly match what is on the image.

If you are building furniture in SketchUp and it needs to be exact, we recommend requesting detailed AutoCAD drawings and/or detailed dimensions.

2. Delete the guide lines.

3. Use the **Arc** tool (shortcut *A*) to create the curved details in the corners based on the image.

    As you are adding the arches, a new face may appear in the opening of the arm. Delete that face as well as the edges that make up the original corners. When you are done, you should have just one face with curved corners, as shown in *Figure 8.19*.

Figure 8.19: Add the curved details using the Arc tool

4.   **Push/Pull** (shortcut *P*) the face .75" away from you, toward the inside of the chair.

5.   Triple-click what you just built and group it. Make the group a component and name it `Chair-Side Frame`.

     We just built one side of the metal frame. The next step is to copy the component we just built to the other side of the chair:

6.   Select the `Chair-Side Frame` component and **Copy + Move** it 26" on the green/y-axis.

7.   Use the **Tape Measure** tool (shortcut *T*) to make sure that the overall distance from one end of the frame to the other end is a total of 2' 2 3/4" (26.75"). Adjust it if needed.

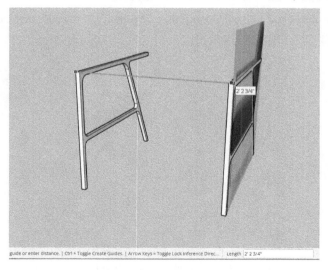

Figure 8.20: Total width should be 2′ 2¾″

Now, we will connect the two side frames by adding stretchers, starting with the upper back stretcher:

8. Turn off the visibility for the tag named `Chair-Imported Image`.

9. Draw a `.75" x .75"` square on the green/y-axis at the top, inside of one of the side frames.

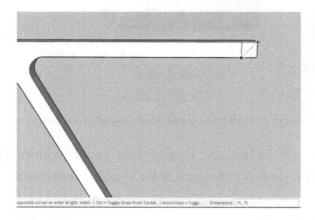

Figure 8.21: Draw a .75" x .75" square on the green/y-axis

10. Activate the **Push/Pull** tool (shortcut *P*) and extrude the square face to meet the inside of the opposite side frame. Remember to snap to an endpoint.

11. Triple-click the object and make it a component. Name it `Chair-Stretcher`.

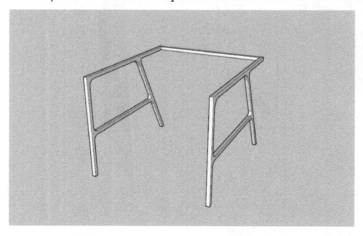

Figure 8.22: Push/Pull the face to the opposite side frame and make it a component

12. Copy the stretcher component with **Move** + *Ctrl* (or *Opt* on macOS) to the lower back of the chair and the lower front of the chair. There should now be a total of three stretchers.

13. Create a new tag called Chair-Frame. Select all parts of the metal frame and assign them to the tag you just created.

We built the metal frame! Here is what your model should look like so far:

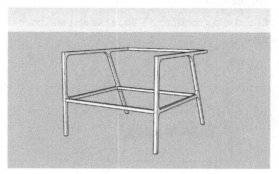

Figure 8.23: Metal frame

Let's soften the edges of the metal frame to add realism.

Softening the metal frame

Softening the edges of the frame will make the chair look more realistic. Small details like this go far in SketchUp:

14. Simply right-click the side frame component and select **Soften/Smooth Edges**. Use the slider in the **Soften Edges** box until all the edges disappear. Remember to check the box next to **Soften coplanar**.

15. Do the same for the stretcher component.

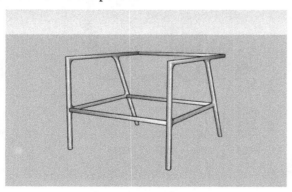

Figure 8.24: Metal frame after softening the edges

Next, we will build the armchair's cushions.

Creating the cushions

Using the tracing technique, we will create the seat and back cushions:

16. Turn on the visibility for the `Chair-Imported Image` tag.

17. Using lines (shortcut *L*) and arcs (shortcut *A*), trace the seat and back cushions to create a new face. Make the face a group.

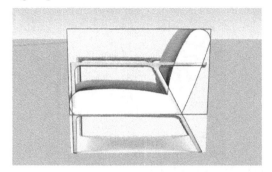

Figure 8.25: Trace the seat and back cushions and make the face a group

> **Tip – turn off tags**
> If the metal frame is getting in the way of tracing the cushions, turn off its visibility and turn it back on after you are done tracing.

18. Get into **Edit** mode of the cushion group and extrude the face `26"` using the **Push/Pull** tool to meet the inside of the opposite side frame.

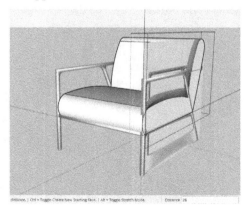

Figure 8.26: Push/pull the face 26" to meet the opposite side frame

19. Still in **Edit** mode of the cushions, select the face that is flush with the imported image. **Push/ Pull** that face .75" away from you so that it aligns with the inside of the metal frame, no longer on the outside of the frame.

20. Turn off the visibility for the Chair-Imported Image tag. Here is what your chair should look like:

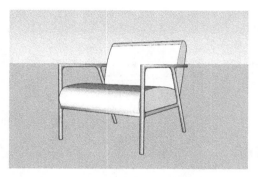

Figure 8.27: Seat and back cushions added

21. Create a new tag named Chair-Cushions. Select the cushion group and assign it to that tag.

22. Make all the chair's groups and components one large group (including the metal frame) and save your model.

You are ready to add the final touch. We will show you an easy way to make the cushions look more realistic using the **RoundCorner** extension by *Fredo6*.

Adding a realistic touch using the RoundCorner extension by Fredo6

Rounding edges and corners can make three-dimensional objects appear less computer-generated. However, the process of curving an edge in SketchUp can be a major headache – especially with organic shapes such as cushions. You end up with multiple **Follow Me** functions plus copying and moving, and so on.

The **RoundCorner** plugin by *Fredo6* is useful for quickly rounding the edges and corners of 3D shapes. This extension will take your models to the next level with just a few easy steps. It is an all-star extension!

> **Note about the RoundCorner extension**
>
> There is a free trial period of 30 days to use **RoundCorner**. After the trial period, you can either purchase the individual plugin or purchase the *Fredo6Bundle* license for access to multiple plugins by *Fredo6*, including **RoundCorner**.
>
> Visit https://sketchucation.com/plugin/1173-roundcorner for an overview of **RounderCorner** and to download the extension.

RoundCorner comes with three different options: **Round**, **Sharp**, and **Bevel**. For this exercise, we are going to use the **Round** option to make our cushions look more convincing.

The following instructions were written with the assumption that you already have the **RoundCorner** extension installed (if you do not have the extension installed, refer to *Chapter 6* for detailed steps on how to install extensions):

23. Get into **Edit** mode of the cushions and double-click on one of the side faces.

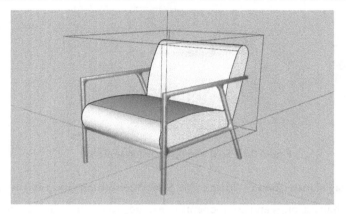

Figure 8.28: Double-click on the cushion's side face

24. Select the **Round Corner** button from the *Fredo6* plugin.

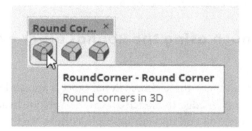

Figure 8.29: Select the Round Corner button

A toolbar will appear with a variety of different settings.

25. Under the **ROUNDING PARAMETERS** option, select the **Offset** button and type 1". Click **OK**. We just set the offset value to one inch.

26. Under the **ROUNDING PARAMETERS** option, select the **# Seg.** button and type 4. Click **OK**. We just set the number of segments for rounding to four. See *Figure 8.30* for what **ROUNDING PARAMETERS** should look like.

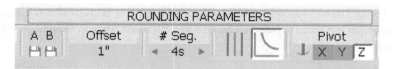

Figure 8.30: Specify 1" for Offset and 4s for # Seg.

27. Click somewhere in open space in your model to run the script. You will see a **Click to Execute** ScreenTip.

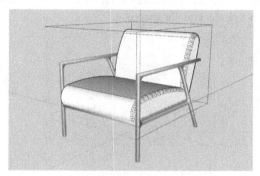

Figure 8.31: The rounded cushion edge after running the script

You may want to experiment with different offset and segment values until you get the look you desire.

28. Follow *steps 23* through *27* to round the edges on the other side of the cushion.

29. Right-click the cushion group and select **Soften/Smooth Edges**. Use the **Soften Edges** slider to soften the cushions less or more.

30. Save your model.

We started with boxy cushions and ended with more realistic, softer cushions by using *Fredo6's* **RoundCorner** extension. Our armchair is now complete. Take a look at the 3D model (on the left) next to the actual RH chair (on the right) in *Figure 8.32*.

Figure 8.32: The completed armchair

Mastering complex furniture takes time and practice. We hope this exercise showed you that there are techniques and tools out there to help you take on any furniture piece in SketchUp. Where there's a will, there's a way.

The next section of this chapter covers how to use radial array by building a decorative tray.

Modeling a decorative tray using radial array

For this exercise, let's model the round decorative tray in *Figure 8.33*. In the process, we will do a radial array, which arranges items in a circle, equally spaced.

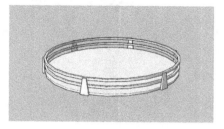

Figure 8.33: Decorative tray

We will start by creating the two-dimensional (2D) framework.

Creating the tray's 2D framework

Open a new SketchUp file, choose the **Architectural Inches** template, and delete the scale figure. Get into **Top** view using the **Views** toolbar or under **Camera | Standard Views | Top**:

1. Draw an 18" diameter circle: Activate the **Circle** tool (shortcut *C*), click and release your mouse anywhere, type 9, and press *Enter*. Group it.

How to adjust the number of edges for a circle

By default, a circle in SketchUp consists of 24 edges. The greater the number of edges a circle has, the smoother its appearance will be. You can adjust the number of sides a circle has by typing a value into the **Measurements** box immediately after activating the **Circle** tool. For example, follow these steps to draw an 18" circle with 40 sides: Activate the **Circle** tool, immediately type 40, press *Enter*, click once to start the circle, type 9 (for the radius), and *Enter*.

Alternatively, you can type 40s into the **Measurements** box immediately after creating the circle while the **Circle** tool is still activated.

For this exercise, create the circle with 24 sides or more.

---

2. Activate the **Tape Measure** tool (shortcut *T*) and hover over the circle's center until you snap to it. Add horizontal and vertical guide lines through the center.

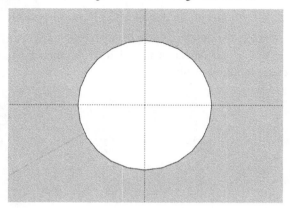

Figure 8.34: Place guide lines through the circle's center

3. Draw a 1" x .25" rectangle just outside the top of the circle. Center the rectangle with the guide line. Then, select the rectangle and make it a component. Name it Tray-Post.

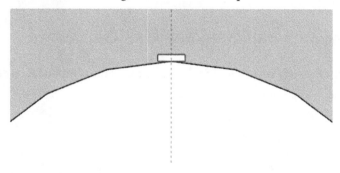

Figure 8.35: Post component centered on the guide line

Next, we will array the post component around the circle.

Making copies with radial array

You are already familiar with creating multiple copies using **Move** and the copy modifier key (*Ctrl* on Windows or *Opt* on macOS). The same process can be used with the **Rotate** command to create a radial array. Let's give it a go!

4. Select the Tray-Post component and activate the **Rotate** tool (shortcut *Q*). Your cursor will change to the *rotate* icon.

5. First, click once in the center of the circle where the two guide lines intersect to select the origin. (Remember to click and release.)

6. The second click should be on the top midpoint of the post component.

7. Immediately tap the *Ctrl* key (or the *Opt* key on macOS) on the keyboard. Your cursor should now be the *rotate* icon with a plus sign at its upper left. Without clicking, move the cursor a bit to the right. Your screen should look like this:

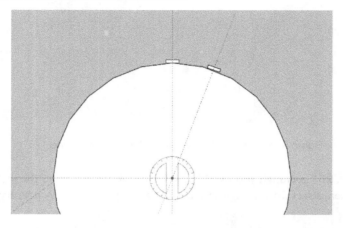

Figure 8.36: Without clicking, move the cursor a bit to the right

8. Type 60 and press *Enter*. We just told SketchUp to rotate the component 60 degrees.

9. Type 5x and press *Enter* to make five copies.

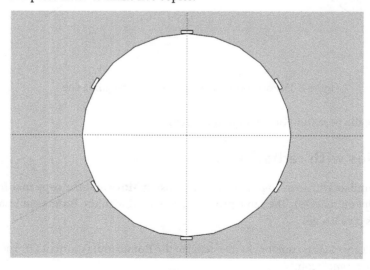

Figure 8.37: Component copied and arranged around the circle

10. Delete the guide lines and save your model.

Time to make the 2D framework 3D.

Extruding the framework and adding final details

In these final steps, we will add depth to the 2D framework and create the final details:

11. Get into **Edit** mode of one of the post components and **Push/Pull** the face up 2 ".

12. Get into **Edit** mode of the circle group and **Push/Pull** the face up .25 ". Then, make it a component and name it `Tray-Circle`.

We will use the **Move + Copy** command to make copies of the circle component.

13. Activate the **Move** tool (shortcut *M*), tap the *Ctrl* key (or the *Opt* key on macOS), click an endpoint on the circle, tap the *up* arrow to lock in the blue/z-axis, move your mouse slightly up, type 1.75, and press *Enter*.

14. Immediately type 2/ and press *Enter*.

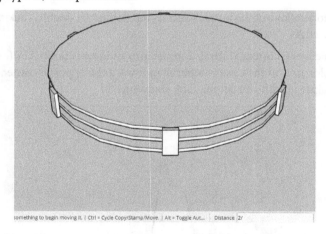

something to begin moving it. | Ctrl = Cycle Copy/Stamp/Move. | Alt = Toggle Aut... | Distance 2/

Figure 8.38: Make a copy of the circle component using Move + Copy and 2/

15. Right-click on the bottom circle component and select **Make Unique**.

16. Get into **Edit** mode of the top circle component. **Offset** (shortcut *F*) the circle .25 " inward and **Push/Pull** (shortcut *P*) the inner face .25 " to cut an opening.

There should now be an opening in the middle circle since the top and middle circles are components.

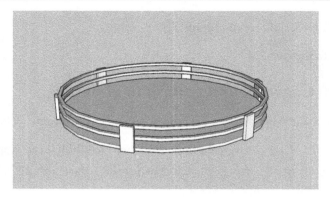

Figure 8.39: Cut openings in the top two circles

17. Select all groups and components of the tray with a selection box and make them a group.

    This looks great, but with just a few extra clicks, we can add more interest. We are going to use the **Scale** tool to taper the vertical posts. In addition to resizing objects, the **Scale** tool can also scale a single selected surface and directly affect the geometry attached to it.

18. Get into **Edit** mode of one of the posts. Select its top surface by double-clicking to activate the face and its four edges.

19. Activate the **Scale** tool (shortcut S). Grab a corner grip and press the *Ctrl* key (or *Opt* on macOS) once, which scales around the center rather than toward the opposite corner. Then, move the grip inward to taper it until you get the look you want.

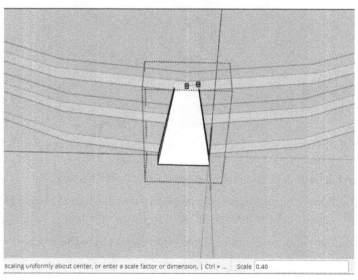

scaling uniformly about center, or enter a scale factor or dimension. | Ctrl = ...   Scale 0.40

Figure 8.40: Use the Scale tool to taper

20. Lastly, to make the tray appear more smooth, you can use **Soften/Smooth**. *Figure 8.41* shows the tray with softened edges.

21. Press *Ctrl* or ⌘ + *S* to save your model.

Place this tray on any coffee table or console to add a more realistic touch. You can add additional accessories to the tray and make it pop more. We will talk about the benefits of adding accessories to your SketchUp models in *Chapter 10*.

Figure 8.41: The finished decorative tray with softened edges and accessories from 3D Warehouse

The next, and final, section of this chapter is dedicated to reviewing helpful extensions for modeling furniture quickly and accurately.

Go-to extensions for modeling furniture

As you learned in *Chapter 6*, utilizing extensions is one way to broaden your SketchUp toolbox. In addition to the **RoundCorner** plugin by *Fredo6*, we use the following extensions when building furniture:

- **CLF Shape Bender** by *Chris Fullmer* – Take any group or component in your model and bend it along a pre-drawn path. This is a simple concept with a very powerful function. We use this extension when building curved furniture, such as organic sofas and circular consoles.

  Here is a link to download CLF Shape Bender: `https://extensions.sketchup.com/extension/8a4d10ff-40f3-4885-b8ba-1dac2b941885/clf-shape-bender`.

- **Soap Skin & Bubble** by *Josef L* – This extension offers the ability to easily create a multi-faceted face and inflate or deflate the created face. It is especially useful for modeling tufted furniture and complex shapes.

  Here is a link to download Soap Skin & Bubble: `https://extensions.sketchup.com/extension/c8d49537-51db-40a7-ac0e-474a244eb525/soap-skin-bubble`.

- **FredoScale** by *Fredo6* – This is another extension written by *Fredo6*. It is essentially an upgraded version of SketchUp's **Scale** tool, offering more scaling options. It also allows you to do things such as twist, stretch, and bend objects.

  Here is a link to download FredoScale: `https://sketchucation.com/plugin/1169-fredoscale`.

  In addition, watch this video for the ultimate guide to FredoScale: `https://www.youtube.com/watch?v=Pn4o5jjMjQs`.

> **Important note**
>
> You will find that the extensions in the preceding list are useful when modeling just about anything, not just furniture.

There are so many amazing extensions out there to help you create a custom and efficient workflow for modeling furniture. New extensions are written all the time; we encourage you to regularly search and add more extensions to the preceding list.

That's a wrap for this chapter!

Summary

Some SketchUp users make an entire career out of modeling furniture. You can even use the software to develop detailed construction documents for furniture builders. Although we don't jump into that realm in this book, this chapter got you moving in the right direction. We built a coffee table from scratch, used manufacturer specifications to model an armchair, created a decorative tray with a radial array, and reviewed some of our favorite extensions for modeling furniture.

In the next chapter, we will experiment with colors and materials and learn how to create custom textures. It is a whole new world when you start seeing your designs in color!

Applying and Customizing Colors and Materials

SketchUp designs come to life in a new way when you start adding colors and materials. In this chapter, we will discuss all things materials, beginning with the **Paint Bucket** tool and SketchUp's built-in material collections, enabling you to experiment with adding color right away. We will also talk about editing materials directly in SketchUp and introduce creating and working with custom materials. Knowing how to apply seamless custom materials is especially handy for showcasing precise finishes, and this chapter shows how to approach this concept effectively. Lastly, we will share best practices and extensions for working with materials.

In this chapter, we will cover the following topics:

- Overview of applying colors and materials in SketchUp
- Repositioning and warping materials
- Editing color, texture, and opacity in the **Materials** tray
- Creating and working with custom materials
- Go-to extensions for working with materials

Technical requirements

This chapter requires the following software and files:

- SketchUp Pro or Studio
- Download the practice file from 3D Warehouse named Chapter 9- Colors and Materials or download it from https://3dwarehouse.sketchup.com/model/65837f6b-0df4-4350-984e-f2a4c1296c44/Chapter-9-Colors-and-Materials

Overview of applying colors and materials in SketchUp

Knowing how to work with colors and materials in SketchUp is an essential skill to add realism to your models. Your models transform into beautifully presented works of art after color is applied. And it all starts with the **Paint Bucket** tool.

Paint Bucket is the SketchUp tool used to apply colors and materials to geometry. To access the **Paint Bucket** tool, click on the paint bucket icon (*Figure 9.1*) in the **Getting Started** toolbar or type *B* for the shortcut. On macOS, you can find it under **Window | Materials**.

Figure 9.1: Paint bucket icon

Once you activate the **Paint Bucket** tool, the **Materials** tray (or **Colors** panel on macOS) will appear.

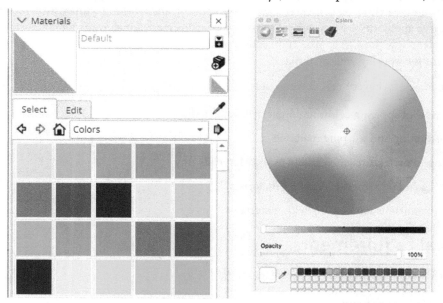

Figure 9.2: The Materials tray on Windows (left) and the Colors panel on macOS (right)

Here, you will find a drop-down menu containing folders of colors and SketchUp's built-in materials. These folders are called *collections* on Windows (or *lists* on macOS). To access the dropdown on macOS, click the brick icon on the right, called the **Textures Palette**.

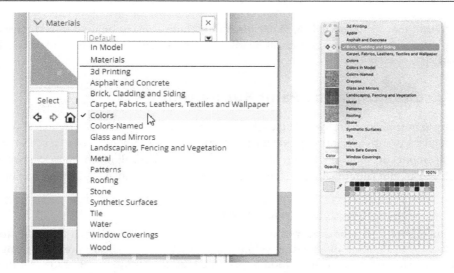

Figure 9.3: Dropdown menu of collections – Windows (left) and macOS (right)

You can think of *colors* like paint, and *materials* are essentially paints that have color and texture. Materials add a realistic look to 3D models.

For example, in *Figure 9.4*, the screenshot on the left shows a breakfast nook painted using only colors, and the screenshot on the right shows the same breakfast nook painted using materials. The one on the right looks more realistic because of the materials.

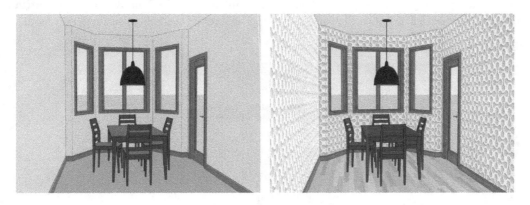

Figure 9.4: Left model is painted with only colors and right model is painted with materials

In the same figure, notice how the flooring in the left model is painted a solid brown, whereas the flooring in the right model appears more realistic, with a brown color and texture that simulates wood flooring. Similarly, the wallpaper, wood trim, and furniture wood in the right model are also materials that have color and texture.

It is worth noting that the terms *colors*, *materials*, and *textures* seem to be used interchangeably by SketchUp users. For our purposes, we will mainly refer to swatches applied to models as colors and materials.

Applying colors using the Paint Bucket tool

The first thing to note about painting in SketchUp is the importance of entering **Edit** mode. We have learned through thousands of hours of modeling that the best way to paint geometry is in **Edit** mode of a group or component. Painting geometry inside a group/component allows for more control over what you are and are not painting, rather than painting loose geometry outside a group/component.

> **The problem with painting groups outside of Edit mode**
>
> If you paint groups or components without getting into **Edit** mode, you forfeit the ability to manipulate the orientation of a texture. While it may work well for solid colors and paint, when dealing with materials such as wood or patterned fabric, it is more logical to paint the faces in **Edit** mode.
>
> Another problem that can arise when painting geometry outside of **Edit** mode is that the interior faces often get painted. This can cause issues down the road when repainting surfaces, using projected textures (we will discuss projected textures in the next section, *Repositioning and warping materials*), or working in photorealistic rendering plugins (which we will discuss in *Chapter 14*).

That being said, applying colors in SketchUp is straightforward. Activate the **Paint Bucket** tool (shortcut *B*), click on a color swatch, and then click on a face to apply the color (make sure you are in **Edit** mode).

Let's practice by painting the umbrella in *Figure 9.5*.

Figure 9.5: Picnic table with umbrella

From 3D Warehouse, download the SketchUp file named Chapter 9- Colors and Materials. You will see a picnic table with an umbrella when you open the model:

1. Click on the scene tab named Picnic Table.

2. Enter **Edit** mode of the umbrella base group. The base group lives within the overall umbrella grouping, so make sure you are editing the correct group.

3. Activate the **Paint Bucket** tool (shortcut *B*). Your cursor should now be a paint bucket.

4. Select the **Colors-Named** collection from the drop-down menu in the **Materials** tray (Windows) or **Colors** panel (macOS).

5. Pick out a color to paint the umbrella base by clicking on a color swatch.

    Whenever you click on a swatch, it becomes the active swatch and appears at the top-left of the **Materials** tray on Windows. On macOS, it is a smaller thumbnail shown near the bottom-left of the window.

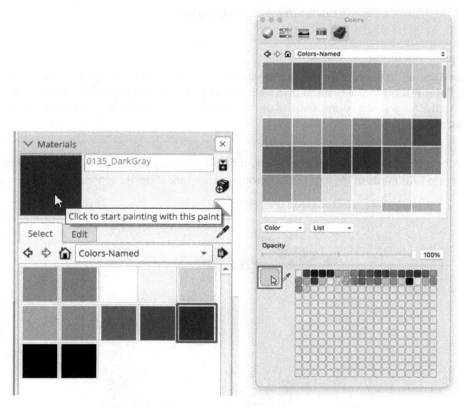

Figure 9.6: Active color swatch in the Materials tray – Windows (left) and macOS (right)

6.   Then, click on a face of the base to apply the color.

Continue by painting the rest of the faces in the base group.

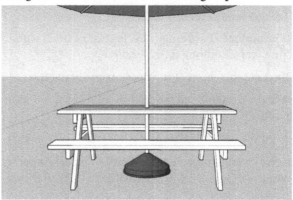

Figure 9.7: Painted umbrella base

Tip for quicker painting

If you are painting all the entities within a group/component the same color, tap the *Shift* key with the **Paint Bucket** tool active and then click on one of the faces to apply the color (in **Edit** mode). All the faces (both connected and unconnected faces) within the group/component will be painted.

7.   Paint the umbrella's pole, rib support system, and canopy, trying out different colors. Remember to get into **Edit** mode of the appropriate group or component before applying the color.

Here are the colors we selected (see *Figure 9.8*):

Figure 9.8: Painted umbrella

Beautiful! We will paint the picnic table in the *Repositioning and warping materials* section. Before that, we want to introduce some helpful painting shortcuts.

Painting tools and shortcuts

There are keyboard shortcuts for almost everything in SketchUp. Here are the painting tools and shortcuts we have found most helpful for interior design:

- To select and paint all the connected geometry within a group quickly, triple-click on a face and then click the **Paint Bucket** tool on one of the faces. All the selected geometry will be painted.

  Alternatively, tap *Ctrl* (Windows) or *Opt* (macOS) with the **Paint Bucket** tool active; then click one of the faces. All the connected geometry will be painted- unless they were already painted with another material.

- On Windows, use the **Sample Paint** eyedropper icon to sample a paint color or material in your model. To use the *sample paint* feature on macOS, tap the shortcut *B*, then tap ⌘ to select a paint color or material. (Do not use the eyedropper on macOS for this purpose because it will not work.)

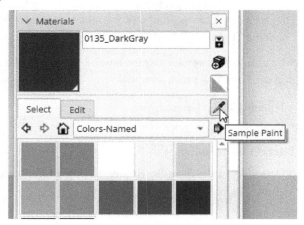

Figure 9.9: Sample Paint eyedropper icon in the Materials tray (Windows)

  Alternatively, for Windows, you can sample a material by tapping *Alt* with the **Paint Bucket** tool active, rather than clicking on the eyedropper icon.

- To repaint multiple, unconnected faces painted the same color within a group/component, tap *Shift* with the **Paint Bucket** tool active and paint one face (in **Edit** mode). Every face with the same color inside the group/component will change to the new color.

> **Important Note**
>
> Later, in the *Go-to extensions for working with materials* section, we will introduce an extension for easily replacing materials throughout your SketchUp model, not just within a group/component.

Try out these different shortcuts to find what works best for your workflow!

Now that we have reviewed the basics of painting in SketchUp, it is time to learn how to manipulate and reposition materials.

Repositioning and warping materials

SketchUp makes it easy to rotate, reposition, and deform materials directly inside the software. Let's take a look at how to modify the orientation of a material using **Fixed Pin** mode.

Modifying a material with Fixed Pins

If you haven't already, take some time to look at the several collections of materials in the **Materials** tray (or the **Colors** panel on macOS). You have probably noticed that the options are limited and not high quality. Later in this chapter, in the *Creating and working with custom materials* section, we will walk through creating our own materials.

For now, we will use SketchUp's built-in materials to learn how to modify a material using **Fixed Pin** mode. Let's begin by opening the *Chapter 9* practice model:

1. Click on the scene tab named `Picnic Table`.
2. Enter **Edit** mode of the picnic table bench.
3. Activate the **Paint Bucket** tool (shortcut *B*).
4. Select the **Wood** collection from the drop-down menu in the **Materials** tray. Take a look at the different wood options.

> **Material names**
>
> When the mouse hovers over a swatch, descriptive names appear. Each material has a name, which is important to know when editing or modifying them.

5. Find the **Wood Cherry Original** material and click on the swatch to select it.
6. Still in **Edit** mode, click on one of the bench faces with the **Paint Bucket** + *Shift* key to apply the wood material. See *Figure 9.10*.

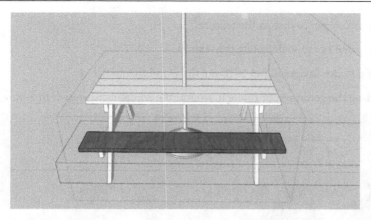

Figure 9.10: Bench painted with Wood Cherry Original material

Notice how the wood grain runs in the wrong direction. Before painting the rest of the picnic table, we are going to modify the orientation of the material so that the wood grain runs in the same direction as the bench.

7.   In **Edit** mode, click once on the top face of the bench to select it, right-click, then choose **Texture | Position**.

A texture editor appears with a grid and four colored pins. See *Figure 9.11*. You are now in **Fixed Pin** mode.

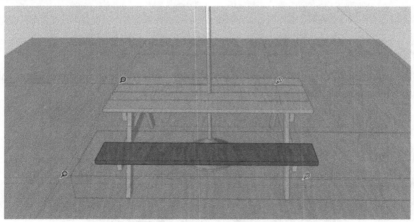

Figure 9.11: Texture editor with the four Fixed Pins

Each pin has a different function:

• Drag the *red pin* to reposition the texture. Note that you can also reposition the texture by clicking and dragging anywhere on the material.

• Drag the *blue pin* to scale/shear the texture.

- Drag the *yellow pin* to distort the texture.

- Drag the *green pin* to scale/rotate the texture.

We are going to use the green pin to rotate the wood material.

8.   Click and drag the green pin to rotate it around the compass, as shown in *Figure 9.12*.

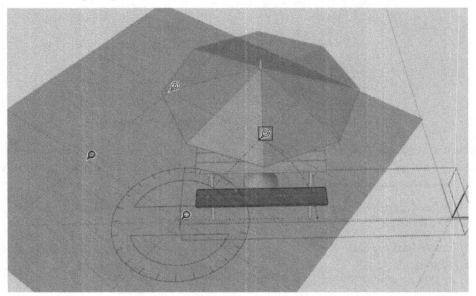

Figure 9.12: Use the green pin to rotate around the compass

9.   Rotate the material 90 degrees so that the wood grain runs in the same direction as the bench. Click anywhere outside the grid to close the texture editor.

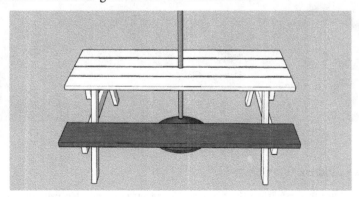

Figure 9.13: Wood grain material rotated 90 degrees

Now, we will sample the wood material that we just rotated to use on the other faces of the bench.

10. With the **Paint Bucket** tool, use *Alt* (or ⌘ on macOS) to sample the top material of the bench. Apply the material to the other faces so that the wood grain runs in the same direction on each face. Adjust the texture as needed using the Fixed Pins.

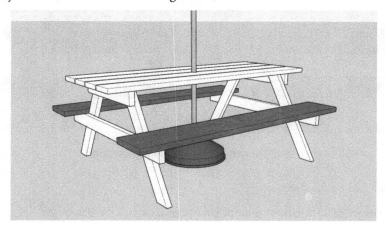

Figure 9.14: Sampled material applied to the rest of the picnic bench

11. Paint the rest of the picnic table using the **Wood Cherry Original** material. Rotate the texture as needed.

Figure 9.15: Painted picnic table and umbrella

In *Figure 9.16*, the left picnic table shows the wood grain oriented correctly, and the right picnic table shows the wood grain oriented in the wrong direction. Compare the difference in appearance.

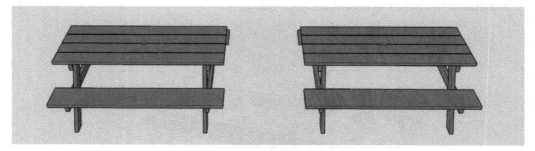

Figure 9.16: Compare the wood grain orientation

These small details make a big difference!

In the next exercise, we will learn how to modify a material using **Free Pin** mode.

Modifying distorted materials with Free Pins

Free Pin mode enables you to adjust the texture between four clear pins. This is particularly helpful for straightening a skewed image. For this example, we are going to take an imported image (we will walk through importing images in the *Creating and working with custom materials* section) and warp it using the Free Pins:

In the *Chapter 9* practice model, click on the scene tab named `Free Pins`.

You will see a wall with an imported image of an angled mural, as shown in *Figure 9.17*.

Figure 9.17: Imported image of a mural, originally photographed at an angle

Ideally, it is best to use images captured from a straight-on perspective rather than angled, but that may not always be an option. This is when SketchUp's Free Pins come in handy. We will use **Free Pin** mode to straighten the mural so that it fits on the wall correctly.

1. In **Edit** mode of the wall, select the face with the mural on it, right-click, click **Texture**, and then choose **Position**.

2. Right-click on the texture again and uncheck **Fixed Pins**. This toggles to **Free Pin** mode; the colored pins change to white pins, as shown in *Figure 9.18*.

Figure 9.18: White pins indicate you are in Free Pin mode

Shortcut to Free Pin mode

Another way to toggle between *Fixed Pins* and *Free Pins* is by tapping the *Shift* key after the texture editor pops up. Using the *Shift* key eliminates having to right-click twice. It also allows you to toggle back and forth between the two modes quickly.

Next, we will move the white pins so that they are on the four corners of the mural. The lower-left and upper-left pins are already in the correct spots (yay!), so we just need to move the lower-right and upper-right pins.

3. Click and release the lower-right pin to select it (do not drag it). The pin should now be attached to your cursor.

4. Move the pin to the lower-right corner of the mural and click and release.

5. Repeat *steps 4* and *5* with the upper-right pin.

    Your screen should look like this, with a white pin in each corner of the mural:

Figure 9.19: Move (not drag) the white pins to each corner of the mural

Now, we will use the pins to stretch the mural so that it fits the wall.

6. Drag the lower-right pin to the lower-right corner of the wall, snapping to the endpoint, as shown in *Figure 9.20*.

Figure 9.20: Drag the lower-right pin to the lower-right corner of the wall

7. Drag the other three pins to their respective corners of the wall. When you are done, click anywhere outside the grid to close the texture editor.

Look at that! The mural fits perfectly on the wall.

Figure 9.21: The mural fits on the wall after using Free Pins

There are so many options to manipulate a material using Fixed Pins and Free Pins. Multiple toggles between the two modes may be necessary to achieve the look you want.

To continue our discussion on warping textures, we will now walk through how to apply materials to curved geometry.

Painting on a curved surface

Have you ever tried to paint a throw pillow in SketchUp using a patterned material? There is a good chance the material looked distorted and did not appear the way you desired. That is because the pillow's geometry was probably rounded.

SketchUp has a couple of tools that help with applying materials to curved surfaces. One method is to use **Texture | Projected**. We will use this tool now to paint fabric onto a throw pillow. Open the practice model:

1. Click on the `Pillow Fabric` scene. On the left, we have a pillow painted with default color and on the right, we have a face painted with the pillow material.

2. Go ahead and paint the pillow using the material. Sample the material with the **Paint Bucket** tool (*B*) + *Alt* (or ⌘ on macOS) or by clicking on the eyedropper (Windows only).

Figure 9.22 shows what it looks like.

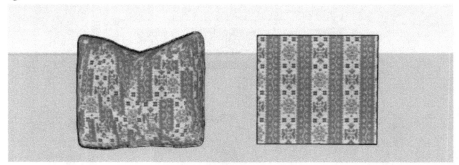

Figure 9.22: Fabric image looks distorted on the pillow

Hmm… That does not look right. The image appears distorted when placed on the pillow.

Let's try again, but this time we will use **Texture | Projected**.

3. Get into **Edit** mode of the grouped face on the right, select the face, right-click, click **Texture**, and then click **Projected**.

4. Try painting the pillow again using the material. You need to re-sample it since we made it *projected*. See *Figure 9.23* for how much better the fabric lays on the pillow now.

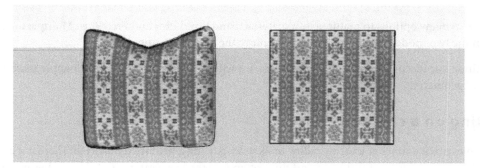

Figure 9.23: The result when you paint the fabric using Texture | Projected

If the material still appears distorted, try again and make sure you re-sample the material after it is projected.

Adding a pattern to draperies or a logo to a curved sign are other examples of when to use **Texture | Projected**.

If painting on curved surfaces is something you do often, or if you need to paint on more complex geometry, check out the section titled *Go-to extensions for working with materials* at the end of this chapter for an extension to use.

Next, we will take a deep dive into using the **Materials** tray (or **Colors** panel on macOS) to edit the color, texture, and opacity of materials. SketchUp makes this process easy!

Editing color, texture, and opacity in the Materials tray

The **Materials** tray (or **Colors** panel on macOS) in SketchUp is very powerful. Do not be deceived by its small size. You can change the coloring, adjust the opacity, create new materials, and much more. The ability to achieve these adjustments directly in SketchUp provides a seamless experience for your workflow.

First, we will review the basics and familiarize ourselves with the interface.

The functions of the **Materials** tray on Windows versus the **Colors** panel on macOS differ quite a bit. We suggest checking out this link for specific macOS features for materials: `https://help.sketchup.com/en/sketchup/adding-colors-and-textures-materials#edit-material`. We will try to cover the basics for both Windows and macOS in this book.

Navigating the Materials tray interface

For Windows users, all materials in the model can be found in the **Materials** tray. Click on the *home* icon (*Figure 9.24*) or select **In Model** from the drop-down menu to display all the materials in your SketchUp file.

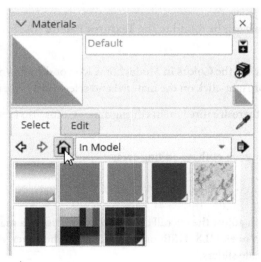

Figure 9.24: Click the home icon or select In Model to view all materials

From here, you can choose a material you want to edit and then click the **Edit** tab (*Figure 9.25*).

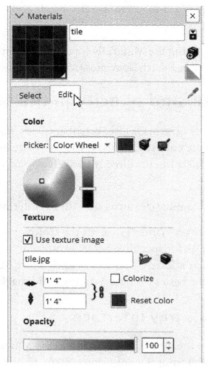

Figure 9.25: The Edit tab in the Materials tray on Windows

For macOS users, all materials can be found in the **Textures Palette** (the brick icon at the far right of the tabs).

To edit a material on macOS, click the **Colors in Model** home icon or dropdown. Then, from the **Color** drop-down list, select **Edit**, or right-click on the material and select **Edit** from the menu that appears.

For both operating systems, there are three main editing areas: **Color**, **Texture** (uses a dropdown on macOS), and **Opacity**.

Let's take a look at how to use each of these editing areas.

Editing color

In the **Color** edit area, you can adjust the overall color and brightness of a material using the **Picker** drop-down options: **Color Wheel**, **HLS**, **HSB**, or **RGB**. (MacOS, however, does not have **HLS** but has **CMYK**. It also has grayscale sliders.)

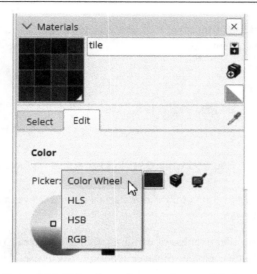

Figure 9.26: Picker drop-down options on Windows

You can customize the color of a material by using the sliders or manually entering specific values for HLS, HSB, and RGB. Color changes happen in real time as you edit.

> **How to get HLS, HSB, or RGB values**
>
> If you want an exact color match and know the HLS, HSB, or RGB numerical code for the color you desire, type the values in their respective boxes in SketchUp.
>
> If you do not know the HLS, HSB, or RGB numerical code for the color you desire, there are online resources you can use to upload an image and select a color from the image to get the exact values. Then, you can simply take note of its numerical code and type it into SketchUp for a color match.
>
> We use the following online source often to get RGB values from an image: `https://imagecolorpicker.com/`

On macOS, the **Colors** panel tabs (or icons) are shown in *Figure 9.27*, from left to right:

- **Color wheel**: Click or drag your mouse around the color wheel to choose a color for painting faces.
- **Sliders**: **HSB**, **RGB**, **CMYK**, and **Grayscale** options to edit an existing color or material.
- **Spectrum**: An image of gradient colors to edit a texture to match colors with real-life objects. Other images can be pulled in to match colors.
- **Colored pencils**: Paint an object with one of the colors shown on the pencil.

- **Textures Palette**: Click the dropdown to find a variety of colors and materials, and find the colors that exist in the current model.

Figure 9.27: macOS Colors panel tabs

Though the placement of where to edit colors and materials on macOS versus Windows is different, rest assured the outcome is the same.

In *Figure 9.28*, you can see the effectiveness of using the **Color** edit area to completely change the appearance of materials and, in turn, change the overall design. This is useful when showcasing clients various design options.

Figure 9.28: Use the Edit functions to change the appearance of materials completely

The wall tile was tweaked using the **HLS** (which stands for **Hue Saturation Light**) sliders (a Windows feature). See *Figure 9.29* for a side-by-side comparison of the HLS values for the wall tiles.

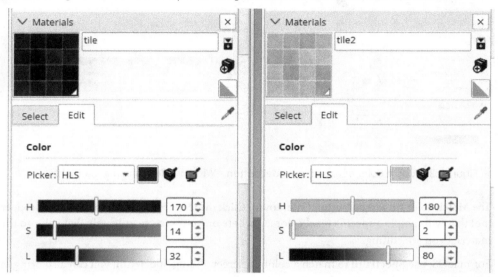

Figure 9.29: Compare the HLS values for the wall tiles

The wood vanity and flooring were also tweaked using the **HLS** sliders. The metal details were adjusted using the **RGB** (which stands for **Red Green Blue**) sliders.

There are two more very useful tools for editing a material's color:

- **The Match Color of object in model button (Windows)**: Click the icon (*Figure 9.30*) to get an eyedropper tool to sample colors from objects in your SketchUp model and apply that color to the material you are editing.

- On macOS, matching the color of an object in a model works slightly differently. In the **Edit** function of the material you are changing, click the eyedropper tool (underneath **Opacity**), near the bottom of the window as shown in *Figure 9.30*. Move your mouse to the color you want to match (be sure to zoom in a bit to pick the correct color) and click once.

> **Note for macOS users**
>
> For macOS users, the *match color* eyedropper performs differently from the *sample paint* feature, used by tapping shortcut *B* and then the ⌘ key, which selects an existing texture in the model.

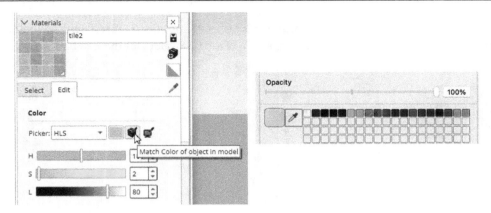

Figure 9.30: Match Color of object in model button – Windows (left) and macOS (right)

- **The Match color on screen button (Windows):** Click the icon (*Figure 9.31*) to get an eyedropper tool that will sample a specific pixel color anywhere on your screen and apply that color to the material you are editing.

    For macOS, use **Spectrum** to match a color on screen. Using **Spectrum**, you can also bring in any image to match colors with.

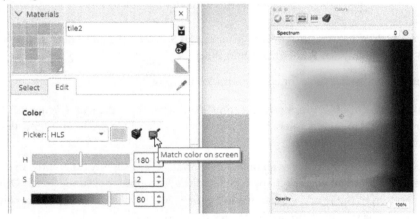

Figure 9.31: Match color on screen button – Windows (left) and macOS (right)

If you sample a textured material using the **Match Color of object in model** feature, sometimes the texture variation disguises the material's color a bit. This is because the tool picks up the overall color of the texture, not just a specific pixel color. It may create results different from what you were expecting. If this happens, use the **Match color on screen** button instead.

These color-matching tools allow you to create cohesive designs with colors that match or complement one another perfectly.

The last tool to introduce in the **Color** edit area is the **Undo Color Changes** button. Click this button to undo all color changes during a single edit session.

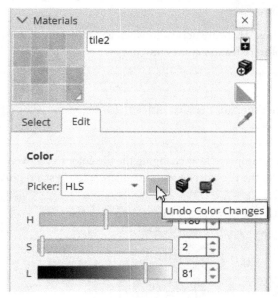

Figure 9.32: Undo Color Changes button (Windows)

Next, we will discuss the tools and features in the **Texture** edit area.

Editing texture

There are some useful tools that enable you to tinker with a material's texture in the **Texture** edit area. The ones that we use most often are the following:

- **The dimensions field**: When you paint using a material, the material image tiles (repeats) to cover a face. Type a value in the width or height box to change the size of the material tile.

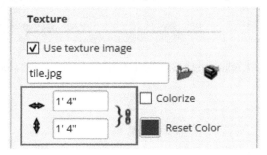

Figure 9.33: Type a value in the dimensions field to change the size of the material

The material image's aspect ratio is maintained (linked) by default, meaning when you change one dimension, the other will change proportionately. Click the **Unlock Aspect Ratio** link to break that relationship.

- **The Colorize checkbox**: There are occasions when a material is not displaying colors properly. This is when the **Colorize** feature comes into play.

> **Note for Mac users**
>
> There is no **Colorize** checkbox for macOS. Instead, use any of the color tabs to select a color and apply it to your material.

Figure 9.34 shows an example of how changing the tile color to yellow resulted in an unwanted outcome with some of the tiles displaying unrealistic splotches and pink areas.

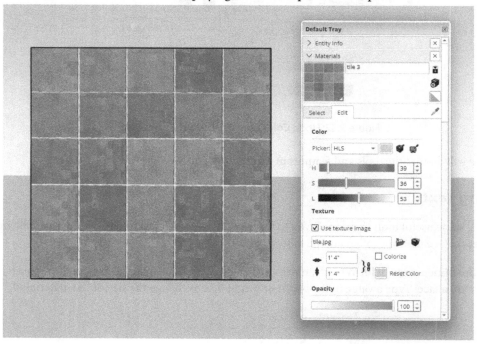

Figure 9.34: Yellow tile has unrealistic splotches and pink areas

Clicking the **Colorize** checkbox applies the color to the entire material and usually fixes the problem of strange splotches. See *Figure 9.35* for how the tiles appear after using **Colorize**. The splotches and pink areas are gone and overall the coloring looks more visually appealing.

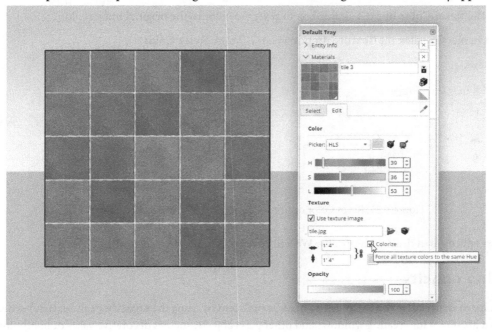

Figure 9.35: Splotches and pink areas are gone after checking Colorize

It is worth noting that sometimes using the **Colorize** option still does not result in the look you want. If this happens, we recommend editing your material in an external image editor, which leads us to the next tool.

- **The Edit texture image in external editor button**: When you click this button, SketchUp opens the currently selected material in your preferred external image editor.

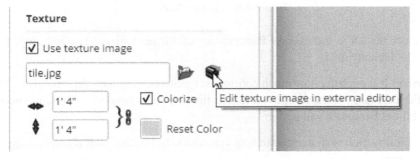

Figure 9.36: Edit texture image in external editor button

Go to **Window | Preferences | Applications** to define your preferred image editor. This is yet another way SketchUp provides a seamless experience when editing materials, even while involving external software.

- **The Reset Color box**: Click this box to reset the color to the original image color.

On macOS, click the **Texture** dropdown and choose **Reset Color**.

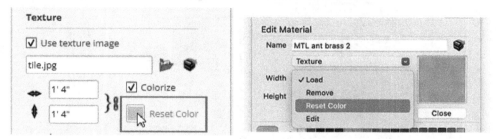

Figure 9.37: Reset Color option – Windows (left) and macOS (right)

The last editing area deals with opacity. We will cover that in the next section.

Editing opacity

Any color or material in SketchUp can be made translucent by using the **Opacity** (translucence) slider. This is a great tool for creating windows and other glass objects, such as decorative vases or lightbulbs.

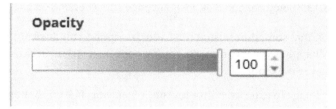

Figure 9.38: Opacity slider

Move the slider to the left to increase the transparency of the material. Alternatively, type a number up to 100 in the **Opacity** field.

There you have it! It is amazing how much control over materials you have directly inside SketchUp solely using the **Edit** tab. We encourage you to take the extra time needed to acquaint yourself with all these capabilities because it will pay off.

The last part of this section is an exercise to help you create the healthy habit of duplicating materials before editing them.

Fun exercise – Painting Becca and Dana by creating new materials

You can have multiple versions of one material in SketchUp, each with different properties tailored to your design needs. Creating new materials in SketchUp essentially involves duplicating an existing material. By duplicating a material before editing it, you preserve the original material.

In the following exercise, we will show you how to get in the groove of creating new materials before customizing them by painting us, the authors of this book (see *Figure 9.39*)!

Open the SketchUp file named Chapter 9- Colors and Materials from 3D Warehouse. Click on the Becca and Dana scene. You will see two scaled figures (Becca on the left and Dana on the right). Everything is painted the default color except for Becca's skin.

Figure 9.39: Becca and Dana, the book authors, as scaled figures in SketchUp

> **Important note**
>
> Psst… Notice how when you orbit around the scaled figures, they always face you. That is because we used the **Always face camera** feature, which we will touch on in the *Creating and working with custom materials* section.

We will make a duplicate of the color swatch used for Becca's skin to create a new material. Then, we will edit the color of the new material to use for Becca's pants:

1. Using the **Sample Paint** eyedropper, sample the color used for Becca's skin to make it the active swatch. It is named Becca_Skin.

2. Click on the box with a plus sign in the **Materials** tray to duplicate the active material.

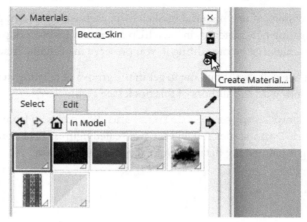

Figure 9.40: Create a new color swatch by clicking on the box with a plus sign

3. A window pops up with **Create Material...** at the top. Type `Becca_Pants` to name the new material.

4. Select **RGB** from the **Picker** drop-down list.

5. Type `173, 109, 100` for the **RGB** value.

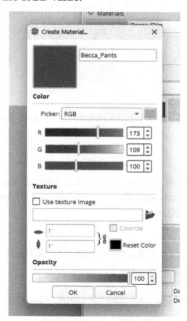

Figure 9.41: Properties for Becca_Pants

6. Click **OK**.

7. Enter **Edit** mode of the `Becca` component and paint her pants using the `Becca_Pants` color swatch that we just created.

Paint the rest of Becca by creating new materials and adjusting the RGB values. Do the same for Dana's scaled figure. See the **RGB** values to use in *Figure 9.42*.

```
Becca_Accessories...... 255, 255, 255        Dana_Backpack.......... 81, 81, 81
Becca_Hair............. 185, 166, 136        Dana_Bandana.......... 143, 28, 43
Becca_Pants........... 173, 109, 100        Dana_Bracelet......... 192, 155, 92
Becca_Shirt........... 0, 0, 0              Dana_Hair............. 174, 130, 95
Becca_Shoes........... 0, 0, 0              Dana_Pants............ 50, 58, 81
Becca_Skin............ 218, 197, 184        Dana_Shirt............ 35, 35, 35
                                            Dana_Shoes............ 69, 84, 87
                                            Dana_Shoes Laces....... 41, 70, 76
                                            Dana_Shoes Soles....... 128, 112, 97
                                            Dana_Skin............. 199, 175, 166
                                            Dana_Socks............ 165, 167, 167
```

Figure 9.42: RGB values

Here is what the scaled figures should look like when you are done:

Figure 9.43: Completed scaled figures of Becca and Dana

Creating new materials is that easy. Remember, it is best practice to create new materials before editing them to preserve the original material.

If you feel inspired, create your own scaled figure that looks like you and paint it by creating new materials! Upload it to **3D Warehouse** so we can see what you created!

Next up, we will dive into the topic of custom materials. Now it starts getting really fun!

Creating and working with custom materials

Figure 9.44 shows a living room 3D model designed by *Kelly Hohla Interiors* and built in SketchUp by *Carré Design Studio*.

Figure 9.44: Living room SketchUp model built by Carré Design Studio and designed by Kelly Hohla Interiors. Website: www.carredesigns.com

You may have noticed that none of the materials in this 3D model can be found in SketchUp's built-in collections. You are right. The space is dripping in custom materials from head to toe. Just about everything from the draperies to the coffee tabletop to the ceiling wallpaper was imported into SketchUp as a custom material.

This section is dedicated to working with custom materials in SketchUp. We will walk through the simple process of creating and importing images to use as custom materials, as well as share creative and unexpected ways to use materials in your workflow. Let's begin!

Creating custom materials

Basically any image can be used as a SketchUp material and then applied to a face using the **Paint Bucket** tool. The key is knowing what makes an image a good material.

What makes an image a good SketchUp material?

Beautiful SketchUp materials are ones that are seamless. A *seamless material* is an image that can be repeated infinitely without any noticeable seams or edges. Each side of the image should meet and match perfectly, allowing the image to be tiled across a large area.

Figure 9.45 is an example of a non-seamless material. The repeated image has a noticeable seam, and it is easy to see where one copy of the image starts and ends.

Figure 9.45: Non-seamless material

Figure 9.46 is an example of a *seamless material*. It is difficult (and maybe impossible) to see where the image starts and ends. Seamless materials are more aesthetically pleasing than non-seamless materials.

Figure 9.46: Seamless material

Another feature of a good SketchUp material is the resolution. Higher-resolution images are going to appear better, but they can also impact the performance of your SketchUp model. We recommend no more than 2,000 KB as the maximum file size and as little as 15 KB for a minimum file size.

Where to find seamless images for SketchUp materials

Here are ways to find good seamless images to use as SketchUp materials:

- **Search online**: Simply search online for images using an image search browser such as Google Images. We recommend adding the words `texture seamless` at the end of your search. For example, if you are looking for an image to use as carpet, type `carpet texture seamless` in any search engine. Or, add more details to filter the results, such as `blue patterned carpet texture seamless`.

- **Manufacturer website**: Lots of brands provide images of their fabric, wall coverings, and other finishes on their website. It is best to use an image of the material straight-on versus rolled or wrinkled.

- **3D Warehouse materials**: You can download materials from **3D Warehouse**. Pretty cool! Visit `https://help.sketchup.com/en/3d-warehouse/browsing-and-downloading-materials` to learn how to browse and download **3D Warehouse** materials.

- **SketchUp texture sites**: One of our favorites is SketchUp Texture Club (`https://www.sketchuptextureclub.com/`). Create a free login to download up to 15 materials per day that are perfect for any SketchUp object. The paid membership gives even more options and up to 50 daily downloads.

  Other major texture websites include Adobe Substance, PixPlant, 3D Textures, and Architextures.

- **Rendering plugins**: Should you decide to create photorealistic renderings of your SketchUp designs, many rendering plugins offer seamless materials. We will cover how to prepare SketchUp textures for photorealistic rendering in *Chapter 14*.

- **Photograph a material**: Take your own photos and import them to use as materials. This is especially helpful if you have a physical swatch of a patterned material but cannot find a seamless version online.

Lastly, did you know you can create your own seamless materials right in SketchUp? Here's how.

Using Combine Textures to create your own seamless materials

You can create your own seamless materials directly in SketchUp. This exercise will show you how. Open the *Chapter 9* practice file:

1. Go to the scene named `Combine Textures`.

    Here, you will see a marble tile pattern on the left and a blank 12' × 12' square on the right, as shown in *Figure 9.47*.

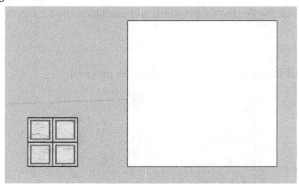

Figure 9.47: The scene named Combine Textures

We want to tile the marble pattern across the 12' × 12' square to use as a floor material. Now, we could just make multiple copies of the marble group. Or, instead, let's create a custom seamless material.

2. Enter **Edit** mode of the marble pattern group. Triple-click on one of the faces to select all the faces.

3. Right-click and select **Combine Textures**.

4.   A popup will appear asking whether you want to erase the interior edges. Click **Yes**.

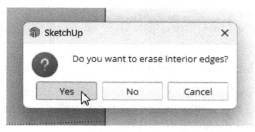

Figure 9.48: Click Yes to allow SketchUp to erase the interior edges

5.   SketchUp just created a new tiling material. Now you can sample the new material and paint it onto the 12' x 12' group, as shown in *Figure 9.49*.

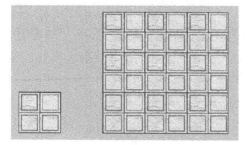

Figure 9.49: Sample the new material and paint it on the 12' x 12' face

How easy!

Head over to the **In Model** folder, and you will see the new material.

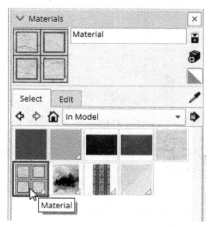

Figure 9.50: You can find the new material in the In Model folder

Here, you can rename the material and edit its color, texture, or opacity using the **Edit** tab (like we learned in the previous section named *Editing color, texture, and opacity in the Materials tray*).

The **Combine Textures** feature works best with simple, coplanar patterns. We recommend using external editors to create more complex seamless materials.

More ways to create seamless images

We will introduce an awesome tool in the *Go-to extensions for working with materials* section to use for creating seamless images.

Next, let's walk through the steps for importing an image from your computer to use as a SketchUp material.

Importing custom materials

So, you have a seamless image you want to use to create a material in SketchUp. Save the image to your computer, and now you are ready to import it into your SketchUp file. There are two methods to do this, and here are the steps for one of them:

1. Select a face you want for the material (in **Edit** mode).

2. Click on **File | Import**. A browser window appears. Make sure **All Supported Types** is selected from the dropdown.

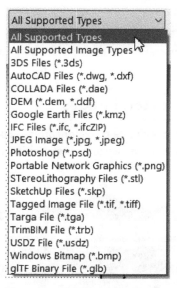

Figure 9.51: Select All Supported Types from the dropdown

3.   Navigate to the image file, click on it to select it, and then select **Texture** under **Use Image As** (as seen in *Figure 9.52*).

Figure 9.52: Select Texture for Use Image As

4.   Click **Import**.

5.   You will notice the material is attached to your cursor. Click once on an endpoint of the face to start placing the material. Move the cursor until the material size looks right to you and then click a second time to apply the material. You can adjust the tile size as needed by using Fixed Pins or the **Edit** tab.

If you look at the materials in the **In Model** folder, you will see the image you just imported. Here, you can name and edit the material just like any other material.

> **Importing materials into SketchUp through the Materials tray**
>
> The second way to import materials into SketchUp is in the **Materials tray**. Click the **Create Material** button and use the file folder to upload an image. The file folder is under the **Texture** area. When you hover your cursor over the icon, the **Browse for Material Image File** ScreenTip appears.

In addition to importing seamless images to use as materials, here are some out-of-the-box ways to use imported images in SketchUp.

Creative ways to use imported images

Creating materials for complex textures can be time-consuming. For example, imagine the time it would take to create aesthetically pleasing and accurate materials to match all the colors and textures on the antique bench in *Figure 9.53*.

Figure 9.53: Image of an antique bench

Instead, for this example, we recommend using the image of the bench as a SketchUp material. See *Figure 9.54* for the bench built in SketchUp with the image used as a material.

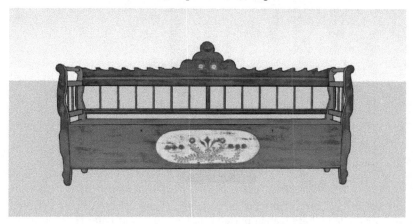

Figure 9.54: Antique bench built in SketchUp

Not only does this look great, but the process is quicker than creating multiple custom materials.

You can even use this technique with intricate light fixtures or table lamps. For example, how would you build the intricate lamp base in *Figure 9.55*?

Figure 9.55: Intricate lamp base

Wow! It would be a huge undertaking to build that lamp base from scratch. Instead, remove the background of the image using an external image editor and then save the image as a PNG with a transparent background. Then, import the PNG file as a material into SketchUp.

See *Figure 9.56* for the result. (Make sure to hide the edges of the face with the imported image.)

Figure 9.56: The lamp base is an imported PNG file with a transparent background

Removing an image background

In addition to using an external image editor, such as Photoshop, there are also online resources that will remove image backgrounds for free, such as this one: https://www.remove.bg/.

From here, make the object a component and check the **Always face camera** option. This feature enables you to create 2D objects that automatically rotate to always face the viewport (just like the scaled figures from the previous section, *Editing color, texture, and opacity in the Materials tray*, did). Then, when you orbit around the model, the lamp base will always face the camera.

Additional information and resources about Always face camera

It is worth noting that the **Always face camera** feature does not always render properly for some photorealistic rendering plugins. In these instances, we recommend using the native assets of the rendering software you select.

Watch this video to learn how to use the **Always face camera** feature: https://www.youtube.com/watch?v=WX0mHEOpjFk.

In *Chapter 6*, we discussed how to incorporate a client's brand into your SketchUp projects, in the *Carrying a client's brand from inside to outside* section. Importing branded logos and images to use as custom materials is an easy way to add the client's personality.

The final SketchUp features we will cover in this chapter are the **Image** and **New Matched Photo** options under **Use Image As**.

Remember the **Texture** button you selected under **Use Image As** when we discussed importing materials? You may have noticed the other two options, **Image** and **New Matched Photo** (see *Figure 9.57*).

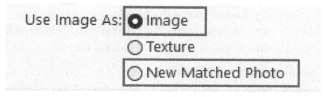

Figure 9.57: Use Image As options

When you import an image to use as an **Image** in SketchUp, there is only one instance of the image. In other words, images do not tile (repeat) like textures do.

We select the **Image** feature for things such as wall art, an exterior window view, or a drawing to trace. To turn the image into a texture, select the image, right-click, and choose **Explode**. The swatch will appear in the **In Model** folder, and it will behave just like any other material.

Use the **New Matched Photo** button to create a model from a photo. This is helpful when you want to build an existing structure in SketchUp but only have images of the structure and no 2D plans or elevations.

Refer to *Chapter 3* for a breakdown of the capabilities of **Match Photo**. After you get the hang of this feature, it can enable you to build spaces you may have otherwise found too difficult to build.

And now, for the last section, let's discuss some of our favorite extensions for materials.

Go-to extensions for working with materials

Here are some must-have extensions for working with SketchUp materials (review *Chapter 6* for how to install extensions):

- **Material Replacer by ThomThom**: As you learned from the painting shortcuts in the *Overview of applying colors and materials in SketchUp* section of this chapter, SketchUp has a feature to replace one material with another within a group/component. However, this feature is limited to replacing materials only within a group/component. Material Replacer lets you replace one material with another throughout your entire model, not just within a group/component. We use this extension daily.

  Here is a link to download Material Replacer: `https://extensions.sketchup.com/ extension/4137f7fc-a81f-4ef9-9ec8-b6dd8a0d9086/material-replacer`.

- **ThruPaint by Fredo6**: When SketchUp isn't projecting a material properly, try ThruPaint. This extension applies materials to complex geometry and allows you to scale and move the material easily on geometry.

Here is a link to download ThruPaint: `https://extensions.sketchup.com/extension/ee037966-cd1c-45cc-9bd5-825d0d93942f/thru-paint`.

- **Material Resizer by SketchUp Team**: Material Resizer allows you to resize materials in your model quickly. A SketchUp file can run slow and have glitches when it is bloated with large material files. We use this extension to reduce large materials and in turn see a performance increase.

  Here is a link to download Material Resizer: `https://extensions.sketchup.com/extension/77b60f26-2352-407e-8c0c-9862c9716111/material-resizer`.

- **Architextures for SketchUp by Architextures**: Create and edit seamless textures, bump maps, and hatches easily using Architextures for SketchUp. This extension offers high-quality textures to choose from, or you can purchase the pro version for more features, such as importing your own textures.

  Here is a link to download Architextures for SketchUp: `https://extensions.sketchup.com/extension/1a0e0f80-7186-48da-8dd4-f6337dac0873/architectures-for-sketch-up`.

Remember, there are new extensions and updates written all the time. Keep exploring!

Summary

We covered a lot in this chapter. (Believe it or not, we could have covered more!) We used SketchUp's **Paint Bucket** tool and learned how to edit and manipulate colors and materials in the **Materials** tray. In addition, we walked through creating and importing images to use as custom materials. Lastly, we shared creative ways to use materials and go-to extensions for working with materials.

Up next, in *Chapter 10*, we will discuss adding final touches to your SketchUp models to prepare for presentations. Plus, you will have the opportunity to explore a professionally built model, complete with interior details and materials.

10

Enhancing a Model with Details for Final Presentation

If you have made it to this point in the book, you should feel proud of your progress! You can tackle a lot in SketchUp, such as creating 3D models based on 2D plans, building furniture from scratch, adding colors and custom materials, plus more in between. *Chapter 10* focuses on tools and techniques for enhancing your SketchUp projects to prepare for a final presentation.

In the first section of this chapter, we will experiment with SketchUp's impressive shadow tools to create real-world shadows. Additionally, we will introduce an extension that enables you to create the perfect shadows in any SketchUp model. Then, we have an exercise to practice adding accessories to your 3D designs. Last but not least, we will begin using and editing SketchUp styles to create presentation renderings.

In this chapter, we will cover the following topics:

- Adding shadows and using sun for shading

- Accessorizing your 3D models

- Exploring SketchUp's **Styles** panel

- Enhancing 3D designs outside of SketchUp

Technical requirements

This chapter requires the following software and files:

- SketchUp Pro or Studio

- Download the practice file from 3D Warehouse named *Chapter 10- Shadows and Styles* or download it from https://3dwarehouse.sketchup.com/model/ bc63a6ab-bf41-4749-bb29-ccf71d783cbf/Chapter-10-Shadows-and-Styles

Adding shadows and using sun for shading

Manipulating light is a crucial element in interior design. A common goal is to incorporate ample natural light. Natural sunlight can make a space feel warm and inviting, and a room with very little natural light can feel cold. I bet you are not surprised to learn that SketchUp has a **Shadows** feature (or maybe you already knew)!

With SketchUp's **Shadows** feature, you can add sunlight to your models with just a click of a button.

> **By default, shadows are turned off**
>
> The **Shadows** feature can increase load times and produce lags. For this reason, we advise keeping shadows turned off until you need them. By default, shadows are turned off.

After you turn **Shadows** on, you can see how the sun casts shadows during different months and at different times of day. Let's try it out!

SketchUp's Shadows feature

From 3D Warehouse, download the practice file, *Chapter 10- Shadows and Styles*. When you open the file, you will see a room from **Top** view. This is what the model looks like when opened:

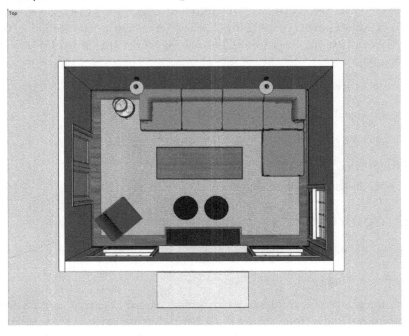

Figure 10.1: Chapter 10- Shadows and Styles practice file

Look familiar? If you completed the exercises in *Chapter 7*, this model will look familiar to you. As promised, here is the living room SketchUp file from *Chapter 7*, professionally built, complete with interior details, furnishings, and materials. We even included the coffee table and armchair we built in *Chapter 8*, with materials added.

Take some time to explore the model. Look at how groups and components are created and organized, check out the tags, and view the materials in the **In Model** folder. You can learn so much by simply viewing others' work.

Did you notice the side table lamp? We imported a transparent PNG file of the lamp rather than building it, and then we used the **Always face camera** feature (which we touched on in *Chapter 9*, section *Creating and working with custom materials*).

We are going to play around with the shadow options using the living room:

1. Start by clicking the scene tab named No Shadows.

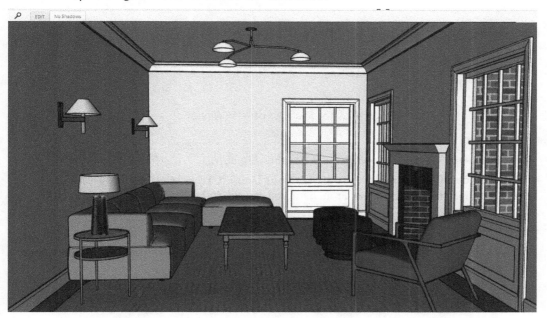

Figure 10.2: Click the No Shadows scene

Follow these steps to turn on shadows:

2.   Open the **Shadows** panel in the **Default Tray**. (On macOS, find it under **Window | Shadows**.)

Figure 10.3: The Shadows panel in Windows

Windows users – If the Shadows panel is not showing up...

If the **Shadows** panel is not showing up in your **Default Tray**, select **Window | Manage Trays...** to open the tray manager. From here, you can check the **Shadows** box to add it to the **Default Tray**.

3.   Click the **Show/Hide Shadows** button in the upper left to display shadows. This button toggles the shadows on and off.

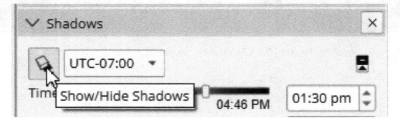

Figure 10.4: Click the Show/Hide Shadows button to toggle shadows on and off

Your model should now have shadows:

Figure 10.5: Shadows turned on

From here, you can see how the sun casts shadows during different times of the year by adjusting the **Time** and **Date** sliders.

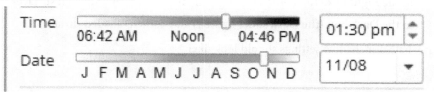

Figure 10.6: Time and Date sliders in the Shadows panel

Note about the Coordinated Universal Time (UTC) drop-down menu

This dropdown allows you to choose a specific time zone. If you are not familiar with the UTC time zones, we included a map to help you (*Figure 10.7*). You can also search the internet for more information.

At the end of this section, we will talk about how to use the **Add Location** feature to set custom locations and shadows in SketchUp.

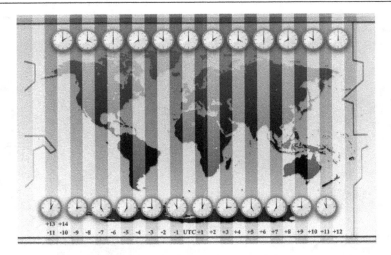

Figure 10.7: UTC time zone map

We are going to create a few new scenes, each with different shadow settings:

4. Set the time to 08 : 30 am by either dragging the slider or typing in the **Time** box.

5. Set the date to 11/08 (if it isn't already) by either dragging the slider or typing in the **Date** box.

6. Type 75 in the **Light** box. The **Light** slider lightens and darkens illuminated surfaces.

7. Type 55 in the **Dark** box. The **Dark** slider lightens and darkens shaded surfaces.

Here is what your shadow settings should look like:

Figure 10.8: Shadows set to 08:30 am on 11/08

And here is what the model will look like:

Figure 10.9: SketchUp model with 8:30 am shadows

Do your shadows look different than ours?

The shadows in your model may cast differently than the shadows shown in *Figure 10.9*, even if you followed the steps properly. If you are in a different time zone than UTC-07:00, then your shadows will look different than ours. That's OK! This exercise is intended simply to study the different property options.

We will now create a new scene with the preceding shadow settings:

8. Right-click on the scene tab called No Shadows.

9. Click **Add…** to add a new scene.

10. Right-click on the new scene and select **Rename**. Name the scene Shadows 8:30am and press *Enter*.

11. Save your model.

12. Create another new scene and name it Shadows 12:30pm. Use the shadow settings in *Figure 10.10* for this scene. (Make sure to adjust not only the time of day but the **Light** and **Dark** sliders as well.)

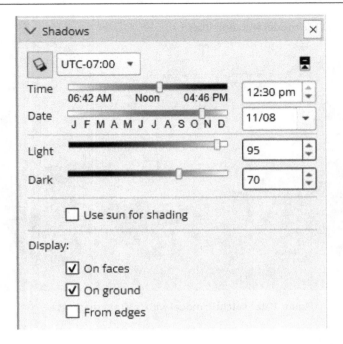

Figure 10.10: Settings for Shadows 12:30pm scene

And here is what the model will look like:

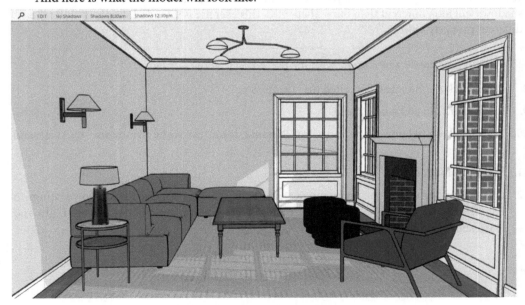

Figure 10.11: SketchUp model Shadows 12:30pm scene

13. Right-click on the scene you just created (named Shadows 12:30pm) and select **Update** to save the new shadow settings.

14. Create one more scene, name it Shadows 4:30pm, and use the shadow settings in *Figure 10.12*. Remember to update the scene after you set the new shadows.

Figure 10.12: Settings for Shadows 4:30pm scene

And here is what the model will look like:

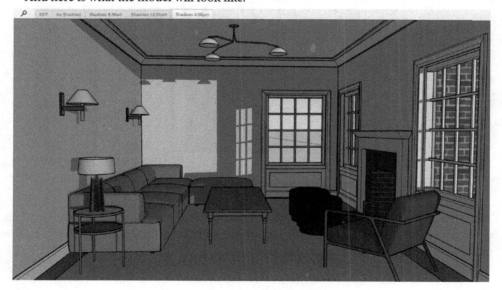

Figure 10.13: SketchUp model Shadows 4:30pm scene

You should now have three scenes showcasing shadows at different times of the day with varying brightness levels.

There are a few more attributes that you can customize in the **Shadows** settings. They are as follows:

- **The On faces checkbox**: This checkbox enables faces to cast shadows on other faces. Shadows must be turned on in order to check this box.

- **The On ground checkbox**: This checkbox enables geometry to cast shadows on SketchUp's ground plane. To view the changes from this checkbox, you may need to zoom out to view the exterior shadows produced by the walls and ceiling, as seen in *Figure 10.14*.

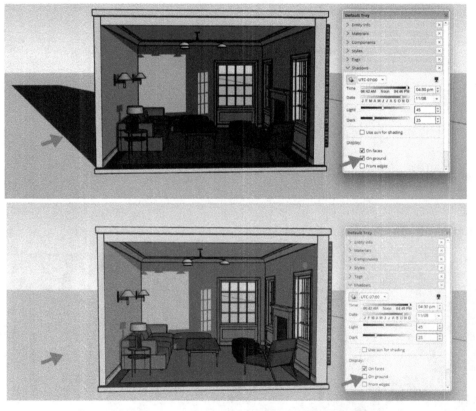

Figure 10.14: On ground checked (top) and unchecked (bottom)

- **The From edges checkbox**: This checkbox controls whether loose edges cast a shadow. Generally, we do not use this feature for interior design, and by default, the option is toggled off. Shadows must be turned on in order to check this box.

- **The Cast Shadows button**: We can also control whether a face, edge, group, or component cast shadows in the **Entity Info** toolbar. There is a toggle at the bottom right of **Entity Info** (see *Figure 10.15*). You can use this feature with ceilings so the room does not appear as dark.

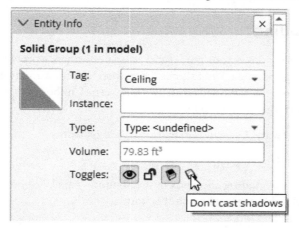

Figure 10.15: Control whether a group/component casts shadows in the Entity Info toolbar

The last checkbox in the **Shadows** panel is **Use sun for shading**. This checkbox enables SketchUp's simulated sun to shade your model even when **Show/Hide Shadows** is toggled off.

Figure 10.16: Use sun for shading checkbox

We utilize the **Use sun for shading** setting all the time. It does not gobble up your graphics card's processing power in the same way that casting shadows does, while still brightening up a space. Let's take a look at how this feature impacts the living room model.

Using sun for shading

Turning on shadows can slow down your model and cause performance problems. Another option is the **Use sun for shading** checkbox. Use this checkbox when shadows are turned off to maximize the performance of your computer. We will create two new scenes in the practice file to see how they compare to our scenes with shadows turned on.

Follow these steps to see how the **Use sun for shading** checkbox works:

1. Click on the No Shadows scene.

2. Check the **Use sun for shading** checkbox in the **Shadows** panel. See how much brighter and warmer the model feels after toggling on this feature.

Figure 10.17: SketchUp model with the Use sun for shading box checked

3. Right-click on the No Shadows scene and add a new scene. Name the new scene Shading-Light.

    Let's customize the Shading-Light scene a bit more to explore the other options.

4. Set the **Light** slider to 30 and the **Dark** slider to 30.

Figure 10.18: Set the Light and Dark sliders to 30

Moving these sliders to the left results in the space feeling much darker, as shown in *Figure 10.19.*

5. Right-click on the Shading-Light scene and add another new scene. Name it
    Shading-Dark.

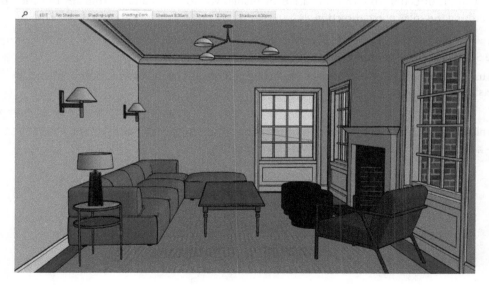

Figure 10.19: Shading-Dark scene

6.   If you have not already, save your model.

Now we have six scenes from the same perspective saved with different sun and shadow settings. Compare the differences. Which one do you like best? Remember which settings are your favorite so you can replicate them in the future.

> **Finding the perfect balance**
>
> You may need to finesse the **Light** and **Dark** sliders along with the **Time** and **Date** features to achieve the look you desire. There is nothing wrong with doing that! Just make sure to use scenes so the changes are saved.

The shadows are casting nicely in the living room practice model, but this will not always be the case for other SketchUp models. Sometimes, you will work in 3D models that have little to no direct sunlight. That's when the **Solar North** extension comes into play.

The Solar North extension

Solar North is an extension created by **SketchUp Team**. With Solar North, you can alter the solar north direction in your SketchUp model. This extension is especially useful when the model axes do not align with the cardinal directions for whatever reason.

It is also a helpful tool to use if your SketchUp model is not casting shadows the way you want. Sometimes, no matter how much you adjust the **Time** and **Date** sliders, you just can't get shadows to display in the direction you want. Solar North enables you to cast shadows from any direction by simply editing the solar north direction.

> **Use Solar North for photorealistic renders**
>
> We use this extension all the time when producing photorealistic renders to achieve aesthetically pleasing shadow lines.

To download Solar North, visit `https://extensions.sketchup.com/extension/393f5153-ba5f-4f5f-849f-46b32cf64bd4/solar-north`.

The Add Location feature in SketchUp

With SketchUp's **Add Location** feature, you can geolocate your model to a specific location anywhere in the world. Once your model is geolocated, SketchUp knows how the sun will shine on your model from that precise location, casting real-world shadows.

Although it may sound like a complex feature, the **Add Location** tool is very easy to use. Click on **File | Add Location**. You can add a location from anywhere in the world. Type an address or a landmark in the search box. Then, you can zoom in and out and move the blue location pin until you find the area you want to use; click **Continue**. If you are geolocating your model solely to cast real-world shadows, we recommend clicking **Skip Import**. With this option, you avoid adding unnecessary imagery and information to your model while still geolocating it.

Casting real-world shadows is one benefit of geolocating your model using the **Add Location** feature. You can also use this tool to import satellite images and site context, providing a reference for modeling surrounding terrain, buildings, roads, and other elements. Visit `https://help.sketchup.com/en/sketchup/add-location-sketchup-desktop-0` to learn more about importing site context with **Add Location**.

To add a location manually, go to **Window | Model Info** and select the **Geo-location** option from the list on the left. Click the **Set Manual Location...** button. Here, you can enter the **latitude** and **longitude** of a specific city or location. SketchUp will use this data to geolocate your model.

> **How to find the latitude and longitude**
>
> You can find the latitude and longitude in decimal format for a specific address or location by searching online.

As mentioned in *Chapter 6*, **Add Location** was updated with simplified workflows and expanded features with SketchUp 2024. If you are using an older version of SketchUp, you may not have access to some of the newer features.

We are ready to continue our conversation on enhancing a SketchUp model for a presentation by talking about the power of adding accessories and art to your 3D designs.

Accessorizing your 3D models

Accessories are the icing on the cake for most designs, adding interest and detail. The same is true for SketchUp designs. Simply adding accessories and artwork to 3D models can make a project feel complete.

Figure 10.20: Accessories can make a space pop with personality

The kitchen on the left without accessories in *Figure 10.20* feels unloved, while the kitchen on the right with accessories pops with personality. The accessories elevate the design and enable you to better imagine what the space would feel like in real life.

Tips for adding accessories in SketchUp

Here are some tips and best practices for adding accessories to SketchUp projects:

- Use **3D Warehouse** to download accessories. There are hundreds of files available to download and use for styling. When searching for accessories on **3D Warehouse**, we recommend typing a descriptive word in front of the word `accessories`. For example, type `bathroom accessories` in the search field for objects such as towels and soap dispensers.

  Remember to use the tips from *Chapter 7*, in the *3D Warehouse II – Downloading, reviewing, and importing* section, to evaluate and clean up **3D Warehouse** models before importing them into your working model.

Create your own 3D Warehouse collection

You can create an *accessories* collection and add models to it for future use. We will cover **3D Warehouse** collections in *Chapter 15*, when we talk about how to organize your SketchUp models.

- As always, you can build objects for styling from scratch.

- Nothing should be floating. For example, do you see how the vases are floating above the fireplace mantel in *Figure 10.21*? This is not ideal and unrealistic. The bottom of the vases should be touching the top face of the mantel, just as they would in real life.

Figure 10.21: A common SketchUp mistake is when objects are floating, such as these vases

- Import images to use as artwork. If your client has a piece of art that must be incorporated into the design (which is almost always the case!), take a picture of the artwork and import the image into SketchUp. When possible, use the exact artwork that you are proposing. To take it a step further, add a frame around it (just a rectangle with added depth).

- Assign the accessories to tags. You may want to add them all to an Accessories tag, or maybe you want to put the wall art on the corresponding wall tags. It's up to you!

With these tips under our belt, let's put them to practice in the next section.

Putting it together – Adding accessories and wall art to our model

Let's practice by adding accessories and wall art to the *Chapter 10* practice model:

1. Click on the EDIT scene, turn on the visibility for the Accessories tag, and update the scene. We added the decorative tray from *Chapter 8* to the coffee table. It is assigned to the Accessories tag.

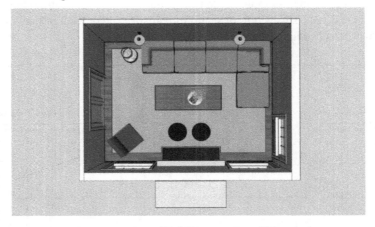

Figure 10.22: EDIT scene with the Accessories tag turned on

2. Add artwork on the wall between the two sconces. You can either find something in **3D Warehouse** or build a picture frame and import an image to use as art. Use any measurements that look proportionate to the area.

3. Add accessories on and/or over the fireplace mantle, on the walls as you see fit, and anywhere else in the model.

4. When you are done, assign the objects to the Accessories tag and save your model.

See *Figure 10.23* to compare the room with and without accessories.

Figure 10.23: No accessories (left) versus accessories added (right)

The right image also has the **Use sun for shading** feature turned on.

Adding accessories can go a long way toward helping your models communicate what they are supposed to.

For the latter half of this chapter, we will talk about SketchUp styles and presentation renderings.

Exploring SketchUp's Styles panel

So, you've built a beautiful 3D model with elaborate details and custom materials, and now it's time to decide how to present your completed model. You can make your models appear loose and sketchy, super technical, or anything in between using SketchUp's **Styles** panel.

SketchUp styles add depth and interest to 3D designs, so it is no surprise that they can slow down the processing speed of your computer. While you work on your model, make sure you are using a **Fast Style**. Style settings that slow down your SketchUp model are disabled for Fast Styles. When a style qualifies as a Fast Style, SketchUp displays a badge in the lower-right corner of the thumbnail. The badge is a small green stopwatch. If you hover your mouse over the green stopwatch, the **this is a fast modeling style** ScreenTip will appear, as shown in *Figure 10.24*.

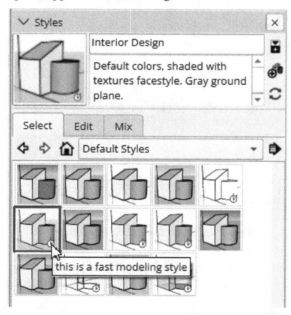

Figure 10.24: SketchUp displays a stopwatch badge in the lower-right corner for Fast Styles

We recommend saving a scene in your working model dedicated to editing with a Fast Style to optimize performance. As an example, the *Chapter 10* practice model includes a scene tab named EDIT with a Fast Style.

We are ready to start styling! In this section, you will learn how to select, edit, and mix styles. Let's begin with the basics, selecting a style.

Selecting a style

SketchUp has dozens of built-in style options that you can easily apply to your model. Each predefined style is a compilation of display settings that changes the model's aesthetic. Open the **Styles** panel in the **Default Tray** to view SketchUp's built-in style options. (On macOS, find the **Styles** panel in **Window | Styles**.)

If you do not see the **Styles** panel in your **Default Tray**, choose **Window | Default Tray | Styles**.

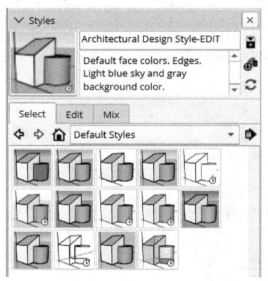

Figure 10.25: SketchUp's Styles panel

You will see a thumbnail, name, and description at the top of the panel, which is the currently selected style. In *Figure 10.25*, the currently selected style is named **Architectural Design Style-EDIT**.

Click the **Select** tab if it is not already selected. From here, you can view the different style collections using the drop-down menu.

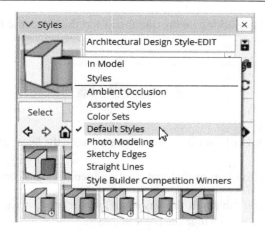

Figure 10.26: Drop-down menu for Style Collections

From a collection, click on a style thumbnail to apply the style to your model. Peruse the different collections of SketchUp's built-in styles to see what is available.

If you can't quite find what you're looking for in SketchUp's built-in styles, you can also customize styles in the **Styles** panel by editing and mixing existing ones.

Editing and mixing styles

We are going to walk through the **Edit** and **Mix** tabs found in the **Styles** panel to demonstrate how to customize SketchUp styles.

Figure 10.27: Use the Edit and Mix tabs to customize styles

Select a style you want to edit by clicking on the thumbnail and then click the **Edit** tab. There are five boxes at the top (*Figure 10.28*).

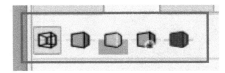

Figure 10.28: Five boxes at the top of the Edit tab in the Styles panel

Here are the five boxes and a list of properties that can be edited in each (from left to right):

- **Edge Settings**: Here, you can adjust the way edges are displayed by checking and unchecking different boxes. You can also change the color of edges.

- **Face Settings**: Click this box to edit the way faces appear in your model. The face style options include wireframe, hidden line, shaded, shaded using textures, shaded using all same, and X-ray. Additionally, toggle global **Material transparency** on or off and adjust the **X-ray opacity**. Lastly, there is an option to check the **Ambient Occlusion** box, which is a fantastic style feature that enhances the visual impact of edge and face interactions in your models through shading techniques, thus boosting realism in SketchUp. You can also use pre-built styles in the **Ambient Occlusion** style collection. We will take a closer look at this feature in the next section, *Exercise – Adding styles to the living room model*.

> **Pro tip**
>
> Have you ever noticed faint white lines that outline various edges throughout a SketchUp model when you turn off **Profiles** and **Edges**? That is the default color from the interior faces of objects seeping through the edges. To hide those faint white lines, change **Back color** in **Face Settings** to a dark gray or black.

- **Background Settings**: Change the background settings, such as sky color and ground color, in this editing area. With the **Ground** box checked, you can use the **Transparency** slider to adjust how much you can see underneath the ground plane. This is a particularly helpful feature for exterior perspectives (we use it in the *Chapter 6* practice file).

- **Watermark Settings**: Insert a company logo, a background image, or an artistic border by adding a watermark. You can learn about watermarking a SketchUp model here: `https://help.sketchup.com/en/sketchup/watermarking-model`.

- **Modeling Settings**: Here, you can adjust display colors, visible geometry, and Match Photo options. Many of the properties in this tab can be accessed in different menus as well. (*Chapter 6* briefly addresses some of these properties while discussing **sections**.)

Use the **Mix** tab to bring aspects of one style into another. For example, you may want to use only the edge settings from one style but none of the other settings. You can use the **Mix** tab to accomplish this.

Let's practice editing and mixing styles in an exercise.

Exercise – Adding styles to the living room model

Now that you've learned about the features found in the **Styles** panel, let's practice adding a few different styles to the Chapter 10 - Shadows and Styles practice model:

1. Click on the scene tab named No Shadows.
2. In the **Styles** panel, select **Style Builder Competition Winners** from the collections drop-down list.
3. Apply the style named **Tech Pen Endpoints** by clicking on it.

> **Looking for a specific style name?**
> If you hover your cursor over any of the style thumbnails, SketchUp will display the style name.

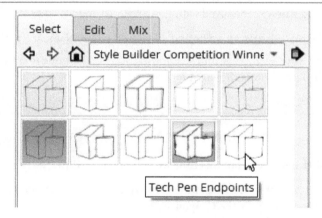

Figure 10.29: Hover your cursor over a thumbnail to see the style name

4. Now, let's splash some sunlight onto it. Go to the **Shadows** panel and toggle on the **Show/Hide Shadows** button.

Figure 10.30: Tech Pen Endpoints style with shadows turned on

Remember, every time you make a visual change within a scene, such as adding shadows or modifying a style, you should either update the scene or add a new scene. For this exercise, we are going to add a new scene saved with these style settings.

5. Right-click on the No Shadows scene and add a new scene. Name it Style A.

6. Right-click on the Style A scene and select **Move Right**. Continue to move the scene to the right until it is the last scene as shown in *Figure 10.31*.

Figure 10.31: Move Style A scene to the right

Let's create another new scene but this time we will practice editing a style:

7. Click on the No Shadows scene again. In the **Styles** panel, select **Sketchy Edges** from the drop-down list. Find and apply the **Crayon** style.

8. Go to the **Edit** tab and click on **Face Settings**. Select the **Display shaded using textures** option by clicking on it. It may take a few seconds to load the textures.

9. Go to **Background Settings** and check the **Sky** and **Ground** boxes. Adjust the colors for the sky and ground to whatever you think looks good.

10. Open the **Shadows** panel and click the **Use sun for shading** checkbox.

11. Lastly, turn on the visibility for the Accessories tag.

12. Right-click on the Style A scene and add a new scene.

This time, a warning popup appears asking what you would like to do with your style changes. Select **Save as a new style.** and click **Create Scene**.

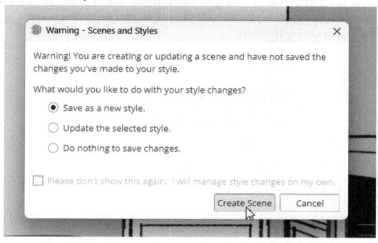

Figure 10.32: Select Save as a new style. and Create Scene

By saving your style changes as a new style, you are preserving the original style settings. Now you can go to the styles **In Model** folder and update things like the style name and description.

13. Rename the new scene `Style B`.

Figure 10.33: Style B scene

Looks great!

Now we will create a final scene by mixing styles:

14. This time, click the Shadows 12:30pm scene. In the **Styles** panel, click on the **Mix** tab. The **Styles** panel expands when you click this tab. A second drop-down menu appears at the bottom of the panel; see *Figure 10.34*.

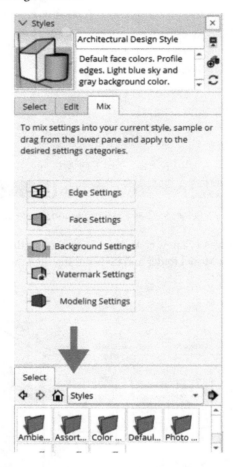

Figure 10.34: A second drop-down menu appears when you click on the Mix tab

15. From the second drop-down list at the bottom of the panel, select the **In Model** folder or click on the home icon.

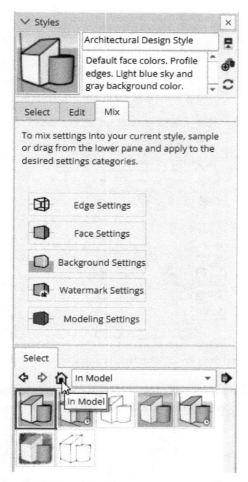

Figure 10.35: Select the home icon from the bottom menu

16. Find the **Pencil With Border and Trees** style **In Model**. What we want to do is apply only **Watermark Settings** from this style to our current scene.

    To do this, click and drag the **Pencil With Border and Trees** thumbnail to the **Watermark Settings** option, as shown in *Figure 10.36*.

Figure 10.36: Click and drag Pencil With Border and Trees to Watermark Settings

If done properly, a white border will appear along with a view of trees outside the window, which are the watermark settings from the **Pencil With Border and Trees** style.

Figure 10.37: Mixing watermark settings

We are going to edit a few more settings to complete this style.

17. Go to the **Edit** tab in the **Styles** panel and click on the **Edge Settings** icon. Match the settings from *Figure 10.38* to your SketchUp model by checking the same boxes and adjusting the numbers as needed.

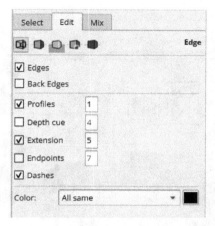

Figure 10.38: Replicate these Edge Settings

18. Now, we are going to use the **Ambient Occlusion** feature. Click on the **Face Settings** icon, check the **Ambient Occlusion** box, and adjust the **Distance** and **Intensity** sliders as you see fit.

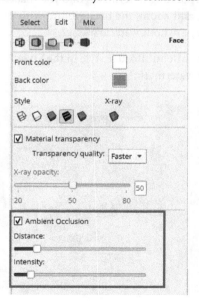

Figure 10.39: Adjust the Distance and Intensity sliders for Ambient Occlusion

19. Turn on the visibility for the `Accessories` tag.

20. And lastly, hide the axes by clicking **Axes** from the **View** menu.

21. Right-click on the `Style B` scene and add a new scene. (Select **Save as a new style** again.) Name it `Style C`.

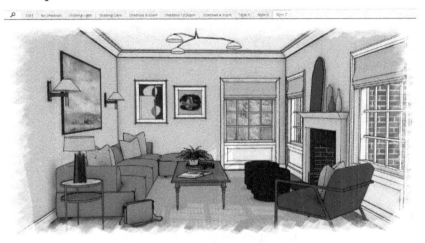

Figure 10.40: Create a new scene named Style C

Zoom out to see the effects of incorporating watermarks into your SketchUp model (see *Figure 10.41*). Notice how when you orbit, pan, and zoom, the background with the trees and the white border remains static? That is because they are both watermarks.

(Credit to the **Pencil Edges With Whiteout Border** style in the **Style Builder Competition Winners** collection for the whiteout border watermark.)

Figure 10.41: Zoom out to see the impacts of adding watermarks

Let's compare `Style C` with the original 3D model before we added shadows, accessories, and styles.

Figure 10.42: Original 3D model without shadows, accessories, and styles (top) versus Style C (bottom)

Can you believe it is the same room? We did that all inside SketchUp!

If that isn't enough, you can create your own sketchy styles from lines you have drawn yourself using **Style Builder**. If you are a SketchUp Pro user, Style Builder is part of the package. Visit `https://help.sketchup.com/en/style-builder/style-builder` to learn more.

Purge unused styles

Every style clicked in the model remains in it, increasing the file size. Remember to purge unused styles every now and then by clicking the corresponding option from the **Details** arrow. Review *Chapter 3*, the section *Learning lesser-known timesavers*, for how to use **Purge Unused**.

When you combine the ability to create your own SketchUp styles and then edit and mix them with other styles, the possibilities are endless!

To take it a step further, consider using external resources to enhance your SketchUp designs. That is what we will talk about in the final section of this chapter.

Enhancing 3D designs outside of SketchUp

Combine your SketchUp designs with other mediums, such as Photoshop or even pen and paper, to create presentation renderings.

Photoshop renderings

You can export 2D images of your SketchUp model and then use those images to import into Photoshop. (We will cover how to export images from SketchUp in the next chapter, *Chapter 11*.) Then, in Photoshop, add shading, color correction, light glows, and other effects to enhance your presentation renderings.

Figure 10.43 shows an example of an exported SketchUp model rendered in Photoshop.

Figure 10.43: An exported SketchUp 2D image rendered in Photoshop by
SketchUp School (www.sketchupschool.com) based on a real-world design
by Martha Picciotti of Picciotti Design (www.picciottidesign.com)

Photorealistic renderings

Create a *wow* effect by using third-party programs to produce photorealistic renderings of your SketchUp models. There are multiple rendering plugins for SketchUp; popular ones include SU Podium, Enscape, V-Ray, KeyShot, and 3ds Max. We discuss the basics of how to produce photorealistic renderings using SU Podium in *Chapter 14*.

See *Figure 10.44* for a kitchen SketchUp model rendered in SU Podium to create a photorealistic effect.

Figure 10.44: A SketchUp model rendered in SU Podium by Nat Ellis, Head of
3D Visualization at jbA Architecture. Website: www.jbarch.co.uk

If you like the character and imperfections that only handcrafted work can produce, give hand-drawn renderings a try.

Hand-drawn renderings

Use your handy-dandy notebook (and pen) to create whimsical pieces of art. Print a hard copy of your SketchUp scene and trace over it for a hand-drawn look. The dreamy result will feel like a piece of art and enhance your presentations.

Figure 10.45 shows an exported SketchUp image traced with a pen.

Figure 10.45: SketchUp model exported as a 2D image and hand rendered with a pen. Design by Heather Hilliard Design and render by Carré Design Studio (courtesy of https://carredesigns.com/)

Figure 10.46 shows a model traced with a pen and then further edited in Photoshop. This is an example of combining multiple mediums to showcase your SketchUp designs.

Figure 10.46: SketchUp model exported as a 2D image, hand rendered
with a pen and edited in Photoshop. Design by JayJeffers Inc and render
by Carré Design Studio (courtesy of https://carredesigns.com/)

We hope this chapter got your creative juices flowing! There are so many powerful techniques to enhance your SketchUp models.

Summary

Experimenting with how to present your SketchUp designs can be fun and satisfying. In this chapter, we discussed how to use SketchUp's **Shadows** panel and the power of adding accessories to your models. We also took a deep dive into SketchUp's **Styles** panel and shared examples of utilizing external resources to enhance your SketchUp models.

In the next chapter, we will cover exporting SketchUp images and printing to scale. We will also walk through how to create moving animations to help clients better understand proposed designs.

Part 4: Presenting SketchUp Designs

Conveying your design vision effectively involves showcasing your ideas in a visually appealing and understandable manner. In this part, we discuss how to create walkthroughs using SketchUp's animation features and prepare an impressive presentation or construction document with SketchUp LayOut. Discover the art of generating stunning photorealistic, high-quality images with SU Podium, a widely used rendering plugin. This powerful tool enhances your design workflow and provides clients with a compelling means to visualize the completed project in remarkable detail.

This part has the following chapters:

- *Chapter 11, Exporting Images and Animations*
- *Chapter 12, SketchUp LayOut Part I – The Interface*
- *Chapter 13, SketchUp LayOut Part II – Paper Space Content*
- *Chapter 14, Photorealistic Rendering with SU Podium*

Exporting Images and Animations

In this chapter, we will discuss how to export a single image and a batch of images. We will also learn about the tools and techniques you can use to simulate a person walking through your model with SketchUp animations. You can use exported SketchUp images and animations for presentations, marketing purposes, or post-processing in an outside application. In the last section of this chapter, we will demonstrate how to print and export SketchUp designs to scale, giving step-by-step instructions.

In this chapter, we will cover the following topics:

- Exporting 2D graphics from SketchUp
- Creating walk-through animations
- Exporting SketchUp designs to scale

Technical requirements

This chapter requires the following software and files:

- SketchUp Pro or SketchUp Studio
- Download the practice file from 3D Warehouse named Chapter 11- Images and Animations or download it from https://3dwarehouse.sketchup.com/model/9e00d3c0-b440-45df-836a-9dc5d8448c74/Chapter-11-Images-and-Animations

Exporting 2D graphics from SketchUp

Exporting scenes as 2D images is one of the easiest ways to share snapshots of your model with others. You can use the images internally to help finalize design details, share the images with clients, or select a few favorite perspectives to enhance outside SketchUp (as we discussed in *Chapter 10*, in the *Enhancing 3D designs outside of SketchUp* section). As with many things in SketchUp, exporting an image is intuitive. Let's get started!

Exporting an image

When you export an image in SketchUp, a good rule of thumb is to export a scene. That way, if you need to change an item in the scene and export a new one, you do not have to orbit, pan, and zoom your way to create the same view as before.

What is exported in an image? Everything that can be viewed within the modeling window. That means no toolbars, such as the **Default Tray** or **Measurements** box, will show. You can leave them as-is.

Click on **File | Export | 2D Graphic...** to export an image of your SketchUp model. A browser will appear, enabling you to pick a location to save the image, select a file format, and name the file. From here, you can also adjust the size and quality of the image by clicking the **Options...** button (although choosing **Options...** is not required to produce a nice image).

Figure 11.1: Click the Options... button to adjust the image size

After clicking the **Options...** button, an **Export options** menu pops up. To adjust the pixel width and height, uncheck **Use view size**.

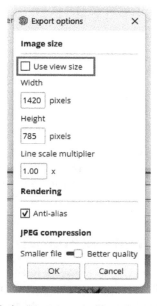

Figure 11.2: Uncheck the "Use view size" box to set the pixel dimensions

The higher the pixel number, the clearer your image will be. The sharpness and quality are especially noticeable when using SketchUp's **Sketchy Edges** collection from the **Styles** toolbar. Take the images in *Figure 11.3*, for example.

Figure 11.3: Higher pixels work better for styles with sketchy edges

Both images in *Figure 11.3* were exported from the exact same SketchUp scene, using the **Brush Strokes Wide** style from the **Sketchy Edges** collection. The only difference between the two images is the pixel dimensions. The left image is 400 x 600 pixels, and the right image is 2100 x 3150 pixels. The right image is much sharper, because it was exported with a higher number of pixels.

> **The magic numbers for pixels**
>
> The magic number for printing a 2D graphic is 300 **PPI** (**pixels per inch**). An image will appear crisp and sharp at 300 PPI. For example, a 4 " x 6 " image should be 1200 x 1800 pixels.
>
> The magic number for web images is 72 PPI. This will display your image crisp and sharp on a screen.

Another export option that is helpful when using a style from the **Sketchy Edges** collection is **Line scale multiplier**.

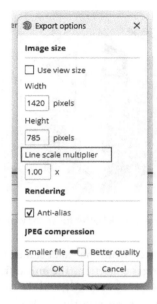

Figure 11.4: Find the Line scale multiplier feature in Export options

The default setting of **Line scale multiplier** is 1.00, and the minimum is 0.25. The lower the number, the thinner the SketchUp lines will appear in the exported image. For example, the left image in *Figure 11.5* is 400 x 600 pixels, with **Line scale multiplier** set to the default 1.00. The right image is also 400 x 600 pixels but with **Line scale multiplier** set to 0.25.

Figure 11.5: Set Line scale multiplier to 0.25 for sketchy edges

Play around with the export settings, and you will soon find your go-to combination!

> **Can you only export scenes?**
>
> No, you can export a 2D graphic from any perspective of your SketchUp model. It does not have to be a saved scene. However, we recommend saving scenes with names so that you can easily return to them.

For those of you who wish to export multiple scenes at once, you're in luck! Continue reading to learn how.

Exporting multiple scenes

It is not uncommon to have a SketchUp file with 15+ scenes. It can be tedious and time-consuming if you want to export every scene as a 2D graphic. Good thing SketchUp has a shortcut!

Before we walk through how to export multiple scenes at once, let's create some client-worthy scenes to export.

In `3D Warehouse`, download the SketchUp model titled `Chapter 11- Images and Animations`. You will see a family room and kitchen from the **Top** view.

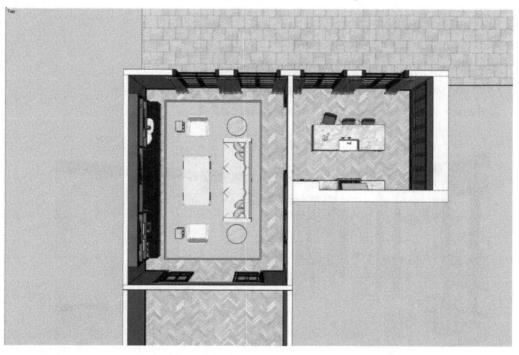

Figure 11.6: The Chapter 11 practice model

For the family room and kitchen, neutral finishes were chosen for most of the furniture, rug, and draperies because, at this point in the design process, we want to focus on the hard finishes and space planning.

In our practice model, we will create scenes from all angles of the two rooms to share with our clients. We have already created four scenes of the family room (named FR-1, FR-2, FR-3, and FR-4) and one scene of the kitchen (named K-1), as shown in *Figure 11.7*.

Figure 11.7: The practice model scenes already created

You will also see an EDIT scene, saved with a Fast Style to optimize performance. (Revisit the *Exploring SketchUp's Styles panel* section in *Chapter 10* for information on Fast Styles.)

For now, you can ignore the FR-ELEVATION scene tab. We will use this scene in the last section of the chapter, *Exporting SketchUp designs to scale*.

To add more scenes of the family room, follow these steps:

1. Click on the scene tab named FR-4.
2. Turn the visibility *off* for the tag named Walls-3.
3. Turn the visibility *on* for the tag named Walls-2.
4. Orbit and pan so that the camera faces northeast, as shown in *Figure 11.8*.
5. Add a new scene to the right of FR-4, and name it FR-5.

Figure 11.8: Create a new scene facing northeast, and name it FR-5

6. Orbit and pan as needed so that the camera faces southeast, as shown in *Figure 11.9*.

7. Add a new scene, and name it FR-6.

Figure 11.9: Create a new scene facing southeast, and name it FR-6

8. Continue around the room by turning off different tags and creating new scenes from each angle. Choose angles that you think look good. Aim for a total of 8–10 scenes (including the scenes already created) showcasing the family room. Remember to name each scene.

See *Figure 11.10* for examples of scene perspectives. Your views will differ, depending on how you choose to angle the camera.

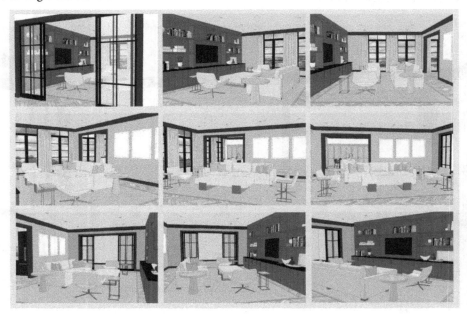

Figure 11.10: Family room scenes

There is a lesser-known zoom tool called **Field of View**. It allows you to adjust the field of view in degrees. It is a helpful tool when working inside small rooms because it lets you adjust how much you can see without bumping into walls and other objects.

Figure 11.11 shows the same perspective of our kitchen from two different fields of view. The **Field of View** setting in the left image is 35 degrees, and the **Field of View** setting in the right image is 60 degrees.

Figure 11.11: The left Field of View setting at 35 degrees versus the right Field of View setting at 60 degrees

You can see more of the space in the right image with the field of view set to 60 degrees. Try using the **Field of View** tool when you aren't quite getting the results you are looking for with the standard **Zoom** tool.

To edit the field of view, select **Field of View** from the **Camera** menu. Click and drag your mouse to visually adjust the field of view, or type a value in degrees. Remember to update your scene after you are done adjusting.

> **Field of view distortion**
>
> Adjusting the field of view can certainly help show more of a small space, but it is important to be aware that it can sometimes cause a *fisheye effect*.

Let's create scenes for the kitchen. Start by clicking on the scene named K-1, and move around the room in the same way you did for the family room. Aim for a total of 5–7 scenes of the kitchen, as shown in *Figure 11.12*. Consider using **Field of View** to capture more of the space.

Figure 11.12: Kitchen scenes

Awesome! Once you finalize your scenes, you are ready to export 2D graphics. Follow these steps to export all the scenes simultaneously:

1. Go to **Window | Model Info | Animation**, and uncheck **Enable scene transitions**.

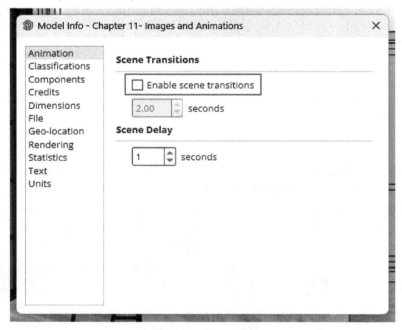

Figure 11.13: Untick the Enable scene transitions box

2. Go to **File | Export | Animation…**
3. A browser will appear. Select **JPEG image set (*.jpg)** from the **Save as type** drop-down menu.

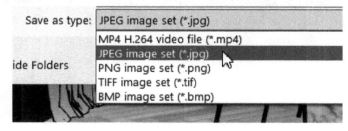

Figure 11.14: Choose JPEG image set (*.jpg)

Next, we are going to adjust the size of the images.

4. Click the **Options...** button.

5. Select **Custom** from the **Resolution** dropdown and **Custom** from the **Aspect ratio** dropdown.

6. Type 1800 for the pixel width.

7. Type 1200 for the pixel height. Click **OK**.

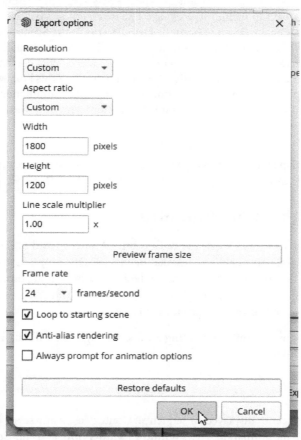

Figure 11.15: Settings for Export options

8. Type Chapter 11- Images and Animations_ in the **File name** field.

9. Pick a location on your computer to save the images, and click **Export**.

Navigate to the folder you selected to view the exported images. They should all be there. No more exporting each scene one at a time!

> **Pro tip – exclude certain scenes**
>
> There may be times when you do not want to export every scene in a JPEG image set. For example, you may not want to include a *working* scene when doing a batch export of scenes. You can control which scenes to include from the **Default Tray** in the **Scenes** panel. To do this, navigate to the **Scenes** panel, and click on a scene that you do not want to include. Then, click on the **Show Details** icon in the upper-right corner of the **Scenes** panel; a list of checkboxes will appear. Uncheck the **Include in animation** box. By unchecking this box, we tell SketchUp to not include this specific scene when exporting multiple images simultaneously. The scene also will be excluded if you create a walk-through animation, which we will cover how to do in the next section.

In the next section, SketchUp animations take center stage! You can get super-creative with this feature, by making animated walk-throughs using different styles and shadows. Let's begin.

Creating walk-through animations

Have you ever wondered how **HGTV** (**Home & Garden Television**) and other home renovation channels create animated walk-throughs and installation videos? One program they use is SketchUp! SketchUp provides a way to explore your 3D designs interactively, by walking through your SketchUp model as if you were actually walking through a space in real life. You can give a seamless tour by using the camera tools and setting up your scenes sequentially.

Before we jump into the ins and outs of creating a walk-through, we will talk about the basics of animating scenes in SketchUp.

Animating scenes

SketchUp animations are scenes displayed in sequence. Context-click any scene tab and select **Play Animation**. To customize the animation, go to **Window | Model Info**, and choose **Animation** in the sidebar. Alternatively, go to **View | Animation | Settings**. Either way, the **Model Info** window will appear with editing options.

Let's take a look at the editing options with our practice model, Chapter 11- Images and Animations:

1. Right-click on the FR-1 scene, and select **Play Animation**. You will see a slideshow of your scenes.

    Instead of a slideshow with still transitions between scenes, we want to see animated transitions. We can change that in the **Model Info** window.

2. Go to **Window | Model Info | Animation**, and check **Enable scene transitions**. (We unchecked this box in the previous section, *Exporting 2D graphics from SketchUp*, when we exported multiple scenes at once. Yours may already be checked.)

3. Type 2 . 50 for the number of seconds under **Scene Transitions**. This sets the length of time from one scene to the next to 2.50 seconds.

    You can also type a number in the **seconds** box under **Scene Delay** to set how long a scene is displayed before transitioning to the next one. For our purposes, you can leave this at 1 second.

4. Close the **Model Info** window by clicking the **X** icon. (The settings automatically save when you close the window.)

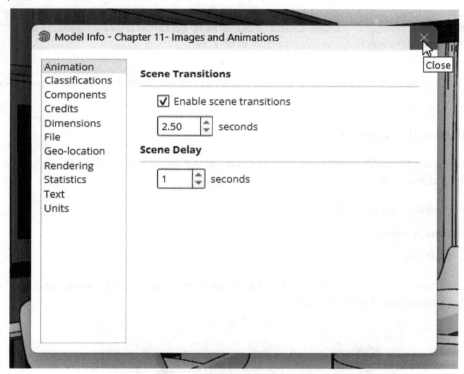

Figure 11.16: Model Info Animation settings

5. Right-click on the FR-1 scene, and select **Play Animation** again.

Did you notice how you travel to each scene rather than cutting to it, like a slideshow? That is because we checked the **Enable scene transitions** box.

Additional info about scene animation

Note that the **Scene Transitions** and **Scene Delay** settings apply to all scenes and cannot be adjusted for individual scenes. Create multiple, consecutive copies of a scene if you want it to display longer in the animation.

There are awesome **extensions** that have additional ways to create animations. **Animate Sections** by *How2SU*, a free extension found at `https://extensions.sketchup.com/extension/877a3ded-a7d5-4b73-aa26-400e6fd3d4d6/animate-sections`, is a great way to animate a section plane to show the construction of any object. **Animator** by *Fredo6*, found at `https://sketchucation.com/pluginstore?pln=Animator`, provides a seamless way to show the assembly of objects.

Next, we will introduce SketchUp's walk-through camera tools and show you how to export scenes as an MP4 file.

Walk-through camera tools

A great way to use SketchUp animations is to pretend you are walking through the model. Here are the SketchUp camera tools that help you accomplish this:

- The **Position Camera** tool
- The **Look Around** tool
- The **Walk** tool

You can find these tools in the **Camera** toolbar, **Large Tool Set,** or under the **Camera** menu. Activate either or both toolbars at **View | Toolbars…**.

Figure 11.17: Position Camera, Look Around, and Walk tools in the Camera toolbar

---

Widen the field of view

We recommend experimenting with the **Field of View** tool before using the walk-through tools. Some perspectives work best when SketchUp's camera has a wide field of view, such as 50 or 60 degrees, so that you can see more of the model.

The rest of this section covers how the walk-through tools work and how to export animations. We will also share an example of an exported SketchUp animation.

The Position Camera tool

The **Position Camera** tool allows you to place the camera at a specific height within your model. The height is meant to represent a person's eye level. You can set it to any height.

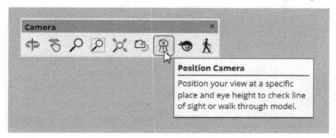

Figure 11.18: The Position Camera icon

There are two ways to use the **Position Camera** tool:

- Click on the icon to activate the tool, and then click anywhere on the floor. Your eye height defaults to 5'-6". If you want a different eye height, type a new value in the **Measurements** box, and press the *Enter* key. With this method, the camera defaults to facing north.

- You can also position the camera to face a specific direction (rather than facing north). With the **Position Camera** tool active, click and hold the mouse where you want to set the camera. Then, drag the cursor to define the direction you want the camera to face. After you release your mouse, you may need to type a new eye level, as it will likely be 0".

  For example, using the *Chapter 11* practice model, let's say you want to simulate the view of someone standing in the kitchen looking into the family room. See *Figure 11.19* for a visual example of how to do that with **Position Camera**.

Figure 11.19: Position the camera facing a specific direction, and then type a new Eye Height

After you set the camera position, the **Look Around** tool automatically activates. This means it's time to look at **Look Around**.

The Look Around tool

The **Look Around** tool simulates looking around a model from a stationary viewpoint, as if you were standing and turning your head. The **Look Around** tool automatically activates after you use the **Position Camera** tool. Otherwise, you need to click the **Look Around** icon to activate it.

When the **Look Around** tool is active, the cursor changes to an eye.

Figure 11.20: The Look Around icon

Click and drag your mouse left, right, up, and down to swivel and view a space. At any point, you can type a different **Eye Height** value in the **Measurements** box and press *Enter*.

> **The Eye Height value**
>
> It is worth noting that the **Eye Height** value is relative to SketchUp's ground plane, not a face in your model.

Let's walk through the final walk-through tool, the **Walk** tool. (Talk about a tongue twister!)

The Walk tool

The **Walk** tool enables you to move through a SketchUp model and turn in different directions, all while staying at a constant eye height. Once you have the camera positioned and eye level set, click on the **Walk** icon to activate it. The cursor changes to a person walking.

Figure 11.21: The Walk icon

Click and drag to walk. Move the cursor up, down, left, or right to explore your model. Did you see the crosshair icon? Move your mouse farther from the crosshair to walk faster; move your mouse closer to the crosshair to walk slower. You can even walk up and down stairs and inclines!

> **Walk through walls and furniture**
>
> Collision detection is on by default. This means you cannot walk through walls or furniture. Hold *Alt* (Windows) or ⌘ (macOS) down while using the **Walk** tool to disable collision detection and move through walls and furniture.

Here are a few more features to try while using the **Walk** tool:

- Hold *Shift* down to visually move the eye level up or down (rather than typing a value into the **Measurements** box)

- Hold *Ctrl* down to run

- Hold the scroll wheel down to use the **Look Around** tool

To see the **Position Camera**, **Look Around**, and **Walk** tools in action, we will share an example of a SketchUp walk-through animation now, along with some tips.

An animation example and tips

We created a walk-through animation of the *Chapter 11* practice model (Chapter 11- Images and Animations) using SketchUp's camera and navigation tools. You can view the exported animation here: https://youtu.be/hhqGtaosDYQ. (We will talk about how to export SketchUp animations next.)

Pretty neat, huh? Imagine this video playing on a loop while presenting to a client.

Here are some notes about the animated walk-through example:

- After exporting the SketchUp animation, we used a separate application for post-processing. We added two SU Podium renderings to enhance the video. (*Chapter 14* covers photorealistic rendering with SU Podium.)

- SketchUp's default eye height is 5'-6". Instead, we used 4'-6" in the video, as we feel it displays the space in a more aesthetically pleasing way.

- We adjusted the field of view multiple times throughout the scenes to showcase more of the rooms.

- **Scene Transitions** are set to 3.50 seconds.

- **Scene Delay** is set to 0 seconds; that way, the animation does not pause on every scene.

- We added shadows to one of the scenes to create an interesting transition of moving shadows. You can also use different SketchUp styles to create interest.

Don't be overly concerned about your walk-through animations being true walk-throughs. If you look up, down, and all around in a SketchUp model in the *exact* way you would in real life, your client or audience is going to feel nauseous. Instead, consider taking a break from *walking* and *looking around* to zooming slowly in or out. This not only gives the viewer a moment to process what they are seeing, but it also gives you the opportunity to highlight a design element visually (or verbally if you are presenting).

Exporting video animations

After you create and sequence your scenes, exporting your animation is easy. It is basically the same as exporting a 2D graphic but with different export options.

Go to **File** | **Export** | **Animation…**. A browser will pop up, enabling you to pick a location to save the animation, select a file format, and name the file. We recommend using **MP4 H.264 video file (*.mp4)** from the **Save as type** dropdown; .mp4 is one of the most supported video file formats.

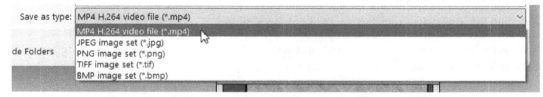

Figure 11.22: MP4 H.264 video file (*.mp4) under the Save as type drop-down list

Click **Options…** to open the **Export options** menu. This is where you can edit the resolution, aspect ratio, and more. Visit https://help.sketchup.com/en/sketchup/animating-scenes#export-video for an overview of the export options.

Exported animations are a great tool to use for client presentations. They may even be helpful for contractors or construction crews, in addition to official construction documents of course. With this knowledge under our belt, we will move on to the final topic for this chapter – exporting SketchUp designs to scale.

Exporting SketchUp designs to scale

With SketchUp Pro or Studio, you can export your 3D designs to scale as a PDF directly from SketchUp. Then, you can print the exported PDF to produce a scaled drawing. If you have attempted this before, you know that it sometimes requires extra attention to ensure your model is, in fact, to scale and not split across multiple pages.

You can also use **SketchUp LayOut** to export to scale, which is very easy and straightforward (and better for larger exports, such as an entire building or a building with geo-located terrain). We will cover LayOut in *Chapters 12* and *13*.

The first step to exporting a SketchUp design to scale is creating a scene with the correct settings.

Setting up a scene to be exported to scale

Follow these steps to set up your scene using the `Chapter 11- Images and Animations` model.

1. Click on the `FR-ELEVATION` scene tab. We are going to export the family room built-ins to ¼" scale.

    To export to scale, your view must be in **Parallel Projection** using the appropriate **Standard View** (Top, Bottom, Front, Back, Left, or Right). Isometric view, or any other 3D perspective view, will not work when exporting to scale. If your view isn't set up properly, you will not be able to define the scale in the properties (they will be grayed out).

    We have already set up the `FR-ELEVATION` scene correctly; it is in **Parallel Projection** with the **Right** camera view setting, using a **Section Cut** with the **Section Plane** hidden. Also, the `Ceiling` and `Floor` tags are turned off.

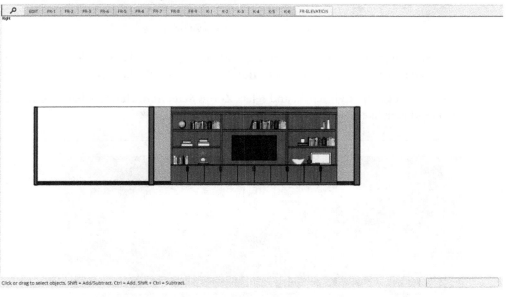

Figure 11.23: The FR-ELEVATION scene

Section Cuts and Section Planes

Section Cuts allow you to slice your model and view interior geometry without hiding any groups or turning off any tags. You can add multiple Section Planes to a model, which is valuable for creating plans and elevations.

Visit *Chapter 6* to review Section Cuts and Section Planes.

SketchUp will export the entire model window. This means if you have a bunch of open white space in the model window, SketchUp will allocate page space for that area. That is how you end up with multiple blank pages. Although the FR-ELEVATION scene is set up with the correct settings, the model window has way too much blank white space, as shown in *Figure 11.24*.

Figure 11.24: There is too much open white space

If we tried exporting this view, we would end up with blank pages and our model split between pages. To avoid this, we will use **Zoom Selection** to zoom in on the built-ins.

2.   Select the built-in group, right-click, and select **Zoom Selection**. Here is what your model window should look like now:

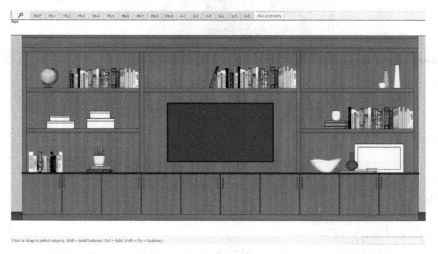

Figure 11.25: Select the built-in group, right-click, and click Zoom Selection

3.   Much better! Update the scene if you haven't yet.

With the scene set up correctly, we are ready to define the export properties.

PDF export options

Follow these steps to define the PDF export options, ensuring that your SketchUp design exports to scale:

1. Click on the FR-ELEVATION scene tab.

2. From the **File** menu, choose **Export**, and then **2D Graphic**.

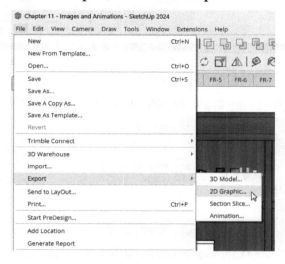

Figure 11.26: The File menu | Export | 2D Graphic

3. In the **Export 2D Graphic** window, choose **PDF File (*.pdf)** from the **Save as type** dropdown. We use a PDF rather than an image file for added accuracy when creating a physical print of a view.

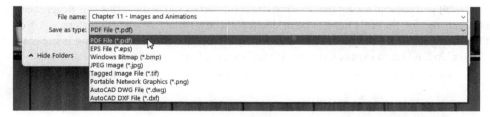

Figure 11.27: Choose a PDF file from the dropdown

> **Important Note**
> Exporting as a PDF is only an option for SketchUp Pro and Studio users.

4. Navigate to where you want to save the PDF file and click once on the folder. Change the file name, if necessary. We should be purposeful with naming files. For example, you could name this one `Family Room Built-ins Elevation`.

5. Click **Options**.

   Any time you are exporting to scale, click **Options…** to make sure the settings are correct.

Figure 11.28: Click Options… before exporting

There is an error message you might see after clicking **Options…**. This is what it looks like:

Figure 11.29: An error window after clicking Options

6. Click **OK** to try to fix the issue in the next step.

Troubleshooting

Sometimes, when first using the **PDF Export options** window, an error message (shown in *Figure 11.29*) will pop up, saying the drawing size is limited to 100 inches. This can either mean that the settings for the scale need to be updated correctly, which we will do in steps 9–10, or that the area you want to export is too large for SketchUp alone to handle. If that is the case, use SketchUp LayOut to export the view. We will discuss LayOut in *Chapters 12* and *13*.

7. A new window called **PDF Export options** will open.

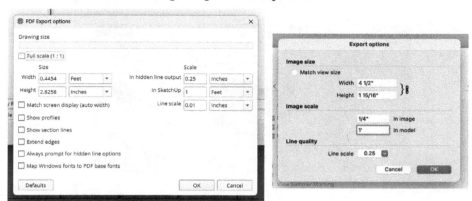

Figure 11.30: PDF Export options for Windows (left) and macOS (right)

If **Scale**, to the right of **Drawing size**, is grayed out, you are not in **Parallel Projection** and cannot change the scale. Click **Cancel** and fix the error in your model.

8. Make sure **Full scale (1:1)** is unchecked.

9. Your **PDF Export options** window might show one, or some, of the checkboxes on the left side of the window either checked or grayed out, such as **Match screen display (auto width)**. You can leave them checked for this export, and then try another export with them unchecked to see what the difference is. (We also show you the difference between **Match screen display (auto width)** checked versus unchecked in *Figure 11.31*.)

10. On the right, underneath **Scale**, change **In hidden line output** to read 0.25, and then hit the *Tab* key on your keyboard.

11. In the dropdown to the right, choose **Inches** (SketchUp will default to this setting in the feet and inches template).

    Double-check that the numbers you typed are correct. Sometimes, for us, it reverts to the original number in the box. If that happens for you, type the numbers in again, and this time they should stick.

12. Next to **In SketchUp**, type 1 and choose **Feet**, or type 12 and keep **Inches**. Again, double check that the numbers you typed are correct.

13. If you unchecked **Match screen display (auto width)**, you will have the option to change the **Line scale** setting, as shown in *Figure 11.30*. The **Line scale** setting impacts how heavy the lineweight appears in the exported PDF. We will leave ours at the default 0.01 setting, just to see what it looks like.

14. Click **OK** to exit this window.

15. Click **Export** in the **Export 2D Graphic** window.

16. Find where you saved the PDF file and open it.

Figure 11.31: The exported PDF with the Match screen display (auto
width) option unchecked (top) versus checked (bottom)

Presto! You have exported your model to scale.

17. Finally, if you plan on printing the PDF document, ensure the settings from your computer's
PDF print menu are set to print the *actual size*, not to fit or *shrink oversized pages*. The scale
will be off if you do not print the actual size.

Follow the preceding steps next time you need to export something to scale.

Summary

This chapter was all about exporting SketchUp images and animations. We discussed multiple export
options, learned about 3D walk-through camera tools, and shared an example of an exported SketchUp
animation. We also covered how to export SketchUp designs to scale for printing.

The next two chapters are dedicated to SketchUp LayOut, a powerful application that comes with a
SketchUp Pro or Studio purchase. LayOut will change the way you create presentations and construction
documents. (*Don't skip these chapters!*)

12

SketchUp LayOut Part I – The Interface

When purchasing SketchUp Pro or SketchUp Studio, users are automatically given a second powerful application, **SketchUp LayOut**. To liken LayOut to **AutoCAD**, LayOut is the paper space to SketchUp's model space. This chapter only begins to scratch the surface of what LayOut can do but gives you helpful information to get rolling in LayOut. In *Chapter 13*, we will pick up where we left off in this chapter by giving a tutorial on one way to format presentation drawings. By the end of both chapters, you will have fallen in love with the simple yet graphically appealing way to use your SketchUp model to create presentations or construction documents.

In this chapter, we will cover the following topics:

- SketchUp LayOut and its templates
- Introducing the tools and toolbars in LayOut
- Document Setup
- Importing files into LayOut
- **Layer**, **Shape Style**, and **Text Style** (or **Fonts**) panels

Technical requirements

To follow along in this chapter, you will need the following:

- SketchUp LayOut (we are working with the 2024 version)
- SketchUp Pro or SketchUp Studio
- Practice exercise file `Chapter 12- LayOut I` in 3D Warehouse or from `https://3dwarehouse.sketchup.com/model/ac3a3f3b-8c1e-440c-9d93-c304c8b416ae/Chapter-12-LayOut`

SketchUp LayOut and its templates

As mentioned in the introductory paragraph, **LayOut** is a second interface that is automatically given to users who purchase SketchUp for Desktop software, whether Pro orStudio.

Figure 12.1: SketchUp logo (left) and SketchUp LayOut logo (right)

The original idea behind LayOut was to use a completed SketchUp model to create construction or presentation documents, just as you would with other CAD software, such as AutoCAD or Revit. When you are in LayOut, you are using a two-dimensional program and no longer able to orbit three-dimensionally.

What LayOut Does

The beauty of using SketchUp with LayOut is the ability to easily share the conceptual or schematic design produced in SketchUp in a format that is typical for people working in the field while allowing the visualization of materials to be clearly understood. That means not only can a SketchUp model with project-specific materials be used, but other file formats, such as spreadsheets, can be imported to reuse specification tables without having to create a new one (though you can). You can also import images of those specification objects, photorealistic renders, and more.

Figure 12.2 is an example of a tile schedule created in LayOut. The viewports are SketchUp models inserted into LayOut. On the elevation and plan views, you can distinctly see the tile texture and how it will be installed.

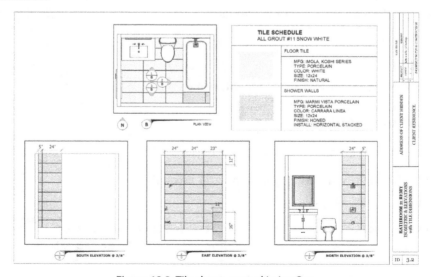

Figure 12.2: Tile sheet created in LayOut

It is important to mention, before we get into the meat of the chapter, that some people find LayOut confusing and hard to use. Many professionals in architecture, residential design, kitchen and bath design, and commercial design have incorporated SketchUp with LayOut as a critical part of their workflow. The majority of issues commonly reported about LayOut boil down to three main factors:

- **Lack of LayOut knowledge**: Users must practice with it often to fully understand how it works.

- **Inadequate SketchUp models**: If your SketchUp model lacks proper construction, including fundamental elements such as groups, tags, scenes, and styles, LayOut may appear ineffective. It's essential to invest effort in crafting precise models that LayOut can interpret accurately. This book will help you do that!

- **Insufficient space on your computer**: Having a minimum of 8 GB of RAM is crucial when working on large LayOut documents. Consider the size of your SketchUp model integrated into LayOut, and multiply that by the number of viewports in the entire document. This figure only grows as you add images or .dwg (DWG) files. Your tolerance for watching the "spinning circle of death" diminishes as your computer's processing units struggle to render everything in the document. The good news is that SketchUp version 2024.0 came out with a major overhaul in the graphics and performance engine. Model lag and the spinning circle of death have significantly diminished. Thank you, SketchUp team! If you are using an older version, be aware of lag times. We cover tips on decreasing them for LayOut in *Chapter 13*.

Keep these factors in mind as you learn a new interface and grant yourself patience as you explore potential unfamiliar territory in this chapter.

Now, let's learn about how to use LayOut!

LayOut templates

To open LayOut, you have two options:

- One way is to double-click on the LayOut application, wherever it is stored on your computer.

- The other method involves accessing LayOut from within the SketchUp model you intend to utilize.

To access LayOut from SketchUp, start by opening the SketchUp file.

From SketchUp, choose **File | Send to LayOut…**.

Alternatively, you can use the **Send to LayOut** icon in the **Getting Started** toolbar (icon with the red box around it in *Figure 12.3*).

Figure 12.3: Send to LayOut from SketchUp options

When LayOut opens, the first thing you see is the **Welcome to LayOut** splash screen on top of the LayOut interface. This screen looks a lot like SketchUp's welcome screen, so it is hopefully familiar to you.

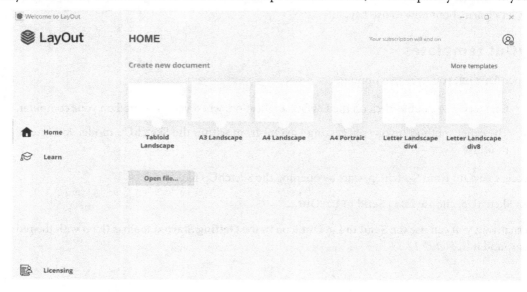

Figure 12.4: Welcome to LayOut screen

This splash screen requires you to either choose a **template** that SketchUp created for you or open your own LayOut template file. You won't be able to access the interface without choosing or opening a template. (You can change this later in LayOut's **Preferences** window, so the splash screen will no longer show when opening LayOut.)

> **Open file option**
>
> When you launch LayOut through **Send to LayOut** within SketchUp, the **Open file** icon shown in *Figure 12.4* is inaccessible. LayOut assumes you are utilizing the SketchUp model you initially began with.

The default templates come in many sizes and styles. Typically, you will find six template icons below **Create new document** for initial selection. The default template options may differ depending on your region (i.e., size and units).

To access additional template options, click **More templates** at the far-right. After clicking **More templates**, there are three tabs to view (*Figure 12.5*).

- **Paper**: From the **Paper** tab, you can choose a template based on size and whether you want graph paper or not. If you choose a paper style without a grid, you can add one later (and vice versa).

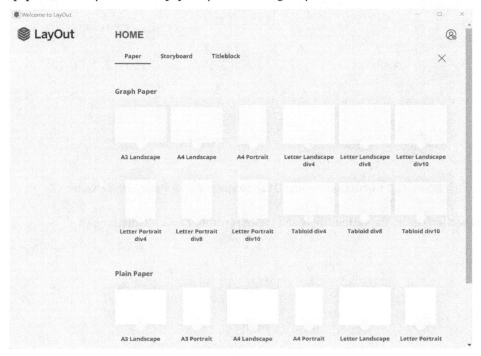

Figure 12.5: More templates window

- **Storyboard:** You can click on **Storyboard** to select a layout that looks like a storyboard (a visual planner with rectangular frames to help determine the order of a project or presentation).

- **Titleblock:** You can click on **Titleblock** to choose a page size with pre-made title blocks. All title blocks are editable, as is almost everything else in the template you choose.

To follow along in the next section of the book, choose **Titleblock**, then scroll down to **Simple** and click once on **ArchD Landscape**.

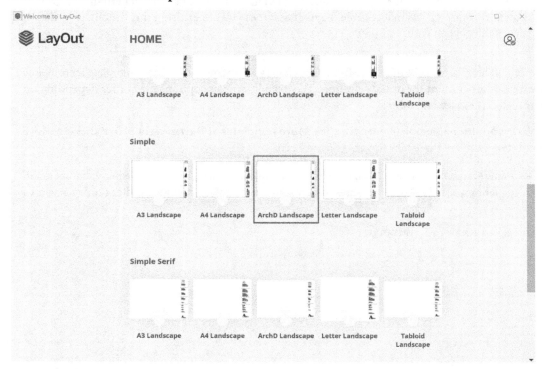

Figure 12.6: Choose Simple ArchD Landscape to follow along in this chapter

Our next section covers the various tools and toolbars within LayOut's interface.

Introducing the tools and toolbars in LayOut

We are now in LayOut! Take a few minutes to look over the interface (or workspace) and get a feel of your mouse. This was mentioned earlier in the chapter, but as a reminder, LayOut is a 2D program. You won't be able to orbit three-dimensionally. The interface looks much like SketchUp's, with the difference being the large document in the middle, rather than a modeling window:

Figure 12.7: LayOut's workspace

Figure 12.8 highlights several of LayOut's primary workspace elements, helping to acquaint you with the software:

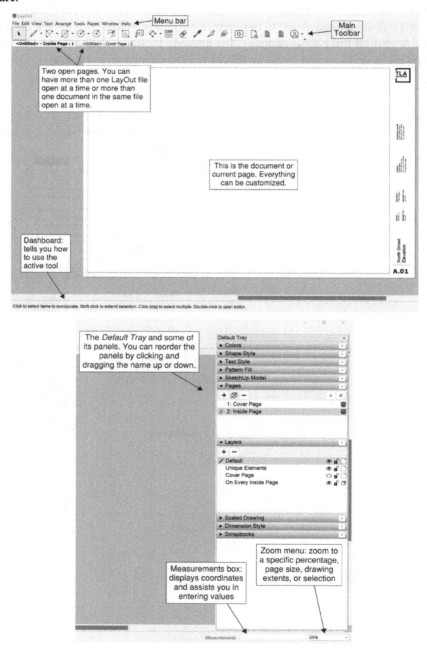

Figure 12.8: The left (top) and right (bottom) sides of LayOut's workspace explained

Let's move on to dissect each toolbar area in LayOut.

Main toolbar

The top of the interface has a format similar to SketchUp, with a menu bar and tool icons. *Figure 12.9* explains the icons you see in the **main toolbar** at the top. A lot of the same SketchUp tools and their shortcuts are used here, such as **Line** (shortcut *L*), **Circle** (*C*), and the mouse shortcut for **Pan** (hold down the scroll wheel and drag). Using Pan in LayOut allows you to move the current page around. The *spacebar* will put you back on the **Select** tool.

Unlike in SketchUp, the main toolbar cannot be moved or swapped for another, though you can customize it (see the bottom figure in *Figure 12.9*). If there is a tool you are looking for that is not shown, check one of the menu dropdowns: **File**, **Edit**, **View**, **Text**, **Arrange**, **Tools**, **Pages**, **Window**, or **Help**.

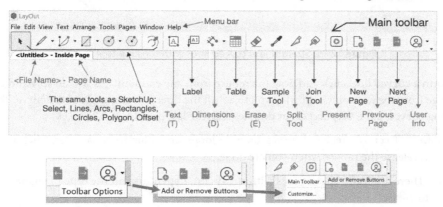

Figure 12.09: LayOut main toolbar (top) and how to customize the toolbar
by clicking the lower arrow next to User Info (bottom)

The list below includes the tools in LayOut and describes what their functions are. All these tools are found in the *main toolbar* or in the **Tools** menu. If shortcuts are available for them, they are denoted in parentheses following their name.

- **Select** (*spacebar*) – To select objects. When you click (select) an object, the tool and cursor will change to the **Move** tool, allowing you to move object(s) around.

- **Line** (*L*) – To draw straight or curved lines. In LayOut, there are the red/x-axis and green/y-axis, like in SketchUp, and they can be locked in with the right or left arrow keys. (Or hold down the *Shift* key to lock in the line horizontally or vertically.) You can also lock in a parallel or tangent line with the down arrow key, which gives you a magenta line.

- In *Figure 12.10*, you can see the red/x-axis while drawing horizontally with the **Line** tool (left), a green/y-axis while drawing vertically with the **Line** tool (middle), and curved lines drawn with the **Line** tool while holding down the cursor, showing the handles (right).

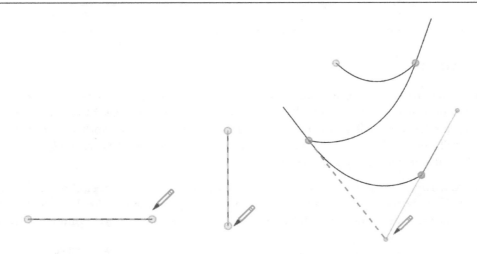

Figure 12.10: Straight and curved lines with the Line tool

To form a curved line, click and drag the mouse from any endpoint. As you do so, handles will emerge from the endpoints, allowing you to adjust the direction and angle of the curve. To stop adding curves, tap *Esc*, *spacebar*, or double-click the last point.

- **Freehand** – To create freehand curves, loop-de-loops, and other irregular lines. Click and drag to draw; release the mouse when you are done.

- **Arcs** – There are four types of arcs within LayOut, depending on the type of shape you are trying to create:

  - **Arc** – An arc based on an angle. Type in an angle measurement or click to end the command.

  - **2 Point Arc** (*A*) – Draw an arc based on the bulge (just like in SketchUp). Type in a bulge measurement or click to stop the bulge.

  - **3 Point Arc** – An arc drawn from a pivot point. For accurate measurements, type the horizontal distance and then the length of the arc.

  - **Pie** – Draw a closed arc that is the shape of a piece of pie or wedge of cheese.

- **Rectangles**: There are four types of rectangle tools within LayOut. Note that using a modifier key will change the shape to a square:

  - **Rectangle** (*R*) – A basic rectangle; holding down the *Shift* key creates a square. Use the **Measurements** box (shown in *Figure 12.8*) to create precise shapes.

> **Important note**
>
> Like in SketchUp, in LayOut, you don't need to click inside the **Measurements** box. You can type the measurement and press *Enter* or *Return* to set the dimensions.

- · **Rounded** – A rectangle (or square using *Shift*) with rounded corners.

- · **Lozenge** – Draw an elongated oval; hold down the *Shift* key to draw a circle.

- · **Bulged** – A rectangle with two parallel sides that bulge out. Holding down *Shift* creates a square with the same result.

- **Circle** (*C*) – Create a circle. To set the size or radius, either click once or click and immediately type the desired radius followed by *Enter* or *Return*.

- **Ellipse** – This takes two clicks, or you can type in the width and height after the first click, followed by *Enter* or *Return*. (For example, typing `10"` comma `20"`, and pressing *Enter* creates a `10"` x `20"` ellipse.) Holding down *Shift* creates a circle.

- **Polygon** – Creates a polygon. It's different from the way you draw a polygon in SketchUp; you need to set the number of sides *after* the first click by typing the number of sides followed by `s`. For example, to create a hexagon, click to start the polygon, then type `6s` and *Enter*.

- **Offset** (*F*) – Offset any edge or shape.

- **Text** (*T*) - Create text. To make a **bounded text box**, click and drag the mouse; release when the box is the size you want. Then start typing. For **unbounded text**, click once and begin typing.

  A bounded text box automatically adjusts its size based on how much text there is, keeping within the confines of the text box you drew. An unbounded text box allows you the freedom to type as much as you want in the direction you began to type, but the text will not wrap to a new line without you tapping *Enter*.

> **Important note**
>
> Currently, LayOut does not include a spellcheck feature. However, some users may have a universal spellcheck feature in their computer settings, which applies to all applications, including LayOut. We always make sure to have someone proofread our work to catch various errors, including spelling and grammar mistakes. Alternatively, you can copy and paste text into other software that offers spelling and grammar-checking functionalities.

- **Label** – Creates a label or leader line.

- **Dimension, linear** (*D*) – Measures the horizontal or vertical dimension across any geometry.

  There is no measuring tool in LayOut. Instead, distances are measured using dimensions in LayOut. Once measured, dimensions can be deleted if they are no longer needed.

- **Dimension, angular** – An angular dimension specifies the measurement of the angle formed by a line or the angle between two or more lines or points.

- **Table** – Create a table. Click and release the mouse to see column and row options attached to the cursor.

- **Erase** (*E*) – Erases any element in the document

- **Style** – Samples one entity's settings and applies them to another. This works for text settings, dimensions, fill or stroke colors, SketchUp model styles (such as shadows), and more.

- **Split** – Splits lines or shapes.

- **Join** – Joins overlapping lines or shapes.

> **Important note**
>
> When using the **Split** and **Join** tools, make sure to check the *Dashboard* for information on how to use them, as well as modifier key options for your operating system.

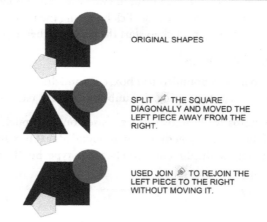

Figure 12.11: Original shapes (top), split (middle), and joined
(bottom) using the Split and Join tools, respectively

Like any new software, it requires practice to become proficient with these tools. While some may not be necessary for your specific needs, others will become indispensable companions over time.

> **Learn more about the toolbar**
>
> Learn how to customize the toolbar and create your own shortcuts here: `https://help.sketchup.com/en/layout/customizing-toolbars-and-menus`

The next section goes through the panels (or toolbars) in the **Default Tray**, which you will use extensively while in LayOut.

The Default Tray

Additional toolbars are found in the **Default Tray**. For Windows operating system users, the Default Tray is not new to you. Our macOS friends are now introduced to the **Default Tray**, which is the extended area of panels (toolbars) on the right side of the interface. Windows users, you can click and drag the entire Default Tray around your drawing but not the individual panels inside the tray. You can, however, click and drag the panels so they are in a different order than shown or collapse or expand them by clicking their name. (Some macOS users can only move the **Colors** panel up or down in the tray). Clicking the **X** in the right corner of each will close the panel. To reopen the **Default Tray**, click the **Window** menu and select **Show Tray**.

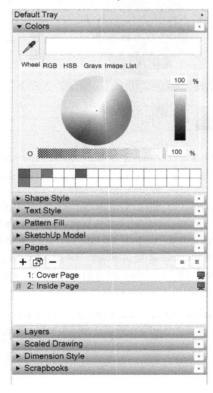

Figure 12.12: Some of the panels within the Default Tray

You can hover at the bottom of a toolbar to reveal an arrow, allowing you to click and drag to adjust the toolbar's length.

Here are the panels in the **Default Tray** and their purposes, listed in alphabetical order:

- **Colors** – This is how you change all colors in the document, whether a font, a shape's stroke, or a shape's fill, by activating the colors box in the coordinating toolbar. You can also add your brand colors to this area for easy access.

  The panel offers various methods to adjust color selection, as indicated by the top row of five tabs in *Figure 12.12*. The smaller grid-like boxes located at the bottom of the panel comprise the color palette. To add colors to them, simply click and drag the active color – denoted by the long box at the top of the panel, called the active color well – down to a palette box.

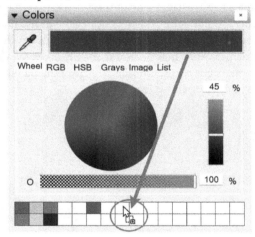

Figure 12.13: Click and drag a color from the active color well at
the top to one of the color palettes at the bottom

  The colors in the palettes remain in all LayOut documents unless you remove or replace them. To remove colors from the palette, you can opt to replace them with either white or a different color by clicking and dragging it to the palette. Furthermore, you can rearrange the colors by dragging from one square of the palette to another. The palette is a great way to save your brand colors for use with other tools in LayOut. Learn more about colors here: `https://help.sketchup.com/en/layout/choosing-colors`

- **Dimension Style** – This toolbar gives you control over how your dimensions look, including their precision, placement of text, and extension offset. We will practice using this toolbar in *Chapter 13*.

- **Layers** – Not to be confused with how layers perform in other CAD software. These layers are similar to Adobe Creative Cloud products (if you are familiar), where their listed order determines the arrangement or visibility of stacked objects. Unlike in SketchUp or CAD, not everything needs to be moved to a layer. That said, the layers control visibility and have options to lock objects to a page, force an object to appear on every sheet (such as a title block), and house elements that belong only on certain sheets (such as the cover sheet).

- **Pages** – This is where you see all your pages or sheets in the drawing set. Putting them in the order you want to present or export is important, as well as naming them according to the document. You can name/rename, add, delete, or duplicate pages here. We will practice using the **Pages** panel in *Chapter 13*.

  To have more than one page in the same file open at one time, use **Window | New Window for <sheet name>**. That will open a duplicate page of what you already have open. Then, in the **Default Tray**, use the **Pages** panel to switch the copy to a different sheet.

- **Pattern Fill** – You can add pre-made patterns to shapes. Once you click the box next to **Pattern** in that toolbar, it will activate (open) the **Pattern Fill** toolbar. Click the dropdown at the top to search for patterns, import a custom pattern, or create your own collection of often-used patterns.

- **Scaled Drawing** – You can use this toolbar to apply a scale to a 2D group or grouping of objects (not including SketchUp or CAD imports). This is a quick way to add a scale without having to do the math (yay!). For example, one way we like to use it is to apply a scale to a LayOut hatch pattern so it corresponds to the scale of the drawing the hatch is covering. Make the pattern, select it, then click **Make Scaled Drawing**. Then apply a scale from the dropdown. Easy! We won't discuss this toolbar further in the book, so use this link to learn more: https://help. sketchup.com/en/layout/creating-scaled-drawing.

- **Scrapbooks** – It's a fun name for what this toolbar does, and you would never guess that this is a library of drawing reference symbols and notes. There are categories of a variety of styles and shapes, including drawing titles, elevation markers, sheet indexes, arrows, and blocks such as people and cars. You can also customize or create your own scrapbooks just by drawing them in LayOut. We will explore the toolbar further in *Chapter 13*.

- **Shape Style** – Change the look of most line types in LayOut here. Change a line's stroke weight or color, make it dashed or dotted, and add an arrow or oblique to the beginning or end of the line. Rectangles can have fillet or chamfered corners, and add pre-made patterns to shapes (i.e., poché or hatching) using **Pattern Fill**. We will practice this method of using a shape with pattern fill in *Chapter 13*.

- **SketchUp Model** – This toolbar will be activated when you select a viewport that is an inserted SketchUp model. We will go through its functions in *Chapter 13*.

- **Text Style** – Change the font type, font size, font color (which activates the **Colors** toolbar), justification, and all document text (including dimension text). Use this toolbar for creating bullet points or a numbered list by clicking the **List** tab inside.

> **Note for macOS users**
>
> MacOS users do not have the **Text Style** panel. Instead, use the **Text** menu to open **Show Fonts**. The **Fonts** panel does not reside in the **Default Tray**. The shortcut to open **Show Fonts** is ⌘ *T*.

Windows SketchUp users are used to seeing the **Instructor** panel in the **Default Tray**. For those unfamiliar with **Instructor**, it is a panel that gives instructions (more than the Dashboard) on using an active tool. There are also graphics to illustrate how to use them. The **Window** menu is where you can reactivate other toolbars in the **Default Tray** that you may have closed.

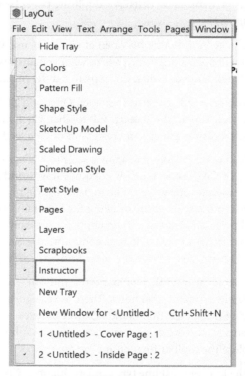

Figure 12.14: Window menu

> **Note for macOS users**
>
> For macOS users, panels under the **Window** menu will not include all those shown in *Figure 12.14*.

The next section shows you how to view the document settings and add project information that can be used across all pages.

Document Setup

Earlier in the chapter, in the *LayOut templates* section, we had you choose a LayOut template that you knew nothing about. If you are curious about the paper size and units – and hopefully you are – choose the **File** menu and click **Document Setup.**.

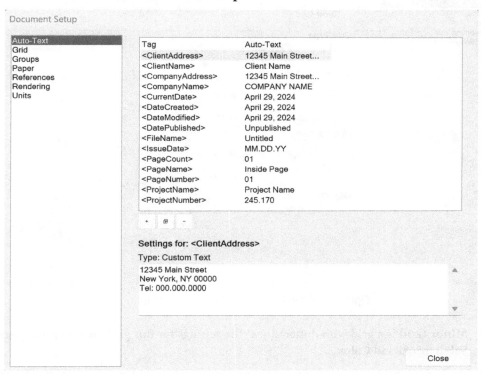

Figure 12.15: Document Setup window

On the left-hand side, within the sidebar, you'll find categories of options for modification. It's worth noting that your operating system may not display all of them as depicted in *Figure 12.15* and listed here:

- **Auto-Text** – Generates text, such as project names and numbers, client or project addresses, page numbers, and ways for you to define your own custom text. This text coordinates with information in the title block and will automatically populate every existing or new page. Learn more about **Auto-Text** here: `https://help.sketchup.com/en/layout/ automate-titleblocks`.

- **Grid** – As mentioned earlier, if you choose a template without a grid but decide you want one later, this is where you can add it. **Show Grid** will already be checked if you chose a template with a grid:

- **Major Grid** is a grid with solid lines. Using **Spacing** and **Color**, you can control the visibility, spacing, and color of the grid.

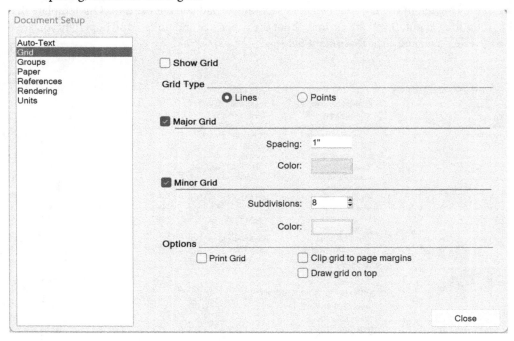

Figure 12.16: Grid settings in Document Setup

- **Minor Grid** is a grid with dotted lines. The settings for this grid are controlled using **Subdivisions** and **Color**.

- **Options** allow you to include the grid in your exported or printed document, clip the grid with page margins, or draw the grid on top of other objects in the document.

- **Groups** – Controls the visibility of other objects when working inside a grouping; you can hide or fade objects outside the group.

- **Paper** – This is where you can edit the settings for your document's size, orientation, paper color, and margins. (If you do not have the **Rendering** menu in the sidebar, it is possible you will see options for output resolution in this window.)

  If you choose to have colored paper, you can also print the color by checking the **Print Paper Color** box.

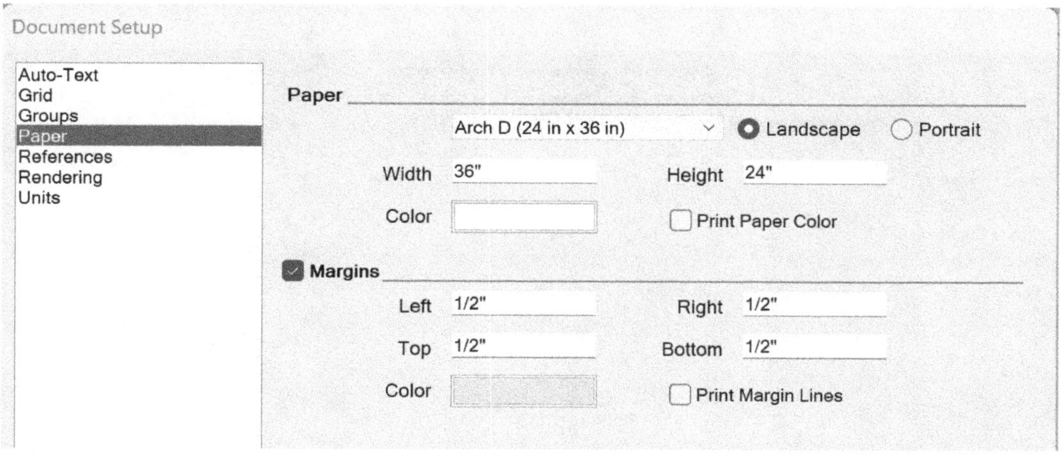

Figure 12.17: Paper settings in Document Setup

Margin lines are shown in the document by checking **Margins**, and those lines are shown when printing by checking the **Print Margin Lines** box.

For our project, we will use the standard **Arch D** margins of 1/2" on all sides except the left, which is 1 1/2". Type 1 1/2 in the left box, then press *Tab*.

Add a space for fractions

Typing dimensions in SketchUp and LayOut looks different than in other CAD software. We do not employ dashes when using a combination of feet, inches, and fractions. For example, instead of typing 6'-7", type 6'7 *Enter* (if using an inches template), or 6'7" *Enter*. If there is a fraction, like 6'-7 ½", add a space between the whole inch and the fraction, like this: 6'7 1/2". Instead of a fraction, you could use a decimal, which would be typed 6'7.5". The counterpart to this comes when there is a foot followed by a fraction – it can be typed with or without the space: 6'1/2", 6' 1/2", 6'.5", or 6' .5".

- **References** – This box is incredibly important once you start inserting anything into LayOut.

The template we chose has an embedded logo as an example. You will see that listed in the **References** area.

Figure 12.18: References menu in Document Setup

When you insert anything into your document, it will automatically be added to this window. Whether a SketchUp model, image file, or other supported content, all insertions will be listed. This is a great place to check whenever you open LayOut, or use for troubleshooting when you do not see an object that you previously inserted. You may have to **Relink**, **Update**, or **Edit** the object. You can also **Relink** and **Update** within the document by right-clicking on the object and selecting the appropriate option.

- **Rendering** – This allows you to choose the settings for display and output resolutions. This applies to all imports, including SketchUp models, image files, and CAD (DWG/DXF) drawings.

Don't have the Rendering menu?

You may find you don't have access to this menu option. Currently, there's an issue where some computers have it available while others do not, regardless of the operating system. If you find yourself without this menu, don't worry. You might find the display and output resolution settings located under the **Paper** menu. Otherwise, you can fix SketchUp model resolution using the **SketchUp Model** panel in the **Default Tray**. Ultimately, we aim to export this document to a PDF, and the image file output can be set to a higher resolution. (Learn more about this at the end of *Chapter 13*, in the section called *Exporting a LayOut file to PDF*.)

- **Units** – Next to **Format**, click the dropdown to choose **Decimal** or **Fractional**.

  The dropdown to its right lets you choose the units of measurement, whether **Inches**, **Feet**, **Millimeter**, **Centimeter**, **Meter**, or **Points**.

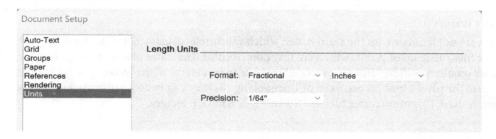

Figure 12.19: Units settings in Document Setup

The **Precision** range depends on the units of measurement. For inches, it ranges from `1"` to `1/64"`.

In our next section, we will begin inserting files into our LayOut template!

Importing files into LayOut

LayOut can import a variety of file types. The most important one, in our humble opinion, is SketchUp models.

LayOut will import the following file types:

- **DWG/DXF files** – We don't have room in this book to go into how to import these CAD files to LayOut, so you can read more about it in SketchUp's help center: `https://help.sketchup.com/en/layout/importing-cad-data-layout`.

- **Image files** in various formats:

  - **BPM or DIB (bitmap formats)** – These are uncompressed **raster** files designed to display high-quality images.

  - **JPG, JPEG, and JFIF** – `JPEG` files are the go-to format for digital images, compressing them down for easy viewing.

  - **GIF** – Did you know this is pronounced *jif*? Yuck. Anyway, they are bitmap rasters that tend to be very pixelated and are mostly used for online posting. While LayOut will import GIF files, don't expect them to display a looped animation. Only a still image will be displayed.

  - **PDF** – This format is only supported for LayOut on macOS (currently). You're lucky!

  - **PNG** – This is a popular format for images because it retains all original color data when compressed, meaning there is no color distortion. It also produces transparent backgrounds.

  - **TIF or TIFF** – This format is used for large image files, typically used for high-quality printing.

- **Spreadsheets/tables** – LayOut can import XLS (Microsoft Excel file) or CSV (text format data) files.

> **Raster images**
>
> If you are not familiar with the word *raster*, which was briefly discussed in *Chapter 4*, they are image files made up of pixels, which are tiny dots of color. The more pixels an image has, the higher quality it will be (and vice versa). You have to be careful when resizing raster images because the pixel numbers are fixed or unchanging, so they can become distorted or blurry when resized. Common raster files are JPEG, PNG, and GIF images.

Now, let's explore the process of inserting a new file.

Inserting a new file into LayOut

To insert a new file into LayOut, use the **File** menu and arrow down to **Insert....**

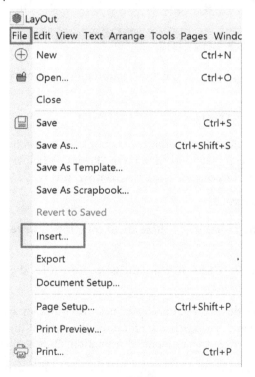

Figure 12.20: Insert from the File menu

The **Open** window will appear. There is a dropdown on the far right that reads **Insertable Content**, so you know all the files showing in your window are files you can bring into LayOut. You won't see files that cannot be inserted, such as PDFs (Windows only) or writing documents such as Microsoft Word.

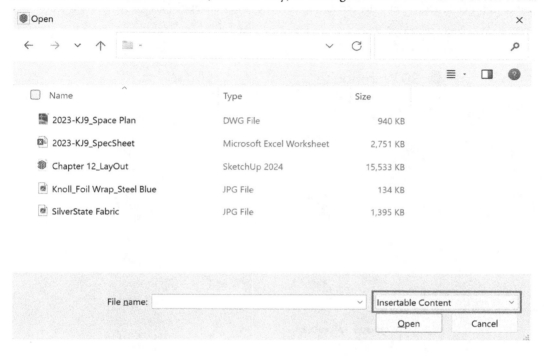

Figure 12.21: Insertable files are shown in the window

If you click the **Insertable Content** dropdown, you will see a list of file types that can be brought in. It is easier, however, to leave the dropdown as **Insertable Content** so you see only what LayOut will accept.

Let's practice inserting a SketchUp model.

Putting it together – Inserting the practice model into LayOut

There is a SketchUp model in 3D Warehouse called Chapter 12- LayOut I. Download it to your computer to accompany the remaining content of this chapter.

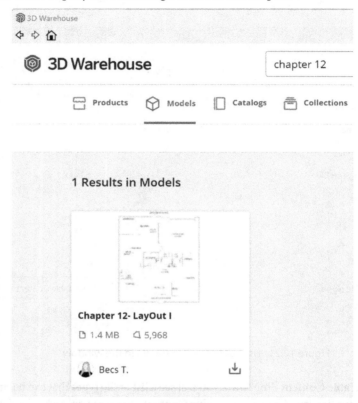

Figure 12.22: The Chapter 12 practice model in 3D Warehouse

Once you've downloaded the practice model, you can open it to view its contents or follow the steps to insert the file into LayOut.

Inserting open files

When you insert a SketchUp file into LayOut, it can also be opened on your computer simultaneously. For instance, inserting an open SketchUp model into LayOut won't create any issues with the original SketchUp file.

Before inserting a file into LayOut, it is helpful to be on the page where you want the file inserted. This saves time that would otherwise be spent cutting and pasting the file onto the appropriate page.

When the LayOut template opened, it put us on a page called **Inside Page**. That's a great place to put the model. We can, however, move or copy files from one page to another.

Here's how to insert a SketchUp model into LayOut:

1. Ensure you are on the LayOut page where you wish to insert the model.

2. Navigate to **File | Insert**.

3. In the **Open** menu, keep the file type as **Insertable Content**.

4. Find where you saved the SketchUp practice file, `Chapter 12- LayOut I`. Double-click on the file to open it, or click on it once and then click **Open**.

5. The SketchUp model will be inserted into your LayOut file. It's as easy as that!

The model will now be considered a viewport for the paper space or document in LayOut. It will show the last saved view in SketchUp. If you played around with the model before inserting it into LayOut, your view might look different from *Figure 12.23*. Also, the content of the viewport might look a little gray or pixelated. Don't worry! We will fix that in *Chapter 13* when we use the **SketchUp Model** panel.

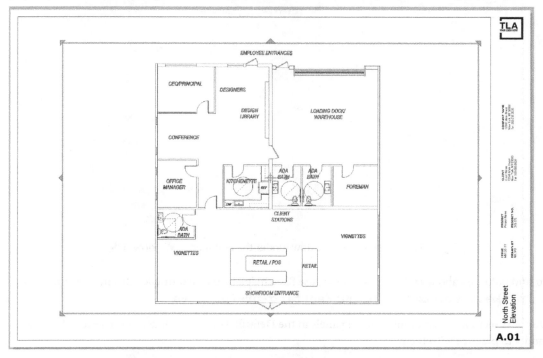

Figure 12.23: Chapter 12 practice model inserted into LayOut

Now that we are going to start working in LayOut, we suggest saving the LayOut file. LayOut will create an automatic backup of the file just like SketchUp does. To change the backup settings – and see additional settings – access the **Edit** menu and arrow down to **Preferences**.

Settings window for macOS users

For macOS, the window called **Settings** is used to change preferences. Use the **Layout** menu | **Settings** to find **Backup** and other options.

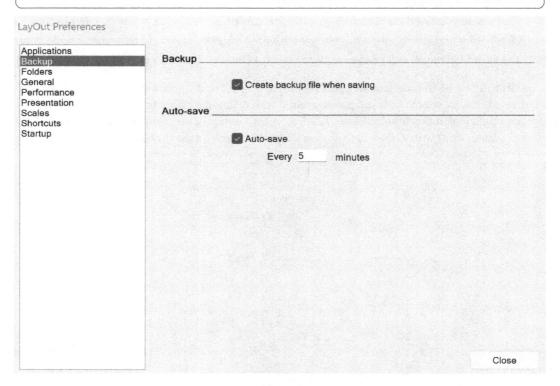

Figure 12.24: Preferences window (under the Edit menu), Windows OS

To find out more about preferences settings, use SketchUp's help center or click this link: https:// help.sketchup.com/en/layout/setting-preferences.

Our next section goes into some of the panels in the **Default Tray**. We will use our inserted SketchUp model to practice with them.

Layer, Shape Style, and Text Style (or Font) panels

Now that we have content inserted into LayOut, let's take the opportunity to practice using three of the panels in the **Default Tray**, or two of the panels if you are on macOS.

Layers panel

We talked briefly about the **Layers** panel earlier in this chapter, in the *The Default Tray* section. The most important thing to remember from that section is that the listing order of layers determines the arrangement or visibility of stacked objects. For example, using the layer order in *Figure 12.25*, if an object on the layer called **On Every Inside Page** is supposed to be arranged on top of an object on the **Unique Elements** layer, it cannot be because **Unique Elements** is listed before **On Every Inside Page** in the **Layers** panel.

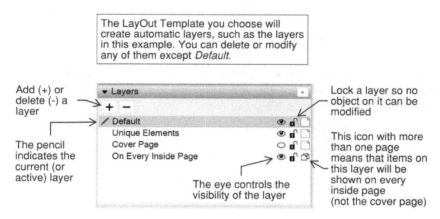

Figure 12.25: Layers panel

You can move the layers around by clicking and dragging the layer up or down.

Here's some more helpful information for the **Layers** panel:

- To add a new layer, click the plus sign (+).

- To delete a layer, select it, then click the minus sign (-).

- To rename a layer, double-click on it, then type the new name.

- To lock a layer so no item can be modified, click the lock icon on that layer so it closes. To unlock it, click the same icon so the lock opens.

- The pencil icon indicates which layer is current/active. To make another layer current, click to the left of the layer name.

- To move an object to a different layer, right-click on the object. Now, let's practice moving the SketchUp viewport to a new layer:

I.   In the **Layers** panel, click the plus sign (+) to add a new layer.

II.   Double-click on the new layer to name it and type SketchUp Models.

The pencil will now be on **SketchUp Models**, indicating it is the current layer. If you want to make **Default** the current layer again, click in the open area to the left of **Default** (*Figure 12.26*).

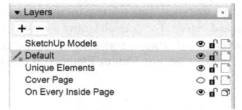

Figure 12.26: Updated Layers panel

III. Click on the SketchUp model viewport in the document. When you do, look at the **Layers** panel. There is a blue dot next to **Default**, which means the object you selected is on that layer (as shown in *Figure 12.26*).

IV.   In the document, right-click on the SketchUp viewport.

A long context menu will appear, offering numerous options for the selected viewport.

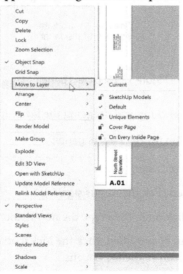

Figure 12.27: Context menu for the SketchUp viewport. The Default layer
has a checkmark next to it indicating it is the current layer

Just like in SketchUp, remember to right-click on objects to see additional tools or settings.

V.   Find **Move to Layer**, then hover or click on it. There will be a checkmark next to **Default**, which is another way for you to see which layer an object is on (shown in *Figure 12.27*). Click `SketchUp Models` to move the SketchUp viewport from the **Default** layer to the `SketchUp Models` layer.

That's all there is to it!

Moving and copying objects in LayOut

To move a text box, image, viewport, and other objects in LayOut, click once on the object (or multiple objects) to select, then click and drag your mouse to move the object(s). Lock in an axis with the coordinating *arrow key* or hold down the *Shift* key to move them horizontally or vertically in a straight line from their current position. You can also nudge them by tapping the arrow keys in the direction you want them to move. To copy an object (or objects), hold down *Ctrl* (Windows) or *Opt* (macOS) *after* clicking the object, and move the copy where you want it placed. Or you can use the universal copy and paste commands of *Ctrl/⌘ C* and *Ctrl/⌘ P*, respectively.

When you clicked on the SketchUp viewport, did you notice that it was surrounded by a cyan-colored box? That color matched the dot in the layers panel to show you which layer the object was on.

Let's see another example. Click on the sheet number text in the title block. It will be surrounded by a maroon box.

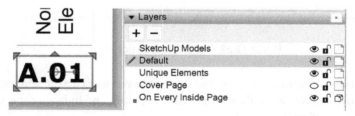

Figure 12.28: Sheet number text surrounded with a maroon box (left) and a maroon dot appearing near On Every Inside Page in the Layers panel (right)

Now look at the **Layers** panel. There is a maroon dot next to **On Every Inside Page**. Objects that are repeated across other pages will be color-coded with maroon. (LayOut has **inferences**, just like SketchUp!)

The next section discusses how to reformat a line using the **Shape Style** panel.

Shape Style panel

In the document, we need to move the left border in so it meets the new 1 1/2" margin we set in the *Document setup* section.

Click on the border. It will be highlighted in maroon, which you now know means it is an object that is on every inside page. The change we make to the border will affect all additional inside pages, if we have any.

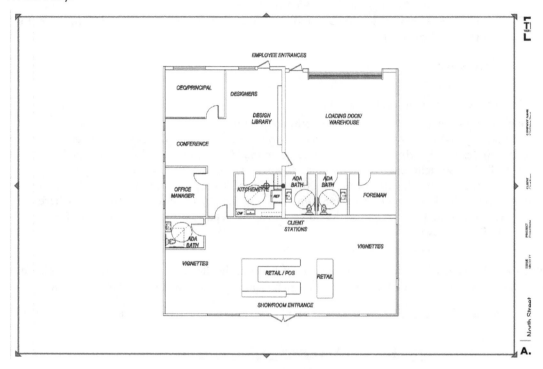

Figure 12.29: Select the page border

There are maroon arrows at various points around the sheet, a result of LayOut automatically merging the lines. These arrows are called **handles**, also known as points, and indicate areas where you can click on the rectangle to adjust its size.

Focus on the left-middle handle by zooming in. As you get closer, your cursor will transform into a small black square with black arrows on both sides, or a double-sided arrow (see *Figure 12.30*). It can also look like the red move tool, depending on where your cursor lies. Move the mouse until the cursor is the double-sided arrow. Click and drag the edge towards the margin line. For precise alignment, zoom in further using your scroll wheel. Once it aligns perfectly with the margin, release your mouse button.

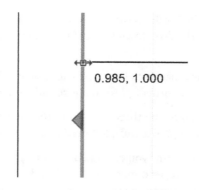

0.985, 1.000

Figure 12.30: The left-middle maroon handle shows a double-sided
black arrow with which to stretch the selected line

Move over to the **Shape Style** panel in the **Default Tray**. The settings and options in this panel can be applied to any line or shape.

Figure 12.31: Shape Style panel

Let's review the options to see if we want to change anything. Make sure the border is still selected so we can see and change its settings:

If we chose the box next to **Fill**, which is white in *Figure 12.31*, it would take us to the **Colors** panel (also in the **Default Tray**).

- Clicking the box to the right of **Pattern** opens or activates the **Pattern Fill** panel. For our purposes, we don't want to fill the border with color or add a pattern, so we will skip those boxes.

- The **Stroke** color is fine as-is, so you don't need to click the black box to change the color. The lineweight is currently at **0.50** pt. Click the dropdown to choose a heavier stroke (a larger number). The dropdown numbers only go up to 2 pt. If you want a heavier stroke than shown in the dropdown, you can type a number in that same box instead. You are not limited to what is shown.

- If you would like to make the border have dashed lines instead of solid, you would click the dropdown next to **Dashes**. The dropdown to the right of that, where it reads **1 x**, changes the length of the dashes.

- **Stroke Style** is where you make changes to the corners of the shape. The default setting, highlighted in blue in *Figure 12.30*, is miter corners. Next to it is round corners, followed by bevel corners.

  For a line or arc with endpoints, the three options to the far right will apply, which are the end options. The default setting is flat ends, followed by round ends, and finally square ends.

- **Start Arrow** and **End Arrow** means you can add or change an arrow or end point to the start point and end point of a line, arc, or dimension. The dropdowns next to them change the size of the points. This does not apply to shapes such as our rectangular border, so we are done with this panel.

We changed the border so it has a lineweight of **2 pt.**, did the same to the line above the sheet number, then stretched the line to meet the page border. We also added a **2 pt.** border around all the title block elements. Here's the result:

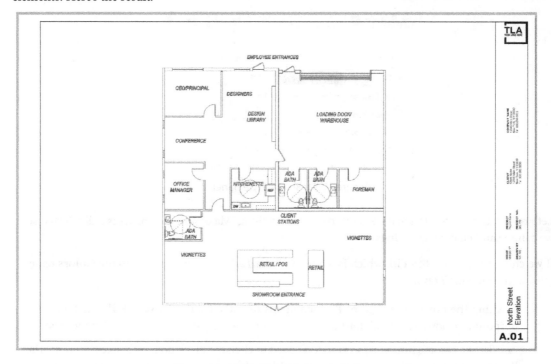

Figure 12.32: Page border shape changes

As a precaution, with the border and any other entity in LayOut, right-click on it and choose **Lock**. This prevents accidental movement, deletion, or alteration of elements. Once locked, the selection color will change from blue to red.

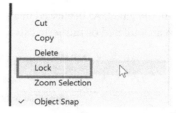

Figure 12.33: Lock an entity in LayOut by right-clicking on it and selecting Lock

To unlock the entity, right-click on it and select **Unlock**.

We are almost done setting up the layout of each sheet. Our final task before moving on to work with viewports (which we will do in *Chapter 13*), is to edit the title block text. That is next!

Text Style panel

Some of the existing title block text is too small. Zoom into that area of the page and open the **Text Style** panel.

Alternatively, you can find many of the same settings in the **Text** menu located at the top of the interface. A useful feature in that menu is the **Find** (shortcut *Ctrl/⌘ F*) or **Find in Document** windows. **Find** allows you to search for content within the document and provides an option to replace specific text with another.

Reminder about macOS fonts

To modify text on macOS, use the **Text** menu to select **Show Fonts**. The **Fonts** panel does not reside in the **Default Tray**. The shortcut to open **Show Fonts** is ⌘ T.

While macOS users may already be aware, it's worth noting that formatted fonts may not consistently translate correctly when accessed on a Windows computer or exported to a PDF. Here's how the **Fonts** panel on macOS looks:

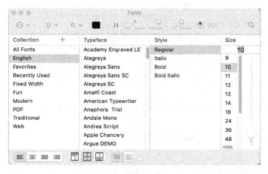

Figure 12.34: Fonts panel on macOS

The **Format** tab is the default tab within the panel. As discussed in an earlier section called *The Default Tray*, the **List** tab is where you can create bulleted or numeric lists.

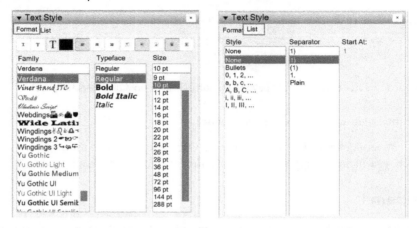

Figure 12.35: Format tab (left) and List tab (right), Windows

For example, typeface shortcuts such as *Ctrl/⌘ B* for bold and *Ctrl/⌘ I* for italics translate to LayOut as well. Use *Figure 12.36* to acquaint yourself with the **Text Style** (Windows) or **Fonts** (macOS) panels:

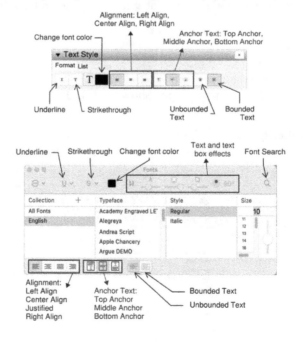

Figure 12.36: Text formatting options in Windows (top) and macOS (bottom)

Create font formatting before adding new text

When you are creating new text, use the **Text Style** box or **Fonts** panel to set up the font formatting before you add new text. That way, the new text you create will already have the settings you want, and you won't have to go back and edit them.

You can edit the formatting for more than one text box at a time: Select one box and hold down the *Shift* key (or *Ctrl* for Windows or *Opt* for macOS) to select additional boxes. *Shift* also allows you to deselect an object.

Now, let's adjust the text formatting within the title block. We will start with the four smaller text boxes in the title block. At first glance, the font size looks a bit small. To change the size of existing text, select the text box. To select more than one text box, use one of the modifier keys (such as *Shift*) to select all four text boxes. Then, open the **Text Style** or **Fonts** panel. It shows us the properties of the font: under **Family** it reads **Arial**, **Typeface** is **Regular**, and **Size** is 14 pt.

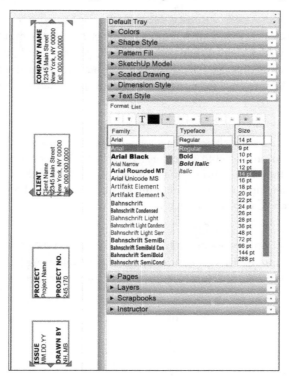

Figure 12.37: Selected text boxes and their font properties (Windows)

To change any of the properties, keep the text boxes selected and choose different options. We will adjust the **Size** to 20 pt and the **Family** to Arial Rounded MT. This will cause the text to overlap the right margin, so we will move it inside the margin by clicking and dragging the mouse until it is positioned where we want.

> **Architectural text height in LayOut**
>
> Determining the correct font size in LayOut based on your CAD standard text height involves some calculations. For instance, a 1/8" text height corresponds to a 9 pt font size. However, remember that the font size may vary depending on the font, as different fonts have unique kerning, glyph properties, and other features.
>
> To help you get started, here are average font sizes commonly used in LayOut: 10-12 pt for basic text (1/8" high), 14-16 pt for labels or callouts, and 14-20 pt for dimensions.
>
> These font size ranges serve as a valuable starting point for your font size selections in LayOut, helping you choose appropriate sizes for the type of text you're working with.

The sheet name text that says North Street Elevation is turned sideways. If you would like to rotate text or other objects, use the rotate point (called the *grip*) near the middle of the box, which is the filled in circle (*Figure 12.37*, left). When your mouse is hovering over it, the cursor will change to a small rotate icon. Click and drag the rotation grip and observe the **Measurements** box located in the lower right corner of the interface. Release the mouse button to finalize the rotation.

> **Precision rotating in LayOut**
>
> You have the ability to rotate any object in LayOut, whether it's a shape, text box, viewport, or another element. To rotate an object to a precise angle without monitoring the **Measurements** box, simply click and drag the rotation grip in the desired direction, then release the mouse button. Immediately after, input the angle you want, for example, 45, and press *Enter* or *Return* to confirm the degree and complete the rotation.

You can mirror objects horizontally or vertically by right-clicking on the object and choosing **Flip**. Explore additional ways to modify LayOut entities by visiting the following link: https://help. sketchup.com/en/layout/arranging-moving-rotating-and-scaling-entities.

Figure 12.38: Rotate any object using the rotation grip (left, middle) and check the measurements box for the angle of the rotation (right)

Rename the sheet name text FLOOR & FURNITURE PLANS by double-clicking the box to initiate editing.

LayOut has a text error inference, denoted by a small red arrow just outside the text box, signifying the presence of text that may not be visible. Alternatively, depending on whether or not the text box is bounded, you may have a lengthy text string that requires shortening by clicking and dragging one of the handles (arrows). Regardless, you must resize the text box to fit the content accordingly.

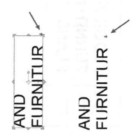

Figure 12.39: Text error indicated with a red arrow in the top right
– text box selected (left) and deselected (right)

Continue stretching the grips, formatting the font styles, and editing other items in the title block until it looks the way you want.

To modify the page number settings, open **Document Setup** from the **File** menu. Click on the **Auto-Text** menu. Since we prefer our sheet numbers not to begin with zero, we scrolled down to locate the tag labeled **<PageNumber>** and adjusted the **Style** settings.

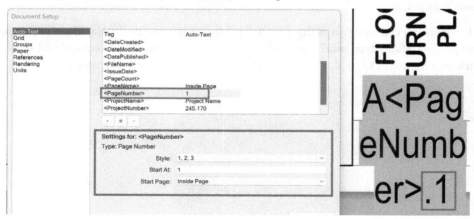

Figure 12.40: We changed the page number settings in the Document Setup Auto-
Text menu (left) and added a period and number 1 to the sheet number (right)

After closing out of **Document Setup**, on the inside page, we edited the sheet number text box by adding a period and 1 after the page number auto-text. We changed the drawing title font to **Arial Rounded MT** and made the title left-aligned. We changed the sheet number font to **Arial Narrow** with a bottom anchor. Our final result is this:

Figure 12.41: Completed sheet name and number edits

And with that, we have completed the initial setup of the LayOut document. We hope you enjoyed exploring the diverse toolbars and settings at your disposal!

Summary

This chapter provided background information on SketchUp LayOut and familiarized you with the interface. We hope you now feel more at ease with the workspace, particularly as we've begun exploring the **Default Tray** panels.

Our next chapter is a continuation of this one, delving into more practical tasks while we continue to go through the **Default Tray** panels. You will learn to dimension the inserted model and adjust its scale, work with images in LayOut, and craft an introductory construction document.

SketchUp LayOut Part II – Paper Space Content

In *Chapter 12*, we introduced you to the SketchUp LayOut interface, including importing files and navigating through the **Layer**, **Shape Style**, and **Text Style** panels. Now that you know how to navigate LayOut, let's work in paper space! This chapter will guide you through two step-by-step tutorials on utilizing the LayOut tools and toolbars. Within LayOut, a multitude of options allows for the incorporation of personal touches and captivating details, offering a rewarding experience for individuals immersed in the creative realm of this industry.

This chapter will cover the following topics:

- Manipulating image files
- Tutorial - Creating presentation or construction drawings
- Troubleshooting viewport warnings
- Adding additional details to drawings
- Presenting the LayOut document

Technical requirements

To follow along in this chapter, you will need the following:

- SketchUp LayOut (we are working with the 2024 version)
- SketchUp Pro or SketchUp Studio
- The Chapter 13- LayOut II practice exercise file in 3D Warehouse or from https://3dwarehouse.sketchup.com/model/1087d8c2-1a86-4223-bbf4-3c9d3d2d7c0f/Chapter-13-LayOut-II

Manipulating image files

In *Chapter 12*, we inserted our `Chapter 12- LayOut I` SketchUp file into **LayOut** using the **Titleblock Template** called **Simple ArchD Landscape**. We put the SketchUp model on a new **Layer** named `SketchUp Models`, and we updated the **Auto-Text** settings of our **Document Setup** window to have our client and project information. We also changed the title block area on *Page 2* to have the information, font family, and *size* we prefer and added an architectural border. Finally, we updated the sheet number font and **Auto-Text** settings.

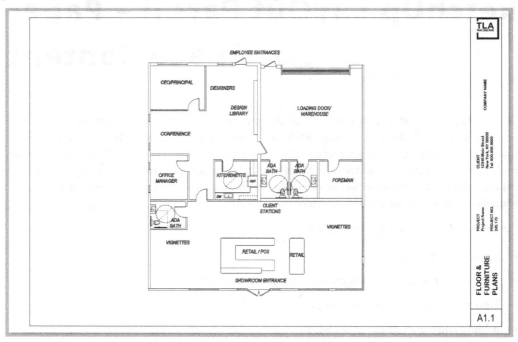

Figure 13.1: The final Chapter 12 LayOut inside page

For this chapter, delete the *Chapter 12* SketchUp file viewport. Instead of using that version of the SketchUp file, we will use the `Chapter 13- LayOut II` file, which has a few more items than the *Chapter 12* file. You can click the viewport and tap *Del* on your keyboard, or right-click on the viewport and select **Delete**.

Insert the `Chapter 13- LayOut II` SketchUp file into LayOut, as practiced in *Chapter 12*.

Figure 13.2 shows where we are starting from in LayOut in this chapter, after the *Chapter 13* SketchUp file is inserted:

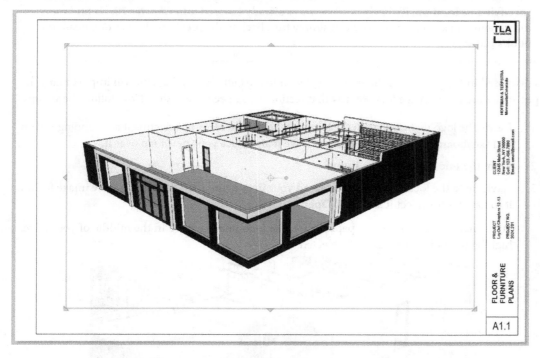

Figure 13.2: LayOut Page 2

After inserting the model, move it to the correct layer. Right-click on the viewport, select **Move to Layer**, and then click `SketchUp Models`. (We added that layer in *Chapter 12*, in the *Layers panel* section. If you do not have it, create one now and move the viewport to that layer.)

In *Chapter 12*, we used the demo logo that came with the template. Now that all our client and project information has been input to LayOut, we will add our logo (or SketchUp's logo) to keep our branding consistent in the documents. Manipulating images in LayOut is similar to the process in other software.

We will now go through the steps to insert an image into LayOut. Before diving in, locate a logo or another image you wish to include in your LayOut document. Then, proceed with this section's tutorial to grasp how to resize and reposition the image.

To use a SketchUp logo as shown in the example (*Figure 13.3*), conduct an image search to find one. We opted for one with a white background, although a version with a transparent background will also work.

> **Information from** *Chapter 12*
>
> Moving forward, if we refer to a LayOut feature without providing background details or specifying its location, it's likely because we've already covered it in *Chapter 12*. To find more information on such features, you can simply turn back to the previous chapter or consult the book's Index.

As discussed in *Chapter 12*, in the *Importing files into LayOut* section, LayOut will import many file types, including raster image files. Review that section if you need a refresher. Now, follow these steps:

1. Delete the logo that came with the template, *Your Logo Here*, by selecting it and tapping *Del* on your keyboard. Alternatively, you can leave it and place your new logo over it.

2. From the **File** menu, choose **Insert**.

3. Navigate to the location where you saved your image, and then double-click the image to add it to LayOut (or select it and click **Open**).

   When inserted into LayOut's paper space, the logo image will be in the middle of your page, highlighted in blue because it is selected:

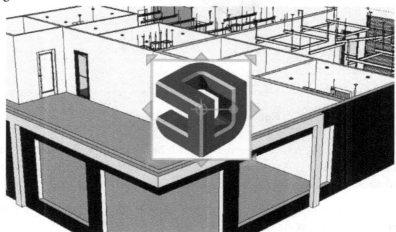

Figure 13.3: The image inserted into LayOut is in the middle of the page

Our image is inserted on top of the viewport on *Page 2*, as shown in *Figure 13.3*. Sometimes, the images might be behind a viewport or other object, and you might have to do a little hunting for them. Use the **Layers** panel to hide objects.

4. Hover your mouse over the selection until the cursor changes to a red move tool.

5. Click and drag the logo away from the viewport toward the top of the title block.

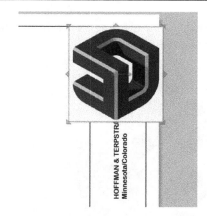

Figure 13.4: The logo at the top of the title block

6. To make the logo image larger or smaller, click and drag one of the blue arrow corner grips to rescale the image.

    Hold down the *Shift* key as you drag the grip in any direction to make the image scale uniformly, ensuring that it is not distorted.

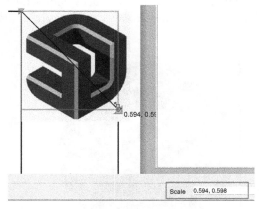

Figure 13.5: Check the measurements box as you rescale the image

If you drag your mouse slowly enough, you will notice that the grip will jump slightly as it hits the *endpoints* of other objects, such as the border around the sheet. This is a great way to know where to stop the scale.

Check the **Measurements** box as you rescale the image. To resize an image accurately without guesswork, click and drag the image, and then hold the *Shift* key while releasing your mouse. Immediately after releasing, type in your desired scale factor (enter a decimal number greater than 1.01 to enlarge or less than 0.999 to reduce the size), and press *Enter/Return*.

Move and resize the logo image until it fits inside the page margins.

7.   If you want to distort the image, click and drag one of the middle grips, or click and drag a corner grip *without* holding down *Shift*.

Figure 13.6: The logo image was distorted by clicking and dragging a middle grip

8.   You can also rotate an image, like a text box is rotated, by finding the blue dot near the middle of the picture. Once your cursor has hovered over the blue circle, the cursor will change to look like SketchUp's rotate tool icon:

Figure 13.7: Rotate an image by finding the blue circle near the middle

Watch your measurements box to know when to stop the angle or type an angle after releasing your mouse. Alternatively, you can eyeball the rotation and release your mouse to stop the rotation.

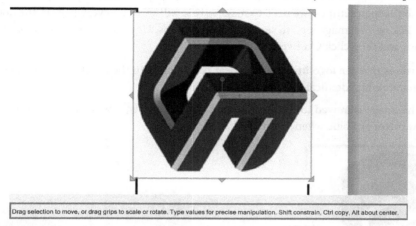

Drag selection to move, or drag grips to scale or rotate. Type values for precise manipulation. Shift constrain, Ctrl copy, Alt about center.

Figure 13.8: The Dashboard at the bottom helps guide you with tools

The Dashboard can help

Remember the **Dashboard** at the bottom of your screen, which gives you tips when using tools. In *Figure 13.8*, the Dashboard says users (Windows) can use modifier key *Alt* to rotate *about center*.

9. After the logo image is placed and sized as you want, add a **Shape Style** border to the image to match the rest of the title block.

    Open the **Shape Style** panel in the **Default Tray** and select **Stroke** to give the image a border. If the border is too thick or thin, adjust the point dropdown to align with the line thickness. To add a colored border, click the black box next to **Stroke**.

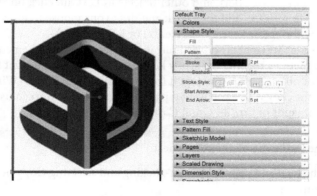

Figure 13.9: Add a border using Stroke under Shape Style

10. If adding a stroke to the image does not fit with the title block, you can add a line (shortcut *L*) to finish out the title block or create a rectangle (shortcut *R*), and then add a stroke to it.

11. To finish the logo settings, we need to make sure it will show on every page of the document. Right-click on the image logo to see additional options. Hover or click your mouse on **Move to Layer**, and then click **On Every Inside Page**.

   This ensures that the logo image will appear consistently in the exact location on every new page, maintaining identical settings across all sheets.

   Once the image is moved to the **On Every Inside Page** layer, it will have a maroon selection window instead of blue whenever it is selected.

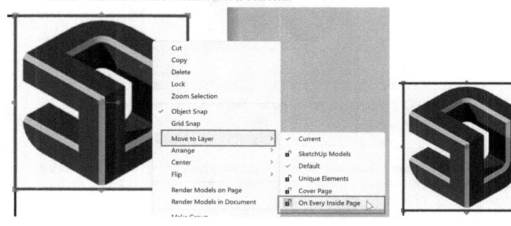

Figure 13.10: Moving the logo image to the On Every Inside Page layer
(left) changes the selection window to maroon (right)

Reminder – Moving and copying objects in LayOut

To move a text box, image, viewport, and other objects in LayOut, click once on the object (or multiple objects) to select it, and then click and drag your mouse to move the object(s). Lock in an axis using the arrow keys – right (red/x) or left (green/y) - or hold down the Shift key to move the object(s) horizontally or vertically in a straight line from their current position. You can also nudge them by tapping the arrow keys in the direction you want them to move. To copy an object (or objects) after selecting it (or them), hold down *Ctrl* (Windows) or *Opt* (macOS) and move the copy where you want it placed. Alternatively, you can use the universal copy-and-paste commands of *Ctrl/⌘ C* and *Ctrl/⌘ P*, respectively.

We also need the logo to be on the cover sheet:

12. Click once on the logo and copy it by right-clicking and selecting **Copy** or using the *Ctrl/⌘ C* keyboard command.

13. In the **Pages** panel, within the **Default Tray**, click once on the line named **Cover Page**.

That will change your sheet view from **Inside Page**, or *Page 2*, to the cover sheet.

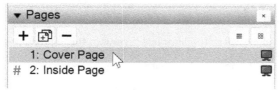

Figure 13.11: The Pages panel

Move your mouse to the sheet.

14. Paste the logo to the cover sheet in the **Edit** menu and click **Paste** or use the *Ctrl/⌘ P* paste keyboard command.

A popup will show, warning you that you are about to paste an object on a hidden layer.

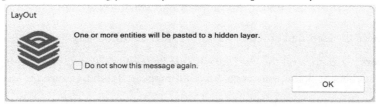

Figure 13.12: A hidden layer warning

Click **OK** to continue. You won't see the logo on the sheet.

15. In the **Layers** panel, turn on the visibility of the **On Every Inside Page** layer by clicking the radio on the right.

The radio will now look like an eye, and the title block from *Page 2* will be visible.

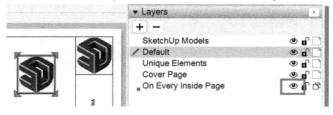

Figure 13.13: The On Every Inside Page layer is visible

Remember how you already made a copy of the logo?

16. Click and hold your mouse on the logo, and then move it away from the title block. There should now be two logos, as shown in *Figure 13.13*.

17. Right-click on the copied logo, select **Move to Layer**, and then click **Cover Page**.

    The logo will now remain on this sheet.

18. At the bottom of the sheet, swap the template logo with the copied logo.

    Select the logo and tap *Del* on your keyboard.

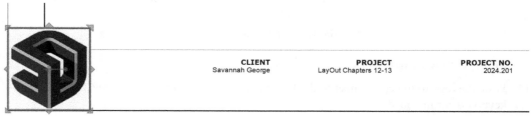

Figure 13.14: Swap the template logo with the new one

You can resize the logo, add or remove a border, or change how it is viewed.

19. In the **Layers** panel, turn off the **On Every Inside Page** layer's visibility by clicking the eye on the right. Double-check that your logo did not disappear. If it did, retrace the steps.

20. Finally, in the **Pages** panel, click back to **Inside Page** so that we can continue editing the viewport.

As a reminder from *Chapter 12*, you can use **Document Setup** under the **File** menu to check your linked or inserted content. You should click **Purge** to remove the link from the *Chapter 12* SketchUp file if you started with it in this chapter. You can find additional information about *references* at this link: `https://help.sketchup.com/en/layout/managing-model-references`.

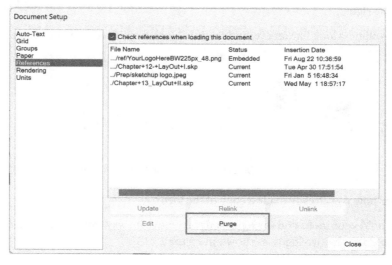

Figure 13.15: Document Setup | References

Now that you have inserted an image and explored the SketchUp practice file (we assume), we should address linking objects to a project folder.

> **Create a project folder**
>
> In *Chapter 12*, we mentioned that any time you insert anything into your document, it will automatically be added to the **References** window. If you are familiar with AutoCAD XREFs or Adobe Links, you know that housing all files associated with a project in one folder is essential, ensuring that you don't have to spend time searching for the source of the link. We suggest creating a project folder for this chapter that houses your SketchUp file, LayOut file, logo, and anything else you might insert into LayOut for this exercise.

In the next section, we will start working with our inserted SketchUp model viewport.

Tutorial – Creating presentation or construction drawings

To dissect the capabilities of LayOut while learning the toolbars, we will now go through a step-by-step scenario for creating drawings.

Revising the SketchUp model to create 2D plan views

We will create two plan view drawing sheets. First, we need to make changes to the SketchUp model. Ensure you are on *Page 2* in LayOut before starting.

1. Open the practice SketchUp model.

    A quick way to open the SketchUp file from LayOut is to right-click on the viewport and choose **Open with SketchUp**.

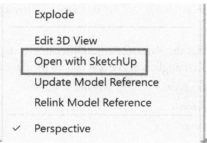

Figure 13.16: Right-click on the viewport and select Open with SketchUp

The *Chapter 13* practice model has three scenes – 3D Iso View, 2D FLOOR PLAN, and LIGHTING.

2. Click on the scene tab named 2D FLOOR PLAN.

3.   Check the **Tags** for this scene. The visibility of the 3D items and 2D furniture is turned off, which is correct. The built-ins and plumbing fixtures should be showing.

But whoops! The flooring texture is still showing. We need to turn it off for this scene.

4.   Click the eye next to the 3D ITEMS folder to close or turn off the visibility of all the items in that folder.

The flooring is in the 3D ITEMS folder, along with other 3D items that are unnecessary for the scene.

Figure 13.17: Use the Tags toolbar to show items for a 2D floor plan view

We only show items necessary for the 2D floor plan view, which means the furniture and accessories are unnecessary.

5.   **Update** the scene with the new tag visibilities.

6.   Choose **Top** view from **Camera | Standard Views** so that we have a 2D flat, orthographic view for this scene.

7.   Make sure the camera angle setting is still set to **Parallel Projection**. This can also be found in the **Camera** menu.

You learned in *Chapter 11* that the **Parallel Projection** camera angle is the only way to export a PDF to scale in SketchUp. That angle is also necessary to produce a scaled viewport in LayOut.

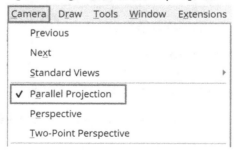

Figure 13.18: The Parallel Projection camera angle is under the Camera menu

Throughout the book, we also reviewed using standard views (such as **Top** or **Left**, but not **Iso**) to set up all drawings accurately. In order to create scaled drawing sets in LayOut, we must use both Parallel Projection and one of the standard views.

8. Change the standard view in the 2D FLOOR PLAN scene to **Top**, then update the scene with this change.

9. **Save** the model.

We always save when changing a SketchUp model that has been inserted into LayOut. Otherwise, the changes will not be reflected in LayOut.

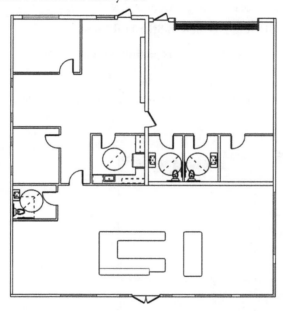

Figure 13.19: The updated 2D FLOOR PLAN scene

Hopefully, you spent time perusing the model and seeing how it is set up. We always do this when given another person's model! Everything you see in the updated 2D FLOOR PLAN scene was drafted in 2D instead of 3D.

> **Drafting in 2D within SketchUp saves time**
>
> Drafting in 2D for construction or presentation documents, especially for space planning, is a great way to save time before building 3D architectural features or furniture. As mentioned in *Chapter 1*, find Becca's Space Plan Items model in 3D Warehouse if you want pre-made space planning items!

Now, let's create a FURNITURE PLAN scene:

10. Right-click on the 2D FLOOR PLAN scene tab and add a new scene.

11. Name the new scene FURNITURE PLAN or FURN PLAN.

12. Make sure you are still using **Top** view in **Standard View**.

    You should also still be in the **Parallel Projection** camera setting.

13. Go back to the **Tags** toolbar.

14. Make all tags visible in the PLAN VIEWS and SHOWROOM tag folders.

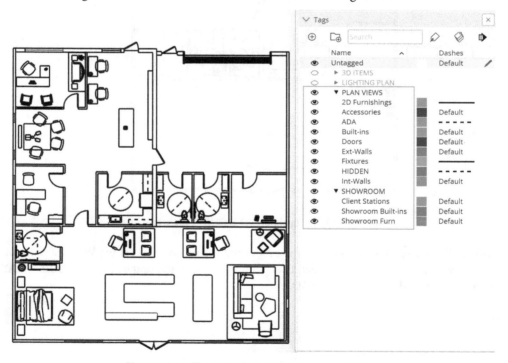

Figure 13.20: The FURNITURE PLAN scene and tags

15. Update the FURNITURE PLAN scene with these changes and save the model.

> **Don't change the view!**
>
> When updating scenes in SketchUp to match LayOut viewports, ensure you don't alter the view. Some users inadvertently update the SketchUp scene with a slight view adjustment. For example, if you select **Zoom Extents** in SketchUp, that will shift the model slightly to the right, causing misalignment in the LayOut viewport.
>
> For a quick resolution when this happens, simply delete the viewport and re-insert it. Before doing so, however, create lines to assist in positioning the new viewport accurately to align with other viewports.

In the next section, we will work primarily in LayOut to add paper space properties.

Using LayOut to create a floor plan

If you're accustomed to CAD software paper space, you're aware of the precision needed to create a comprehensive drawing set. While this chapter won't delve into that level of detail, we will guide you through the essential tools to achieve it:

1. To start, return to your LayOut file.

    The viewport should automatically update based on the linked SketchUp model changes. You can tell that it's updating because you won't be able to use your cursor for a minute.

2. If the viewport does not update, right-click the viewport and choose **Update Model Reference**.

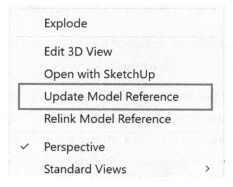

Figure 13.21: Update Model Reference

    You may or may not see changes to the viewport's position. Either way, we will make changes to the viewport soon.

3. Click the SketchUp model viewport to select it.

4. Look in the **Default Tray**; the **SketchUp Model** panel, if it is open, will no longer be grayed out. If the panel is not open, click on the name to expand it.

    Figure 13.22 shows the **SketchUp Model** panel and explains what each of the items in the panel controls. Take some time to become familiar with these settings while playing with the practice file.

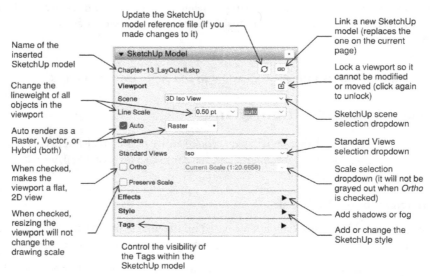

Figure 13.22: The SketchUp Model panel explained

5. Ensure the viewport is still selected, or the text inside this panel will be grayed out.

6. Update the following settings in the **SketchUp Model** panel (settings also shown in *Figure 13.23*):

    I.   **Scene**: Click the dropdown and choose 2D FLOOR PLAN.

    II. Check **Auto** so that your viewport graphics will automatically update based on your changes.

    III. **Standard Views**: Make sure that **Top** is selected. If not, click the dropdown and change it.

    IV. Check **Ortho**. Even when the SketchUp **Scene** is set up as 2D, we still need to tell LayOut we want it to be 2D. Always check **Ortho** for 2D views; otherwise, you won't be able to choose a drawing scale.

    V.   The **Scale** dropdown: Choose **3/16" = 1'-0" (1:64)**.

    VI. Check **Preserve Scale**: When showing a scaled drawing, **Preserve Scale** should always be checked. If you need to move or resize a viewport's border, the drawing scale will not change.

Figure 13.23: Make these changes to your SketchUp Model panel

7. If you do not see the three flyouts at the bottom of the panel, hover at the bottom until you see a white double arrow, and then drag the panel down until you see **Effects**, **Style**, and **Tags**.

8. Click and drag the viewport blue box areas to make the viewport size smaller so it does not fill up the sheet.

    Figure 13.24 shows the before (left) and after (right) states when resizing the blue viewport box.

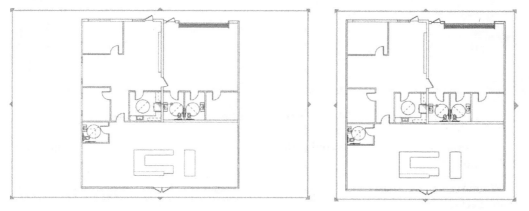

Figure 13.24: Make the viewport size smaller, as shown on the right

As long as you check **Preserve Scale**, the drawing will retain its 3/16" scale.

9. Click and drag (move) the floor plan to the bottom-right, near the title block.

10. Move it so that there is room at the right for dimension lines between the title block and the drawing. There should be room at the bottom for the drawing title. Use *Figure 13.25* to help you determine where it should be placed.

> **Tip**
>
> When moving and aligning objects in LayOut, it helps to create a line for guidance, allowing objects to snap to an endpoint.

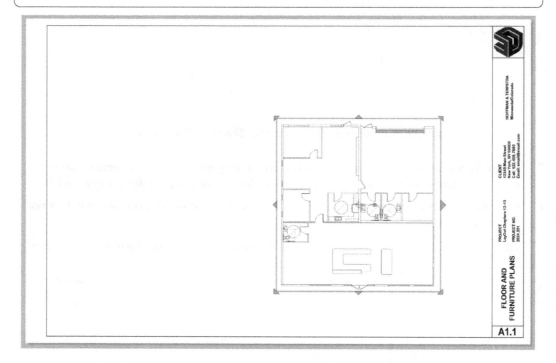

Figure 13.25: Move the viewport near the bottom-right of the sheet

Viewports can be moved, as you did in this step, so don't stress if yours is not lined up exactly like ours.

11. When you are done making changes to the viewport, click the gray area inside LayOut to deselect it.

We will now add text boxes on top of the viewport.

Working with text styles

The **Text Styles** panel (Windows) or **Fonts** panel (macOS) in the **Default Tray** is used for all text inside LayOut, such as labeling rooms, creating legends or notes, or customizing dimension text.

> **Two types of text boxes**
>
> *Chapter 12* mentioned the two types of text boxes. As a refresher, here is that information again.
>
> A **bounded text box** automatically adjusts its size based on how much text there is, keeping it within the confines of the text box you drew. **Unbounded text** allows you the freedom to type as much as you want in the direction you began to type, but the text will not wrap to a new line without you tapping *Enter/Return*.

We will now make room and area labels to add on top of the viewport:

1. Add a new layer and name it Room Labels. Make it the current layer by clicking on it, which will move the *pencil* to the left of the name.

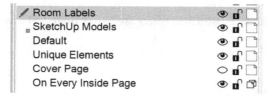

Figure 13.26: Make Room Labels the current layer

Remember that the pencil tells you which layer is currently active.

2. Create a text box using the *T* shortcut. You can also create a text box by clicking the icon in the toolbar.

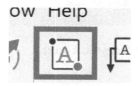

Figure 13:27: The text box icon

To make a *bounded text box*, click and drag the mouse. Release the mouse when the box is the size you want. You can change the size of the text box later.

Then, start typing inside the box.

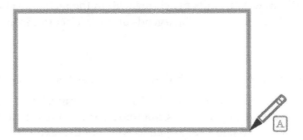

Figure 13.28: Creating a bounded text box

For *unbounded text,* click and release your mouse, and then begin typing where your cursor is.

3.   Create the room labels listed here:

- EMPLOYEE ENTRANCE/EGRESS (there are two of these text boxes)
- CEO/PRINCIPAL
- DESIGNERS
- DESIGN LIBRARY
- LOADING DOCK/WAREHOUSE
- CONFERENCE
- OFFICE MANAGER
- DESIGN STUDIO PUBLIC ENTRANCE
- KITCHENETTE
- ADA BATH (there are three of these text boxes)
- FOREMAN
- CLIENT STATION 1
- CLIENT STATION 2
- VIGNETTES (there are two of these text boxes)
- RETAIL/POS
- RETAIL
- SHOWROOM ENTRANCE

Figure 13.29 shows where each room label should reside.

> **Copying in LayOut**
>
> Create one text box, and then copy and reuse it for the next room.
>
> To copy, either use the universal copy/paste commands, *Ctrl*/⌘ *C* for copy and *Ctrl*/⌘ *V* for paste. Alternatively, after selecting the box and starting to move it, hold down *Ctrl* (Windows) or *Opt* (macOS) as you drag your mouse to where the copy should be placed. Release your mouse to stop the copy. One great thing about text boxes is that you can *nudge* them in smaller increments using your keyboard arrow keys!

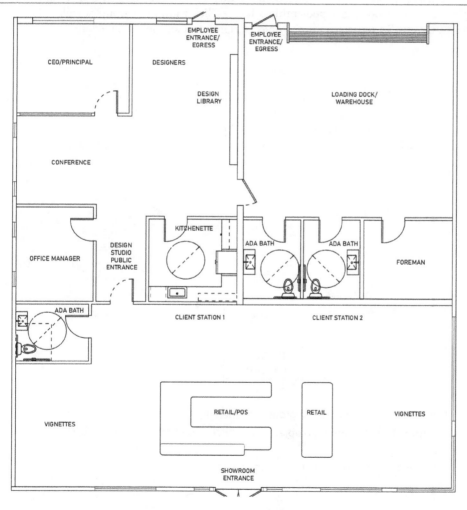

Figure 13.29: Where to place the room and area labels

While crafting your labels, take a moment to experiment with the **Text Style** (or **Font**) settings, as covered in *Chapter 12*. Explore options such as adding a stroke or border to the text box, incorporating stroke or fill colors, and adjusting the font style or size.

Grouping entities

LayOut enables us to group various entities together, irrespective of their layer placement. This feature proves useful in numerous situations, such as consolidating all room names for duplication or moving in unison across additional viewports, a task we will tackle later. To consolidate entities, either drag a bounding box around them or hold *Shift* and select each one (like in SketchUp), and then right-click on any entity and choose **Make Group**, as illustrated in *Figure 13.30*. To modify grouped entities, double-click within the group or right-click and select **Edit Group**. To separate grouped objects, right-click and select **Ungroup**.

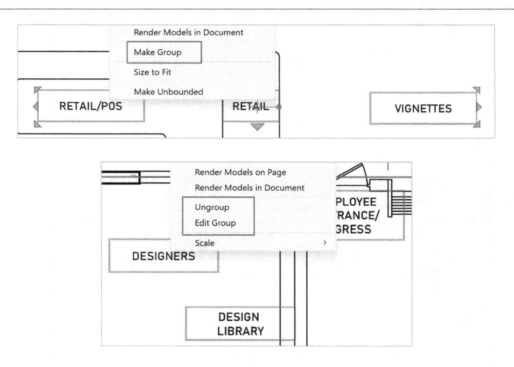

Figure 13.30: Select entities to group, and then right-click and select Make Group (top). To edit or ungroup objects, select Edit Group or Ungroup (bottom)

Now, let's start dimensioning items that are in the viewport.

Dimensioning in LayOut

Dimensioning in LayOut requires clicking on *points* (endpoints or midpoints) to create the dimension. That means if your SketchUp model has edges turned off, turn them on, or you won't be able to dimension. We will dimension the exterior elements: walls, windows, and doors:

1. Create a new layer in LayOut and call it `Dimensions`.

2. Make it the current layer by ensuring that the pencil is to the left of the layer name. If not, click the layer name.

3. Move the layer above the `SketchUp Models` layer by clicking and dragging the layer name. That way, the dimensions will be arranged on top of the model instead of underneath.

    Before we start adding multiple dimensions, it is helpful to decide how we want them to look. If we don't do this beforehand, we'll have to tweak each dimension's settings separately later, slowing down our workflow.

    The following panels can be used when setting up dimensioning styles:

    *   **Shape Style** (how the line should look)

    *   **Dimension Style** (how the dimension should display)

    *   **Text Style**

    To set up the styles of all future dimensioning in this document, we begin by activating the **Dimension** tool:

4. Open the **Dimension Style** panel in the **Default Tray**.

5. Activate the **Linear Dimension** tool by clicking the **Dimensions** icon in the toolbar.

    Alternatively, you can activate dimensions by tapping shortcut *D* on your keyboard.

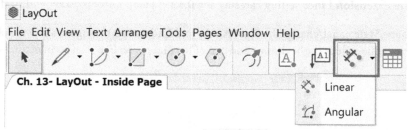

Figure 13.31: The Dimensions icon in the toolbar

If you want to create angled dimensions, click the dropdown next to the icon and choose **Angular** dimensions (shown in *Figure 13.31*).

6. In the **Dimension Style** panel, choose the settings shown in the following screenshot, or create your own dimension style:

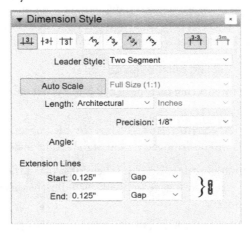

Figure 13.32: Dimension Style settings

These are the steps we took to create the settings in *Figure 13.32*:

I.   Select the icon that shows the dimensions above the dimension line.

II. Change **Leader Style** to **Two Segment**.

III. Click **Auto Scale** so that the dimensions match the scale of the drawing, locking them in at **Full Size (1:1)**.

IV. For **Length**, select **Architectural**.

V.   Change **Precision** to **1/8"** or **1/16"**, whichever you prefer.

VI. The **Extension Lines** setting can stay at a **0.125" | Gap** for both **Start** and **End**.

7. In the **Shape Style** panel, change the **Start Arrow** and **End Arrow** settings to show the **oblique** at **2 pt**. The oblique style at the beginning and end of the dimension line is an architectural standard:

Figure 13.33: Shape Style settings

8. Open the **Text Style** panel. Choose any font and text height for the dimensions.

    How do you know which text height to choose for architectural standards in LayOut? As mentioned in *Chapter 12*, it depends on the font, of course, but typical sizes are 14 to 16 pt for labels and between 14 and 20 pt for dimensions.

    For reference, we are using the **Bahnschrift** font at 18 pt. for dimensions in this tutorial. (Note that macOS does not have this font.)

    Now, we can start dimensioning!

9. Dimension the width of all the walls, windows, and door openings along the North wall, across the top of the drawing (*Figure 13.34*). Click the endpoints of the SketchUp model. Zoom in and out to be precise (and to access the endpoints better).

Not seeing the correct measurements?

If you dimension a wall that you know is 6 " wide and it measures incorrectly, check the **Dimension Style** panel. You may need to deselect **Auto Scale** and then click the scale dropdown to choose the precise scale of your viewport.

Figure 13.34 shows our top row of dimensions after dimensioning endpoint to endpoint and before fixing the overlap.

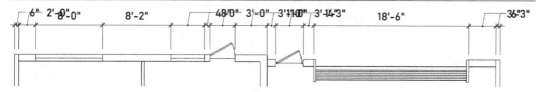

Figure 13.34: Create the top row of dimensions along the North wall

If you do not like how your dimension style looks after placing the first dimension, undo, fix the style, and start dimensioning again with new settings.

Having trouble with Dimension Styles?

In *steps 5* through *8*, you set up the dimension appearance, so that whenever you click the **Dimensions** icon in the toolbar or tap shortcut *D*, all dimension settings should be how you want them. (To restart a new setting for multiple dimensions, follow the same steps.) In the realm of technology, however, exceptions to rules are commonplace. Despite adhering to the correct steps, some macOS users have discovered that dimension style settings may not remain locked. Fortunately, there's a simple solution – activate the **Style** tool, represented by an eyedropper icon in the main toolbar. By selecting a dimension with your preferred styles, the cursor transforms into a bucket, enabling you to effortlessly paint other dimensions with all the attributes of the original. There is a second way to achieve the same result, shown in *Figure 13.41*, by selecting the dimension with your preferred styles, going to **Edit | Copy Style**, selecting the dimensions to change, and then using **Edit | Paste Style**.

To fix a dimension so that it does not overlap, double-click once so only the text box is highlighted:

10. Click, hold, and drag the box where you want it placed.

11. Release your mouse to stop moving the text, and then click on a blank area of the sheet to exit editing the dimension.

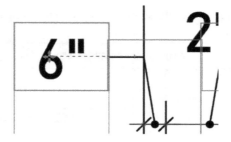

Figure 13.35: Move the text box by clicking and dragging

12. Do the same for the rest of the overlapping dimensions along the top.

All dimensions should line up with each other whenever possible. Using lines (the *L* shortcut) to guide you is helpful.

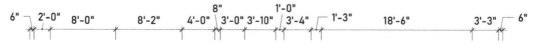

Figure 13.36: The top row of dimensions after fixing the overlap

Add TYP. after the 6 " dimension annotation for the two exterior wall dimensions. (This means that all exterior walls are typically 6 " deep unless otherwise noted.) That way, you do not have to dimension other 6 " exterior walls.

13. Double-click the dimension, and then double-click the text box to edit the annotation.

Type TYP. (in uppercase) after the <> symbols.

Figure 13.37: Type TYP. after the <> symbols

You might need to move the text box again, so it fits better with the other dimensions.

14. Tap *Esc* a couple of times to stop editing the dimension or click on a blank area of the sheet until you are out of the edit.

15. Add TYP. to the second 6 " wall notation or delete it by selecting it once and tapping *Del* on your computer. You can also right-click on the dimension and choose **Delete**.

16. Add a callout or leader line, called **Label** in LayOut, at the top of the drawing, where there is a 7 " difference between the back exterior wall depths.

The text font and height usually match the dimension style. Select the same font settings that you used when creating the dimensions.

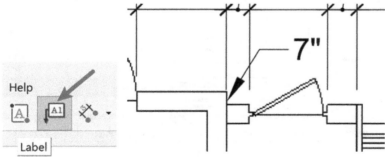

Figure 13.38: The Label icon (left), and adding a Label indicating the 7" wall jog (right)

If you want the **Shape Style** settings for **Start Arrow** and **End Arrow** to match ours, we chose the first arrow style in the **Start Arrow** dropdown with a **4 pt** setting.

Create all the exterior door, wall, and window dimensions around the building, as shown in *Figure 13.39*.

We made sure no dimensions overlapped; the dimension style was consistent throughout and included overall dimensioning of the drawing's left, top, and right sides.

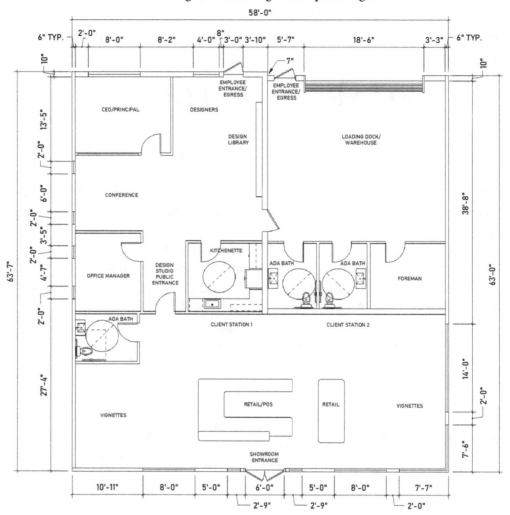

Figure 13.39: The completed dimensions

17. Add a label (leader line) at the bottom-right of the drawing that says GLASS TO GLASS FRAMELESS CORNER WINDOW @ SOUTHEAST.

Write the note in uppercase:

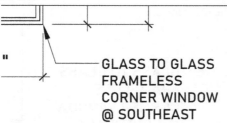

Figure 13.40: Add a note at the bottom-right corner using a Label

18. The label style should match the initial one you created earlier. To accomplish this, follow these steps:

I.   First, create the label and add the text regarding the window.

II.   Then, select the first label you created (the 7" dimension callout).

III.   Go to the **Edit** menu and select **Copy Style**.

IV.   Click the new label.

V.   Go back to the **Edit** menu and select **Paste Style**.

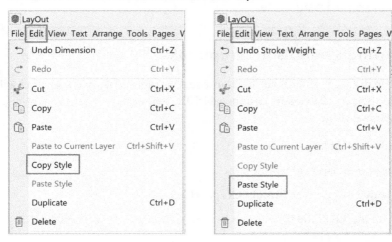

Figure 13.41: Copy and paste a previously used style

You will likely need to adjust the label's text box size so that it does not run into the title block.

19. To adjust the text box, double-click the leader line of the label, *not* the text box.

20. Then, use the blue grips on the text box to move it over, down, and so on, until it fits inside the sheet and not on top of the title block.

Figure 13.42: Adjust the text box by clicking and dragging the blue grips

To modify the font of all dimensions or labels after creating them, select them using a bounding box. Then, open the **Text Style** (or **Fonts**) panel, and make the changes. You can use other panels to adjust the styles of one or more dimensions or labels after creating them, such as **Colors**.

> **Learn more**
>
> To find more dimensioning tips, use this link: `https://help.sketchup.com/en/layout/marking-dimensions`.

Finding drawing symbols in scrapbooks

LayOut has built-in drawing symbols, tables, blocks such as cars and people, and other helpful tools in the **Scrapbooks** toolbar. All items are customizable! The following steps take you through selecting and modifying a drawing title:

1. Create a new LayOut layer called `Drawing Symbols`.

    Make it the current layer (hint – the pencil).

2. In the **Default Tray**, find the **Scrapbooks** panel.

    Under one of the **TB** (**Title Block**) style headings, choose **Auto-Text Enabled**.

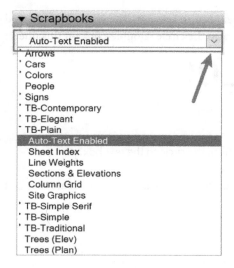
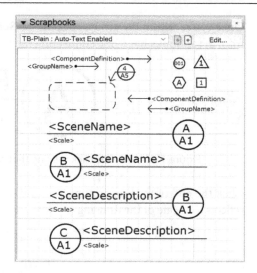

Figure 13:43: A Scrapbooks title block

There are a variety of styles you can look through. Find one that matches your brand or your style. All items can be modified.

3. Click a *drawing title* icon to select it, move your mouse to the sheet, and click again to place the drawing title under your floor plan. (You might have to click and drag the drawing title, depending on your version of LayOut.)

    The drawing title will still remain attached to your cursor, allowing you to place it more than once. When you are done placing the object, tap the *spacebar*.

    If you do not like the drawing title you chose, delete it or *undo*, and then find another.

4. If you want to use **Colors**, **Shape Style**, or other panels to edit your drawing title, go for it! All drawing titles are grouped, so you will need to double-click each element within to alter its text or appearance.

5. Change the drawing title text to match the following information:

    -   The sheet letter is A

    -   The drawing title is FLOOR PLAN

    -   The scale is 3/16" = 1'-0"

6. Double-click the drawing title group to link or **Auto-text** the drawing title information to your document. For this example, we will link the **Scale** text box to the drawing scale.

Once you're within the group, click on the **Scale** text box to select it. The symbol we selected from **Scrapbooks** has a line connecting the text box to the circle. Double-click on this line:

Figure 13.44: Double-click the line that goes from the circle to the text box

7. Click the end of the line on the circle and drag it up to the drawing until the **Scale** text box reflects the scale of the drawing.

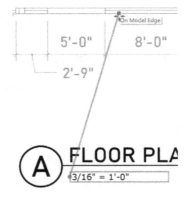

Figure 13.45: Click and drag the line up to the drawing

8. Release your mouse, tap *Esc*, or click outside the group a couple of times until you can no longer edit the group.

9. In **Scrapbooks**, find a *north arrow*, and add it to the left of the drawing title.

    North arrows are usually found under **Site Graphics** or **Drawing Symbols**.

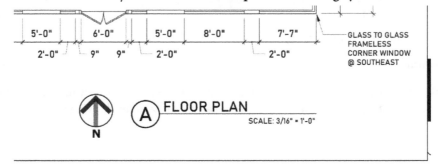

Figure 13.46: Drawing title A and the north arrow

You can edit the north arrow to fit your style, such as its size, color, and shape stroke. Just remember to double-click to edit, or right-click the group and select **Edit Group**.

This floor plan is coming along!

Adding a wall hatch or poché and a new lineweight

Now, let's practice adding a new lineweight and other CAD-type attributes:

1. Add a new layer, and name it `Hatching` or `Poche`.

2. Make it the current layer.

3. Draw rectangles (shortcut *R*) over the exterior walls, between the window and door openings.

4. In the **Shape Style** panel, click the box to the right of **Pattern**. That will open the **Pattern Fill** panel.

5. Use **Pattern Fill** to add a **Cast-in-place Concrete** material to each rectangle.

6. Return to the **Shape Style** panel to change the stroke of each rectangle to `1` or `1.50` pt.

This creates a heavier lineweight for the exterior walls.

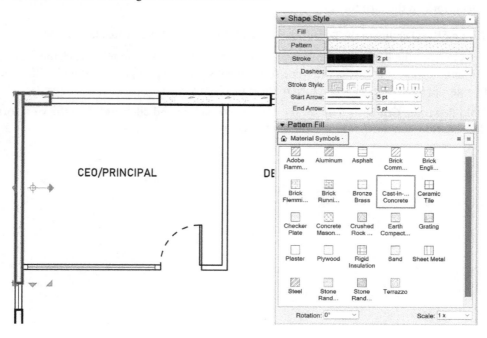

Figure 13.47: Use Shape Style and Pattern Fill to add hatching and a heavier lineweight

Add rectangles, hatching, and stroke around the entire peimeter of the building.

The only exterior wall areas where you should *not* add rectangles are at the entrance to the Warehouse, highlighted in red in *Figure 13.48*.

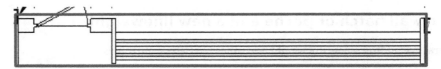

Figure 13.48: Do not add a hatch or fill to the Warehouse entrance or loading dock

One way to streamline the hatching is to create the rectangles and then turn off the **Dimensions** and **SketchUp Models** layers. Then, select all the rectangles at once and apply **Fill** and **Stroke**.

We are done modifying the floor plan.

Copying a viewport

Now, we will work on the furniture plan:

1. Turn off the visibility to the Dimensions and Hatching (or Poche) layers.

2. Click to select the Floor Plan viewport, hold down the *Shift* key, and then click the drawing title and north arrow to select all three simultaneously. If you grouped the room labels, select that group; otherwise, we will return to them in a later step.

3. Hold down the *Ctrl* key (Windows) or *Opt* key (macOS) and click and drag the viewport, drawing title, and north arrow to the left (*Figure 13.49*).

4. Once your mouse finds the red axis, hold down the *Shift* key to keep everything aligned along the red axis with the originals.

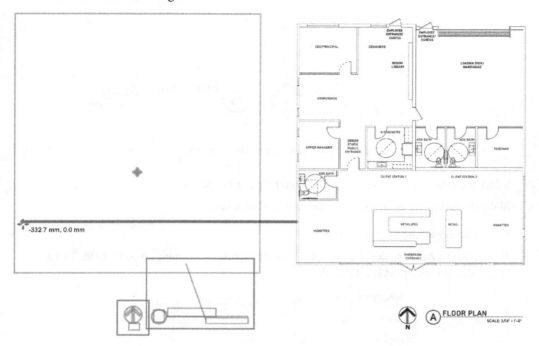

-332.7 mm, 0.0 mm

Figure 13.49: Copy the viewport, drawing title, and north arrow to the left

You can also use pre-made lines to snap to endpoints.

5. Change the drawing title to FURNITURE PLAN.

6.   Change the drawing letter to B.

Figure 13.50: The renamed drawing title

7.   Select the new viewport and open the **SketchUp Model** panel.

8.   Make the following changes in the **SketchUp Model** panel:

   I.   Change **Scene** to FURNITURE PLAN.

   II.   Next to **Auto**, click the dropdown that says **Raster** and change it to **Hybrid**. This affects how the viewport is rendered.

Figure 13.51: Make changes to the SketchUp Model panel for the new viewport

   III.   Change the FLOOR PLAN viewport rendering also to **Hybrid**.

9.   Copy the room labels to FURNITURE PLAN, just like you copied the viewport and other elements (if you did not copy them already). Move them around the plan, if necessary, so that they are not on top of furniture.

When you are done moving, adding, or deleting the room labels, the plan should look similar to *Figure 13.52*:

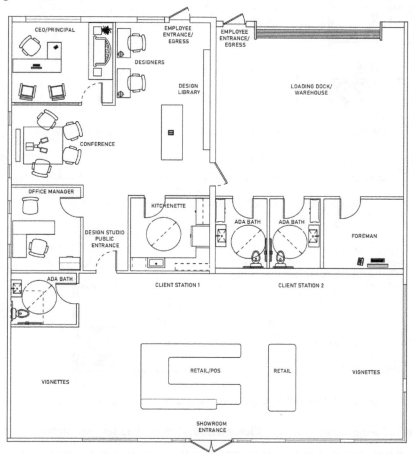

Figure 13.52: The FURNITURE PLAN viewport

It looks like the foreman's desk is not showing in FURNITURE PLAN. We need to go back to SketchUp to fix that.

10. Back inside SketchUp, click on the FURNITURE PLAN (or FURN PLAN) scene tab. The foreman's desk is still not showing.

11. Open the **Outliner** toolbar.

The desk component, called <3 Desk w Chair>, is listed at the top of the **Outliner** toolbar because it starts with the number 3. As demonstrated in *Figure 13.53*, if you click on the component's name, you will see a blue outline of where the desk should be in the foreman's office.

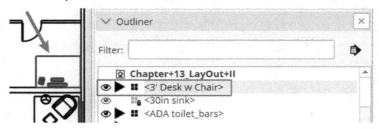

Figure 13.53: The Outliner toolbar shows 3′ Desk w Chair at the top

The odd thing is that even though it is listed in *Outliner*, the desk cannot be seen in the SketchUp model. The desk and chair will have dotted lines if hidden geometry is not visible.

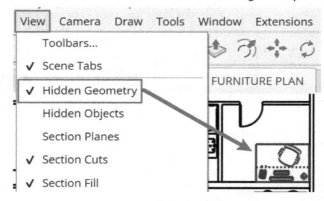

Figure 13.54: The desk and chair appear with Hidden Geometry visible

To show hidden geometry, use the **View** menu and check **Hidden Geometry**.

12. Go into **Edit** mode of the chair.

Select all the dotted edges of the chair, right-click, and choose **Unhide**.

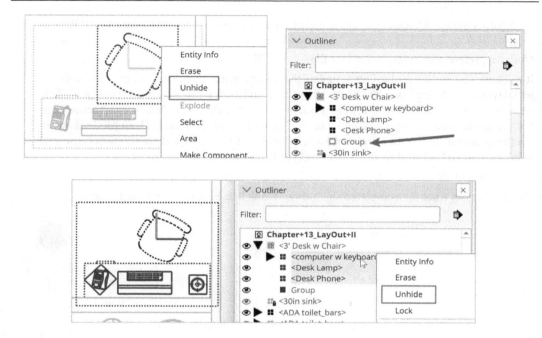

Figure 13.55: Unhide the edges of the chair (top), use Outliner to Unhide the edges of the desk (bottom)

13. Unhide the desk edges as well. Try using **Outliner** to unhide the desk's edges by getting into **Edit** mode of the desk and selecting all objects inside the group (*Figure 13.55 bottom*).

14. Get out of **Edit** mode and update the scene.

15. **Save** your model so that LayOut will update with the change.

16. Go back to LayOut.

LayOut should automatically begin updating the viewport with the change made in SketchUp.

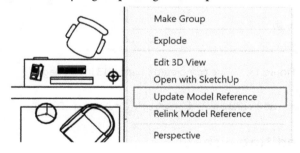

Figure 13.56: Update Model Reference

If it does not update automatically, right-click on the viewport and select **Update Model Reference**.

Updating references in larger LayOut files

It will take a bit of time for LayOut to update the reference, mainly because we are now working with **Hybrid** rendering instead of **Raster**. Be patient, and don't try to click inside LayOut while it renders. If your computer is lagging too much or crashing often, change the viewport renderings back to **Raster**. Alternatively, as mentioned in *Chapter 12*, you can **Enable Draft Mode** (**Layout | Settings** in macOS or **Edit | Preferences** in Windows), which is a great substitute because you won't have to go back and fix the rendering type before presenting or exporting.

Figure 13.57 shows what the completed sheet should look like, depending on your additions:

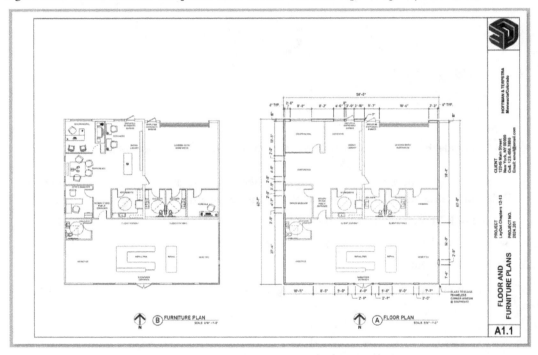

Figure 13.57: The completed Chapter 13 inside page

We will now add a new page and create a `Reflected Ceiling Plan`.

Duplicating and editing a sheet

LayOut makes it easy to keep your drawing sheets consistent simply by duplicating the page.

In LayOut's **Pages** dialog box, duplicate the **Inside Page** sheet:

1. Click **Inside Page**.
2. Select the button between the *plus* and *minus* buttons, called **Duplicate selected page**.
3. Click once to *duplicate* the page.

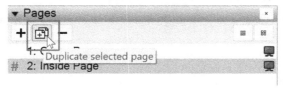

Figure 13.58: Duplicate selected page

A new sheet will appear underneath the original. It will automatically be named Page 3.

4. Rename Inside Page (or Page 2) to Floor & Furniture Plans by double-clicking the original name to edit.
5. After renaming, tap *Enter* or *Return* to keep the new name.
6. Rename the new page, Page 3, to Reflected Ceiling Plan.
7. Make Reflected Ceiling Plan the page you are working on by clicking on it once so that it is highlighted.

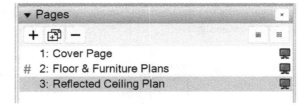

Figure 13.59: Click the new page to make it current

Now, we will work on the final sheet of the tutorial, Reflected Ceiling Plan.

Creating a Reflected Ceiling Plan with stacked viewports

When drafting a **Reflected Ceiling Plan** (**RCP**), it's helpful to have the furniture showing at a lighter lineweight than the lighting.

Before we start that, however, we need to edit the duplicated sheet a bit to eliminate information that does not pertain to the RCP:

1. Select and delete all dimensions, leaders, and hatching, but don't delete the **Dimensions** or **Hatching** layers. Otherwise, that will delete the dimensions, labels, and hatching for the floor plan on *Page 2*. Keep the room labels where they are.

2. To simplify selection, temporarily disable the **SketchUp Models** and **Room Names** layers and re-enable them afterward.

3. Change the drawing title to REFLECTED CEILING PLAN: DESIGN STUDIO.

4. Change the drawing letter to C.

5. You will have to extend the text box and line to make them fit. Zoom in closely to select the line, after double-clicking the multiple groups within the drawing title grouping.

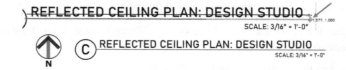

Figure 13.60: Click the line's handle to stretch it (top) and the finalized Drawing C title on Page 3

If you want to omit **DESIGN STUDIO** from the title, that's okay.

6. Change the title block sheet name to Reflected Ceiling Plan. Double-click the sheet name, and then type over the selection.

Figure 13.61: Change the title block sheet name

Note that the sheet number is updated automatically. Yay! (If not, you may have accidentally moved the sheet number from the **On Every Inside Page** layer.)

7. Delete the FURNITURE PLAN viewport and drawing title on the left. We won't need them for this sheet. Also, delete the room and area labels from the left viewport area.

8. Select the viewport and open the **SketchUp Model** panel. Make the following changes in the panel:

    I.   Change the scene to FURNITURE PLAN.

II.   Open the **Tags** flyout. Turn off the visibility to all tags in the PLAN VIEWS folder except 2D Furnishings and Built-ins. In the SHOWROOM folder, turn off the visibility of the entire folder.

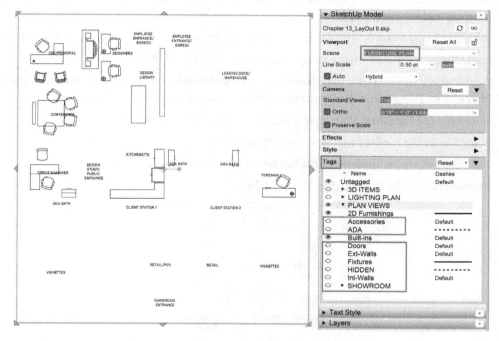

Figure 13.62: The new FURNITURE PLAN viewport

Use *Figure 13.62* to guide you on which tags to turn off.

9.   Create a new LayOut layer, named Furniture Plan. Move the viewport to that layer.

10.   Create another new LayOut layer, named RCP.

Make sure that the **RCP** layer is *above* the **Furniture Plan** layer.

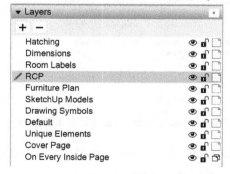

Figure 13.63: The RCP layer should be above the Furniture Plan layer

To align with the stacking of viewports in the upcoming steps, the **RCP** layer should be positioned above the **Furniture Plan** layer for visibility.

11. Copy the `Furniture Plan` viewport using either *Ctrl/*⌘ *C* or by right-clicking on the viewport and selecting **Copy**.

12. Paste the viewport exactly where the other viewport is by using *Ctrl/*⌘ *V* or through **Edit | Paste**.

13. Immediately right-click on the viewport and move it to the **RCP** layer.

14. Double-check that you have two viewports on two different layers by turning off the **Furniture Plan** and **RCP** layers and then turning on one at a time to see whether they appear.

15. Show only the **Furniture Plan** layer. Click the viewport to select it.

16. In the **SketchUp Model** panel, open the **Styles** flyout.

17. Click the dropdown underneath the header and choose **Styles**.

18. Double-click on the `Straight Lines` folder.

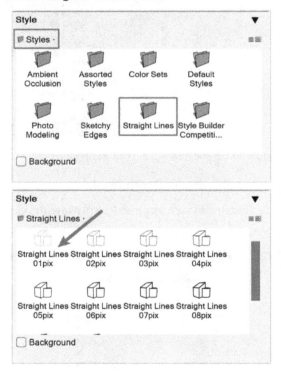

Figure 13.64: Choose the Straight Lines folder (top) and Straight Lines 01pix style (bottom)

Another window will open, with 10 different types of straight line styles.

19. Select the style named **Straight Lines 01pix**.

20. Up near the top of the **SketchUp Model** panel, next to **Line Scale**, click the dropdown and select **0.10 pt**.

The furniture and built-ins in the viewport should now be a lighter lineweight than they were initially.

21. *Lock* the viewport. (*Figure 13.65* has a blue arrow pointing to the lock icon.)

After you lock the viewport, the selection box turns from blue to red.

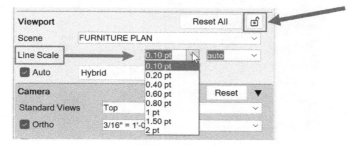

Figure 13.65: Change the Line Scale setting and lock the viewport

Have you been saving your LayOut file? If not, make sure to do that now.

22. In the **Layers** panel, lock the **Furniture Plan** layer:

Figure 13.66: Lock the Furniture Plan layer

23. Turn on the visibility of the **RCP** layer and open the **SketchUp Model** panel.

Change the scene to LIGHTING.

24. Under **Tags**, click the white **Reset** button dropdown.

    Select **Reset Visibility**.

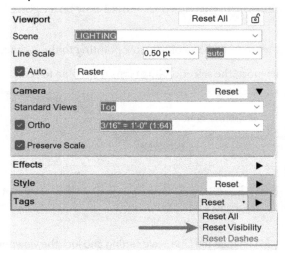

Figure 13.67: Reset the Tags for the RCP viewport

Let's set up the tags for the RCP viewport.

25. Show/turn off the visibility of the tags, as shown in *Figure 13.68*:

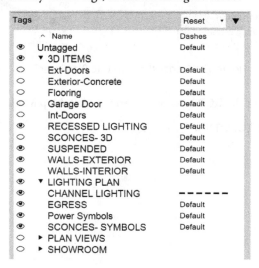

Figure 13.68: Set the visibility of the tags as shown in this figure

You do not need to open the PLAN VIEWS or SHOWROOM folders; just make sure the visibility to the folders is off.

26. Move the room labels around so that they do not obstruct the lighting.

    We cannot see where the walls and windows are on the plan because we are using a scene with 3D models instead of 2D shapes. Because of this, we will change the style to **Wireframe** to pick up the edges we cannot see through the walls in a standard 3D view.

27. In **Style | Default Style**, search for and choose the default style called **Wireframe**.

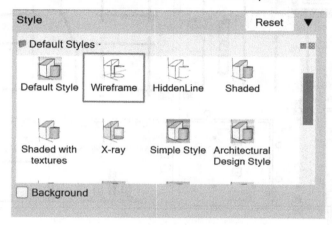

Figure 13.69: Select the Wireframe style

You should now be able to see the window and door lines in the floor plan.

28. Change **Line Scale** to **1.50 pt**.

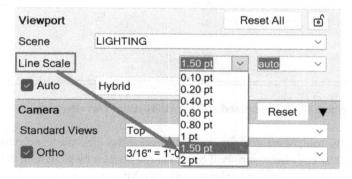

Figure 13.70: Change Line Scale to 1.50 pt

The two stacked viewports should look like this:

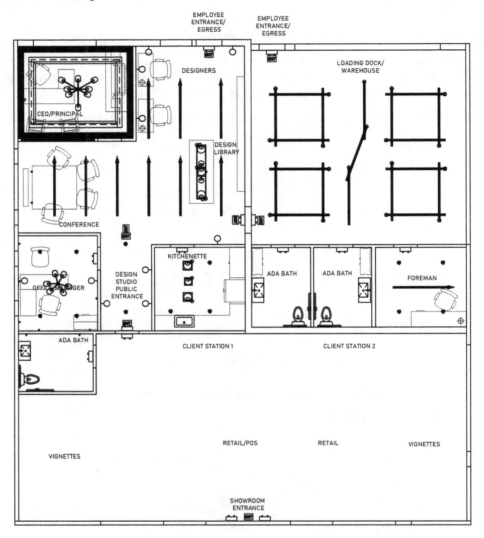

Figure 13.71: The stacked RCP and FURNITURE PLAN viewports

LayOut is a remarkable tool, offering many creative possibilities that can be efficiently harnessed. The step-by-step tutorial ends here, and we'll conclude the chapter by providing valuable insights on optimizing your document. Prepare to elevate your LayOut game with the final tips that follow.

Troubleshooting viewport warnings

As mentioned earlier, our choice to render SketchUp models as **Hybrid** could result in the file lagging, mainly as multiple viewports are introduced. If using **Enable Draft Mode** is not for you, there is another option:

Experienced LayOut users often utilize two layers to render output viewports – one labeled `Raster` and the other `Hybrid/Vector`. That is because a viewport will not update until it is visible on the sheet. To expedite document updates without waiting for a higher-quality rendering, simply toggle off the visibility of the hybrid/vector layer. When preparing to process a high-output visual, disable the raster layer and enable the hybrid/vector layer.

In the event that a yellow warning symbol appears beside your viewport during the modeling process, as depicted in *Figure 13.72*, don't panic! This indicator highlights a viewport issue that can be resolved through a variety of methods, depending on the underlying problem.

- Right-click on the viewport and choose **Render Model**
- Right-click on the viewport and choose **Update Model Reference**
- Right-click on the viewport and choose **Relink Model Reference**

Figure 13.72: A warning error in LayOut and right-click options to fix the error

For pages with stacked viewports. such as the `REFLECTED CEILING PLAN` page, you must determine which viewport has the issue. Because the `FURNITURE PLAN` viewport is locked, you have to unlock both the layer and viewport before fixing the problem.

Should these solutions prove ineffective, consider exiting LayOut and allowing your computer to rest before reopening the file. This might resolve the issue. If it persists, you may need to remove the viewport and insert it again. However, this is a rare occurrence, so it's not something to be overly concerned about.

Adding additional details to drawings

Typically, when crafting an RCP, we would include dimensions for lighting, details on each fixture, and ceiling height indicators, among other things. However, this chapter will not cover these aspects, as it is already quite extensive. Instead, we'll point out some areas for further independent exploration, mainly focusing on expanding knowledge about **Scrapbooks**, creating **tables**, **clipping masks**, and inserting content.

First, however, we want to show you a workaround for hyperlinks.

Adding a hyperlink

The preceding lead-in was a bit misleading. You can add a **hyperlink** to LayOut, but only by copying the URL and pasting it to LayOut. Currently, there is no way for Windows users to right-click on a set of text and add a hyperlink to it, or a hyperlink to an object (such as an image).

The copy-and-paste approach is acceptable if you want to show the hyperlink text. In *Figure 13.73*, we see two examples of hyperlinks in a LayOut PDF export. The hyperlink on the left is where the URL was copied from a lighting website, and the text was pasted *underneath* an image of the corresponding light fixture. The URL paste does not underline the text, but you can add that in **Text Styles** or **Fonts**.

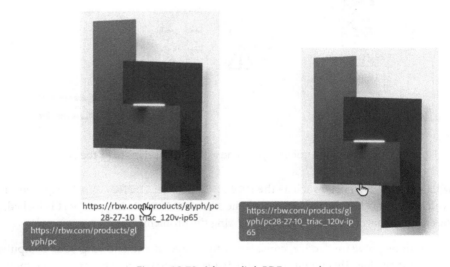

Figure 13.73: A hyperlink PDF example

The hyperlink on the right comes from the image. How did we make this happen? Follow these steps to find out:

1. Copy the URL link and paste it into LayOut. It automatically creates a text box without having to start one yourself.

2. Using the **Layers** panel, create two different layers.

    We named one Hyperlinks and the other one Product Image.

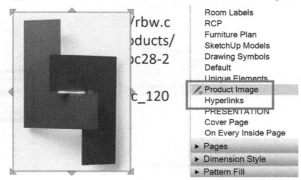

Figure 13.74: Create new layers - Hyperlinks and Product Image

We like to make the text bigger, so the hyperlink is visible when a mouse hovers over the image on the PDF.

3. Make sure the image layer is above the hyperlink layer, as shown in *Figure 13.74*.

4. Move the image over the text so that the text is hidden.

    There are times when we turn the text white to make it invisible. This little trick also lets us sneak hyperlinks into different parts of the sheet without messing up the look.

5. Test out the hyperlink when you are done working in LayOut and exporting the PDF.

Hopefully, the link will work every time!

Clipping masks

If the term *clipping mask* is unfamiliar to you, it refers to a technique used to restrict or isolate a specific portion of an existing element, leaving the rest of the element trimmed or concealed. This is useful for trimming unwanted information or referencing areas in a document by making them larger than the original.

Many software programs, such as Adobe and AutoCAD, have their interpretation of and uses for clipping masks. SketchUp LayOut allows us to clip anything in the model, whether it is an image, SketchUp model, drawing, or more. The *mask* portion comes from using a shape to create the clip or trim. And don't worry- the clipping mask does not permanently alter the object you are using it for.

In *Figure 13.75*, a clipping mask is shown to the left of the RCP, calling out an image of the pendant light fixture in the CEO's office.

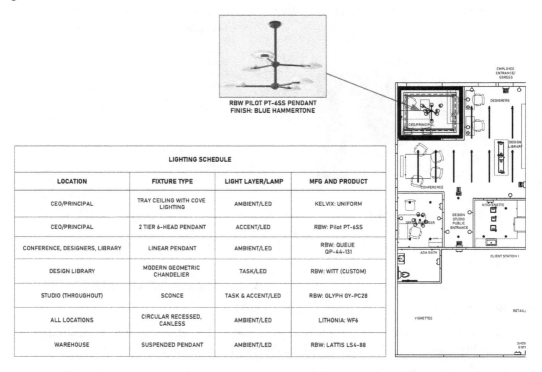

RBW PILOT PT-6SS PENDANT
FINISH: BLUE HAMMERTONE

LIGHTING SCHEDULE			
LOCATION	**FIXTURE TYPE**	**LIGHT LAYER/LAMP**	**MFG AND PRODUCT**
CEO/PRINCIPAL	TRAY CEILING WITH COVE LIGHTING	AMBIENT/LED	KELVIX: UNIFORM
CEO/PRINCIPAL	2 TIER 6-HEAD PENDANT	ACCENT/LED	RBW: Pilot PT-6SS
CONFERENCE, DESIGNERS, LIBRARY	LINEAR PENDANT	AMBIENT/LED	RBW: QUEUE QP-44-131
DESIGN LIBRARY	MODERN GEOMETRIC CHANDELIER	TASK/LED	RBW: WITT (CUSTOM)
STUDIO (THROUGHOUT)	SCONCE	TASK & ACCENT/LED	RBW: GLYPH GY-PC28
ALL LOCATIONS	CIRCULAR RECESSED, CANLESS	AMBIENT/LED	LITHONIA: WF6
WAREHOUSE	SUSPENDED PENDANT	AMBIENT/LED	RBW: LATTIS LS4-88

Figure 13.75: A clipping mask showing a visual of the real pendant light fixture

The steps to create the clipping mask are as follows:

1. Copy one of the SketchUp model viewports, insert an image, or add another type of insertable content.

    You can change the scene or view of the viewport if desired.

2. Create a shape, whether a rectangle, square, polygon, or series of edges.

3. Position the shape over the area of the viewport (or other element) to keep, ensuring that it has no *fill* so that we can see through it.

4. Select both the shape and the viewport (or other element).

5. Right-click on them and select **Create Clipping Mask**. Both must be selected, or you will not have the option to create the clip. You can also find this tool under the **Edit** menu.

6. The clipping mask will be applied. You can move it, adjust its size, add a border (*stroke*), or implement other modifications to enhance the clip.

Clipping masks are easy to use and a great addition to your professional document!

Adding your work to scrapbooks

Once we've added SketchUp models, images, or AutoCAD drawings, it's essential to dedicate time to refining, modifying, or developing new elements. This effort ensures the creation of an impressive document that we can proudly share.

Creating your own set of often-used symbols that are not readily available in LayOut saves drafting time in the future.

For example, the egress **EXIT** signs from SketchUp aren't great. We created our own in LayOut, using shapes and text, and added a directional arrow from **Scrapbook**. These small details make our drawings better.

Figure 13.76: We created two different exit symbols in LayOut

After making the signs, we saved them as a new **Scrapbook** item so that they appear in each LayOut file we open. Yes, you can design your own scrapbook items to use again!

To do that, add those elements to a blank LayOut file. Using the **File** menu, click **Save As Scrapbook…**. Make sure to save the file with a name that matches the items. Afterward, check the **Scrapbooks** panel to see your creation. It will be available every time you open LayOut on your device!

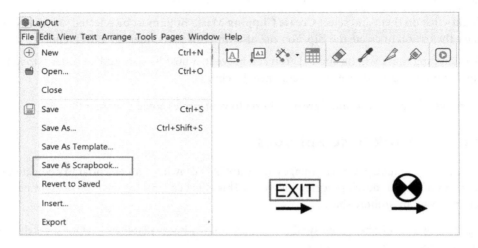

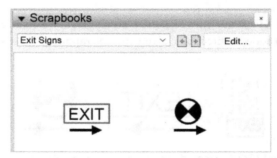

Figure 13.77: Save your creation as a scrapbook (top), and then check the Scrapbooks panel (bottom)

Another important element missing from LayOut, at least for people who prepare construction documents, is a revision cloud. We are sorry to say that, at the time of writing, a revision cloud is not an available feature (but it should be!). We have figured out a workaround for it – by creating a series of overlapping circles, and then using the **Split** and **Join** tools to make our own revision cloud. You can learn how to create your own by watching this video by SketchUp: `https://youtu.be/VpCvYRFYx1w?si=wlK7Wlg-U9fUWUCp`.

If you do not have time to create your own, you can download a LayOut file of our exit signs and revision clouds from Dropbox: `https://www.dropbox.com/scl/fi/hx0icdvilx3lbn3tk6te9/Chapter-13-Scrapbooks.layout?rlkey=9dkbxe2cqawcnqvidw4ect27t&st=q538lyz3&dl=0`.

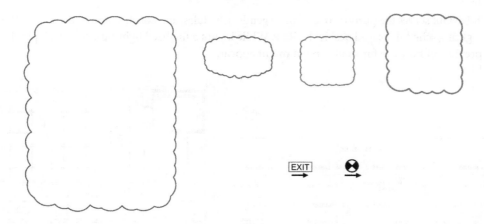

Figure 13.78: Download our Chapter 13 Scrapbooks LayOut file

After downloading the file, add them to your own *scrapbooks* by following the steps covered previously (*Figure 13.77*). You can adjust the *size, stroke color, weight*, and other options mentioned in this chapter and *Chapter 12*.

> **Want more?**
>
> You can buy handy scrapbooks made by other users! Matt Donley of **Master SketchUp** has an electrical scrapbook on his website (`https://mastersketchup.com/product/electrical-symbol-scrapbook/`), as well as a huge library of construction details and assemblies by LayOut expert Nick Sonder (`https://mastersketchup.com/product/sonder-detail-scrapbooks/`). There are more downloads out there waiting for you to find them!
>
> Learn more about scrapbooks here: `https://help.sketchup.com/en/layout/working-scrapbooks-reusable-entities`.

Creating a table and inserting a spreadsheet

This chapter is long, so we won't go into much detail on how to add a table or insert a spreadsheet into LayOut. We will give you links and a few tips to help.

To create a table, click the toolbar icon, or use the **Tools** menu and click **Table**.

Figure 13.79: The table icon in LayOut

A *table* in LayOut serves the purpose of crafting legends, schedules, and construction notes. *Figure 13.80* shows a lighting schedule placed beside the RCP. While it's not a finalized lighting schedule, it provides a rapid preview of how the finished version might appear.

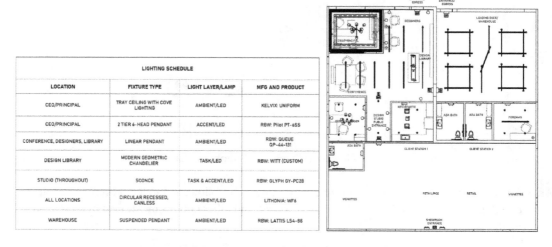

Figure 13.80: An example of a schedule next to the RCP

Tables are managed the same way text, lines, and other LayOut entities are edited – by using **Text Styles**, **Shape Styles**, **Pattern Fill**, **Color**, and other panels.

Learn more about tables

Use the following links to create a table or insert a spreadsheet:

`help.sketchup.com/en/layout/adding-tables-document`

`https://help.sketchup.com/en/layout/adding-tables-document#import-data`

Readers, we aim for transparency in this book, and we'll maintain that honesty. Frankly, we're not big fans of tables in LayOut. They can be a bit of a headache, requiring extra time to tweak a single cell, let alone wrestling with the whole table to make it match your style. So, if you're in need of a schedule, our advice is to either import a spreadsheet or get creative with shapes and text boxes to whip up your own.

In *Figure 13.81*, an Excel spreadsheet imported into LayOut is depicted. It was very easy to import the Excel document, which was already complete. After importing, we had the option to change the font styles without it affecting the original document.

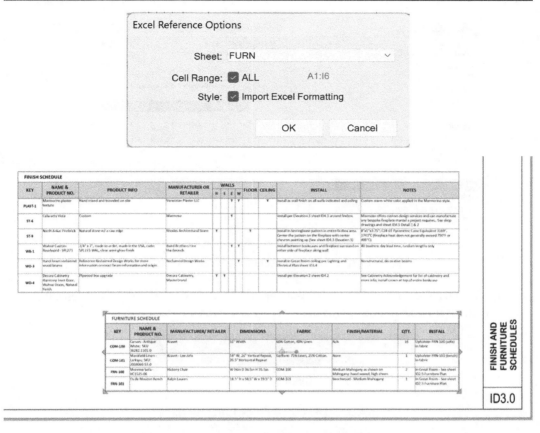

Figure 13.81: An Excel spreadsheet inserted into LayOut. Schedule
information provided by Madeleine Draper, Interior Designer.

The presentation of the imported spreadsheet is notably cleaner and more legible, and making changes is far easier than working with a table directly in LayOut.

Using a scrapbook table for the sheet index

The scrapbooks **sheet index** transforms creating a cover sheet index into a seamless and visually engaging experience, making setup easy and aesthetically pleasing.

Wait, didn't we just say we don't like tables in LayOut? Yes, we did. The difference with this table is that we don't have to modify much because it automatically adds the sheet number and name based on how they are set up in **Pages**.

Now, on the cover page, or *cover sheet* as we call it, open **Scrapbooks** and search for **Sheet Index** under any of the **TB** menus. Like other scrapbook items, click on the table and add it to the sheet.

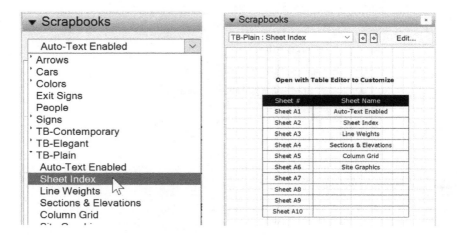

Figure 13.82: Search for Sheet Index in Scrapbooks

We changed the fill color for the header rows and font style, and now our sheet index is done. It took us three minutes from start to finish.

SHEET #	SHEET NAME
Sheet A0.0	COVER SHEET
Sheet A1.1	FLOOR & FURNITURE PLANS
Sheet A2.1	REFLECTED CEILING PLAN

Figure 13.83: The modified sheet index

As long as your **Pages** panel has the sheets in the correct order and they are already named, LayOut does the rest for you.

Finishing the cover sheet

Throughout this book, we've touched on the **Add Location** feature several times. To recap, it allows you to bring a specific geographical location into your SketchUp model, complete with site imagery and data. This is particularly useful for adding a detailed site plan to your cover sheet (or other pages) in LayOut.

However, as we explored in *Chapter 12* and in the first section of this chapter, *Manipulating image files*, there's another route you can take by importing an image file. Inserting a site map image file directly into LayOut is a quick way to show existing and proposed buildings. Additionally, or as a complementary approach, you can utilize scenes from your SketchUp model to craft exterior elevation views of your building.

And let's not forget the impact of a photorealistic rendered image of your project. Incorporating such an image can truly elevate the presentation document, leaving a lasting impression!

Figure 13.84 shows a cover sheet with a **SketchUp Diffusion** rendered exterior image of the practice file:

Figure 13.84: A SketchUp Diffusion AI-generated render of the project exterior

Chapter 15 will introduce you to *SketchUp Diffusion*, an **Artificial Intelligence (AI)** rendering extension, and give introductory tips on how to use it.

Managing linked items

The last thing we want to mention in this section is the **Document Setup** dialog box. We mentioned this window many pages ago at the tutorial's beginning but want to circle back to it, now that we have inserted more content.

Make sure to check **Document Setup** whenever you have a linking issue. It's also good to click the **Purge** button now and then to purge your file of unused links.

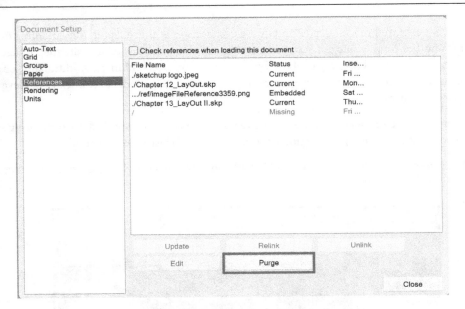

Figure 13.85: Before clicking Purge

Take a look at the files under **File Name** in *Figure 13.85*. Having multiple SketchUp files inserted into LayOut causes the file size to bloat. *The best practice is to have one SketchUp file with multiple scenes, and then copy the same viewport throughout LayOut as needed.* Also, don't drag and drop files into LayOut. Use **File | Insert** when you are inside LayOut, or **Send to LayOut** inside SketchUp.

If you don't follow a proper workflow, LayOut will lag heavily, the **Status** of objects will show **Missing**, as does the one in our example, or your file will be prone to issues such as crashing. Keep in mind there is no way to delete links, such as our **Missing** link. Links will be purged if not used in LayOut, but there is no *delete* button.

To prevent modifications in the SketchUp or image file from affecting your LayOut document, break the link by selecting the reference and choosing the **Unlink** option. That will cause the status to change to **Embedded**.

The next and final section of the chapter explores exporting the LayOut file to a PDF and using the **Presentation** tool.

Presenting the LayOut document

There are two methods to present your document. One way is by creating a PDF export. The second way is to use the presentation tool in LayOut.

Exporting a LayOut file to a PDF

Exporting your document to a PDF is generally a seamless and straightforward task. However, you might experience a delay when the document contains multiple pages loaded with detailed content, which can extend the time needed for the export process.

Here are the steps to export:

1. From the **File** menu, choose **Export**, and then select **PDF....**

    There are other ways to export, as you see from *Figure 13.86*. You can export LayOut pages as images or export them to a DWG/DXF CAD file.

> **Learn more**
>
> Learn more about exporting to CAD here: https://help.sketchup.com/en/layout/exporting-cad-data-layout.
>
> Learn about exporting image files at this link: https://help.sketchup.com/en/layout/exporting-or-printing-your-layout-document.

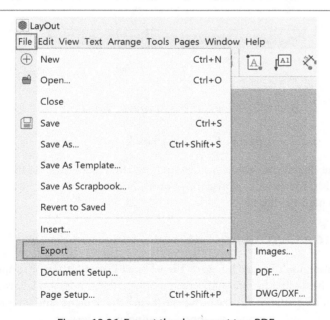

Figure 13.86: Export the document to a PDF

2. The first window that pops up asks you to choose a place to save the export.

3. The second window, **PDF Export options**, is the last one before the export begins:

    I. Under **Pages**, you can export all pages at once or a smaller range, next to **Range**.

II.   Decide the **Image compression quality** setting you want using the slider. (This is where you can generate a higher output image if the **Rendering** menu is not available in **Document Setup**). The higher the output, the longer the export will take.

III.   If you want to export the layers to the PDF, check the box under **Layers**.

IV.   To open the PDF export immediately upon finishing, check the box underneath **Finish**.

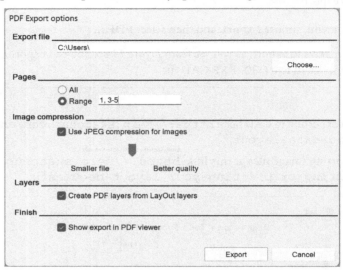

Figure 13.87: The PDF Export options dialog box

4.   Click **Export** to start the export or **Cancel** to go back.

The larger your LayOut document, with viewports, images, and other elements, the longer the export process will take to finish. You can take a break from your computer, confident that LayOut is diligently working to generate a high-quality file.

Presenting inside LayOut

To utilize the presentation tools in LayOut, go to **View | Start Presentation**, or simply click the **Start Presentation** icon on the toolbar to enter full-screen mode. In this mode, you'll have access to several handy features for your presentation. These features enhance the dynamic and interactive capabilities of your LayOut presentations, making them more engaging and informative.

- **Page navigation**: Easily move through your presentation pages using the arrow keys or your mouse:

  - *Right arrow* = go to the next page (regular mouse click)

  - *Left arrow* = go back (right-click)

- *Up arrow* = go to the first page

- *Down arrow* = go to the last page

- **Annotation tools**: The **Freehand** tool becomes active in **Presentation** mode, allowing you to draw directly on your pages and highlight important aspects of your project. The **Freehand** tool used in LayOut is identical to the one in SketchUp, so there's no need to familiarize yourself with a new tool.

  Once your presentation concludes, you can save any annotations you made during the presentation.

- **Animation playback**: If your SketchUp model includes animation, it can be played during your LayOut presentation. To do this, double-click the SketchUp model, right-click, and choose **View Animation** from the menu.

To exit **Presentation** mode at any time, tap the *Esc* key.

Only three presentation preferences are found in the **Edit** menu | **Preferences** (Windows) or the **LayOut** menu | **Preferences** (macOS). These preferences specifically pertain to the number of monitors in use.

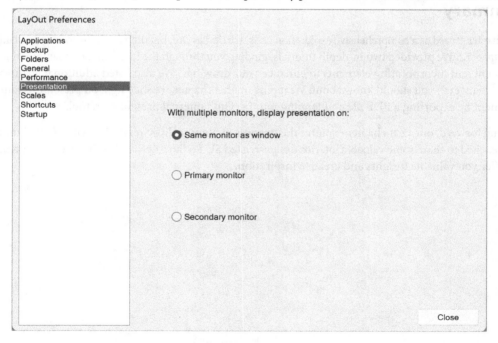

Figure 13.88: Presentation preferences

Before presenting, make sure to choose one of the three options. A description of their settings are as follows:

- **Same monitor as window**: This default setting ensures that your presentation will be shown on the monitor displaying most of the LayOut document window.

- **Primary monitor**: If you've got more than one monitor hooked up, this option tells LayOut to show your presentation on the main one. Not sure which is your primary monitor? Just check your system's display settings to see which one it is.

- **Secondary monitor**: If you pick this option, LayOut will display your presentation on your extra monitor. On Windows, it usually identifies as monitor 2 in your display settings. For macOS, it's the monitor without the menu bar across the top.

And that wraps it up! We've journeyed through SketchUp LayOut from start to finish, though it's interesting to think that we've only touched on the basics. We sincerely hope this experience has been as enjoyable and informative for you as it has been for us.

Summary

This chapter served as a comprehensive exploration of SketchUp LayOut, building upon the foundation laid in *Chapter 12*. We provided two in-depth tutorials, guiding you through the insertion and manipulation of content and incorporating elements to enhance your drawings. We also listed additional features (game-changers!) you should know about. Wrapping up this chapter, we shed light on presenting your document by exporting a PDF file and tapping into LayOut's internal presentation tool.

Looking forward, our next chapter explores the nuances of photorealistic rendering with SU Podium. We're excited to share some valuable interior design-related SU Podium tips, and we believe the content will offer you valuable insights and creative inspiration.

14
Photorealistic Rendering with SU Podium

This chapter teaches you how to create renderings by adding photorealistic qualities to your SketchUp models. There are entire books dedicated to photorealistic rendering, so this chapter is not meant to cover everything. It is designed to get you started and be a guide for those who are either rendering for the first time or want to learn more.

There are many rendering plugins available for use with SketchUp. We focus on **SU Podium** in this chapter. In the final section of the chapter, we will share information about other rendering plugins should you want to explore further. Once you know how to use one photorealistic rendering software, learning how to use others is much easier.

You will learn step-by-step instructions for how to prepare a SketchUp model for photorealistic rendering, such as setting up the lighting, adding material properties, and fine-tuning render options. This preparation can be used for other rendering plugins as well.

In this chapter, we will cover the following topics:

- Introduction to photorealistic rendering
- SU Podium plugin
- Preparing a SketchUp model to be rendered
- Final renderings
- Tips, tricks, and troubleshooting
- PodiumxRT and other photorealistic rendering plugins

Technical requirements

This chapter requires the following software and files:

- SketchUp Pro or Studio

- SU Podium (we are using the current version, **SU Podium V2.6 Plus**)

- Download the practice file from 3D Warehouse named Chapter 14- Rendering or download it from https://3dwarehouse.sketchup.com/model/21ccb8da-151f-45b0-81f5-795625977253/Chapter-14-Rendering

Introduction to photorealistic rendering

What is **photorealistic rendering**? It is the process of creating lifelike 2D images from three-dimensional models using a **render engine**. A high-quality photorealistic rendering can be mistaken for good photography even by experienced experts. Let's take a look at some examples of photorealistic renderings.

Here's an exported image of a SketchUp model:

Figure 14.1: SketchUp model by Nat Ellis, Head of 3D Visualization
at jbA Architecture. Website: www.jbarch.co.uk

And here's the same model rendered using the SU Podium plugin:

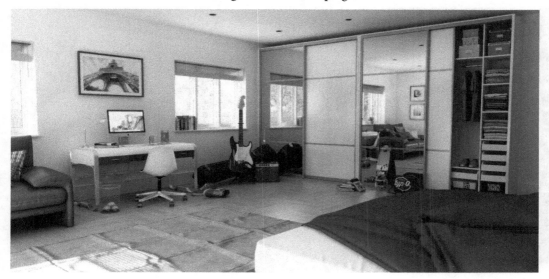

Figure 14.2: SketchUp model rendered in SU Podium by Nat Ellis, Head of 3D
Visualization at jbA Architecture. Website: www.jbarch.co.uk

Here's an example of an exterior SketchUp model:

Figure 14.3: Exterior SketchUp model by Nat Ellis, Head of 3D Visualization
at jbA Architecture. Website: www.jbarch.co.uk

And here's the same exterior model rendered using the SU Podium plugin:

Figure 14.4: Exterior SketchUp model rendered in SU Podium by Nat Ellis, Head
of 3D Visualization at jbA Architecture. Website: www.jbarch.co.uk

The level of realism for any given rendering will vary and is influenced by multiple factors, such as the amount of detail in the model, materials and textures, modeling accuracy, render resolution, render engine, post-processing, and more. Each rendering artist has their own workflow, which usually includes a compromise between render speed and render quality.

In addition, achieving realistic results requires attention to detail, time, and patience. Experimenting with settings, adjusting, and refining the scene all contribute to better final images as well. Let's see some more examples.

Here's an interior SketchUp model built by *Carré Design Studio*:

Figure 14.5: SketchUp model by Carré Design Studio (design by Kelly Hohla Interiors). Courtesy `https://carredesigns.com/`

And here's the same model rendered using SU Podium:

Figure 14.6: SU Podium render by Carré Design Studio (design by Kelly Hohla Interiors). Courtesy https://carredesigns.com/

You can even render floor plans, as shown in *Figure 14.7*.

Figure 14.7: Floor plan rendering by Carré Design Studio using SU Podium
(design by Kelly Hohla Interiors). Courtesy https://carredesigns.com/

Here's an example of a rendering achieved using Enscape:

Figure 14.8: Design, SketchUp model, and Enscape rendering by Madeleine Draper, Interior Designer

This final example features an interior pool design to showcase what water can look like when rendered. Here is the SketchUp model:

Figure 14.9: SketchUp model by Nat Ellis, Head of 3D Visualization
at jbA Architecture. Website: www.jbarch.co.uk

And here's the same model rendered using SU Podium:

Figure 14.10: SketchUp model rendered in SU Podium by Nat Ellis, Head of
3D Visualization at jbA Architecture. Website: www.jbarch.co.uk

Photorealistic rendering is an art form, and there is a learning curve, so don't expect expert results immediately. As with anything, the more time and energy you put into learning how to generate realistic images, the better your results.

The rendering process

You are not alone if you feel intimidated by the idea of learning how to transform your SketchUp scenes into realistic images, but the good news is, you have already done most of the work! The bulk of the work needed to successfully produce a rendering is done in Sketchup; this includes building the model, adding details and materials, and setting up initial scenes. At its simplest, you can render just about any SketchUp model with just a few clicks. Now, it may not convince anyone besides your grandma that it is a real photo, but it's a starting point!

The rendering process can be broken up into three phases:

1. Building the SketchUp model.

2. Preparing the SketchUp model to be rendered using a rendering plugin and pressing the *render* button.

3. Enhancing the generated image using external software, such as Photoshop.

There are several rendering plugins available for SketchUp. We use **SU Podium** for this chapter.

SU Podium plugin

SU Podium is a rendering plugin developed by **Cadalog, Inc.** designed for SketchUp, and SU Podium V2.6 Plus is the current version while writing this book. A few of the biggest draws to SU Podium versus other rendering plugins are as follows:

- It costs much less than other options.

- It has been available since 2006, making it one of the most established rendering plugins for SketchUp.

- It produces some of the most beautiful interior renderings.

> **Terminology used in this chapter**
> In this chapter, Podium and SU Podium refer to **SU Podium V2.6 Plus**.

With Podium, you can add realistic lighting, reflections, and materials to SketchUp models and generate lifelike images. Here is a link to SU Podium's website: `https://suplugins.com/`.

Figure 14.11: The SU Podium website

Understanding the modeling and rendering process is more important than which rendering plugin you choose to use. Many have similar tools and processes, so once you learn how to navigate one rendering plugin, learning another is much easier. We will share other popular plugin options at the end of the chapter, in the *PodiumxRT and other photorealistic rendering plugins* section.

You will need to download SU Podium to follow along with the practice exercises for the remainder of the chapter. Remember to check hardware requirements and recommendations before downloading new software onto your computer.

Downloading SU Podium

First-time users can download a free, 30-day trial of SU Podium here: `https://suplugins.com/free-evaluation.php`. There are no minimum hardware requirements. The main thing to be aware of is which version of SketchUp you are using:

- If you are using SketchUp 2018, 2019, 2020, 2021, 2022, 2023, 2024 (Windows or macOS) or SketchUp 2017 (Windows only), download **SU Podium V2.6**
- If you are using SketchUp 2014, 2015, or 2016 (Windows or macOS), download **SU Podium V2.5**

Since we are using SketchUp 2024 for this book, we downloaded SU Podium V2.6. If you are using SU Podium V2.5, our instructions and screenshots will still make sense for you to follow along.

Although there are no minimum hardware requirements to install SU Podium, the Podium website recommends 64-bit Mac or Windows operating systems. In addition, here is some guidance for current hardware recommendations:

- Processor: Multi-core processor with 3 GHz or faster
- RAM: 8 GB of free RAM or more (the authors prefer more free RAM for faster rendering)

- Graphics card: A dedicated GPU with 2 GB or more of VRAM for improved rendering performance (an NVIDIA graphics card is best for SketchUp and other types of photorealistic rendering plugins, such as *Enscape*)

- Monitor resolution: A high-resolution monitor is recommended for detailed work

In general, the more processors and RAM you have, the faster your computer can produce a rendering. However, a high-tech computer with lots of processors and RAM is not necessary for the type of renderings we will do in this chapter. Should you decide to make a career out of photorealistic rendering, then you may want to consider investing in a different computer.

Keep in mind that software versions and updates can occur over time. For the most accurate and up-to-date information regarding hardware requirements and recommendations, please check the official SU Podium website (`https://www.suplugins.com/`) or contact the software's support team.

After you've downloaded the SU Podium extension, installing it follows the same process as any other extension through the **Extension Manager**. Subsequently, you will need to activate the license by navigating to **Extensions | SU Podium V2.6 Plus | License**.

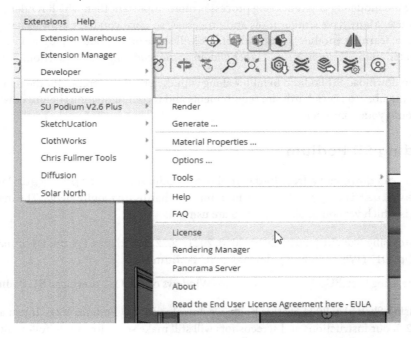

Figure 14.12: Activate your Podium license through the Extensions menu

Enter the license key or serial number you received when you purchased Podium, and follow any on-screen prompts to complete the activation process. Once the activation is successful, you will see a message on your computer screen confirming that your license has been activated. If you downloaded the 30-day trial version, you do not need to activate the license and can skip this step. Now, you are ready to move on and learn about the software's toolbar and options menu.

Podium toolbar

After Podium is downloaded and installed, SketchUp will display the Podium toolbar.

Figure 14.13: Podium toolbar in SketchUp

Here is a summary of the Podium tools in *Figure 14.13* from left to right:

- **Render Current Scene**: This is essentially the *render* button. Click this to begin rendering the current viewport. Note that Podium will render your current *viewport*, regardless of what scene you have selected.

- **Generate Current Scene**: An alternative way to produce renderings. It is especially useful for remote rendering.

- **Material Properties**: Click this to open the **Material Properties** dialog box. We will use this tool to assign realistic material properties to the SketchUp textures in your scene. (We cover this process in the *Adding realistic material properties to SketchUp textures* section.)

- **Options**: Click this to open the **Options** dialog box. This is an important menu where you can choose most of the render settings. We will walk through it in detail after we review the rest of the tools found in the Podium toolbar.

- **Analyse model**: Use this tool for troubleshooting issues that may occur during the rendering process. (Find information about this tool in the *Tips, tricks, and troubleshooting* section.)

- **Podium Browser**: **Podium Browser** is a large, render-ready content library. Here, you can find render-ready materials, furniture, lighting, and more. It is similar to **3D Warehouse**, except everything you find in **Podium Browser** is preconfigured with SU Podium render properties. We will explore this powerful resource in the *Podium Browser* section.

- **Podium Light System Panel**: Use this panel to create and insert artificial lights, such as *omni* and *spot lights*. (We cover this process in the *Setting up the lighting with shadows and artificial light* section.)

You can also access these tools by selecting **SU Podium V2.6 Plus** from the **Extensions** menu.

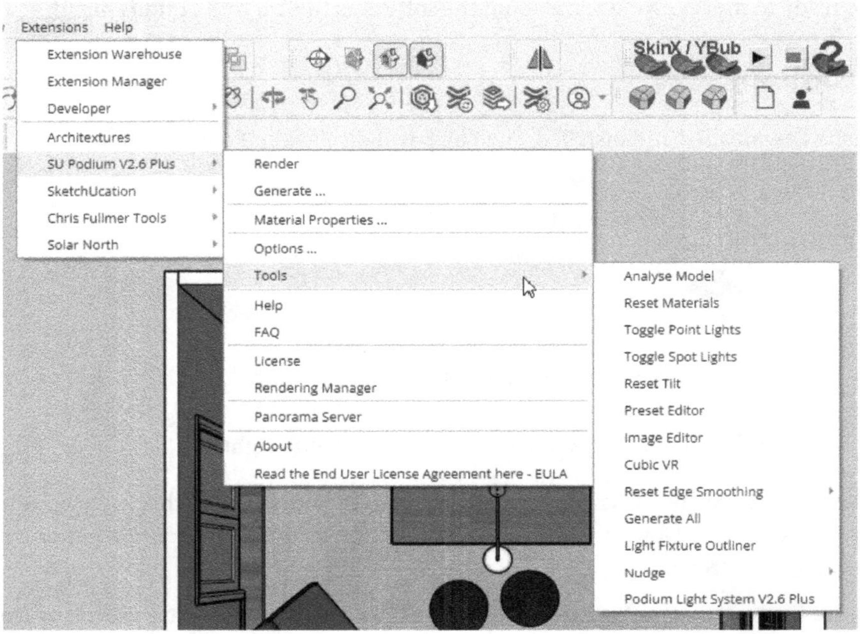

Figure 14.14: Find Podium tools from the Extensions menu

Here, you can also find additional tools not found in the toolbar to help you model faster in SketchUp and set up the camera view. Some of them are **Nudge**, **Generate All**, **Light Fixture Outliner**, **Cubic VR**, and **Reset Tilt**. Another great Podium feature is **EditInPlace**, which allows you to edit small groups/components in large models without interference from a clipping plane. Select a group or component, right-click, and select **Edit In Place...** to use this feature. You can learn about these tools on SU Podium's website: `https://suplugins.com/podium/free-plugins.php`.

We will not address every tool and feature that Podium offers in this chapter. Instead, the goal is to share processes and techniques to help you generate immediate rendering results that are easily replicable.

Now, we will take a closer look at the **Options** menu and render presets.

Options menu and Podium presets

Most of this chapter will focus on preparing a SketchUp model to be rendered, but before we get started, we need to first practice using the **Options** dialog box and Podium presets. A critical part of preparing a SketchUp model for photorealistic rendering is running test renders throughout the process. To run test renders, you must understand how to use and select render options and presets.

> **What is a test render?**
>
> In the context of photorealistic rendering, a test render is a preliminary render or draft that is created to assess the lighting, materials, and overall composition before committing to a full, final rendering. Test renderings help identify any issues or areas for improvement. They are also useful for experimenting with new or different rendering techniques to determine the most effective approach for a project.
>
> We recommend using low-quality rendering settings and presets for test renders as a time-saving strategy. We will cover render presets in the *Render presets* section.

If you have been following along from the beginning of the book, the *Chapter 14* practice model will be familiar to you; it is the same living room from *Chapter 7* and *Chapter 10*. Download the SketchUp file titled `Chapter 14- Rendering` from `3D Warehouse`. As always, familiarize yourself with the model.

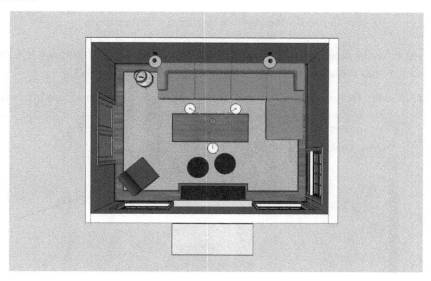

Figure 14.15: Chapter 14 practice model

You may notice some subtle differences between this practice model and the *Chapter 10* practice model, even though they are the same space. For this chapter, we added more detail to the windows, lampshades, and rug. For example, the rug now has rounded edges and a border painted with brown carpet material. We also staggered the ottomans in front of the fireplace. In the real world, nothing is perfect. Adding purposeful imperfections, such as staggering the ottomans, and extra detail, such as rounding the rug's edges, will make our renderings more realistic.

Let's begin by looking at the Podium **Options** menu.

Options menu

Click the *gear* icon in the Podium toolbar to open the **Options** menu.

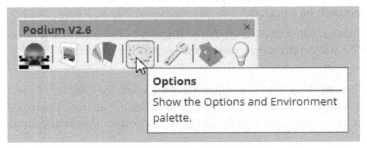

Figure 14.16: Click the gear icon to open the Options menu

At the top of the **Options** menu, you can select a render preset from the drop-down list. (We will experiment with Podium presets after we finish discussing the **Options** menu.)

In the **Output** tab of the **Options** menu, you can set the image size, format, and save location.

Figure 14.17: Output tab

> **Pro Tip: Render with transparency**
>
> With the **.png** format selected, you can check the **Transparent** box to create rendered images that have transparent backgrounds. This makes adding your own background image in an external photo editor very easy.
>
> Visit `https://suplugins.com/podium/help/transparency.php` to learn more about rendering with a transparent background.

The **Environment** tab within the **Options** menu is where you can control and customize settings related to the background, sky, and other miscellaneous elements that impact the overall lighting and atmosphere of rendered images. In the next section, *Render presets*, we will play around with some of these settings in an exercise.

Figure 14.18: Environment tab

Keep **Rendering Mode** set to **Fast**. **Slow** mode is the older processing scenes employed before SU Podium V2.5 and V2.6. On rare occasions when you are trying to resolve rendering issues, you may consider using **Slow** mode. However, it is worth noting that the authors have never needed to use this mode. Visit `https://suplugins.com/podium/tutorials/slow-mode.php` to learn more about **Rendering Mode** options.

Checking **Clay** is a fun way to view your model without any textures. You do not need to remove textures when you check **Clay**; SU Podium will automatically remove the textures and instead render the model with the front-face SketchUp Default color.

We recommend checking the **Information Bar** checkbox for all test renders. It provides valuable details about the rendered image, such as preset used, render time, and image resolution.

Checking **Automatic Materials** is helpful because it assigns certain SketchUp standard materials pre-defined SU Podium photorealistic properties, such as reflection, refraction, blur, and bumps. This lessens the amount of work you have to do to add realism to those materials. (You can also edit the settings on them. We will cover how to edit Podium material properties in the upcoming section, *Adding realistic material properties to SketchUp textures.*)

HDRI/IBL tab in the Options menu

High Dynamic Range Imaging (HDRI) and **Image-Based Lighting** (IBL) are useful techniques for more realistic and dynamic lighting, especially in exterior scenes where the lighting conditions vary. We will not use the **HDRI/IBL** tab in this chapter; visit `https://www.suplugins.com/v26/hdri-interface.php` for a video introduction.

OK, are you ready to check out the render presets? This means we get to produce our first rendering together!

Render presets

Understanding how to select render presets plays a significant role in succeeding with Podium. **Presets** are preconfigured settings for lighting, materials, shadows, and other rendering parameters designed to simplify the rendering process. This allows users to achieve a desired outcome without having to manually adjust individual settings.

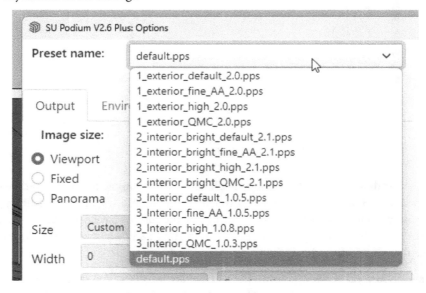

Figure 14.19: Podium render presets

There are a total of 13 presets. They range in quality, with the highest quality requiring the most time to render and the lowest quality rendering the fastest (see *Figure 14.20*).

Preset Type	Render Speed	Render Quality
Preview (only in v2.5)	Fastest	Lowest
Default	Fast	Moderate
Fine AA	Slow	Best edge anti-aliasing
High	Slow	Best
QMC	Slowest	Good to best

Figure 14.20: Preset comparison

The four *default* presets should be used for test renders since they render fast and produce moderate results. We recommend a higher preset for final renders when quality is more important. In this chapter, we will primarily use the default presets.

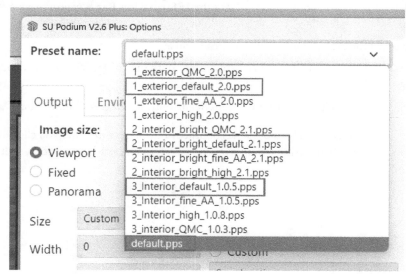

Figure 14.21: The four default render presets

For our first rendering, we will generate an image of the Chapter 14- Rendering practice model using the **default.pps** preset:

1. Click on the scene tab named Presets.
2. Click the **Options** icon in the Podium toolbar.
3. Select the **default.pps** preset from the **Preset name** drop-down menu.

4. Select **Viewport** under **Image size**.

5. Select **.png** under **Image format**.

6. We are going to run multiple test renderings. Create a folder on your computer named `Podium preset comparison` to save the test renderings.

Figure 14.22: Create a folder on your computer and name it Podium preset comparison

7. Under **Image save location**, click **Custom** and select the `Podium preset comparison` folder you created by using the **Browse** button.

8. Next, click on the **Environment** tab. Check the **Information Bar** box and leave everything else as-is.

9. Click **Save** and the dialog box will automatically close.

10. Save your SketchUp model. This is an essential step. With the 30-day trial version, Podium will not render anything until you've saved your model.

11. Ready, set, *render!* Click the **Render Current Scene** button in the Podium toolbar.

Two popups will appear consecutively, and a series of processes will initialize after you click the *render* icon. The first popup is the **Processing Scene** window, which often only appears for a split second; blink, and you might miss it!

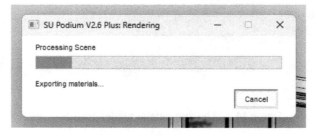

Figure 14.23: Processing scene popup

Podium License Error

If your Podium license hasn't been activated yet, you'll see a **Podium License Error** window appear on your screen. You can activate your license via the **Extensions** menu in SketchUp. For more details on how to activate your license, refer to the *Downloading SU Podium* section. Start again with *step 1* after you successfully activate your license.

If you are using the 30-day trial version, you can ignore this error and simply click OK to continue rendering.

Next, Podium opens up a connection with OOPR (the **Podium Rendering Manager** window). This is where you can watch in real time as Podium works through the various rendering processes. Do not click around in SketchUp while you wait for Podium to generate the rendered image because it slows down the process and may cause SU Podium to stall.

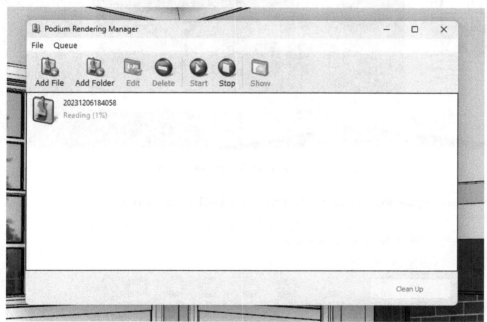

Figure 14.24: The OOPR/Podium Rendering Manager popup

If the `Podium Rendering Manager` **dialog box does not open…**

If you click the render button and only encounter the **Processing Scene** window without seeing the OOPR/**Podium Rendering Manager** dialog box, it is possible that an antivirus or firewall is blocking this process. Don't worry, the render is still taking place in the background. You can find information on unblocking your firewall and resolving other potential processing issues in this link: `https://suplugins.com/podium/help/processing-issues.php`.

Although you are unable to see the full-quality render results until Podium is done processing the image, you can view a preview image of the render progress. Click on the **Show** button in the **Podium Rendering Manager** for a preview image; the preview image will be smaller than the final rendered image.

Figure 14.25: Click Show for a preview image

Your render is complete when you see **Total time** in the **Podium Rendering Manager**.

Figure 14.26: Seeing the total render time means your rendering is done

Navigate to the `Podium preset comparison` folder you created on your computer to view the rendered image. Seeing your SketchUp model as a photorealistic rendering for the first time is pretty awesome, even when the results need a lot of work!

Figure 14.27: default.pps rendering

Our rendering is reading very dark and blue. First, let's cover why it is reading blue. In the **Environment** tab in the **Options** menu, we set the render **Background** as **Default (set in SketchUp)**. This means Podium will use the current SketchUp background color for the background color of the rendered image. Since the background in the `Presets` scene is set with a blue sky, our rendered image has an unrealistic blue glow to it. As a best practice when learning how to render, always set your background as white. We will do that now:

12. In the **Styles** panel, select the style named `Construction Documentation Style-Rendering` in the **In Model** folder.

13. Update the `Presets` scene.

14. Repeat *steps 1-11* to produce another rendering. *Figure 14.28* shows the rendered image with the background as white.

Figure 14.28: default.pps rendering with white background

The coloring appears more natural now, but the overall image is still very dark. For the next rendering, we will change the preset:

15. Click on the `Presets` scene and open the Podium **Options** menu.

16. Select **3_Interior_default_1.0.5.pps** from the preset drop-down list. Keep all other settings as-is. Make sure the `Podium preset comparison` folder is still selected for the **Image Save Location**.

17. Click **Save** in the **Options** dialog box and save your SketchUp model.

18. Click **Render Current Scene**.

Figure 14.29: Interior default preset rendered

Looking better!

19. Let's generate two more images using the last two default presets (**2_interior_bright_ default_2.1.pps** and **1_exterior_default_2.0.pps**); follow *steps 15-18*, but swap out the preset.

Tip for long render times

If you are spending lots of time waiting for the computer to complete a rendering, use the **Fixed** radio button under **Image Size** when choosing your render settings in the **Options** dialog box. Select **Custom** from the **Size** picklist and type a low-resolution pixel **Width** and **Height**, something like 900 x 450 or even less. The rendering quality will be lower, but the rendering time will be faster.

Figure 14.30 shows the interior bright default preset rendered:

Figure 14.30: Interior bright default preset rendered

And *Figure 14.31* shows the exterior default preset rendered:

Figure 14.31: Exterior default preset rendered

Examine each of the renderings we just produced on their own and side-by-side. Which rendering is your favorite? Why is it your favorite? Which preset was used to produce your favorite rendering? Which preset took the longest to render? Make note of these things. (The **Information Bar** can help remind you of the settings, if you forget.)

With this next batch of renderings, we will turn on shadows and try a different render background:

20. Click on the scene tab named Presets.

21. Open the SketchUp **Shadows** panel. Set the **Time** to `12:15` pm and **Date** to `11/08`. Click the **Show/Hide Shadows** button to turn shadows on.

22. Update the `Presets` scene.

23. Open the Podium **Options** menu and select the **default.pps** preset.

24. In the **Environment** tab, change the **Background** to **Podium Physical Sky 1** and click **Save**.

Physical Sky feature

When you set the render **Background** to **Podium Physical Sky 1** or **Podium Physical Sky 2**, Podium will ignore the SketchUp background colors and instead use the time of day and year to simulate sunlight and skylight based on real-world physics. SketchUp shadows must be turned on to use the Physical Sky feature.

Visit `https://www.suplugins.com/help2/environment.php#physical` to learn more about the Physical Sky feature and to compare rendered images using **Physical Sky 1** versus **Physical Sky 2**.

---

25. Click the *render* icon.

Figure 14.32: default.pps preset with shadows on and Physical Sky 1

Figure 14.32 shows the rendered image. The splash of sun makes a dramatic impact. Turning on shadows not only brightens the rendering but also makes it appear more real.

26. Generate three more rendered images with shadows on using the other three default presets (**3_Interior_default_1.0.5.pps**, **2_interior_bright_default_2.1.pps**, and **1_exterior_default_2.0.pps**). Use **Podium Physical Sky 1** for the render background.

When you are done, study all nine renderings, making note of which are your favorites and the settings associated with them. If you feel inspired, continue experimenting with the different preset and environment settings.

Here are some ideas for further testing:

- With shadows on, render each default preset using **Podium Physical Sky 2** for the **Background**. Do you like the results from **Physical Sky 1** or **Physical Sky 2** better?

- Edit the **Time** and/or **Date** in SketchUp's **Shadows** panel to see how it affects the rendering. Remember to update the scene and save your model before rendering.

- Change the **Intensity** and **Exposure** sliders in the **Environment** tab. By default, they are both set to 50. The **Intensity** slider adjusts the brightness of the sun, and the **Exposure** slider adjusts the brightness of indirect light and the surrounding environment. SketchUp shadows must be turned on. You can compare how the two sliders impact rendered images on the SU Podium website: `https://suplugins.com/podium/help/int-exp.php`.

Another helpful resource on the SU Podium website is the preset comparison page, where you can compare two presets side by side: `https://www.suplugins.com/podium/preset-comparison.php`.

You should now have a good understanding of how to navigate the render options and presets. In the next section, we will cover multiple practice exercises with test renderings to showcase the entire process of preparing a SketchUp model for final renders.

Preparing a SketchUp model to be rendered

The goal of this section is to provide you with step-by-step instructions on how to set up a SketchUp model for rendering. We will generate multiple test renders, demonstrating what a typical workflow looks like during the rendering process.

Interior versus exterior renderings

The *Chapter 14* practice model features an interior space. While the methods and tools used for interior renderings are transferrable to exterior models, exterior rendering comes with its own challenges, such as landscaping, large-scale environments, and weather conditions.

We recommend checking out these tips when you are ready to tackle exterior scenes: `https://suplugins.com/podium/tutorials/advanced-exterior-tips.php`.

There are three main areas to prepare a SketchUp model to be rendered:

- Composing a SketchUp scene

- Adding realistic material properties to SketchUp textures

- Setting up the lighting with shadows and artificial light

Just like most things SketchUp related, there are multiple methods and ways to accomplish some of the processes outlined in this chapter. We are sharing one way in hopes that after you spend some time using the software, you will find your own artistic roadmap to photorealistic rendering.

We will begin with scene composition.

Composing a SketchUp scene

In the Chapter 14- Rendering practice model, click on the scene tab named Render. We will use the Render scene for the exercises in this section. It is the same perspective as *Chapter 10*, when we explored SketchUp's **Styles** panel, as shown in *Figure 14.33*.

Figure 14.33: Chapter 10 scene using a sketchy style

Here are some things worth noting about the Render scene:

- The SketchUp **Background** is set to white. As a reminder, setting the background as white helps to avoid unwanted colors in the rendering.

- The accessories were strategically placed throughout the space to look aesthetically pleasing from this specific vantage point. How you decide to compose the placement of accessories and components helps determine the focus in a rendering, just like it does in real-life photography.

- Speaking of photography, when you are finalizing the perspective of a scene, position the SketchUp camera from the same angle you would position a camera if you were actually standing in the room. For example, *Figure 14.34* shows an unrealistic camera angle.

Figure 14.34: Unrealistic camera angle

The only way to capture a viewpoint like the one shown in *Figure 14.34* is to stand on a chair. Beautiful renderings can be ruined by unrealistic perspectives; likewise, mediocre renderings are taken to the next level by proper camera angles. In summation, if you understand photo composition, use it to your advantage.

- The intentional imperfections in this scene will make the final rendering appear more realistic:

  - The roman shades are each scaled to different lengths; they are not uniform.

  - The ottomans in front of the fireplace are slightly staggered instead of in a straight line.

  - The book on the coffee table is left open, rather than neatly closed.

- Lastly, setting up the exterior window views is part of composing a scene for rendering. Turn on the tag named EXT-RENDER (inside the PODIUM tag folder) to view a 180-degree background component we downloaded from **Podium Browser**. We also downloaded a climbing rose component and placed it outside the window on the right to add extra interest. We will run a test render with this tag turned on when we set up the lighting in an upcoming exercise.

Use the preceding notes for the future when you are composing a scene to be rendered.

Next, we will add realistic properties to the SketchUp textures using Podium's **Material Properties** tool and, in the process, run the first test renders.

Adding realistic material properties to SketchUp textures

Adding Podium properties to SketchUp materials elevates the realism of the rendering and enables more accurate visualization of how objects interact with light, shadows, and their surroundings. Before we apply any realistic property materials, we are going to run a test render to view our starting point.

Running a test render before adding material properties

Follow these steps to run a test render:

1. Click on the Render scene.
2. Open the Podium **Options** menu and match the **Output** tab and **Environment** tab settings from *Figure 14.35*. (You decide where to save the image on your computer.)

3. Click **Save**.

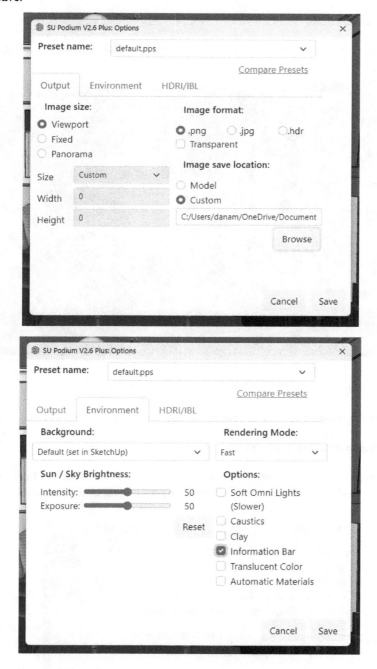

Figure 14.35: Use these render settings for the Output tab (top) and Environment tab (bottom)

4. Save your SketchUp model.

5. Render the scene.

Go to where you saved the rendered image on your computer to view it. *Figure 14.36* shows what it looks like, which is flat and dull.

Figure 14.36: First test render complete

Now, let's look at an overview of the material properties that are available and how to use the dialog box.

Overview of the material properties

Adding material properties will help create a richer, deeper image. We will use the **Material Properties** dialog box to accomplish this. Click on the **Material Properties** icon in the Podium toolbar to open the dialog box.

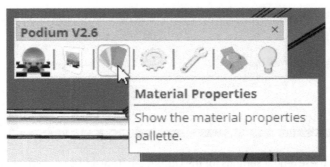

Figure 14.37: Material Properties icon in the Podium toolbar

Select a SketchUp material by using the eyedropper tool directly from the dialog box (see *Figure 14.38*). Alternatively, you can select a material by selecting the face the material is on or sampling the material with the eyedropper tool from SketchUp's **Materials** tray.

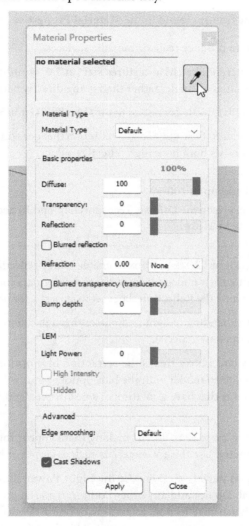

Figure 14.38: Use the eyedropper in the Material Properties dialog box to select a SketchUp material

The material name will appear at the top of the **Material Properties** dialog box. Sometimes you need to select the SketchUp material more than once before it appears.

Once you have a SketchUp material selected, you can start applying and editing reflections, bump maps, and other realistic properties to it by using the sliders and checkboxes. The three main sliders at the top under the **Basic Properties** area are **Diffuse**, **Transparency**, and **Reflection**. These sliders are connected to each other, and the combined value should equal 100% for best results. When you decrease one of the sliders, make sure to manually update the other two sliders so that they total 100% (sometimes they update automatically). Instead of using the sliders, you can type a number into the box.

Here is a quick overview of the features found in the **Material Properties** dialog box:

- **Material type**: Use this to produce realistic metallic surfaces.
- **Diffuse**: All non-transparent SketchUp textures start at 100% diffuse by default. Diffuse is reflective light that reflects at an angle, rather than going directly back to the camera.
- **Transparency**: This slider is directly connected to the **Opacity** slider in SketchUp's **Materials** tray.
- **Reflection**: Move this slider to the right to add a reflection that goes directly back to the camera. Mirror and chrome materials both have high reflective values.

> **Reminder: Sliders should add up to 100%**
>
> This is a reminder to keep an eye on the **Diffuse**, **Transparency**, and **Reflection** sliders regularly to ensure they always equate to 100%.

- **Blurred reflection** checkbox: Check this box to enable blurry reflections instead of sharp and clear reflections. It is particularly noticeable for surfaces such as glass and water, and some metals, such as brass. (You must have the **Reflection** slider set to at least 1 for blurry reflections to work.)
- **Refraction**: Refers to the bending of light as it passes through different mediums, such as air, water, glass, or any transparent material.
- **Blurred transparency** checkbox: This is the refraction blur option that adds noise to the material. It will take longer to render with the blur option, but it will look very realistic. This is a useful setting for items that have a mixture of smooth yet slightly rough texture, such as sheer linen drapery.
- **Bump depth**: Add bump maps to materials making them appear rough and bumpy without adding additional geometry. Use this for materials such as carpet or brick.
- **LEM (Light Emitting Material)** section: Use the **Light Power** slider to add light-emitting properties to a material. Do not add any other Podium material properties listed under the **Basic properties** area (such as reflection, refraction, or bump depth) to LEMs. This can cause SketchUp and Podium to crash or produce unwanted black surfaces in a rendered image.
- **Edge smoothing**: Here, you can edit the default anti-aliasing value of individual materials. Anti-aliasing is part of the rendering process used to reduce the jagged edges and lines in a rendering, helping to refine the image.

> **Important note**
>
> It is worth noting here that when a view is photorealistically rendered, no matter which rendering engine you choose, edges (or lines) are removed. Because of this, we sometimes must be dramatic with the depth of objects, such as cabinetry door fronts, to distinguish one depth from another.

- **Cast Shadows** checkbox: Use this toggle if you do not want a specific material to cast shadows in the rendering.

- **Apply** button: Click **Apply** to save the material properties.

> **More information**
>
> For a more detailed explanation of each of these features, visit https://suplugins.com/podium/help/material-properties.php.

Adding material properties to the practice model

Let's apply Podium property materials to the `Chapter 14- Rendering` SketchUp model. We will begin by focusing on the furnishings and ignoring the accessories:

1. Click on the `Render` scene and turn off the visibility for the tag named `Accessories`.

2. Click the **Material Properties** icon in the Podium toolbar.

3. We will start with the wall sconce materials. Select the brass material on the sconce, named `brass 01`:

    I.   Change the **Material Type** to **Metallic**.

    II.   Type 50 in the **Reflection** box..

III.   Click the **Blurred reflection** checkbox.

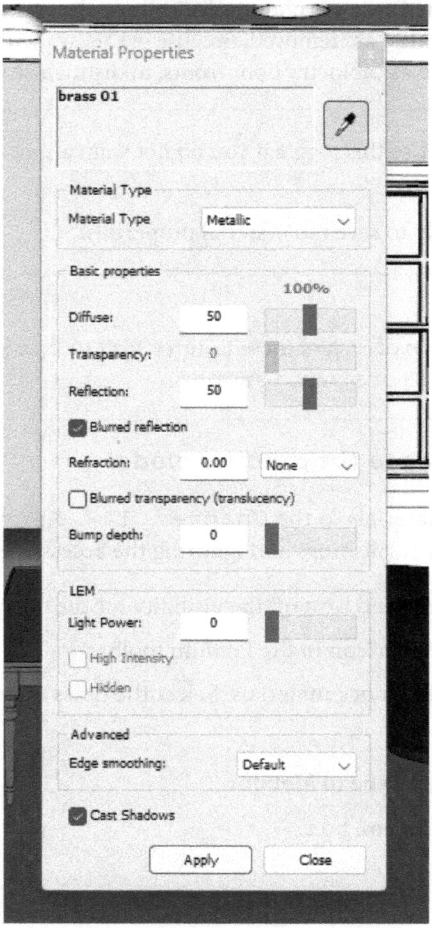

Figure 14.39: brass 01 Podium material properties

IV.   Click **Apply** at the bottom of the **Material Properties** dialog box.

This is an important step. If you do not click **Apply**, no properties will be applied.

> **Podium properties are assigned to every instance of a material.**
>
> Any instance in which brass 01 is used in the entire model will automatically have these same Podium properties. For example, brass 01 is also used on the side table legs and on the ceiling light fixture. You will not need to add Podium properties to them individually.

4. Next, select the `bronze 01` material on the sconce:

    I.   Change the **Material Type** to **Metallic**.

    II.   Type `40` in the **Reflection** box.

    III.   Check **Blurred reflection**.

    IV.   Click **Apply**.

5. Now, select the `lamp shade 01` material:

    I.   We are going to add a bump map so that the lampshade appears bumpy. To do this, type `10` in the **Bump depth** box.

    II.   Click **Apply**.

6. Continue around the room, adding Podium material properties to the materials shown in *Figure 14.40*.

Not every material needs Podium properties, and sometimes adding unnecessary Podium properties has unhelpful results that appear grainy or unrealistic in rendered images. With that said, we won't add Podium properties to every material **In Model**.

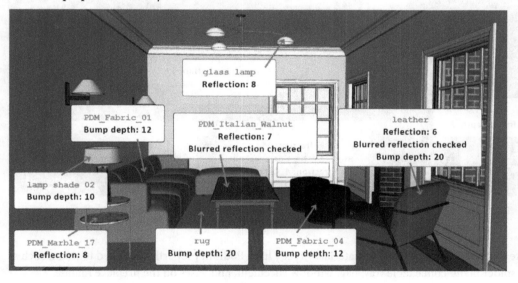

Figure 14.40: Material properties to use for the Render scene

> **PDM materials**
>
> You may notice that certain materials in the **In Model** folder contain PDM in their names. This indicates that the material originated from Podium, potentially from **Podium Browser**.
>
> Materials from **Podium Browser** usually come with pre-assigned properties, but we have removed them for this exercise to allow you to practice adding material properties.

Note that we already assigned Podium properties to some of the architectural materials, such as the windows, fireplace materials, and wood floor, in order to save time and streamline the process.

Next, let's focus on the accessories. Follow these steps to add material properties to accessories:

7. Click the `Render` scene and turn off the visibility for the tag named `Furnishings`.

8. Assign Podium properties to the accessory materials shown in *Figure 14.41*.

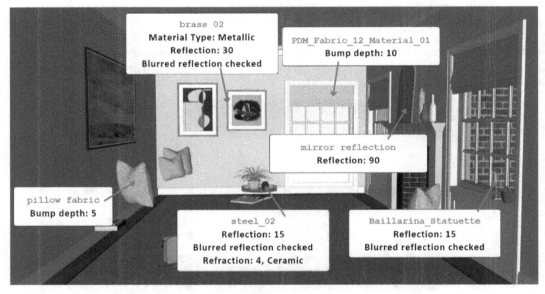

Figure 14.41: Accessory material properties for Podium

Note that some of the accessory materials already have Podium properties assigned to them, such as the spider plant, coffee table tray, bag, window succulent, and vases on the fireplace mantle.

Now that we added Podium material properties, we can run another test rendering of the `Render` scene.

Running a test render after adding material properties

Let's run a test render to view the impact of adding Podium material properties.

1. Close the **Material Properties** dialog box by either clicking the **Close** button or the **X** in the upper-right corner.

2. Repeat *steps 1 to 5* in the *Running a test render before adding material properties* section to run another test render. *Figure 14.42* shows the rendered image.

Figure 14.42: Rendering with material properties added

The reflective surfaces look nice (such as the mirror, vases, and metal details throughout), but there are some unwanted splotches and grainy spots on the leather chair and window frames. These issues are usually resolved during the final rendering phase when we use a higher-quality preset. Since our test renderings are done with the *default* presets, we will ignore these imperfections for now.

If there are any materials that are producing undesirable results, this is the time to reopen the **Material Properties** dialog box and adjust the settings. For example, if you want the brass 01 material to appear more reflective, you could increase the **Reflection** slider and click **Apply**. While learning how to render, we advise running additional test renders after updating material settings. This allows you to observe the effects of changes to the end result.

> **Every monitor will display renders differently.**
>
> Do not worry if your rendering color looks slightly different than ours. Rendering colors can appear differently on monitors due to variations in monitor calibration, color profiles, graphics cards, age of the computer, and other display settings.

See *Figure 14.43* for a recommended starting point for Podium material property settings.

ACRYLIC/PLASTIC/PLEXIGLASS:
Diffuse: 50-95
Reflection: 5-50
Blur: check for more glossy plastic, but also increase (slightly) the reflection

CARPET:
Diffuse: 100
Bump: 0-50

GLASS:
Inside looking out
Diffuse: 10, daytime or night
Reflection: 15-20 daytime; 50 night
 Transparency: 75-80 daytime; 40 night

Outside looking in
Diffuse: 30 daytime; 10 night
Reflection: 35-45 daytime; 25 night
Transparency: 25-35 daytime; 65 night

MIRROR REFLECTION:
Reflection: 75-100%. Render with different settings until you find the most realistic percentage for your material.

MIRROR REFLECTION:
Semi-gloss/Egg Shell/Satin

Diffuse:	Semi-gloss 85-95
	Egg Shell 90-95
	Satin 95
Reflection:	Semi-gloss 5-15
	Egg Shell 5-10
	Satin 5
Bump:	Flat 0
	Textured 5
	Stucco 5-15
Blur: check	

For *Flat Paint*, Diffuse should be 100

STONE (NON-POLISHED) AND BRICK:
Diffuse: 100
Bump: Stone 15-75 *typ.*
        Brick 15-50 *typ.*
Blur: if checked, reflection should be >0

STONE/TILE (POLISHED):
Soft Shine (Subtle)
Diffuse: 80-95
Reflection: 5-20

Bright, Polished, Glossy
Diffuse: 70-85
Reflection: 15-30

WATER:
Diffuse: 80-85
Reflection: 15-20

WOOD (EXTERIOR OR ROUGH):
Diffuse: 100
Bump: 25-75 (higher numbers to add roughness)

WOOD (FLOORING AND CABINETRY):
Diffuse: 85-95
Reflection: 5-10
Blur: check
Bump: 5-25 for interior

Figure 14.43: Podium material property settings

> **Important tip**
>
> The material property settings will vary with each color/texture. It is helpful to keep your own list, such as a spreadsheet, of materials and their Podium settings that work for you and your computer. It will save you a lot of trial-and-error time on your next project!

With Podium properties added to materials, the SketchUp model is ready for lighting.

Setting up the lighting with shadows and artificial light

Just like in design, light plays a powerful role in the overall mood and focus of a rendering. The intensity, color, placement, and direction of light can influence the atmosphere and emotional response when looking at a rendering. This is when your unique creative touch really shines.

It is important to understand and acknowledge the purpose of your rendering. Is it to sell your design to a client? Is it for marketing purposes? What do you want the focus of your rendering to be? Depending on your response, the approach you take to illuminating a rendering will likely differ.

For example, if the purpose is to sell your design to a client, adding dramatic direct sunlight with bold shadows might take away from the design itself. Instead, consider adding more harmonious lighting with softer sunlight and shadows. Whereas if the purpose of your rendering is to create a *wow* effect on social media, dramatic sunlight with bold shadows could be the way to go.

For our rendering purposes in this chapter, we want to share an approach that highlights the positive impact direct sunlight can bring combined with the benefits of achieving balanced artificial light. First, we will cover how to use the **Shadows** panel to set up SketchUp's simulated sun for rendering.

Setting natural lighting with shadows

Most rendering plugins, including Podium, reference SketchUp's **Shadows** panel to generate daylight in a rendered image. We are going to turn on shadows in the *Chapter 14* practice model so that the sun casts light through the windows, and then run a test render:

1. Click on the scene named `Render`.

2. Turn on the tag named `EXT-RENDER` (inside the `PODIUM` tag folder). This is a good time to see how the exterior looks when rendered.

3. Turn off the tag named `Accessories`. It is best practice to turn off extra tags during test renders to increase render speed.

4. In the SketchUp **Shadows** panel, set the **Time** to `1:15 pm` and **Date** to `11/20`. Turn on shadows by clicking **Show/Hide Shadows**.

5. Update the `Render` scene.

    Let's do a test render.

6. In the Podium toolbar, open the **Options** dialog box and match the settings shown in *Figure 14.44*. You decide where to save the image on your computer. Click **Save**. (Notice how we selected the interior default preset and changed the **Background** to **Podium Physical Sky 1**.)

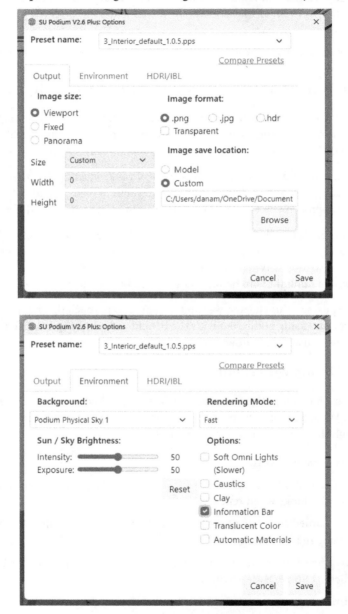

Figure 14.44: Test render settings for the Output tab (top) and Environment tab (bottom)

Reminder for slow rendering

This is a reminder to use a **Custom**, low-resolution pixel **Width** and **Height** for the **Image size** if you are experiencing slow rendering. To do this, choose **Fixed** under **Image size**. This is a good solution, especially for test renders.

7.   Save your SketchUp model and press the **Render Current Scene** button.

Figure 14.45: First test rendering with shadows on

Not only is this way too bright, but it is shows unrealistic shadows. To mimic what shadows would look like if we were physically looking into the room from this angle, we need to add walls, a floor, and a ceiling behind the SketchUp camera to block the sun from pouring in as it is in *Figure 14.45*.

8.   Click on the Render scene. Turn on the visibility for the tag named WALLS BEHIND CAMERA. It is inside the PODIUM tag folder.

9.   Update the Render scene.

Before continuing, take a moment to check out what is on the WALLS BEHIND CAMERA tag. For a better view, use the EDIT scene, turn on the WALLS BEHIND CAMERA tag, and turn off the Wall-West tag.

As shown in *Figure 14.46*, you will see a box that acts as an extension of the room. Its purpose is to block the sun from shining in from anywhere but the windows. There is a hole in one of the walls to allow extra light into the space.

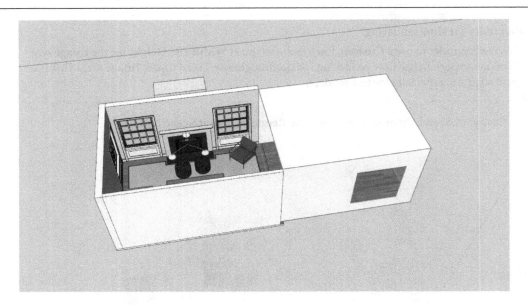

Figure 14.46: Box on WALL BEHIND CAMERA tag

Lastly, the interior of the box is painted using the same floor and paint color as the rest of the room. This is a technique used to ensure the reflective lighting is consistent.

The scene is ready for another test render.

10. Go back to the Render scene.

11. Refer to *steps 6-7* to run another test render.

Figure 14.47: Second test rendering with shadows on

Looks good! The shadows produce a warm glow, and the window views make the rendering feel more realistic.

> **Reminder: Use the Solar North extension**
>
> Achieving the desired light direction is not always possible using just the **Time** and **Date** sliders in the **Shadows** menu. Remember you can alter the direction of North in SketchUp using the **Solar North** extension.
>
> Refer to *Chapter 10*, section *Adding shadows and using sun for shading*, for more details on **Solar North**.

Now, we will add artificial light.

Adding artificial light

There are three main ways to illuminate a SketchUp model with artificial light:

- **LEM** light – LEM (**Light Emitting Material**) light is often used to achieve overall balanced light. LEMs are also used to produce profile and LED strip lighting.
- **Omni** lights – Omni lights emit light evenly in all directions, like a lightbulb.
- **Spot** lights – Spot lights provide directional and focused lighting. Track light fixtures and picture lights usually use spot lights.

It is not necessary to use all three light sources every time you render. Depending on the light fixtures within the space, how many windows there are, and the desired mood, you may only use one or two artificial light sources. Moreover, many rendering artists prefer relying solely on SketchUp's simulated sky and sun for illumination, avoiding artificial light altogether.

With that said, artificial light has some advantages. It can be controlled and directed with more flexibility than natural light. It is very useful for nighttime renderings or areas with no natural light. We want you to see the impact of all three light options, so we will use LEM, omni, and spot lights in the rendering.

LEM lights

The LEM feature allows certain materials to emit light. LEM lights are an easy way to make the overall light harmonious, and they render quickly. In `Chapter 14- Rendering` practice model, we will add a hidden LEM light to brighten the room. In addition, we will use LEM lights on the ceiling fixture to simulate that it is turned on:

1. Click on the scene tab named `EDIT`.
2. Turn off the tag named `Wall-West`.
3. Turn on the tag named `LIGHTS-HIDDEN LEM`.

The LIGHTS-HIDDEN LEM tag contains a large rectangular face that we will use to apply a hidden LEM. The face was purposely built to be about 21" off each wall and placed about 82" above the floor. It extends past the room and into the box behind the camera to ensure an even light spread. You should try not to place any type of SU Podium artificial light source too close to walls and ceilings, to avoid creating a hot spot (a large, unrealistic circle of light).

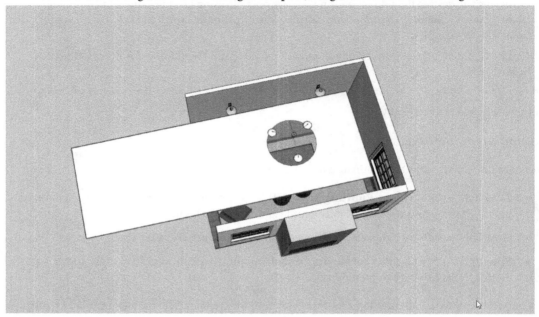

Figure 14.48: Rectangular face on the LIGHT-HIDDEN LEM tag

There is a circular hole cut out of the face directly under the light fixture. This is a method used to avoid unwanted noise produced by the LEM lights. To make a hidden LEM, we need to create a new material.

4. In SketchUp's **Materials** tray, choose a light gray paint color from the **Colors** collection and make it the active swatch. Make a duplicate of the gray color by clicking **Create Material**. Name it LEM-hidden.

    (Refer to the *Fun exercise – Painting Becca and Dana by creating new materials* section of *Chapter 9* to review the process for creating a new material.)

5. Apply the `LEM-hidden` material to the bottom face of the rectangular group, as shown in *Figure 14.49*.

Figure 14.49: Apply LEM-hidden to the bottom face

6. Create another new material, this time with the `LEM-hidden` material as the active swatch. Name it `transparent top`.

7. Apply `transparent top` to the top face of the rectangular group.

8. Create one more new material, again with the `LEM-Hidden` material as the active swatch. Name it `LEM-ceiling lamp`.

9. Apply `LEM-ceiling lamp` to the bottom face of the ceiling glass lamp component, as shown in *Figure 14.50*.

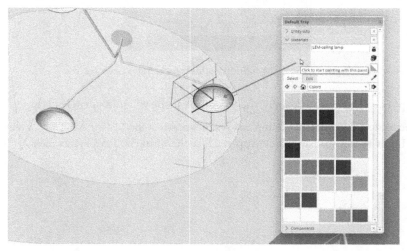

Figure 14.50: Paint LEM-ceiling lamp to bottom face of the ceiling glass lamp component

10. Set the **Opacity** to 0 for the `transparent top` material.

11. Open the **Material Properties** dialog box and select the `LEM-hidden` material.

12. Set the **Light Power** to 4, click the **Hidden** checkbox, and uncheck **Cast Shadows**.

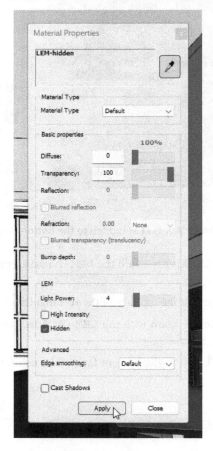

Figure 14.51: LEM-hidden Podium material properties

13. Click **Apply**. When you click apply, the face of the shape will immediately disappear. That's ok!

14. With the **Material Properties** dialog box still open, select the `LEM-ceiling lamp` material. Set the **Light Power** to 2 and click **Apply**. Close the **Material Properties** menu.

> **Reminder: LEM should have no other properties than LEM properties**
>
> Do not add any other Podium material properties to LEMs.
>
> For example, you may have considered adding reflective properties to the `LEM-ceiling lamp` texture to create more realism. However, since the `LEM-ceiling lamp` texture already has LEM properties applied to it, do not add reflection or any other material properties under **Basic properties** to it.

We are ready to run another test render.

15. Click on the `Render` scene.

16. Turn on the `LIGHTS-HIDDEN LEM` tag and update the scene.

17. Open the **Options** dialog box and match the previous test render settings (refer to *Figure 14.44*).

18. Click **Save** and **Render Current Scene**.

   See *Figure 14.52* for the rendering.

Figure 14.52: Test render with Hidden LEM set to Light Power 4

This is too bright and overexposed. Reducing the light power of the hidden LEM should do the trick.

19. Change the **Light Power** to 2 for the `LEM-hidden` material. Remember to click **Apply** afterward.

Before running one more test render, we are going to discuss and incorporate omni and spot lights.

Omni and spot lights

Omni and **spot** lights are the two types of artificial lights that can be created and inserted from the **Podium Light System Panel**. Click on the *lightbulb* icon from the Podium toolbar to open the dialog box.

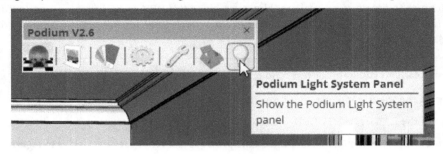

Figure 14.53: Click the lightbulb icon in the Podium toolbar

An omni light produces light rays uniformly in all directions, and a spot light casts a cone-shaped beam in one direction.

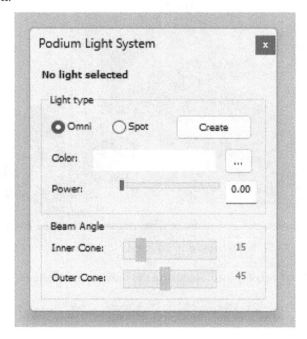

Figure 14.54: Podium Light System Panel

We have already added omni and spot lights to the `Chapter 14- Rendering` model (see the `LIGHTS-OMNI + SPOT` tag within the `PODIUM` tag folder).

For future reference, here is an overview of how to insert omni and spot lights into a design. Let's start with omni lights:

1. Choose **Omni** from the **Podium Light System Panel** and set the **Color** and **Power** level. Adding a color is optional, but setting the power is not. Omni power settings can be a decimal ranging from 0.01 all the way to 100. (The **Beam Angle** section is for **Spot** lights only, so it will be grayed out for **Omni**.)

2. Click **Create**. It requires two clicks to place an omni light:

    I.   The first click is to set an inference point that will help you position the light.

    II.   The second click is to insert the light.

> **Important Note**
>
> An omni comes in as a component. It can be copied and used in other areas. However, changing the power level of one omni does not simultaneously adjust the power level of all the duplicated omnis, as might be expected. To change the power level or color of multiple omnis, each omni component must be individually selected and edited.

Omni lights are small and, because of this, can be difficult to find. We sometimes make them larger using the **Scale** tool so that they are easier to locate. Scaling an omni light does not change the light properties; it only changes the visual representation. It is also important to place omni lights on a coordinating tag as soon as it is placed, to control its visibility. If you happen to lose an omni, use the **Light Fixture Outliner** to find, hide, and unhide. Go to **Light Fixture Outliner** in the SU Podium **Tools** menu, found under the **Extensions** menu in SketchUp.

Next, let's move on to spot lights:

1. To create a spot light, choose **Spot** from the **Podium Light System Panel** and set the **Color** (optional), **Power**, **Inner Cone**, and **Outer Cone**. The power settings for spot lights can be a decimal ranging from 0.01 to 100.

> **Beam angles**
>
> The spot light projects a cone-shaped light on a specific area you select. The **Inner Cone** feature determines the circumference of light that is shining on an object or area. The **Outer Cone** feature is the shadowing around the outside of the light coming from the inner cone. SU Podium tutorials refer to it as the *light drop-off area*. For softer shadowing, keep the outer cone number higher than the inner cone number. If you want a sharper or more defined look to the outer cone, make it a smaller number than the inner cone.

2. Click **Create**. It requires three clicks to place a spot light:

    I.   Choose an inference point for the first click.

    II. The second click is to set the location for the light source. After the second click, you will see a line attached to your cursor from the light source. This line represents the beam of light.

    III. The third and final click should be on the face that you want the spot light to illuminate. (Unlike omni lights, do not copy and reuse spot lights in other areas because the beam angles will be different for each spot.)

To edit an existing omni or spot light, select the grouped light in SketchUp and open the **Podium Light System Panel**:

- For omni lights, you can change the **Color** and **Power** level.

- For spot lights, you can change the **Color**, **Power**, **Inner Cone**, and **Outer Cone**. You cannot adjust the angle of the light.

There is no *apply* button; your changes automatically save when you close out of the **Podium Light System** window.

More information

Watch this video for more information about Podium artificial lighting: `https://suplugins. com/v26/vids/v26-06-artificial-lights.php`.

In the *Chapter 14* practice model, turn on the `LIGHTS-OMNI + SPOT` tag within the `PODIUM` tag folder.

There are three omni lights in the practice model:

- Two of the omni lights are used in the wall sconce component. The **Power** is set to `0.06`.

- The third omni light is for the table lamp, with the **Power** set to `0.13`.

There are three spot lights in the practice model:

- All three spot lights are in the ceiling light fixture. The **Power** is set to `1.00`, and the **Beam Angle** was left at the default levels.

Let's run the last test render to see how the lighting looks with the hidden LEM turned down to 2 and the omni and spot lights turned on:

1. Go to the `Render` scene.

2. Turn on the `LIGHTS-OMNI + SPOT` tag and update the scene.

3. Go ahead and run the final test render using the same settings (refer to *Figure 14.44* for the settings).

Figure 14.55 shows the rendered image.

Figure 14.55: The final test render

If you want the table lamp or sconce lighting to be less or more dramatic, adjust the **Power** in the **Podium Light System Panel**. Or, if you want the space to be darker overall, decrease the **Light Power** to 1 for the LEM-hidden material. This is up to you and your personal preference. We will leave ours as-is.

> **Editing the wall sconce omnis and ceiling spot lights**
>
> In order to adjust the light power levels of the wall sconce omni lights, you must get into **Edit** mode of the wall sconce component and zoom inside of the lightbulb to select the Omni light. To adjust the light power levels of the ceiling spot lights, you must get into **Edit** mode of the ceiling glass lamp component to select the Spot light.

The scene is composed, the materials have Podium properties, and the lighting is set. We are all systems go for a final rendering!

But before we dive into the final rendering, we want to highlight an incredibly powerful Podium resource that you can utilize to prepare your file for rendering. It is called **Podium Browser**.

Podium Browser

Podium Browser is like **3D Warehouse** in the sense that it is a content library filled with 3D models that you can download into your SketchUp model. The difference is that everything you find in **Podium Browser** is render-ready. This means it already has Podium material properties assigned. In addition, the models are high-quality and built by advanced SketchUp users.

If you have a **SU Podium V2.6** license, you have access to **Podium Browser**. Click on the **Podium Browser** icon in the Podium toolbar to open it. (It requires an internet connection to function.)

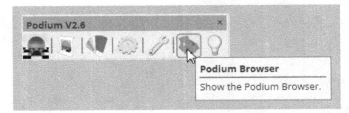

Figure 14.56: Podium Browser icon in the Podium toolbar

After clicking the **Podium Browser** icon, the home page appears. From here, you can search thousands of premium 3D models from the categories and subcategories, such as light fixtures, furniture, appliances, 3D and 2D plants and trees, materials, electronics, cars, decorations, and much more.

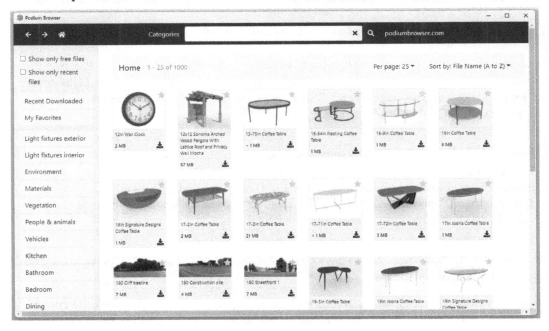

Figure 14.57: Podium Browser

The following objects from the *Chapter 14* practice model were downloaded from **Podium Browser**: sectional, brass wall art frames, spider plant, coffee table book, side table books, vases and mirror on the fireplace mantle, fireplace logs, accessories on the window sill, 180-degree background component, exterior climbing rose, plus various materials.

> **Important notes**
>
> **Podium Browser** content is *not* included in the 30-day, free SU Podium trial. Visit `https://suplugins.com/v26/trial-content.php` for how you can use **Podium Browser** during the 30-day trial.
>
> To further explore the content found on **Podium Browser**, visit `https://podiumbrowser.com/`.

Now, let's jump back into the final rendering process.

Final renderings

At this point, we have worked our way through the rendering process, which has included a series of test renders combined with refining Podium properties and details. Creating photorealistic renderings can be time-consuming, with lots of time waiting for the computer to produce an image. With more practice, you will better understand the factors that affect render speed. You will also start eliminating test renders throughout the process as you determine your go-to Podium properties and settings.

Final render settings

Final render settings frequently depend on the time available for rendering. Some projects may require overnight render times to achieve the desired quality, while others may opt for faster render settings with slightly reduced quality for quicker results. This is ultimately up to you. Most rendering artists find a balance between the level of realism they desire and the time available.

Here are the steps and settings we recommend using for the *Chapter 14* final rendering:

1. Click on the scene tab named `Render`.
2. Turn on the `Accessories` tag and update the scene.

3. Feel free to orbit or pan the view to fit your desire for the final render. We adjusted the vantage point so that it is lower and slightly angled, as shown in *Figure 14.58*. Remember to update your scene if you orbit or pan.

Figure 14.58: Orbit or pan the view to fit your desire for the final render

4. Click on the **Options** icon in the Podium toolbar.

5. Select **3_Interior_fine_AA_1.0.5.pps** from the **Preset** drop-down menu.

The 3_Interior_default_1.0.5.pps preset

If you prefer to prioritize render speed over quality, use **3_Interior_default_1.0.5.pps** preset. The *default* preset still produces reasonably good images and is significantly faster than the *fine* preset.

---

6. Click the **Fixed** radio button under **Image size**.

7. Select **Custom** from the **Size** drop-down menu. Type 1960 in the **Width** box and 1080 in the **Height** box.

8. Use **.png** for the **Image format**.

9. Choose an **Image save location** on your computer.

Figure 14.59: Output tab for final render

10. In the **Environment** tab, choose **Podium Physical Sky 1**.

11. Set the **Intensity** Slider to 50 and the **EXPOSURE** slider to 50.

12. Check **Soft Omni Lights (Slower)**. Uncheck all other boxes.

Figure 14.60: Environment tab for final render

13. Click **Save**.

14. Press the **Render Current Scene** button.

Figure 14.61: The final render generated in Podium

Voilà! The final render is generated.

Postproduction

Most photorealistic renders are touched up after using any rendering engine in order to enhance the rendering by modifying light, color, contrast, and more.

SU Podium has a built-in image editor called the **Podium Image Editor**, or **PIE**. You can auto-enhance an entire image, add a vignette, change the hue and saturation, and more. One incredible tool is the light level sliders, which can be used to manually fine-tune the lighting. These sliders are effective in correcting areas that are overly bright or too dark. Using PIE can significantly reduce the need for extensive re-rendering, saving you valuable time.

> **More information**
> Learn more about PIE here: `https://www.suplugins.com/podium/help/pie-help.php`.

You can also import rendered images into Photoshop or other photo-editing software.

Figure 14.62: Watercolor effect added to the Podium rendering in Photoshop

Some rendering artists spend more time editing a rendered image in the postproduction phase than they do on rendering it in the first place. Post-processing can make a dramatic impact, especially on exterior renderings. You can add atmospheric effects, enhance grass and terrain, and adjust backgrounds. We encourage you to explore online and published resources if you are interested in learning about postproduction rendering methods.

Additional renderings

Once a SketchUp file is prepared for rendering, you can generate additional scenes quickly. See *Figure 14.63* for a perspective showcasing the chair we built in *Chapter 8*.

Figure 14.63: Additional perspective rendered

Or, you can crop renderings for social media platforms and websites that favor vertical orientation, as shown in *Figure 14.64*.

Figure 14.64: Create vertical renderings

Another SU Podium feature is **Panorama VR**. Panorama VR enables you to experience a panoramic rendering in a virtual 360 environment on any device. To view a Panorama VR of the *Chapter 14* practice model, visit `https://www.panopdm.com/viewer.php?application=panorama&id=4dae44eee6190cda8b61b1e58c3445a3f1f65bb9`:

- If you are viewing the Panorama VR on your computer, click and use the mouse to spin around the room.
- If you are viewing the Panorama VR on your phone, move your device to rotate around the room.

Amazing, right? Don't be deceived by the impressive ability to view the space in a 360 capacity; the process for creating a Panorama VR is not much different than what you did in this chapter. In fact, you have already done most of the work.

And yes, the SU Podium Panorama VR feature is included with a Podium license! Go to `https://suplugins.com/podium/pano.php` to get started. (Most other popular rendering plugins also offer a similar feature.)

In the next section, we share extra tips and solutions for solving common issues.

Tips, tricks, and troubleshooting

Here is a list of helpful tips, tricks, and troubleshooting techniques you can use to improve your render workflow and images.

Line overlay

Overlaying SketchUp lines on a rendering is a quick way to stylize a final image. That is one way to use the PIE, mentioned in the *Postproduction* section.

Figure 14.65: Rendered image with line overlay

Line overlay can be completed in just a few steps. Go to `https://suplugins.com/v26/line-overlay.php` for instructions.

Lift up furniture

One method to create contact shadows under furniture and other objects on the floor is to move them up by about 1/8". For example, looking at the *Chapter 14* practice model, the coffee table, ottomans, and side table are slightly lifted off the rug.

Rendering with shadows

Do not work in SketchUp with shadows turned on. Working with shadows will slow performance, even in small models. If you want to utilize shadows in a rendering, consider duplicating the render scene so that you have two render scenes: one for editing the scene (with shadows off) and one for the final render (with shadows on).

You can forgo shadows altogether and add them in postproduction. This will speed up the rendering time.

Harsh sunlight

If the shadows in your rendering are too harsh, you can adjust the sunspot to create a softer shadow transition by manually editing the Podium preset. Watch this video tutorial for how to control the softness of sunspots: `https://www.youtube.com/watch?v=D4pLqRN_bxM`.

Adding texture imperfections

Texture imperfections can significantly enhance the realism of photorealistic renderings. These imperfections, such as scratches, dents, stains, and irregularities in shade, mimic the natural variations and flaws found in real-world materials. You can use Photoshop or other image-editing software to add texture imperfections to your material images and 3D models.

Materials not displayed properly/reverse faces

First, double-check that the material properties are, in fact, what you want them to be. As a reminder, Podium applies material properties globally to textures. If you forget to create a new gray material for a texture used as a mirror and apply reflective properties to it, every surface in the entire model with that same gray material will also have reflective properties.

Another reason your render is displaying a material incorrectly could be if the interior face of a group is painted a texture other than SketchUp's *default* color. This usually happens when painting geometry outside of **Edit** mode. To fix the issue, repaint the inside surfaces *default*. You may have to explode the group if the faces are not changing to *default*. Then re-group the geometry.

Light seeping through

Modeling walls, ceilings, and floors without any volume can cause light leaks in a rendering. To prevent this, model your walls, ceilings, and floors with some thickness rather than leaving them as planar surfaces.

Rendering with tag folders

If you want a tag not to be rendered, you must specifically turn it off, even if it is inside a tag folder that is turned off. If you only turn off the tag folder and not the individual tag, the objects on the tag will still be rendered.

Analyse model

The **Analyse model** feature is designed to help users identify potential issues in their SketchUp models before rendering. You can find this tool in the SU Podium toolbar. Visit `https://suplugins.com/podium/pdm-tools/analyse-tool.php` to watch a video overview of Podium's **Analyse model** tool.

Adding light switches and outlets

Adding extra details, such as light switches and power outlets, will enhance the rendering's believability.

Now that you understand SU Podium, you can explore other rendering programs.

PodiumxRT and other photorealistic rendering plugins

PodiumxRT (Extended Real-Time) is another extension developed by Cadalog, Inc. that offers real-time rendering capabilities. This means that as you make changes to your SketchUp model, such as adjusting materials or lighting, you can see the results instantly in the rendering window. This real-time rendering functionality results in a quicker and more interactive rendering experience.

The PodiumxRT extension is a separate product from SU Podium with its own licensing structure. However, it relies on SU Podium's material settings since it lacks a dedicated interface for creating and editing material properties. To set material properties for PodiumxRT, use the SU Podium **Material Properties** dialog box and make adjustments there. If you don't own an SU Podium license, you can download and install the free trial. Once the trial expires, you will no longer be able to render with SU Podium, but you'll retain access to the material and lighting interface for PodiumxRT rendering.

Due to its added features and real-time rendering option, PodiumxRT is priced higher than SU Podium. Additionally, it has its own hardware requirements. PodiumxRT prioritizes CPU-based rendering, so having a higher number of CPU cores will enhance its performance. For a comprehensive overview of PodiumxRT's capabilities, pricing, and hardware requirements, visit `https://podiumxrt.com/`.

In addition to Podium, there are many excellent rendering programs available for SketchUp users, and most offer free trials. Here are some other popular options:

- **V-Ray** (`https://www.chaos.com/vray/sketchup/`) – Owned by Chaos. V-Ray is known for its versatility and ability to produce high-quality renderings. It offers the feature of previewing the final render before the actual rendering process, known as real-time rendering. V-Ray also integrates with Revit.

- **Enscape** (`https://enscape3d.com/`) – Owned by Chaos. Enscape allows users to interact with and navigate the rendering in real time, just like V-Ray. It differs from V-Ray because it is meant to produce a fast-rendered visual rather than a higher-quality rendering, like V-Ray. The great thing is because they are both owned by Chaos, if you start adding materials and scenes in Enscape, you can transfer a scene to V-Ray (if you have both plugins). Like V-Ray, Enscape integrates with Revit.

- **Twilight Render** (`https://www.twilightrender.com/`) – Twilight Render is known for its user-friendly interface and a variety of material and lighting options. It has additional add-ons, such as Terrain and Denoising.

- **Lumion** (`https://lumion.com/`) – Lumion is popular for its ease of use and fast rendering. It offers an upgrade called *LiveSync*, which is its version of real-time rendering. At the time of writing this book, Lumion is available only for Windows operating systems.

- **Twinmotion** (`https://www.twinmotion.com/en-US`) – Twinmotion is designed to be relatively accessible in terms of hardware requirements compared to some other high-end rendering software. It offers real-time rendering and integration with CAD and other 3D modeling programs.

> **System requirements**
>
> Before installing any of these plugins, it's advisable to refer to the plugin's website for the latest information on system requirements.

Rendering is an extensive topic, with a wealth of resources available if you are interested in taking your skills to the next level. Many rendering plugins offer dedicated blogs that keep users updated on changes and provide free asset downloads. There are also plugin forums where users can gather online to discuss topics related to the software, share tips and tricks, and seek help or advice from other users. Here is a link to the SU Podium forum: `https://supodiumforum.websitetoolbox.com/`.

Each plugin comes with its own selling points, unique features, learning curve, and pricing, but rest assured, there is a rendering program to suit every need and budget.

Summary

The benefits of photorealistic rendering are numerous and extend across various industries. There is a lot to discover in the world of photorealism, and we hope this chapter planted a seed. We covered render options and presets, scene composition, realistic material properties, lighting techniques, and final render settings – using SU Podium as the rendering plugin example. The last two sections focused on tips, troubleshooting, and other rendering plugin options.

In the next and final chapter, we will share extra modeling tips and tricks we have learned through the years and provide helpful links, books, and courses for continuing education. We will also touch on *SketchUp Diffusion*, which uses a SketchUp model and text prompts to create AI-generated images.

Part 5: Bonus Tips for Quicker Modeling

The final part features a bonus chapter, filled with valuable insights and best practices accumulated from our experiences over the years. We couldn't fit it all into the main content, so consider it a little extra treat! It includes tips for maintaining clean and organized SketchUp files and an introduction to SketchUp Diffusion. We have compiled a list of recommended extensions, some already discussed in the book, which we have consolidated for reference. Lastly, we have included helpful resources for your ongoing education.

This part has the following chapter:

- *Chapter 15, Tips and Tricks to Up Your SketchUp Game*

Tips and Tricks to Up Your SketchUp Game

This final chapter is loaded with extra tips and tricks we have learned through the years. We will discuss best practices for keeping SketchUp models clean and organized to avoid Bug Splats and improve performance. In addition, we will introduce SketchUp Diffusion (Beta version), which uses generative **Artificial Intelligence (AI)** to create rendered images of your SketchUp models in seconds. Although we have seen multiple AI features of SketchUp released, **Diffusion** is the first one to come directly from SketchUp. The last two sections include lists of must-have extensions, helpful links, books, and courses to explore for continuing education.

In this chapter, we will cover the following topics:

- Keeping your models clean and organized
- SketchUp Diffusion
- Helpful extensions and plugins
- Continuing education

Technical requirements

You do not need anything to complete this chapter. If you want to check out SketchUp Diffusion or any other extensions, you will need SketchUp Pro or Studio, Trimble Connect, and internet access.

Keeping your models clean and organized

SketchUp files comprise so much more than what you see in your viewport. They include hidden geometry, group and component information, tags, scenes, styles, materials, and so on. SketchUp is actively processing and displaying the content in your model whenever you orbit, pan, or zoom. The greater the number of edges, faces, materials, and other elements, the more data SketchUp has to render, which leads to longer load times and sometimes more of the dreaded Bug Splats. There are things you can do and ways you can model to improve SketchUp's performance.

In this section, we share tips for how to keep your model clean and organized, starting with how you build objects.

Polygon count

In SketchUp, the term **polygon count** refers to the total number of faces that make up a 3D model. Polygons are flat, two-dimensional shapes with three or more sides. In the context of SketchUp, they form the faces of objects in a model. A higher polygon count generally means a more detailed and complex model, but it can also impact the performance of your SketchUp project. When building anything in SketchUp, use the minimal amount of geometry required while maintaining the desired detail level. The goal is to keep the polygon count as low as possible.

For example, by default, a circle in SketchUp is made up of 24 edges. The more edges a circle has, the smoother it will appear (which is good), but also it will have a higher polygon count (which can slow down your model). Like with most things SketchUp-related, it's about finding a balance. (Refer to *Chapter 8* for how to adjust the number of edges for a circle.)

Check out the two wall sconces in *Figure 15.1*. Although they look almost identical, the sconce on the right comprises substantially more faces and edges (a higher polygon count).

Figure 15.1: These sconces look very similar, but the right one has a much higher polygon count

Figure 15.2 shows the **Hidden Geometry** toggled on.

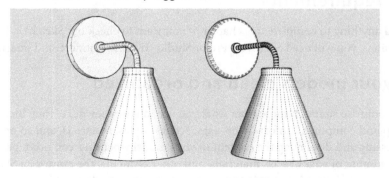

Figure 15.2: Hidden Geometry toggled on

Each sconce was built by starting with a circle for the back plate. Following this, the sconces were both constructed using the same four SketchUp tools: **Push/Pull**, **Offset**, **Follow Me**, and **Autofold**. The left sconce is made up of 192 faces and 467 edges. The right sconce is made up of 1,124 faces and 2,400 edges. If the two sconces were constructed using essentially the same steps, why does the right one have a higher polygon count? Great question! Here are the two major differences between the sconces:

- The circle for the left sconce's back plate has 24 edges (the default), whereas the circle for the right sconce's back plate has 40 edges.

- The right sconce includes rounded edges on the backplate and shade. Adding rounded edges to an object adds more detail, but in turn, it creates more faces, resulting in a higher polygon count.

If an entire model is made up of extra, unneeded edges and faces, it can become bloated and hard to work with. It is important to understand the intended use of an object in a model and build it appropriately from the beginning.

Next, we will share the recommended settings for a working scene.

Creating a working scene

Create a scene in your SketchUp model dedicated to modeling and editing. Name the scene working, edit, or something similar. Save the scene with the following settings to optimize model efficiency and SketchUp performance:

- Use a simple style, such as a **Fast Style**. Refer to *Chapter 10*, in the *Exploring SketchUp's Styles panel* section, to review Fast Styles.

- Turn shadows off. The **Shadows** tool should be used as a precision instrument. Turn shadows on only when you are assessing light or exporting images.

- Turn unneeded tags off. For example, if your focus is on building the interior architecture of a space, turn off any exterior elements, such as vegetation or landscaping, for your working scene.

You can update the working scene as you develop your model and focus on different elements by toggling off and on tags and perhaps adjusting the camera perspective.

Removing unneeded data

The more unneeded data in your SketchUp model, the more likely you will experience performance degradation. Use **Zoom Extents** to view all stray groups or geometry and delete unwanted objects.

Purge unused styles, components, materials, and tags. We discuss **Purge Unused** in *Chapter 3*, in the *Learning lesser-known timesavers* section. You can also purge individual categories by clicking the **Details** arrow and selecting **Purge** within the **Materials**, **Components**, and **Tags** toolbars.

> **Purge unused components before materials**
>
> If you purge unused materials before components, any materials applied to the purged components will still be in your model. You will need to purge unused materials again to remove them. We recommend either purging unused components first or purging everything at once using the **Model Info** window (as shown in *Chapter 3*).

Imported images

When importing images into your model, steer clear of `TIFF` files due to their tendency to have large file sizes, requiring more computing resources to display. We advise `JPEGs` and `PNGs`, with a maximum file size of `2,000` KB and a minimum file size of `15` KB.

Organizing furniture and accessory models

As you know by now, staying organized in SketchUp is essential for efficiency, file size management, and overall workflow optimization; this means creating an organized library of SketchUp models ready to be imported. Here are some ways you can organize your go-to models:

- **3D Warehouse collections**: Collections are groups of related models that users can create to organize their content. You can edit the name and description of a collection and easily modify it by adding or removing models based on your preferences. Collections are public and available for all 3D Warehouse users to view. For a private option, opt for a 3D Warehouse folder rather than a collection.

- **3D Warehouse folders**: 3D Warehouse folders are like collections but are private and only available for viewing and editing. There is a **Convert to Public Collection** option should you want to make your private folder available to others.

- **Trimble Connect**: Trimble Connect is a great option for collaboration. It is a collaborative platform that allows users to store and share project data and models. It integrates with SketchUp, among other applications. Users can organize SketchUp models into projects and folders, control who can access specific projects or folders, and add comments to models directly within the platform. (Trimble Connect is included when you purchase a SketchUp subscription.) Ways to use Trimble Connect are mentioned in *Chapter 3*.

- **Use your personal device**: Of course, you can always use your personal device to create a SketchUp library. We have personal SketchUp libraries on our devices filled with hand-selected, go-to models organized in categorical folders. Depending on your computer storage, this option can be limiting if you want to curate an extensive library with hundreds of models.

No matter your chosen method, we recommend dividing your models into categories. Category examples include accessories, doors, light fixtures, vegetation, and more. You may consider creating subcategories. For example, within the light fixtures category, you could add subcategories such as floor lamps, table lamps, wall sconces, and pendants. Some users prefer organizing models based on rooms. Spend some time finding what works best for you!

Creating your own SketchUp template

Many users never explore beyond SketchUp's default templates, but you can save time setting up your SketchUp workspace by creating a custom template. For example, you can move toolbars or panels around to your liking, fix a background style, turn off the axes, or change the mouse settings. A bonus: it is easy to create your own template!

> **More information**
>
> Find out more about customizing your workspace by searching on YouTube or visiting: `https://help.sketchup.com/en/sketchup/customizing-your-workspace`.

And don't forget, you can set your preferences, such as how often your model auto-saves, in the SketchUp **Preferences** window. On Windows, it's found under the **Window** menu and **Preferences**. For macOS, use the **SketchUp** menu and then **Preferences**.

Re-saving SketchUp files each day

Regularly saving your SketchUp files is good practice for several reasons. The most obvious reason is to ensure that you don't lose too much work in the event of an unexpected interruption. In addition, regularly saving your model with a new name is a form of project documentation. You can track the evolution of your model over time and access different stages of a project. We recommend changing the date at the end of the SketchUp filename whenever you save new versions. All in all, the extra work to re-save SketchUp models is worth the peace of mind, allowing you to focus on your design. (And don't forget about **Version History**, mentioned in *Chapter 3*.)

Using the most recent SketchUp version

Make sure you are using the latest version of SketchUp. Updates often include performance improvements. To check for updates, use the **Help** menu in Windows (**SketchUp** menu on macOS) and arrow down to **Check for Update**.

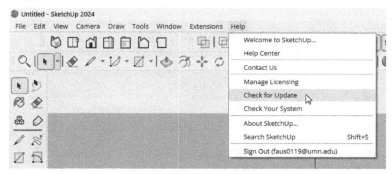

Figure 15.3: Check for Update

By following the tips in this section, you should have a cleaner SketchUp model and a smoother modeling experience. In the next section, we will introduce SketchUp's latest release, SketchUp Diffusion, which uses generative AI.

SketchUp Diffusion

Generative AI has revolutionized workflows across countless industries, including interior design and architecture. **SketchUp Diffusion** incorporates this technology into SketchUp's familiar interface, enabling users to create AI-generated images using an active model's viewport and a text prompt. You can find SketchUp Diffusion in the Extension Warehouse.

Installing SketchUp Diffusion

SketchUp Diffusion requires an active SketchUp Go, Pro, or Studio subscription and internet connection. It is available on SketchUp for Desktop, SketchUp for iPad, and SketchUp for Web.

Use the following steps to install SketchUp Diffusion on SketchUp for Desktop:

1. Open **Extension Warehouse**.
2. Type `SketchUp Diffusion` in the search bar. Click on the extension.

SketchUp Diffusion
Create concept visuals in seconds with Generative AI.
1,000,630 Views   Free

Figure 15.4: SketchUp Diffusion in the Extension Warehouse

3. Click **Install**.

After SketchUp Diffusion is installed, the toolbar will appear. See *Figure 15.5*.

Figure 15.5: SketchUp Diffusion toolbar

You can also access the toolbar by selecting **Diffusion** from the **Extensions** menu. If **Diffusion** is not listed as an option under the **Extensions** menu, then you need to close out of SketchUp and restart it. Check again after you restart it.

Once Diffusion is up and running, you are ready to start experimenting.

How to use SketchUp Diffusion

The SketchUp Diffusion interface is simple. At the top of the **Diffusion** window is a box to enter a text prompt, as shown in *Figure 15.6*.

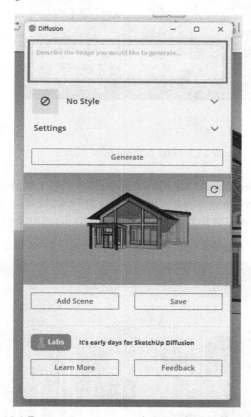

Figure 15.6: Type a text prompt at the top of the Diffusion window

Use the text prompt field to describe the visual elements you desire for your generated image.

> **All text prompts should be in English**
>
> Diffusion is trained in English, so all text prompts should be written in English.

Then click **Generate**. After about 15 seconds (give or take), Diffusion presents the results as thumbnails. Click on a thumbnail to make the image larger and display it in the main section of the preview pane. From here, you can finetune the text prompt and click **Generate** again to edit and build upon the generated images further.

At any point in the process, you can click the **Refresh Input View** button at the upper-right of the preview image to reset and start from the original SketchUp model.

Figure 15.7: Refresh Input View button

It is important to offer clear direction and use natural language for the text prompt field. For example, we used the following three text prompts with the *Chapter 14* practice model to see what SketchUp Diffusion would produce. (We used the **Refresh Input View** button between each of these text prompts.)

As a reminder, here is what the original *Chapter 14* practice model looks like:

Figure 15.8: Chapter 14 SketchUp model

Here's the result with text prompt #1: `modern sleek design with sunlight and city views`:

Figure 15.9: Modern sleek design with sunlight and city views (text prompt)

Here's the result with text prompt #2: `rustic mountain cabin with wood elements and cozy vibes`:

Figure 15.10: Rustic mountain cabin with wood elements and cozy vibes (text prompt)

Here's the result with text prompt #3: `southwest new mexican design with terracotta floors, stucco walls, desert views, and santa fe inspired art`

Figure 15.11: Southwest New Mexican design with terracotta floors, stucco walls, desert views, and Santa Fe inspired art (text prompt)

Pretty neat! To assist further in generating visuals, SketchUp Diffusion provides multiple Style Presets and settings, eliminating the pressure to create the perfect text prompt. All Style Preset options can be found directly under where you enter a text prompt. Hover over each preset to see a quick blurb on how it generates an image. Select a Style Preset from the list and click **Generate** to view the results.

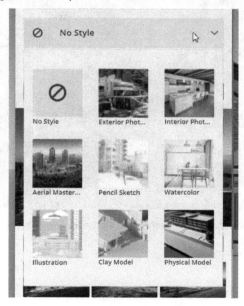

Figure 15.12: Style options for Diffusion (Beta version)

The **Settings** tab can be found just below the available Style Presets. You will see two sliders: **Respect Model Geometry** and **Prompt Influence**. Use these two sliders to tell Diffusion how much to respect your SketchUp model geometry and how much to prioritize the text prompt when generating an image.

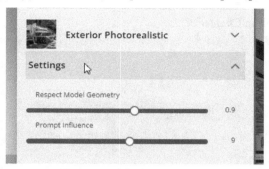

Figure 15.13: The Diffusion Settings tab is found directly under the Style Preset options

Tweak these settings to find a balance between your original SketchUp geometry and the creative input of SketchUp Diffusion. Once you're happy with the results, you can create a new scene containing the generated image. The new scene is a **Match Photo** image. An especially cool feature is the ability to use the generated image to apply textures to surfaces in your SketchUp model. Watch this YouTube video to learn how: https://www.youtube.com/watch?v=CW6LETkJ4Pk.

In addition to creating a new scene of the generated image, you can also save it on your device or share it with others. Saved and shared images use the exact resolution as your SketchUp viewport.

Closing SketchUp Diffusion or SketchUp

If you close the SketchUp Diffusion window or your SketchUp model, the generated images will no longer appear in the Diffusion panel. Generated images are only available in the Diffusion panel during an active session or if you create a scene, save them to your device, or share them.

Some limitations of SketchUp Diffusion (Beta version) include the following:

- It does not always respect your SketchUp materials, even when you include material descriptions in the text prompt.
- The variance in textures is sometimes unnatural.
- People often turn out incorrectly formed.
- It is difficult to change or edit generated images.
- Overall, there is a lack of control and precision in the rendering process.

If you want more control over what final renders look like, we recommend using rendering software, such as SU Podium (covered in *Chapter 14*), Enscape, or V-Ray.

Let's look at some examples of AI-generated images using SketchUp Diffusion.

Examples of AI-generated images using SketchUp Diffusion

Remember the chair we built in *Chapter 8*?

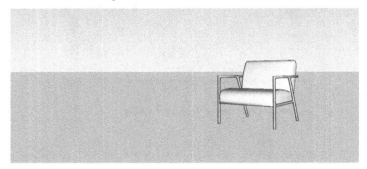

Figure 15.14: The RH Thaddeus Track Armchair built in Chapter 8

In SketchUp Diffusion, we typed `scandinavian living room with christmas tree and presents, fireplace, furry rug, christmas accessories` into the text prompt and selected the **Watercolor** preset. *Figure 15.15* shows the results.

Figure 15.15: Chapter 8 chair rendered in Diffusion with the Watercolor preset

Diffusion is a great tool to turn to when you are feeling stuck creatively. It can spark inspiration. As another example, let's see how Diffusion can bring the *Chapter 11* practice model to life. Here is an exported image of the family room from the SketchUp model:

Figure 15.16: Chapter 11 SketchUp practice model

Here is the same model rendered using SketchUp Diffusion with the text prompt `contemporary design with wood millwork, sunset atmosphere`:

Figure 15.17: Contemporary design with wood millwork, sunset atmosphere (text prompt)

Try using the **Clay Model** preset to view your model without colors and textures. This preset helps enable designers to explore different design iterations by highlighting the model with simple, monochrome surfaces.

Figure 15.18: Clay Model preset with no text prompt

You get to see Diffusion stretch the possibilities with exterior models. In *Chapter 13*, the finalized LayOut cover page included a Diffusion-rendered exterior image. After adding showroom furniture through the windows and a roof and concrete decorative blocking to the exterior, we let Diffusion set the stage for the rest of the exterior.

Figure 15.19: Chapter 13 SketchUp model with exterior additions

The prompts for the *Chapter 13* exterior model with Diffusion's **Exterior Photorealistic** preset were: urban landscape, exterior, downtown, parking lot, sidewalk, daytime. This was the result:

Figure 15.20: Exterior Photorealistic preset

Using the preset called **Physical Model**, which says it will *Turn your model into a wooden physical architectural model*, we first tried it without adding a prompt. This is what the model looked like:

Figure 15.21: Physical Model preset – no prompts

To see what the preset could do with some of the suggested prompts and a couple of our own, we typed `architectural presentation, balsa wood, soft shadows, foam core`. This was the result:

Figure 15.22: Physical Model preset – with prompts

The current Beta version of SketchUp Diffusion has limitations with render control and accuracy, but there is no denying the burst of creativity and imagination it can ignite. The generated images can be helpful for brainstorming during the design process, especially during the early conceptual stages. The images can also be used for extra project visuals and to communicate your vision. Experiment with the settings and see what you come up with!

Up next, we will share an extensive list of extensions and plugins we have used over the years and can confidently recommend.

Helpful extensions and plugins

Extensions offer a wide range of tools and features, allowing users to customize their workflow, add new capabilities, and streamline various tasks within SketchUp. We discussed how to find and install extensions in *Chapter 6* and have introduced multiple extensions throughout the book. For your convenience, we compiled the following list, which includes all extensions referenced in the book, plus more that we and fellow SketchUp users have found helpful. The list is geared toward SketchUp for interior designers and architects, but several extensions are used across many other industries, such as product design, woodworking, landscaping, and more.

> **Extension prices**
>
> While many extensions on this list are free, some do cost money. Those usually offer a free trial period to test the tools before purchasing.
>
> For the most up-to-date pricing and license requirements for any given extension, users are encouraged to check the official **Extension Warehouse** page or the official **SketchUcation Plugin Store**.

Keep in mind that an extension's availability and specific functionalities may evolve as developers continue to create new and innovative tools for SketchUp.

1001bit Tools by GOH C.

1001bit Tools includes a collection of tools helpful for quickly modeling architectural details and elements, such as staircases, doors, rafters, and more.

Extension Warehouse page: `https://extensions.sketchup.com/extension/e5b1211a-8d1a-4813-bdc3-b321e5477d7b/1001bit-tools-freeware`

Referenced in *Chapters 5* and *6*.

3D Text Editor by ThomThom

The **3D Text Editor** allows users to edit 3D text easily at any point.

Extension Warehouse page: `https://extensions.sketchup.com/extension/40a79eb9-ee97-4d1a-bc1c-cf534042a5b5/3d-text-editor`

Referenced in *Chapter 6*.

Animate Sections by How2SU

The **Animate Sections** extension facilitates creating section animations with an automated process. It streamlines a tricky task into an automated process with just a few clicks. Use Animate Sections when creating animations with sections!

Extension Warehouse page: `https://extensions.sketchup.com/extension/877a3ded-a7d5-4b73-aa26-400e6fd3d4d6/animate-sections`

Referenced in *Chapter 11*.

Animator by Fredo6

Animator is a great extension to use to show the assembly of objects.

From **SketchUcation** only: `https://sketchucation.com/plugin/1839-animator`

Referenced in *Chapter 11*.

Architextures for SketchUp by Architextures

Use the **Architextures for SketchUp** plugin to create and edit seamless textures, bump maps, and hatches directly inside SketchUp. There are a variety of high-quality seamless textures to choose from, or you can purchase the pro version for additional features, such as uploading custom textures.

Extension Warehouse page: `https://extensions.sketchup.com/extension/1a0e0f80-7186-48da-8dd4-f6337dac0873/architextures-for-sketch-up`

Referenced in *Chapter 9*.

Bezier Curve Tool by SketchUp Team

Bezier Curve Tool is used to create true and complex curves, shapes, and surfaces using control points. It is a great extension for building turned legs.

Extension Warehouse page: `https://extensions.sketchup.com/extension/8b58920d-0923-42f8-9c72-e09f2bba125e/bezier-curve-tool`

CleanUp3 by ThomThom

CleanUp3 focuses on optimizing and cleaning up your SketchUp models. It helps remove unnecessary geometry, textures, and components, ultimately reducing the file size.

Extension Warehouse page: `https://extensions.sketchup.com/extension/046175e5-a87a-4254-9329-1accc37a5e21/clean-up`

CLF Scale and Rotate Multiple by Chris Fullmer

CLF Scale and Rotate Multiple allows you to apply random scale and rotation factors to objects in your model. For example, it is great for quickly scaling exterior vegetation, such as plants and shrubs. You can also scale and rotate objects uniformly.

Extension Warehouse page: `https://extensions.sketchup.com/extension/652f2598-503a-47e4-94c0-45bc20f4666c/clf-scale-and-rotate-multiple`

CLF Shape Bender by Chris Fullmer

CLF Shape Bende is designed to bend a group or component along a specified path or curve. CLF Shape Bender is particularly useful for creating twisted shapes and curvy furniture.

Extension Warehouse page: `https://extensions.sketchup.com/extension/8a4d10ff-40f3-4885-b8ba-1dac2b941885/clf-shape-bender`

Referenced in *Chapter 8*.

Click-Change 1 by Dynamique Agencement

Click-Change 1 is designed to draw and then customize 3D kitchens quickly, choosing all the details.

Extension Warehouse page: `https://extensions.sketchup.com/extension/d76677c3-f9b2-451b-8a51-8423e3ed248c/click-change`

ClothWorks by Anton_S

Use **ClothWorks** to simulate fabric or cloth in your 3D models. It allows users to drape cloth over 3D objects or furniture and create realistic fabric simulations. You can adjust various parameters of the cloth, such as stiffness, gravity, and more. ClothWorks comes in handy when modeling tablecloths and draperies.

From **SketchUcation** only: `https://sketchucation.com/plugin/2053-clothworks`

Eneroth View Memory by Eneroth3

The **Eneroth View Memory** extension can help you save and recall specific views in your SketchUp model for future reference, even across different models. It allows you to save camera positions, field of view, styles, and more, so you can return to those views later. This can be particularly useful for duplicating scene perspectives from a previous project or establishing consistent scenes across multiple models.

Extension Warehouse page: `https://extensions.sketchup.com/extension/7f6577c2-634c-4adb-afa9-a3b2e5d38a99/eneroth-view-memory`

FredoScale by Fredo6

FredoScale provides a variety of scaling options within SketchUp. It offers advanced techniques for transforming objects more sophisticatedly than SketchUp's standard **Scale** tool.

From **SketchUcation** only: `https://sketchucation.com/plugin/1169-fredoscale`

Referenced in *Chapter 8*.

MAJ FollowMe by Majid M.

The **MAJ FollowMe** plugin extends the native SketchUp **Follow Me** tool with several additional functions. It creates complex curved shapes and structures, such as railings, stairs, and more.

Extension Warehouse page: `https://extensions.sketchup.com/extension/7f38db24-aca5-4f5f-ba51-f10c23513f60/maj-follow-me`

Referenced in *Chapters 3 and 5*.

Material Replacer by ThomThom

Material Replacer has a user-friendly interface, making it super easy to replace materials in your SketchUp models. It is quick to replace one material with another throughout an entire model.

Extension Warehouse page: `https://extensions.sketchup.com/extension/4137f7fc-a81f-4ef9-9ec8-b6dd8a0d9086/material-replacer`

Referenced in *Chapter 9*.

Material Resizer by SketchUp Team

Material Resizer gives you a list of all the materials within your SketchUp model, as well as information about the size of the materials. Then, you can use the extension to resize large materials and set maximum dimensions. Try Material Resizer if your SketchUp model is running slow.

Extension Warehouse page: `https://extensions.sketchup.com/extension/77b60f26-2352-407e-8c0c-9862c9716111/material-resizer`

Referenced in *Chapter 9*.

Medeek Wall by Medeek Engineering Inc.

Medeek Wall is designed to assist users in creating detailed wall assemblies, which include accurate framing geometry within SketchUp. In addition, you can use the extension to add doors, windows, beams, stairs, plus more.

Extension Warehouse page: `https://extensions.sketchup.com/extension/e662b5c8-28ec-48e2-b26f-d7f72550787d/medeek-wall`

Referenced in *Chapters 5* and *6*.

Revit Importer by SketchUp Team

Revit Importer makes it easy to import a Revit file (newer than 2011) directly into SketchUp with a SketchUp Studio subscription. No Revit license is required.

> **Windows compatibility**
> At the time of writing this book, Revit Importer is available only on Windows computers.

Extension Warehouse page: `https://extensions.sketchup.com/extension/83ac914b-cea0-4c1f-8fe0-c18bd741df31/revit-importer`

Referenced in *Chapter 4*.

RoundCorner by Fredo6

Use the **RoundCorner** extension to add rounded corners and beveled edges to 3D shapes. It includes a variety of customizable parameters such as bevel radius, number of segments, and other settings to achieve the desired look.

Extension Warehouse page: `https://extensions.sketchup.com/extension/043331df-2bb3-492f-95e3-ac8320fae172/round-corner`

Referenced in *Chapter 8*.

Skatter by Lindalë

Skatter is designed to facilitate the process of scattering objects in SketchUp. It is another excellent tool for creating natural landscapes, vegetation, and other scenes where you want to distribute elements in a more randomized and realistic manner. In addition, a *render only* feature sends all the scattering data directly to rendering engines, skipping SketchUp altogether. This allows users to render large quantities of objects without compromising SketchUp performance.

Extension Warehouse page: `https://extensions.sketchup.com/extension/23339f53-a400-40a4-a9c1-2aad7dc0213d/skatter`

SketchPlus by mind.sight.studios

Known for its SketchUp-like user interface, **SketchPlus** offers 30+ helpful tools to add to your SketchUp workflow, including select, move, and material tools.

Extension Warehouse page: `https://extensions.sketchup.com/extension/3b1e7d7b-c1f0-43ce-aa99-86a1b0a13ee4/sketch-plus`

Soap Skin & Bubble by Josef L

Use **Soap Skin & Bubble** to create surfaces that appear inflated or deflated. The plugin enables you to generate surfaces that resemble bubbles stretched between a series of edges. It is commonly used for modeling complex shapes and objects, such as tufted furniture.

Extension Warehouse page: `https://extensions.sketchup.com/extension/c8d49537-51db-40a7-ac0e-474a244eb525/soap-skin-bubble`

Referenced in *Chapter 8.*

Solar North by SketchUp Team

Solar North allows users to easily set and adjust the geographic orientation of a SketchUp model to match the real-world solar north. It is also used for shadow studies and creating visually appealing shadows. It is a popular extension to use when producing photorealistic renderings.

Extension Warehouse page: `https://extensions.sketchup.com/extension/393f5153-ba5f-4f5f-849f-46b32cf64bd4/solar-north`

Referenced in *Chapters 10* and *14.*

Solid Inspector² by ThomThom

Solid Inspector² analyzes your model and identifies any areas where geometry is not solid. It provides tools to help fix these issues, such as automatically filling holes, closing gaps, and repairing faces. Use this plugin to ensure that your SketchUp models are correctly constructed and ready for further use.

Extension Warehouse page: `https://extensions.sketchup.com/extension/aad4e5d9-7115-4cac-9b75-750ed0902732/solid-inspector`

Referenced in *Chapter 3*.

ThruPaint by Fredo6

ThruPaint is an upgraded version of SketchUp's **Paint** tool, offering more functions. Users can apply materials to complex and curved geometry and then easily scale, rotate, and move the material directly on the geometry.

Extension Warehouse page: `https://extensions.sketchup.com/extension/ee037966-cd1c-45cc-9bd5-825d0d93942f/thru-paint`

Referenced in *Chapter 9*.

TrueBend by ThomThom

TrueBend is designed to bend or deform geometry along a curve or path. It often provides a real-time preview of the bending operation, allowing users to visualize the changes before applying them. It is an excellent plugin for creating organic and curved shapes.

Extension Warehouse page: `https://extensions.sketchup.com/extension/c9135b56-4492-449e-ac63-8c26b734ba39/true-bend`

As you can see, the SketchUp Extension Warehouse hosts a wide variety of plugins and tools created by developers from around the world. New extensions are introduced regularly to help users take their skills to the next level. We encourage you to spend more time adding to the list provided. You never know when you might discover an extension that integrates seamlessly into your SketchUp workflow.

Now, let's move on to our final section (of the book!) about continuing education.

Continuing education

It goes without saying that continuing education is prudent in any profession to remain competent, relevant, and adaptable. We – the authors – strive to learn new tools and techniques to grow as SketchUp modelers in this ever-evolving industry. In the following list, we share various forms of continuing education, including forums, online courses, YouTube channels, books, and a conference.

Forums

SketchUp has incredibly active online communities where users post messages, ask questions, share information, and converse about 3D modeling and related topics. The two largest forums are **SketchUp Community** (the official SketchUp forum) and **SketchUcation**.

SketchUp Community

SketchUp Community has a variety of subforums covering different aspects of SketchUp, including general discussions, specific versions of the software, extensions, and more. It is a valuable resource for beginners and experienced users looking to connect with others, seek advice, or showcase projects.

Visit `https://forums.sketchup.com/` for SketchUp Community.

SketchUcation

The *SketchUcation* forum is known for hosting a vibrant community of SketchUp enthusiasts. It was founded in 2007 and is solely managed by SketchUp users; it is jam-packed with knowledge, troubleshooting solutions, extensions, and answers to just about any SketchUp question you have.

Visit `https://sketchucation.com/forums/` for the SketchUcation forum.

Online courses

Online courses are an attractive option for continuing education, given the flexibility, accessibility, and cost-effectiveness. You can often go through the materials at your own pace, which is a significant benefit for those of you with busy schedules and other commitments. There are some fantastic SketchUp instructors out there creating new learning content daily. We cannot highlight them all, but here are three popular options.

Becca's LinkedIn Learning

If you enjoyed this book, you will certainly enjoy **Becca's LinkedIn Learning** courses as they incorporate a similar teaching style, plus lots of videos! (As a reminder, Becca is a co-author of this book ☺.) Becca currently has two LinkedIn Learning courses:

- *SketchUp Pro Lunchtime Lessons*

  A collection of 26 videos, all less than 10 minutes long, with quick tips designed to help users enhance their SketchUp skills in their spare time.

- *SketchUp Pro: Interior Design Detailing*

  In this course, Becca teaches how to create a basic floor plan, build it up three-dimensionally, populate the space with furniture and fixtures, and create the documentation needed to deliver it to a client or contractor. As with many design programs, diving into a project is one of the best ways to learn; Becca provides custom-made exercise files to guide you through the tutorials. After this course, you'll have a better understanding of what SketchUp Pro has to offer designers, as well as clients.

All LinkedIn Premium subscriptions include access to LinkedIn Learning courses at no additional charge. Visit `https://www.linkedin.com/help/linkedin/answer/a1355837` for instructions to create a Premium account. Once you create an account, you will have access to LinkedIn Learning and can search for Becca's course titles.

SketchUp for Interior Designers

SketchUp for Interior Designers offers direct access to a SketchUp expert, Tammy Cody. Tammy's hands-on approach includes exercises and step-by-step instructions to learn SketchUp, which is designed specifically for interior designers. The lessons are entirely self-paced, so you decide when you start and finish. The SketchUp for Interior Designers social media accounts are also great resources for quick modeling tips.

Visit `https://sketchupforinteriordesigners.com/` to learn more about SketchUp for Interior Designers.

MasterSketchUp

MasterSketchUp is known for stellar SketchUp tutorials by Matt Donley, many of which are geared toward architecture. The tutorials are in written and video format for users to follow along at their preferred learning style and pace. In addition to tutorials and online courses, MasterSketchUp also offers the option to become a free member. Members have access to sample files and templates.

Visit `https://mastersketchup.com/` to learn more about MasterSketchUp.

YouTube channels

There is a YouTube video for almost every SketchUp query you can think of. You can learn so much by watching another modeler do their thing.

The SketchUp Essentials

Our personal favorite, **The SketchUp Essentials**, is a YouTube channel created by Justin Geis. Justin shares his 3D modeling expertise to help users improve their skills. Tutorials cover topics ranging from basic to advanced techniques. Each video tutorial is thorough yet straightforward. Plus, his positivity and enthusiasm about SketchUp are contagious.

Visit `https://www.youtube.com/@Thesketchupessentials` to subscribe to The SketchUp Essentials YouTube channel.

SketchUp

This is the official **SketchUp** YouTube channel; it is updated weekly with new, high-quality training videos, case studies, and even weekly live streams. Our favorite thing about this channel is the unique 2-hour live modeling sessions.

Visit `https://www.youtube.com/user/SketchUpVideo` to subscribe to the SketchUp YouTube channel.

Books

We might be a little bit biased, but we love SketchUp books! Here are five we recommend:

- *Getting Started with SketchUp Pro* by David S. Sellers

  - Purchase here: `https://www.amazon.com/Getting-Started-SketchUp-Pro-practices/dp/1789800188`

- *SketchUp for Dummies* by Bill Fane, Mark Harrison, and Josh Reilly

  - Purchase here: `https://www.amazon.com/SketchUp-All-Dummies-Aidan-Chopra/dp/1119617936/`

- *SketchUp to LayOut* by Matt Donley

  - Purchase here: `https://www.amazon.com/SketchUp-LayOut-beginners-guide-Pro-dp-0996539336/dp/0996539336/ref=dp_ob_title_bk`

- *Taking SketchUp Pro to the Next Level* by Aaron Dietzen

  - Purchase here: `https://www.amazon.com/Taking-SketchUp-Pro-Next-Level/dp/1803242698`

- *The SketchUp Workflow for Architecture* by Michael Brightman

  - Purchase here: `https://www.amazon.com/SketchUp-Workflow-Architecture-Visualizing-Construction-dp-1119383633/dp/1119383633/ref=dp_ob_title_bk`

3D Basecamp conference

If meeting face-to-face with other SketchUp fanatics from around the globe for a week-long trip intrigues you, check out **SketchUp's 3D Basecamp**. At 3D Basecamp, which typically happens every two years, attendees have the opportunity to learn from experts, participate in collaborative projects, explore the latest developments in SketchUp, network, and have fun! Previous 3D Basecamp locations include Vancouver (Canada), Palm Springs, and Boulder.

Visit `https://3dbasecamp.sketchup.com/` to learn more about 3D Basecamp.

Summary

We have shared our final SketchUp tips and tricks of the book in this chapter (there's more, but sadly we have to end the book). The bulk of this chapter is dedicated to extensions and plugins. There is a detailed list of must-have extensions, with a featured section dedicated solely to SketchUp Diffusion. When and if you are ready to continue learning, review the *Continuing education* section for SketchUp forums, online courses, and more.

Final words

That concludes our exploration of SketchUp for interior design and architecture (for now)! We want to take a moment to thank you for reading this book. We are immensely grateful to be part of your journey with SketchUp and hope that the knowledge gained within these pages equips you to take your SketchUp modeling to places you dream of. If you can design it, you can build it (in SketchUp)!

Connect with us on LinkedIn. We would love to see what you create!

Becca: `https://www.linkedin.com/in/rebecca-terpstra/`

Dana: `https://www.linkedin.com/in/danamhoffman/`

Index

Symbols

packtpub.com

Subscribe to our online digital library for full access to over 7,000 books and videos, as well as industry leading tools to help you plan your personal development and advance your career. For more information, please visit our website.

Why subscribe?

- Spend less time learning and more time coding with practical eBooks and Videos from over 4,000 industry professionals

- Improve your learning with Skill Plans built especially for you

- Get a free eBook or video every month

- Fully searchable for easy access to vital information

- Copy and paste, print, and bookmark content

Did you know that Packt offers eBook versions of every book published, with PDF and ePub files available? You can upgrade to the eBook version at packtpub.com and as a print book customer, you are entitled to a discount on the eBook copy. Get in touch with us at customercare@packtpub.com for more details.

At www.packtpub.com, you can also read a collection of free technical articles, sign up for a range of free newsletters, and receive exclusive discounts and offers on Packt books and eBooks.

Other Books You May Enjoy

If you enjoyed this book, you may be interested in these other books by Packt:

Getting Started with SketchUp Pro

David S. Sellers

ISBN: 978-1-78980-018-0

- Build massing 3D models and preliminary designs
- Identify optimal methods to boost productivity and efficiency with SketchUp Pro
- Explore SketchUp tools and understand their diverse functionality
- Get a complete walkthrough of editing tools, materials, and components in SketchUp
- Create and edit components and explore component options
- Get acquainted with SketchUp extensions, 3D Warehouse, and additional tools and resources

Taking SketchUp Pro to the Next Level

Aaron Dietzen aka 'The SketchUp Guy'

ISBN: 978-1-80324-269-9

- Recap the basics of navigation and SketchUp's native modeling tools
- Modify commands, toolbars, and shortcuts to improve your modeling efficiency
- Use default templates, as well as create custom templates
- Organize your models with groups, components, tags, and scenes
- Analyze your own modeling workflow and understand how to improve it
- Discover extensions and online repositories that unlock the advanced capabilities of SketchUp
- Leverage your existing SketchUp Pro subscription for even better results

Packt is searching for authors like you

If you're interested in becoming an author for Packt, please visit authors.packtpub.com and apply today. We have worked with thousands of developers and tech professionals, just like you, to help them share their insight with the global tech community. You can make a general application, apply for a specific hot topic that we are recruiting an author for, or submit your own idea.

Share Your Thoughts

Now you've finished *The SketchUp Handbook for Interior Design*, we'd love to hear your thoughts! Scan the QR code below to go straight to the Amazon review page for this book and share your feedback or leave a review on the site that you purchased it from.

https://packt.link/r/1-837-63187-5

Your review is important to us and the tech community and will help us make sure we're delivering excellent quality content.

Download a free PDF copy of this book

Thanks for purchasing this book!

Do you like to read on the go but are unable to carry your print books everywhere?

Is your eBook purchase not compatible with the device of your choice?

Don't worry, now with every Packt book you get a DRM-free PDF version of that book at no cost.

Read anywhere, any place, on any device. Search, copy, and paste code from your favorite technical books directly into your application.

The perks don't stop there, you can get exclusive access to discounts, newsletters, and great free content in your inbox daily

Follow these simple steps to get the benefits:

1. Scan the QR code or visit the link below

https://packt.link/free-ebook/9781837631872

2. Submit your proof of purchase
3. That's it! We'll send your free PDF and other benefits to your email directly

Printed in the USA
CPSIA information can be obtained
at www.ICGtesting.com
CBHW080722101124
17181CB00041B/1225

9 781837 631872